DEVELOPING *style*

AN EXTENSION OF *personality*

LLOYD A. FLANIGAN

SYLVIA A. HOLLADAY

Holbrook Press, Inc. *Boston*

Library of Congress Catalog Card Number: 72-153751

contents

preface ix

I STYLE: A WAY OF LIFE AND AN ANGLE OF VISION 1

formal
8 Johann Gottlieb Fichte / *The Ego*

informal
16 Desmond Morris / *The Childlike Adult*

colloquial
26 Russell Baker / *Wanted: New Heads for Old Ivy*

II ELEMENTS OF STYLE 31

Point of View 33

first person singular
38 Freeman Dyson / *Human Consequences of the Exploration of Space*

first person plural
54 E. B. White / *The Age of Dust*

second person
58 William H. Whyte, Jr. / *You, Too, Can Write the Casual Style*

third person subjective
66 John J. Corson / *Social Change and the University*

third person objective
75 Ernest J. Sternglass / *The Death of All Children*

third person objective (technical report)
92 Edwin A. Joyce, Jr. / *Commercial Shrimping*

Mood and Tone 102

Poetry 104

joyful

105 William Shakespeare / *When in Disgrace with Fortune*

106 William Wordsworth / *My Heart Leaps Up*

107 Emily Dickinson / *I Taste a Liquor Never Brewed*

Prose 110

somber
110 John Updike / *The Assassination*

humorous
115 James Thurber / *University Days*

ironic
123 Jonathan Swift / *A Modest Proposal*

satiric (Horatian)
134 John Updike / *No Dodo*

satiric (Juvenalian)
139 Art Buchwald / *The Trial of Jack the Ripper*

sarcastic (individual)
143 Jack Richardson / *Joe Namath and the Problem of Heroic Virtue*

sarcastic (group)
149 Earl Cameron Winchell / *Acapulco Confidential*

sentimental (of self)
154 Barry Farrell / *Confessions of a Kite Hustler*

sentimental (of other person)
159 James Baldwin / *Sweet Lorraine*

Diction 166

denotative language
169 Council for National Cooperation in Aquatics / *Artificial Respiration*

connotative language
177 E. B. White / *Rediscovery*

figurative language (analogy)
182 E. B. White / *The Distant Music of the Hounds*

figurative language (imagery)
187 John Updike / *Central Park*

scientific language
191 Albert Rosenfeld / *Beyond the Moon*

Language Patterns 197

normal word order sentences: simple and compound
201 Ernest Hemingway / *Bull Fighting a Tragedy*

subordination and variation of word order in sentences
213 William Faulkner / *On Privacy: The American Dream, What Happened to It?*

emphasis in sentences
227 Laurence A. Jolidon / *Decade of Destiny*

III METHOD AND STYLE 233

Description 235

Narration 236

Exposition 237

Argument 238

objective description
240 Thomas Henry Huxley / *A Piece of Chalk*

subjective description of a place
244 John Updike / *Spring Rain*

subjective description of a person
248 Deems Taylor / *The Monster*

historical narration
254 Edward Gibbon / *Rome Besieged*

speculative narration
260 Thomas Carlyle / *The Fall of the Bastille*

experiential narration
266 John Keats / *On Running Away*

reminiscent narration
279 John Updike / *The Lucid Eye in Silver Town*

tight exposition
291 James Baker / *Alienation: Sign of Sickness or Symbol of Health?*

loose exposition
298 George Frazier / *John Steinbeck! John Steinbeck! How Still We See Thee Lie*

formal process
310 Laurence C. Blenheim / *Television Teaching by Professional Performers?*

informal process
316 *Changing Times* Staff / *How to Hunt for Bargains*

formal argument of process
326 C. Vann Woodward / *American History (White Man's Version) Needs an Infusion of Soul*

formal argument of policy
343 Carolyn Dillon / *The Professional Name Game*

informal argument
351 K. Ross Toole / *I Am Tired of the Tyranny of Spoiled Brats*

emotional argument
360 Anonymous / *A Declaration of Liberation*

IV FICTION AND CRITICISM 363

short story
367 John Steinbeck / *Flight*

critical essay
387 Dan Vogel / *Steinbeck's "Flight": The Myth of Manhood*

critical essay
391 Chester F. Chapin / *Pepé Torres: A Steinbeck "Natural"*

short story for analysis
393 John J. Iorio / *The Man in the Black Apron*

V SELECTIONS FOR ANALYSIS OF STYLE: ANGLES OF VISION 405

407 Frederick Douglass / *A Child's Reasoning*

415 Eleanor Wait / *Ellie: An Inventory of Being*

419 E. B. White / *The Sword*

421 Povl W. Toussieng with Arthur Henley / *Defiant Kids Will Make the Best Adults*

427 Arthur Schopenhauer / *On Women*

439 Sara Davidson / *An Oppressed Majority Demands Its Rights*

451 Sue Smart / *Certain Women*

452 e. e. cummings / *mrs*

454 Rupert Brooke / *Jealousy*

456 Howard Luck Gossage / *Tell Me, Doctor, Will I Be Active Right Up to the Last?*

463 James Thurber / *The Night the Ghost Got In*

469 Winston Weathers / *For Those of You Who Are Obviously Smarter Than I Am: A Sonnet*

470 Marshall McLuhan / *Sight, Sound and Fury*

480 Charles A. Fairbanks / *Liberalism: Too High a Price?*

484 Langston Hughes / *Evenin' Air Blues*

485 Charles Gordone / *A Quiet Talk with Myself*

499 e. e. cummings / *!blac*

500 Frank Trippett / *The Epic of Garbage*

504 Ralph Nader / *Fashion or Safety*

510 W. H. Auden / *Moon Landing*

author-title index 513

index of terms 517

preface

This book demonstrates, in simple terms, various styles to the novice writer. We include exemplary essays for him to analyze and imitate while on his way to developing his own style.

The book mainly contains short current essays, although we have included some poetry and prose classics that exhibit certain ideas and stylistic points. Short, uncomplicated introductions to each of the first four parts define terms and explain stylistic techniques. Following each essay in the first three parts—STYLE: A WAY OF LIFE AND AN ANGLE OF VISION, ELEMENTS OF STYLE, and METHOD AND STYLE—is exercise material on the style and content of the essay and suggestions for writing. Part IV, FICTION AND CRITICISM, consists of two examples of literary criticism on John Steinbeck's short story *Flight,* which is also included. The purpose of Part IV is to give the student an introduction to the method of literary criticism and an opportunity to write his own criticism of John Iorio's short story *The Man in the Black Apron.* Part V, SELECTIONS FOR ANALYSIS OF STYLE: ANGLES OF VISION, provides the student with material for further analyzing style and generating ideas.

Our intention is to offer the student a means to develop his own style, to be himself and to express himself in the most effective way. We do not claim that any one author's style is more acceptable than another's. We are not prescribing taste; we are simply explaining and describing style in terms we hope will aid the student.

LLOYD A. FLANIGAN

SYLVIA A. HOLLADAY

PART ONE

Style: A Way of Life and an Angle of Vision

STYLE: A WAY OF LIFE

Hey, baby, how ya making it?
Good afternoon, how are you?
What d'ya say?
Hi there, how are you?
Hey, man, gladda seeya!
Hello, it's good to see you.

Each of these greetings expresses a clue to the personality of the speaker; each hints at a certain life style, a mode of living.

If you try to imagine the first speaker's appearance, you will likely picture a figure wearing a beard, beads, head band, and various unmatched articles of clothing. By contrast, you probably see the second speaker as a close-shaven man with neatly trimmed hair. His clothing consists of a conservative business suit and carefully matched accouterments—possibly even a bowler hat and black umbrella. These images are evidence that we think of style as an extension of personality. We might hastily and incorrectly stereotype someone by what seems to suggest his life style; but more frequently than not, we can expect the bearded bead wearer to be less *uptight* than the well-groomed bowler wearer.

Style, consequently, tells us much. For instance, we hear a basketball fan comment on a player's ability to put one through the hoop in a virtually impossible scoring situation: "That's style, man; that's what you call real style." This fan has expressed his approval of the player's ability to score in a manner unlike that of most others. The player's "style" distinguishes him from other players in the same game.

What then is style? Style is our manner of self-expression in a given circumstance. Sometimes we adopt a certain style to fit into a certain social setting; at other times, we use a distinctive style that attracts attention. Many manners of self-expression are open to us. On one occasion we might say, "How do you do?" and on another, "Hey, man, how's it goin'?" The bank teller, the bulldozer operator, the artist, the musician, the engineer, and the writer all use different styles in various situations; but it is also likely that each has some overall distinctive style, some special mannerisms that set him apart from others in his trade or profession, mannerisms that make him not exactly like everyone else in society. And one person may be more distinctive than another. Often the one with a distinctive style has been unusually aware and desirous of being set apart from all the rest. With conscious effort, he has developed his style, his way of expressing himself.

In written composition, style is *how* we say what we have to say; style is an integral part of our communication. In a broad sense, it is the manner in which a writer expresses his attitude—both emotional and logical, both unconscious and conscious—toward a subject. Style is the total effect of a writer's effort to be understood, his effort to communicate. In the words of an eighteenth century French critic: "Style is the man himself."

Any writer—of whatever capability—will surely agree that the major purpose of writing is clear communication; and that to accomplish clear communication, he must be able to control effectively the basic writing conventions of language: the structure of the word order, the punctuation system, the capitalization system, and the spelling system; and he must be able to determine and logically organize material relevant to his subject.

> He (the writer) must be correct, because without correctness he can be neither agreeable nor intelligible. Readers will expect him to obey those rules which they, consciously or unconsciously, have been taught to regard as binding on language; and unless he does obey them, he will disgust.
>
> Anthony Trollope: *Autobiography*

In seeking to develop his style, the writer need not abandon all conventions of language—and thereby "disgust"—for the sake of individualism. He can express his own thought within the bounds of the conventions that contribute to lucid composition.

> Altogether, the style of a writer is a faithful representative of his mind; therefore, if any man wish to write a clear style, let him be first clear in his thoughts; and if any would write in a noble style, let him first possess a noble soul.
>
> Johann Wolfgang von Goethe:
> *Conversations with Eckermann*

STYLE: AN ANGLE OF VISION

If we think of style as an extension of personality, we must consider what affects certain personalities. In other words, we need to know our audience's angle of vision, how our reader or listener looks at things. For example, a salesman is likely to miss a sale when he tries to convince a woman who says she "knows nothing about cars" that the car he is selling is superior in horsepower, gear ratio, carburetor efficiency, torsion bars, and wide-tracking. All of these technical aspects of his car may well contribute to economy, safety, comfort, and design, but such technical language bewilders this customer. She will buy her new car from the man who explains the car's advantages so she "can understand what he's talking about." She will respond to his style: "Ma'am, this car floats along the road—but economically—and when you step on the brakes, you stop in plenty of time." A mechanical engineer, on the other hand, might be more inclined to buy his car from the man who gives the specific technical data. Thus, to make a sale, we need to know our audience, the person to whom we want to communicate our thoughts. Knowing his angle of vision enables us to find a common basis for understanding each other.

The reader's angle of vision is important to us for another reason. Knowing our audience's attitude about a subject tells us what to say and what level of language to use. If we know our audience is friendly and shares our views, we approach him in a manner entirely different from that used with the audience who is hostile toward us and repulsed by our attitudes. We react differently to each of these types. A spokesman for a group of teachers seeking money for education, for instance, approaches another group of teachers by appealing to and encouraging feelings of loyalty and camaraderie. Before a group of legislators, his response might be defensive, or aggressive, or both; in any case, he might well feel embattled. And in trying to rouse an apathetic public, the spokesman would likely combine two approaches: aggressiveness to stir them and camaraderie to sustain them.

The writer then must know who his audience is, what it thinks, and how it thinks. When he writes, he aims at a certain audience; and this audience helps the writer determine what he has to say and how he has to say it.

A writer intending to reach colleagues familiar with his subject matter will express himself in terms familiar to his colleagues, but unfamiliar to others. He will respect his colleague's knowledge and views and use language that might seem esoteric to the layman who, although perhaps well educated, lacks familiarity with the intricacies of the writer's subject. However, the writer can inform the larger audience of laymen by expressing himself in language familiar to the audience. He can define terms and simplify and clarify concepts. These two ways of expressing the same material—these two *styles*—we can consider formal and informal. A third style—the colloquial—has a conversational quality; at times, it even has a *buddy-buddy* quality that sounds much like the *good old backhome* speeches of politicians.

Formal style:	Symptoms of acute inflammation of the veriform appendix were evident and an appendectomy was performed, establishing that a severe catarrhal condition was present.
Informal style:	The doctor operated on the patient, who had symptoms of appendicitis, and established the appendix was badly inflamed.
Colloquial style:	He had pains in his stomach and they cut out his appendix, which was real bad.

Each of the three styles has a particular audience. The formal style (serious, dignified, organized with special attention to logical development) is the surgeon's official report to the general practitioner who made an early diagnosis; the informal style (less serious, less dignified, looser in structure) is the general practitioner's report to the patient's wife; and the colloquial style (conversational, uses slang, lacks dignity) is the wife's report to her neighbor. Each person was aware —consciously or unconsciously—of how his audience would respond to the level of language used. But imagine the general practitioner's reaction to the surgeon's official report written in the colloquial style. He would likely revise his way of looking at the surgeon and perhaps encourage the AMA to investigate the surgeon's qualifications.

The writer's angle of vision depends on who his audience is, as well as who he himself is.

Johann Gottlieb Fichte (1762–1814) was a German philosopher and metaphysician. He studied theology at several German universities. In 1810, he was given a chair of philosophy at Berlin University and became the second rector of the University. His most important philosophical work is *Grundlage der Gesammten Wissenschaftslehre* (Fundamental Principles of the Whole Theory of Science). Fichte believed that the world itself has no independent self-existence: the sole purpose of the world is to provide man the opportunity to realize the ends of his existence.

The Ego *(Formal)*

JOHANN GOTTLIEB FICHTE

[1] We have to search for the absolute, first, and unconditioned fundamental principle of human knowledge. It cannot be proven, nor determined if it is to be absolute first principle.

[2] This principle is to express that *deed-act* which does not occur among the empirical determinations of our consciousness, nor can so occur, since it is rather the basis of all consciousness, and first and alone makes consciousness possible. In representing this deed-act it is not so much to be feared that my readers will *not* think what they ought to think, as that they will think what they ought not to think. This renders necessary a *reflection* on what may perhaps for the present be taken for that deed-act, and an *abstraction* from all that does not really belong to it.

[3] Even by means of this abstracting reflection, that deed-act which is not empirical *fact* of consciousness, cannot become fact of consciousness: but by means of this abstracting reflection we may recognize so much; that this deed-act must necessarily be *thought* as the basis of all consciousness.

[4] The laws according to which this deed-act must necessarily be thought as basis of human knowledge, or, which is the same, the rules according to which that abstracting reflection proceeds, have not yet been proven as valid, but are

for the present tacitly presupposed as well known and agreed upon. As we proceed we shall deduce them from that fundamental principle, the establishment whereof is correct only if they are correct. This is a circle, but an unavoidable circle. And since it is unavoidable and freely admitted, it is also allowable to appeal to all the laws of general logic in establishing this highest fundamental principle.

[5] In undertaking this abstracting reflection, we must start from some proposition which every one will admit without dispute. Doubtless there are many such. We choose the one which seems to us to open the shortest road to our purpose. In admitting this proposition, the deed-act, which we intend to make the basis of our whole science of knowledge, must be admitted; and the reflection must show *that* this deed-act is admitted the moment that proposition is admitted.

[6] Our course of proceeding in this reflection is as follows: Any fact of empirical consciousness, admitted as such valid proposition, is taken hold of, and from it we separate one of its empirical determinations after the other, until only that remains, which can no longer be separated and abstracted from.

[7] As such admitted proposition we take this one: A is A.

Every one admits this proposition, and without the least hesitation. It is recognized by all as completely certain and evident.

[8] If any one should ask a proof of its certainty, no one would enter upon such a proof, but would say: This proposition is *absolutely (that is, without any further ground) certain;* and by saying this would ascribe to himself the power of *absolutely positing something.*

[9] In insisting on the in-itself certainty of the above proposition, you posit *not* that A *is*. The proposition A is A is by no means equivalent to *A is*. *Being* when posited without predicate is something quite different from being when posited with a predicate. Let us suppose A to signify a space enclosed within two straight lines, then the proposition A is A would still be correct; although the proposition A *is* would be false, since such a space is impossible.

[10] But you posit by that proposition: *If* A is, *then* A is. The question *whether* A is at all or not, does not, therefore, occur in it. The *content* of the proposition is not regarded at all: merely its *form*. The question is not whereof you know, but *what* you know of any given subject. The only thing posited, therefore, by that proposition is the *absolutely* necessary connection between the two A's. This connection we shall call X.

[11] In regard to A itself nothing has as yet been posited. The question, therefore, arises: Under what condition *is* A?

[12] X at least is in the Ego, and posited *through* the Ego, for it is the Ego, which asserts the above proposition, and so asserts it by virtue of X as a law, which X or law must, therefore, be given to the Ego; and, since it is asserted absolutely, and without further ground, must be given to the Ego through itself.

[13] *Whether* and *how* A is posited we do not know; but since X is to designate a connection between an unknown positing of A (of the first A in the proposition A is A) and a positing of the same A, which latter positing is absolute on condition of the first positing, it follows that A, *at least in so far as that connection is posited,* is posited *in* and *through* the Ego, like X. Proof: X is only possible in relation to an A; now X is really posited in the Ego; hence, also, A must be posited in the Ego, in so far as X is related to it.

[14] X is related to that A, in the above proposition, which occupies the logical position of subject, and also to that A which is the predicate, for both are united by X. Both, therefore, are posited in the Ego, in so far as they are posited; and the A of the predicate is posited *absolutely* if the first one is posited. Hence the above proposition may be also expressed: If A is posited *in the Ego,* then *it is posited,* or then it *is.*

[15] Hence, by means of X, the Ego posits; that A *is* absolutely for the asserting Ego, and *is* simply because it is posited in the Ego: or that there is something in the Ego which always remains the same, and is thus able to connect or posit: and hence the absolutely posited X may also be expressed, Ego=Ego, or I am I.

[16] Thus we have already arrived at the proposition

I *am;* not as expression of a deed-act, it is true, but, at least, as expression of a *fact.*

[17] For X is absolutely posited; this is a fact of empirical consciousness, as shown by the admitted proposition. Now X signifies the same as I am I; hence, this proposition is also absolutely posited.

[18] But Ego is Ego, or I am I, has quite another significance than A is A. For the latter proposition had content only on a certain condition, namely, *if* A is posited. But the proposition I am I is unconditionally and absolutely valid, since it is the same as X; it is valid not only in form but also in content. In it the Ego is posited not on condition, but absolutely, with the predicate of self-equality; hence, it is posited, and the proposition may also be expressed, I *am.*

[19] This proposition, *I am,* is as yet only founded upon a fact, and has no other validity than that of a fact. If "A=A" (or X) is to be certain, then "I am" must also be certain. Now, it is fact of empirical consciousness that we are compelled to regard X as absolutely certain; hence, also "I am" is certain, since it is the ground of the X. It follows from this, that the *ground of explanation of all facts of empirical consciousness is this: before all positing, the Ego must be posited through itself.*

[20] I say of *all* facts; and to prove this I must show that X is the highest fact of empirical consciousness, is the basis of all others, and contained in all other facts; which, perhaps, would be admitted by all men, without proof, although the whole science of knowledge busies itself to prove it.

[21] The proposition A is A is *asserted.* But all asserting is an act of the human mind; for it has all the conditions of such an act in empirical consciousness, which must be presupposed as well known and admitted in order to advance our reflection. Now, this act is based on something which has no higher ground, namely X or I am.

[22] Hence, that which is *absolutely posited and in itself grounded* is the ground of *a certain* (we shall see hereafter of *all*) acting of the human mind; hence its pure character; the pure character of activity in itself, although abstracting from its particular empirical conditions.

[23] The positing of the Ego through itself is, there-

fore, the pure activity of the Ego. The Ego *posits* itself; and the Ego is by virtue of this mere self-positing. Again, *vice versa:* the Ego *is* and *posits* its being, by virtue of its mere being. It is both the acting and the product of the act; the active and the result of the activity; deed and act in one; and hence the *I am* is expressive of a deed-act; and of the *only possible* deed-act, as our science of knowledge must show.

[24] Let us again consider the proposition *I am I.* The Ego is absolutely posited. Let us assume that the first Ego of this proposition (which has the position of formal subject) is the *absolutely posited* Ego, and that the second Ego (that of the predicate) is the *being* Ego; then the absolutely valid assertion that both are one signifies: the Ego is, *because* it has posited itself.

[25] This is, indeed, the case according to the logical form of the proposition. In A=A the first A is that which is posited in the Ego, (either absolutely, like the Ego itself, or conditionally, like any non-Ego) and in this positing of A the Ego is absolutely subject; and hence the first A is also called the subject. But the second A designates that which the Ego, in now making itself the object of its own reflection discovers thus *as* posited in itself, (since it has just before itself posited the A in itself). The Ego, in asserting that proposition A=A, predicates in truth not something of A, but of itself, namely, that it has found an A posited in itself; and hence the second A is called predicate.

[26] The Ego in the former and the Ego in the latter significance are to be absolutely Equal. Hence, the above proposition may be turned around, and then it reads: The Ego posits itself simply *because* it is. It posits itself through its mere being, and *is* through its mere being posited.

[27] This, then, will explain clearly in what significance we here use the word Ego (I), and will lead us to a definite explanation of the Ego as absolute subject. The Ego as absolute subject is *that, the being, essence, whereof consists merely in positing itself as being.* As soon as it posits itself, it is; and as soon as it is, it posits itself; and hence the Ego is for the Ego absolute and necessary. Whatsoever is not for itself is not an Ego.

[28] The question has been asked, What *was* I before I became self-conscious? The answer is, *I* was not at all, for I was not I. The Ego is only, in so far as it is conscious of itself. The possibility of that question is grounded upon mixing up of the Ego as *subject,* and the Ego as *object* of the reflection of the absolute subject; and is in itself altogether improper. The Ego represents itself, and in so far takes itself up in the form of representation, and now first becomes a *somewhat,* that is, an object. Consciousness receives in this form of representation a substrate, which *is,* even without the real consciousness, and which, moreover, is thought bodily. Such a condition is thought, and the question asked, *What* was the Ego at that time? that is, what is the substrate of consciousness? But even in this thought you unconsciously *add in thinking* the *absolute subject* as looking at that substrate; and hence you unconsciously add in thought the very thing whereof you wanted to abstract, and thus you contradict yourself. The truth is, you cannot think anything at all without adding in thought your Ego as self-conscious; you cannot abstract from your self-consciousness; and all questions of the above kind are not to be answered, since maturely considered, they cannot be asked.

[29] If the Ego *is* only so far as it posits itself, then it also is only *for* the positing, and posits only for the being Ego. *The Ego is for the Ego;* but if it posits itself absolutely, as it is, then it posits itself necessarily, and is necessary for the Ego. *I am only for me; but for me I am necessarily.* (By saying *for me,* I already posit my being.) *To posit itself* and *to be* is, applied to the Ego, the same. Hence, the proposition I am because I have posited myself, can also be expressed; *I am absolutely because I am.*

[30] Again, the Ego as positing itself and the Ego as being are one and the same. The Ego is as *what* it posits itself and posits itself as *what* it is. Hence, *I am absolutely what I am.*

[31] The immediate expression of the thus developed deed-act may be given in the following formula: *I am absolutely because I am, and I am absolutely what I am for myself.*

[32] If this narration of the original deed-act is to be

placed at the head of a science of knowledge as its highest fundamental principle, it may perhaps be best expressed thus:

[33] *The Ego posits originally its own being.*

(In other words, the Ego is necessarily identity of subject and object; is itself subject-object; and it is this without further meditation.)

[34] We started from the proposition A=A, not as if the proposition, I am, could be proven by it, but because we had to start from some one certain proposition given in empirical consciousness. And our development, also, has shown that A=A does not contain the ground of "I am," but, on the contrary, that the latter proposition is the ground of the former.

[35] By abstracting from the content of the proposition I am, and looking merely to its form, namely, the form of drawing a conclusion from the being posited of something to its being, as we must abstract for the sake of logic, we thus obtain as *fundamental principle of logic* the proposition A=A, which can only be proven and determined through the science of knowledge. *Proven:* for A is A because the Ego which has posited A is the same as the Ego in which A is posited. *Determined:* for whatever is, is only in so far as it is posited in the Ego, and there is nothing outside of the Ego. No possible A (no *thing*) can be any thing else but an A posited in the Ego.

[36] By abstracting, moreover, from all asserting as a determined acting, and looking merely to the general *manner* of acting, of the human mind, which is given through that form, we obtain the *category of reality*. Every thing to which the proposition A=A is applicable has reality, *in so far as that proposition is applicable to it.* That which is posited through the mere positing of any thing (in the Ego) is its reality, its essence.

EXERCISES—*THE EGO*

Content

1. What is Fichte's purpose in writing *The Ego*?
2. Explain Fichte's use of the word "absolute."

3. In your own words, what does this quotation mean (paragraph (31))? "I am absolutely because I am, and I am absolutely what I am for myself."

Style

1. For whom is this essay written; who is Fichte's audience? Explain your choice.
2. Describe the author's level of language.
3. Why do no contractions appear in this essay?
4. For what reasons can you call this a formal essay?
5. Why does the author use the personal pronoun "we" in this essay: ". . . , we must start from some proposition . . ." (paragraph (5))?
6. Why does Fichte shift the person in which he writes?

Application of Stylistic Techniques

1. Choose an informal or colloquial essay and rewrite a portion of it in a formal style.
2. As if for a formal essay, write a paragraph about something you know well for other persons likely to be equally knowledgeable (coaching a sport; doing some kind of work: electrical, sewing, carpentry, mechanics; engaging in some pastime: chess, bridge, poker, deep sea fishing, football, wrestling, basketball, diving, dancing, playing a musical instrument, etc.)

Suggestions for Writing

1. Write a formal essay in which you challenge or support Fichte's concept of the ego.
2. Imitating Fichte's formal style, in an essay explain your concept of selfishness, love, hate, war, or death.
3. Select a topic on which you feel yourself an authority (anything from davenport wrestling to nuclear physics) and write a formal essay expressing an opinion.

Desmond Morris (1928–   ) was born in Wiltshire, England and obtained a degree in zoology from Birmingham University. In 1951, he joined Niko Tinbergen's animal behavior group at Oxford and began work on his doctoral thesis, concentrating on the reproductive behavior of fish. He became curator of mammals for the Zoological Society in 1959. His research into mammalian behavior problems led him to consider the human animal and eventually to write *The Naked Ape,* a worldwide best-seller. He has published more than fifty scientific papers and his previous books include *The Biology of Art and the Mammals: A Guide to the Living Species.* With his wife Ramona, he has written *Men and Snakes, Men and Apes*, and *Men and Pandas.*

The Childlike Adult *(Informal)*

DESMOND MORRIS

[1] In many respects the play of children is similar to the Stimulus Struggle of adults. The child's parents take care of its survival problems and it is left with a great deal of surplus energy. Its playful activities help to burn up this energy. There is, however, a difference. There are various ways of pursuing the adult Stimulus Struggle, one of which is the invention of new patterns of behaviour. In play, this element is much stronger. To the growing child, virtually every action it performs is a new invention. Its naivety in the face of the environment more or less forces it to indulge in a non-stop process of innovation. Everything is novel. Each bout of playing is a voyage of discovery: discovery of itself, its abilities and capacities, and of the world about it. The development of inventiveness may not be the specific goal of play, but it is nevertheless its predominant feature and its most valuable bonus.

[2] The explorations and inventions of childhood are

usually trivial and ephemeral. In themselves they mean little. But if the processes they involve, the sense of wonder and curiosity, the urge to seek and find and test, can be prevented from fading with age, so that they remain to dominate the mature Stimulus Struggle, over-shadowing the less rewarding alternatives, then an important battle has been won: the battle for creativity.

[3] Many people have puzzled over the secret of creativity. I contend that it is basically no more than the extension into adult life of these vital childlike qualities. The child asks new questions; the adult answers old ones; the childlike adult finds answers to new questions. The child is inventive; the adult is productive; the childlike adult is inventively productive. The child explores his environment; the adult organizes it; the childlike adult organizes his explorations and, by bringing order to them, strengthens them. He creates.

[4] It is worth examining this phenomenon more closely. If a young chimpanzee, or a child, is placed in a room with a single familiar toy, he will play with it for a while and then lose interest. If he is offered, say, five familiar toys instead of only one, he will play first here, then there, moving from one to the other. By the time he gets back to the first one, the original toy will seem "fresh" again and worthy of a little further play attention. If, by contrast, an unfamiliar and novel toy is offered, it will immediately command his interest and produce a powerful reaction.

[5] This "new toy" response is the first essential of creativity, but it is one phase of the process. The strong exploratory urge of our species drives us on to investigate the new toy and to test it out in as many ways as we can devise. Once we have finished our explorations, then the unfamiliar toy will have become familiar. At this point it is our inventiveness that will come into action to utilize the new toy, or what we have learned from it, to set up and solve new problems. If, by re-combining our experiences from our different toys, we can make more out of them than we started with, then we have been creative.

[6] If a young chimpanzee is put in a room with an ordinary chair, for example, it starts out by investigating the

object, tapping it, hitting it, biting it, sniffing it, and clambering over it. After a while these rather random activities give way to a more structured pattern of activity. It may, for instance, start jumping over the chair, using it as a piece of gymnastic equipment. It has "invented" a vaulting box, and "created" a new gymnastic activity. It had learned to jump over things before, but not in quite this way. By combining its past experiences with the investigation of this new toy, it creates the new action of rhythmic vaulting. If, later on, it is offered more complex apparatus, it will build on these earlier experiences again, incorporating the new elements.

[7] This developmental process sounds very simple and straightforward, but it does not always fulfil its early promise. As children we all go through these processes of exploration, invention and creation, but the ultimate level of creativity we rise to as adults varies dramatically from individual to individual. At the worst, if the demands of the environment are too pressing, we stick to limited activities we know well. We do not risk new experiments. There is no time or energy to spare. If the environment seems too threatening, we would rather be sure than sorry: we fall back on the security of tried and trusted, familiar routines. The environmental situation has to change in one way or another before we will risk becoming more exploratory. Exploration involves uncertainty and uncertainty is frightening. Only two things will help us to overcome these fears. They are opposites: one is disaster, and the other is greatly increased security. A female rat, for instance, with a large litter to rear, is under heavy pressure. She works non-stop to keep her offspring fed, cleaned and protected. She will have little time for exploring. If disaster strikes—if her nest is flooded or destroyed—she will be forced into panic exploration. If, on the other hand, her young have been successfully reared and she has built up a large store of food, the pressure relaxes and, from a position of greater security, she is able to devote more time and energy to exploring her environment.

[8] There are, then, two basic kinds of exploration: panic exploration and security exploration. It is the same for the human animal. During the chaos and upheaval of war, a

human community may be driven to inventiveness to surmount the disasters it faces. Alternatively, a successful, thriving community may be highly exploratory, striking out from its strong position of increased security. It is the community that is just managing to scrape along that will show little or no urge to explore.

[9] Looking back on the history of our species it is easy to see how these two types of exploration have helped human progress to stumble on its way. When our early ancestors left the comforts of a fruit-picking, forest existence and took to open country, they were in serious difficulties. The extreme demands of the new environment forced them to be exploratory or die. Only when they had evolved into efficient, co-operative hunters did the pressure ease a little. They were at the "scraping by" stage again. The result was that this condition lasted for a very long time, thousands upon thousands of years, with advances in technology occurring at an incredibly slow rate, simple developments in such things as implements and weapons, for example, taking hundreds of years to take a small new step.

[10] Eventually, when primitive agriculture slowly emerged and the environment came more under our ancestors' control, the situation improved. Where this was particularly successful, urbanization developed and a threshold was passed into a realm of new and dramatically increased social security. With it came a rush of the other kind of exploration—security exploration. This, in turn, led to more and more startling developments, to more security and more exploration.

[11] Unfortunately this was not the whole story. Man's rise to civilization would be a much happier tale if only it had been. But, sadly, events moved too fast and, as we have seen throughout this book, the pendulum of success and disaster began to swing crazily back and forth. Because we unleashed so much more than we were biologically equipped to cope with, our magnificent new social developments and complexities were as often abused as they were used. Our inability to deal rationally with the super-status and super-power that our super-tribal condition thrust upon us, led to new, more sudden,

and more challenging disasters than we had ever known. No sooner had a super-tribe settled down to a phase of great prosperity, with security exploration operating at full intensity, and wonderful new forms of creativity blossoming out, than something went wrong. Invaders, tyrants and aggressors smashed the delicate machinery of the intricate new social structures, and panic exploration was back on a major scale. For each new invention of construction, there was another of destruction, back and forth, back and forth, for ten thousand years, and it still goes on today. It is the horror of atomic weapons that has given us the glory of atomic energy, and it is the glory of biological research that may yet give us the horror of biological warfare.

[12] In between these two extremes there are still millions of people living the simple lives of primitive agriculturalists, tilling the soil much as our early ancestors did. In a few areas primitive hunters survive. Because they have stayed at the "scraping by" stage, they are typically non-exploratory. Like the left-over great apes—the chimpanzees, the gorillas and the orang-utans—they have the potential for inventiveness and exploration, but it is not called forth to any appreciable extent. Experiments with chimpanzees in captivity have revealed how quickly they can be encouraged to develop their exploratory potential: they can operate machines, paint pictures and solve all kinds of experimental puzzles; but in the wild state they do not even learn to build crude shelters to keep out the rain. For them, and the simpler human communities, the scraping-by existence—not too difficult and not too easy—has blunted their exploratory urges. For the rest of us, one extreme follows the other and we constantly explore from either an excess of panic or an excess of security.

[13] From time to time there are those among us who cast an envious backward glance at the "simple life" of primitive communities and start to wish we had never left our primeval Forest of Eden. In some cases, serious attempts have been made to convert such thoughts into actions. Much as we may sympathize with these projects, it must be realized that they are fraught with difficulties. The inherent artificiality of pseudo-primitive drop-out communities, such as those

that have appeared in North America and elsewhere recently, is a primary weakness. They are, after all, composed of individuals who have tasted the excitements of super-tribal life as well as its horrors. They have been conditioned throughout their lives to a high level of mental activity. In a sense they have lost their social innocence, and the loss of innocence is an irreversible process.

[14] At first, all may go well for the neo-primitive, but this is deceptive. What happens is that the initial return to the simple way of life throws up an enormous challenge to the ex-inmate of the human zoo. His new role may be simple in theory, but in practice it is full of fascinatingly novel problems. The establishment of a pseudo-primitive community by a group of ex-city-dwellers becomes, in fact, a major exploratory act. This, rather than the official return to pure simplicity, is what makes the project so satisfying, as any Boy Scout will testify. But what happens once the initial challenge has been met and overcome? Whether it is a remote, rural or cave-dwelling group, or whether it is a self-insulated, pseudo-primitive group set up in an isolated pocket inside the city itself, the answer is the same. Disillusionment sets in, as the monotony begins to assail the brains that have been irreversibly trained to the higher, super-tribal level. Either the group collapses, or it starts to stir itself into action. If the new activity is successful, then the community will soon find itself becoming organized and expanding. In no time at all it will be back into the super-tribal rat-race.

[15] It is difficult enough in the twentieth century to remain as a genuine primitive community, like the Eskimoes or aborigines, let alone a pseudo-primitive one. Even the traditionally resistant European gypsies are gradually succumbing to the relentless spread of the human zoo condition.

[16] The tragedy for those who wish to solve their problems by a return to the simple life is that, even if they somehow contrived to "de-train" their highly activated brains, such individuals would still remain extremely vulnerable in their small rebel communities. The human zoo would find it hard to leave them alone. They would either be exploited as a tourist attraction, as so many of the genuine primitives are today,

or, if they become an irritant, they would be attacked and disbanded. There is no escape from the super-tribal monster and we may as well make the best of it.

[17] If we are condemned to a complex social existence, as it seems we are, then the trick is to ensure that *we* make use of *it*, rather than let *it* make use of *us*. If we are going to be forced to pursue the Stimulus Struggle, then the important thing is to select the most rewarding method of approach. As I have already indicated, the best way to do this is to give priority to the inventive, exploratory principle, not inadvertently like the drop-outs, who find themselves all too soon in an exploratory blind alley, but deliberately, gearing our inventiveness to the mainstream of our super-tribal existence.

[18] Given the fact that each super-tribesman is free to choose which way he pursues the Stimulus Struggle, it remains to ask why he does not select the inventive solution more frequently. With the enormous exploratory potential of his brain lying idle and with his experience of inventive playfulness in childhood behind him, he should in theory favour this solution above all others. In any thriving super-tribal city *all* the citizens should be potential "inventors." Why, then, do so few of them indulge in active creativity, while the others are satisfied to enjoy their inventions second-hand, watching them on television, or are content to play simple games and sports with strictly limited possibilities for inventiveness? They all appear to have the necessary background for becoming childlike adults. The super-tribe, like a gigantic parent, protects them and cares for them, so why is it that they do not all develop bigger and better childlike curiosity?

[19] Part of the answer is that children are subordinate to adults. Inevitably, dominant animals try to control the behaviour of their subordinates. Much as adults may love their children, they cannot help seeing them as a growing threat to their dominance. They know that with ultimate senility they will have to give way to them, but they do everything they can to postpone the evil day. There is therefore a strong tendency to suppress inventiveness in members of

the community younger than oneself. An appreciation of the value of their "fresh eyes" and their new creativeness works against this, but it is an uphill struggle. By the time the new generation has matured to the point where its members could be wildly inventive, childlike adults, they are already burdened with a heavy sense of conformity. Struggling against this as hard as they can, they in turn are then faced with the threat of another younger generation coming up beneath them, and the suppressive process repeats itself. Only those rare individuals who experience an unusual childhood, from this point of view, will be able to achieve a level of great creativity in adult life. How unusual does such a childhood have to be? It either has to be so suppressive that the growing child revolts against the traditions of its elders in a big way (many of our greatest creative talents were so-called delinquent children), or it has to be so un-suppressive that the heavy hand of conformity rests only lightly on its shoulders. If a child is strongly punished for its inventiveness (which, after all, is essentially rebellious in nature), it may spend the rest of its adult life making up for lost time. If a child is strongly rewarded for its inventiveness, then it may never lose it, no matter what pressures are brought to bear on it in later years. Both types can make a great impact in adult society, but the second will probably suffer less from obsessive limitations in his creative acts.

[20] The vast majority of children will, of course, receive a more balanced mixture of punishment and reward for their inventiveness and will emerge into adult life with personalities that are both moderately creative and moderately conformist. They will become the adult-adults. They will tend to read the newspapers rather than make the news that goes into them. Their attitude to the childlike adults will be ambivalent; on the one hand they will applaud them for providing the much-needed sources of novelty, but on the other they will envy them. The creative talent will therefore find himself alternately praised and damned by society in a bewildering way, and will be constantly in doubt about his acceptance by the rest of the community.

EXERCISES—*THE CHILDLIKE ADULT*

Content

1. State Morris's thesis (central idea, controlling idea) in one sentence.
2. According to the author, what is the most significant factor in an individual's being especially creative as an adult? Point out any exception(s) to Morris's view that you know.
3. What kind of society does Morris say nurtures creativity best?
4. Why does he think persons returning to the primitive life—similar to hippie communities—will be unsuccessful in their endeavor?

Style

1. In both *The Ego* and *The Childlike Adult,* Fichte and Morris examine an aspect of man. Judging from what you have read, which man would you rather engage in conversation? By discussing their styles, explain your choice.
2. In what person does Morris write? Is he consistent throughout the essay? Explain.
3. For what reasons can you call this an informal essay?
4. List three sentences from the essay that show the author's ability to put a complex idea into the educated laymen's language. Explain your choices.

Application of Stylistic Techniques

1. Select a portion of a formal essay (perhaps Fichte's *The Ego*) and rewrite it in an informal style.
2. Write a paragraph about something you know well, aiming it at an educated audience who is, however, not familiar with your subject. You might explain the dangers of scuba diving; the game of football (baseball, basketball, etc.); the way to make a putt, to play an instrument, etc.; the reasons for exercising, learning judo, dropping out of society, or becoming politically involved.

Suggestions for Writing

1. Write an informal essay in which you challenge Morris's view of the creative talent.

2. Imitating Morris's use of frequent examples, explain your view of returning to the primitive life, or the idea that for each new constructive invention developed a destructive one offsets it.
3. Consider society as a "gigantic parent" and write an informal essay demonstrating youth's natural rebellion against his parent.
4. Select a topic and write an informal essay.
   The Creative Genius: Only an Intelligent Child?
   The Creative Artist Struggles against Society
   Creative People Are Malcontents
   Serious People Lack Creativity
   Creativity: What's It Done for Us?
   Creative People: Immoral?
   The Value of the Primitive Life
   Progress: Where to Now?
   Civilization: It's Own Enemy?
   Modern Artists: Deserving of Ridicule?

Russell Baker (1925–   ) is a noted American newspaper columnist and satirist. He writes for *The New York Times* and has contributed to *Life*. He is also the author of *An American in Washington, No Cause for Panic,* and *All Things Considered.*

Wanted: New Heads for Old Ivy *(Colloquial)*

RUSSELL BAKER

[1] The other day I was offered a college presidency.

[2] Not at East Oaksap Normal either, mind you. No sir. This was a college that most people, a couple of years back, would have been proud to be president of. You know the scene—a Nobel winner or two on the faculty, luscious drum majorettes, ivy-covered gymnasium—everything that makes a great university.

[3] The way this offer came about was this: I'm sneaking into the office late one morning and bump into this group of glum faces waiting for the elevator. It turns out that they have already been all through the office trying to find somebody to take this college presidency and everybody, including the office boy, has turned them down.

[4] They are on their way downstairs to see if they can interest Pepe, the counterman at Julio's Snack Bar and Carry-Out, in switching jobs when I pop out of the elevator.

[5] "My good man," says an oleaginous fellow. He is the governor of the state in which this university is located, but I do not know that yet. I figure him for an insurance salesman. "My good man," he says, "will you give us a moment of your time to discuss a matter of the utmost urgency to the future of the free world?"

[6] Talking like this, he *has* to be an insurance salesman. Still there is a hairy spiritual-looking fellow with him who is wearing jeans and sandals and cheap jewelry, and how often do you get a chance to resist an insurance pitch from a guy who looks like that? Actually, of course, he is the leader of the student revolution at this college.

[7] I invite them into my cubicle and, to cut through a lot of overinflated rhetoric, the long and short of it is that they have made an intensive search for the one man in America qualified to be president of their college. This man is me.

[8] Now I am as big a fool as the next man, but even the next man knows that being offered a college presidency these days is like being offered a chance to drive a truckload of nitroglycerine over the Andes.

[9] At last count between 60 and 70 college presidents had turned in their resignations this spring, and this doesn't include college presidents who couldn't be reached at the time of the survey on account of being in intensive-care units or being thrown out of windows or being bricked up in their offices.

[10] "Out!" I tell them. "Out! Or I'll call the janitor and have you swept out."

[11] "Please hear us through," says a familiar voice at the rear of the group. On close inspection he turns out to be President Nixon. "Give us a chance," he says, "to tell you why we need you."

[12] When the President speaks to you like that, the least you can do is listen. "This is the leader of the campus revolution," says Mr. Nixon, introducing the hairy, ornamented fellow.

[13] "We need you as a symbol of a corrupt Establishment power structure," the hairy fellow says. "Without a president we have nobody whose office we can tear apart. Nobody whose files we can rifle for letters from the CIA. Nobody whose reputation we can destroy. And without these things, we cannot maintain enthusiasm for the revolution on our campus."

[14] "But I don't even know anybody in the CIA, much less anybody in the CIA who would write me a letter."

[15] "We'll get you some letters from the CIA," says the governor. "We'll supply you with a whole set of files linking you to the power structure so thoroughly that your name will be mud to your own children. You take the job, we'll do the rest."

[16] This from the governor! I don't get it.

[17] "I need you," says the governor. "Without a college president on that campus, the kids will have no incentive to riot. Without a riot, I will have no reason to threaten to have your head unless you use strong police repression to restore law and order. And without being able to call for your head, I won't be able to exploit the anti-intellectualism among the voters of my state and get myself re-elected."

[18] "But I don't have anything against intellectuals."

[19] "Then take the job," says the professor representing the college's faculty. "We of the faculty need you. Without a president, the professors have nobody to turn the student rioters loose on when they become incensed about our going to Europe instead of sitting around that dreary campus teaching and updating our lectures."

[20] "But I've got no sympathy for professors that don't teach."

[21] "Then take the job," says the millionaire representing the college trustees. "We need you. Without a president, the trustees have nobody to fire for indulging in shameful permissiveness toward radical student elements bent on taking control of the college into their own hands."

[22] "But I don't like being without an income."

[23] "Then take the job," says the senator representing Congress in the delegation. "We need you. Without a college president to be the center of riots, to be abused by the faculty and to be fired by the trustees, we in Congress will have no crisis on the American campus to investigate. And since we have nothing to legislate, we'd have a terrible time justifying our pay raises to the folks back home. After you're fired, we'll investigate you and pay you the usual witness's fee."

[24] I omit the arguments of editors, TV cameramen and comedians, as it is fairly obvious what they need with

college presidents, and come to the clincher, who is President Nixon.

[25] "It is clear to every patriotic American," he says, "that this country cannot survive in today's world without college presidents, and it is my duty as Chief Executive to see that this country survives. As you know, I favor a volunteer army. I also favor a volunteer college-president force. Unless decent patriotic Americans are willing to volunteer for this duty, however, I shall have no alternative but to ask Congress for a college-president draft."

[26] After observing that this is one issue on which he will certainly have the unanimous backing of students, professors, trustees, press, television, and politicians of both parties, I tell the President I will mull it over and call him sometime and for him not to call me.

[27] Later that day I duck down to Julio's for a carry-out cheese sandwich and an orange soda pop. "Hey," says Pepe, the counterman, "you won't believe the job I just turned down."

[28] And Pepe rehashes the whole scene over the Wisconsin processed cheddar, concluding that as a patriot, "If they draft me, I'll go."

Not me, Pepe, I'll go to Canada first.

EXERCISES—*WANTED: NEW HEADS FOR OLD IVY*

Content

1. Why did Baker write this essay?
2. Why do the governor and the U.S. senator want the college president to fail in his endeavor to maintain campus tranquility?
3. Explain the author's suggestion of a volunteer college-president force.

Style

1. What characteristics of the colloquial style does paragraph (3) have? Explain your points.
2. From paragraph (6), select words that contribute to Baker's colloquial style. Explain your choices.

3. What stylistic purpose does the author's reliance upon dialogue serve?
4. Explain the author's placing of the phrase "ivy-covered gymnasium" in the fourth sentence of paragraph (2).
5. In what way does the analogy in paragraph (8) contribute to Baker's colloquial style?

Application of Stylistic Techniques

1. Rewrite paragraph (3) as if it were part of a formal essay, then as if part of an informal essay.
2. Rewrite paragraph (9) as if it were written by a scientist for other scientists, then as if by a member of the U.S. Senate writing to an anti-intellectual constituent who contributed to the senator's campaign.
3. Put paragraph (25) into one sentence of "plain English," one without any reliance upon political language.

Suggestions for Writing

1. Select a current controversial event and develop an essay in Baker's colloquial manner, imitating his stylistic techniques.
2. Select a topic and write an essay in the colloquial style.
   The Establishment's Power Structure
   The Hairy Guys with All the Answers
   The Student Revolution
   Majorettes *and* Education?
   The Hazards of Academic Life
   The Value of Ivy-Covered Gymnasiums
   Who Benefits from Unrest?
   Canada: The Answer to Dissent?
   What's Wrong with Patriotism?
   What's Wrong with Hairy Ornamented Fellows?

PART TWO

Elements of Style

Thus far, we have considered style in broad aspects: style as a means of expressing our life styles, our modes of living; and style as an angle of vision, our way of responding to other persons. These two aspects of style are the major ingredients in our concept of style as an extension of personality.

The elements of style—*Point of View, Mood and Tone, Diction,* and *Language Patterns*—are the means the writer uses to extend his personality. From the various facets of these means, the writer selects the tools to accomplish his aim in written composition. The combination of stylistic facets the writer employs in expressing himself constitutes his style, his way of extending his personality into his work.

POINT OF VIEW

Although the terms "point of view" and "opinion" are often used interchangeably, by point of view we mean the writer's way of presenting himself to his reader. For example, a writer might want to create an impersonal or personal relationship with his reader. To remain impersonal, he generally selects an impersonal pronoun (one, anyone, someone, everyone, many, etc.), thereby establishing his point of view. To develop a personal relationship, the writer uses personal pronouns (I, we, and you). Examine the relationship, the point of view, each of the following sentences establishes with the reader.

> One knows now what it is like to live in poverty.
> I know now what it is like to live in poverty.
> We know now what it is like to live in poverty.

The first sentence makes the reader wonder if "one," in his aloof point of view, really knows what it is like to live in poverty. In the second sentence, the reader likely feels a sympathy for the writer. The "we" (meaning you and I, not the editorial "we") of the third sentence creates a camaraderie, an almost intimate relationship with the reader.

The writer can also use the indefinite "you," meaning

"anyone," for the personal relationship; however, the use of "you" sometimes causes a problem. The writer risks confusing the indefinite "you" and the imperative mood "you." While the indefinite "you" often creates an intimacy between reader and writer, the imperative addresses the reader authoritatively, usually delivering instruction, giving admonition, or making an urgent appeal.

Indefinite:	As a writer, you accept a rigorous way of life. (As a writer *a person* (anyone) accepts a rigorous way of life.)
Imperative:	To become a writer, be willing to accept a rigorous way of life. (To become a writer, *you* (understood) *must* be willing to accept a rigorous way of life.)
Confusion of imperative and indefinite:	To become a writer, be willing to accept a rigorous way of life; but you enjoy working with words and ideas.

In the indefinite, frequently used to create a close relationship, the reader is being told how someone—not necessarily the reader—does something; in the imperative the reader is being told how to do something. The confusion in the last example occurs when the writer is uncertain whether he wants to give instruction or explain how *he* did something (his own experience). The problem is that the writer prefers not to use "I" because it is not intimate enough for him, and what he is explaining is the kind of thing anyone might do.

A similar problem arises with the use of "we." A writer must be careful not to confuse the personal "we," meaning "you and I," with the editorial "we" used correctly in editorials and whenever the writer is a spokesman—perhaps self-appointed—for a group.

Personal:	We know the urgency of improving conservation measures, for we have worked together in some of the most industrially devastated areas in this country. ("We" meaning *you and I* would be determined from the whole text.)

Editorial:	We will not rest until the waste makers in this country stop their wanton destruction of our natural resources.
Confusion of personal and editorial:	Together, we have done all we can to make the citizens of this country aware of the crisis, but we will perish by our monomaniacal desire to create our burial mounds of garbage.

In the above example of confused point of view, the writer is consistent in his use of "we" as a word, but confusion results from his use of "we" as a point of view. In the first clause, he likely means "you and I" (probably he and his co-workers), and in the second clause he is a spokesman for the people, using the editorial "we" to mean "we" Americans.

Used appropriately, the editorial "we" is effective, but it can be downright ludicrous when used for a single person. Such a writer sounds phony or as if he belongs in an earlier century.

> We had our tooth pulled yesterday and it was painful.

This kind of writing irritates a reader as much as the nurse irritates a patient by saying, "Now we'll have our shot, won't we?" Only she never gets hers.

Whereas the personal point of view (I, we, you) usually brings the reader and writer closer together, we often think of third person as impersonal, putting distance between reader and writer. Scientific and historical writing are typical of third person impersonal writing, what is frequently called "third person objective." However, third person can also be subjective, putting the writer's point of view somewhere between personal and impersonal. In third subjective, the writer usually avoids the impersonal pronoun "one," which often sounds stuffy, and projects himself into his writing by asserting his opinion. He does not simply disclose facts objectively, letting the reader make conclusions. The writer using third person subjective clearly states his opinion, but avoids the personal pronouns. He likewise, in his subjectivity, avoids the impersonal *one.* The following selection from John J. Corson's *Social Change and the University* demonstrates third person subjective:

> There are forces at work that will change the function of the university, that will substantially expand the university, and that will establish new demands on the university. In coping with that change, some of the most venerated concepts, practices, and traditions of an old, old institution will be altered or abandoned.

A writer, however, sometimes wants to remain objective; that is, he wants to make his point through facts—not rely too heavily on personal feeling and speculation. Often simultaneously, he will prefer not to risk alienating his audience by using *one.* This kind of third person objective point of view does not mean the writer has no opinion; he does. His choice of subject matter alone indicates his special interest; and by careful attention to his audience's need for explanation and clarification, he can establish a close relationship with his readers. This passage from Ernest J. Sternglass's *The Death of All Children* exemplifies a writer's ability to use third person objective and still remain close to the reader. Sternglass avoids using both personal and impersonal pronouns to establish his point of view: his lack of personal pronouns provides objectivity; his level of language and careful explanation and clarification create a closeness with the reader.

> Not only was there a drastic change in overall infant mortality for the U.S. as compared to the rest of the advanced countries, but there were also disturbing patterns of change within the U.S. For example, the infant mortality rate started to level off sharply in the Eastern, Midwestern and Southern states within two years after the onset of atomic testing in Nevada in 1951, while it continued steadily downward in the dry Western states. But this is exactly the known pattern of accumulated strontium on the ground and in the diet, since strontium is most heavily deposited in states of high annual rainfall, especially in those to the east of Nevada.

The most impersonal third person objective writing is the scientific report which, in addition to avoiding a personal pronoun point of view, relies heavily on passive voice. In scientific writing, for example, the performer of the action is often less important than the receiver of the action. Therefore, the writer frequently prefers passive voice to active. And he concerns himself less with establishing a rapport with the audience; his intention is to report information.

Active voice:	The laboratory technician examined the fungus by microscope every thirty-six hours.
Preferred passive voice:	The fungus was examined by microscope every thirty-six hours.

The passive in this example eliminates unnecessary words and the inclination to repeat the "technician-he" combination throughout a report.

However, passive improperly used makes a report wordy and often obscures meaning.

Wordy passive:	An antibiotic was produced by the fungus.
Precise active:	The fungus produced an antibiotic.
Obscure passive:	It was understood that Chemicals Unlimited, Incorporated, would complete their project by 1970.

In the obscure passive, who understood the completion date? Does the writer mean he, or his company (not Chemicals Unlimited), understood; or that Chemicals Unlimited understood (perhaps meaning either they did not meet the date or they agreed to it); or that the two parties agreed on the date; or that the writer is confessing to his misunderstanding of the date? To avoid this kind of problem and wordiness, the scientific or impersonal writer often turns to the active voice, thereby mixing active and passive voice in his report.

Although you should strive to be consistent in voice and point of view, at times you will want to—perhaps have to—shift, as your material develops and your relationship with the reader changes.

In establishing and maintaining your point of view, you will want to be neither too close nor too distant, and although there is no rule about what point of view fits what particular subject matter, there is a way to determine what point of view you will adopt. You analyze your attitude toward the subject, decide who your audience is and what his attitude is, and then select the point of view that best enables you to communicate to that audience.

Freeman Dyson (1923–   ) is a physicist and resides in New Jersey. He received his B.A. from the University of Cambridge in 1945. Mr. Dyson is with the Institute for Advanced Study, Princeton, New Jersey. He has contributed to several scientific publications and is listed in *World's Who's Who in Science.*

Human Consequences of the Exploration of Space *(First Person Singular)*

FREEMAN DYSON

[1] When Columbus set sail into the Atlantic, he knew he was going to do something great, but he did not know what. This remark about Columbus is trite. It has been made a hundred times before by people discussing man's activities in space, yet it is the truest thing that can be said. In my personal view of the human situation, the exploration of space appears as the most hopeful feature of a dark landscape. Everything I say may well be as strong and irrelevant as Columbus' reasons for sailing West. The important thing is that he did sail West and we do go into space. The true historical consequences of these events can only be known much later.

[2] In recent months many thoughtful voices have been heard, questioning the wisdom of pursuing big space projects at a time when so many human problems remain unsolved on earth. Just now, when the direction of space activities after

Reprinted by permission, from Chapter 2 of *Man on the Moon,* edited by Eugene Rabinowitch and Richard S. Lewis, © 1969 by Education Foundation for Nuclear Science, Basic Books, Inc., Publishers, New York.

the Apollo missions is still to be decided, it is important for us to think seriously about the value of such enterprises. This article is an attempt to think ahead, to sketch a possible future for men in space. My intention is not to make my readers believe everything I say, but to provoke them into forming their own judgments, their own visions of human needs and purposes.

[3] I do not think we need to have a generally agreed set of goals before we do anything ambitious. I do not believe that any philosopher-king or hierarchy of committees can dissolve the causes of human discord and give us a universally accepted order of priorities. On the contrary, I consider it natural and right that we shall continue to stumble ahead into space without really knowing why. The ultimate strength of the space program derives from the fact that it unites in a constructive effort a crowd of people who are in it for quite diverse reasons. I am in it partly because I am a scientist and am interested in astronomical problems. But many scientists are indifferent or hostile to the program, while I myself was enthusiastic about space travel long before I became a scientist.

[4] I shall be expressing opinions about matters which are much more human than scientific. I shall put forward a point of view about the social problems of our time, problems which have little to do with science or with space. At the end I will argue that the exploration of space offers remedies to some of our social diseases, but my argument will remain on the level of literature rather than of science.

[5] When I am discussing human affairs, I like to deal in individual people rather than in abstract principles. For this reason I find science fiction more helpful than sociology in suggesting probable futures. Like anybody who is concerned with the long-range future, I owe a great debt to the ideas of H. G. Wells. Wells was an unsuccessful biologist who became a successful novelist. He understood better than most of us the comedy of the individual human being, and yet he never lost sight of his biological background, of the human species emerging from dubious origins and groping its way to an even more dubious destiny. He was no physicist, and he never took space travel seriously, although he used it on occa-

sion as a stage property for his stories. His visions of man's future are earthbound, pessimistic, and quite different from my vision as I shall describe it to you tonight. But I do not need to agree with Wells in detail in order to acknowledge the greatness of his influence. I take his contribution to human thought to be not the description of particular futures, but the awareness of the future as an object of intellectual study, having a depth and breadth as great as the study of the historic past. I am a child of Wells insofar as I cannot think of human destiny beyond the year 2000 as lying outside the scope of my responsibilities.

[6] As an example of the sort of insight into human character that I find more illuminating than sociological analysis, let me mention the Artilleryman who appears briefly in Wells' "War of the Worlds." This is an insignificant man who becomes convinced, as civilization collapses around him, that he can keep everything under control. He has unlimited self-confidence and a fine flow of words, quite out of touch with reality. Recently I met a U.S. diplomat who serves in a country where our policies might charitably be described as being on the point of collapse. At first I wondered, "Now where have I met this man before?"—and then I remembered Wells' Artilleryman. If you listen carefully, you will hear the voice of the Artilleryman wherever human society is facing problems of overwhelming difficulty.

[7] Another splendid example of Wells' insight is the General Intelligence Machine which appears in his story "When the Sleeper Wakes," written in 1899. It did not take much wisdom to foresee in 1899 a machine which would sit in somebody's living room and speak upon request, giving up-to-date news reports concerning the events of the day. Wells' insight is shown in the nature of the information which the machine provides. It puts out a continuous stream of advertising commercials and political propaganda, at such a level of imbecility that the characters in the story refer to it only by the name of "Babble Machine." To give the flavor of the thing, I quote directly from Wells: "Babble Machines of a peculiarly rancid tone filled the air with strenuous squealing and an idiotic slang, 'Skin your eyes and slide,' 'Gewhoop,

bonanza,' 'Gollipers come and hark!'" I find it comforting, when the drivel put out by our contemporary Babble Machines drives me to fury or despair, to reflect that even the worst television commercials are not quite as bad as Wells imagined they would be.

[8] Let me give you a short list of facts which I regard as central to the human situation. Like Wells and other social analysts, I shall select my facts to make my theory plausible.

[9] One fact of human life which is hard to ignore is nationalism. In all parts of the world nationalism is the strongest political force. In most places it is the only effective force making possible the organization of man's efforts for peace or war. Where nationalism is weak, as in Nigeria or Belgium, it is usually because a smaller political unit—a tribe or a province—has usurped the place of the nation in men's minds. The strength of nationalism in the world as a whole has steadily increased during recent centuries, and is probably still increasing.

[10] Another obvious fact of life is race. The events of the last years have made it clear, if it was not clear before, that the problem of race runs deep in our society. No society with a substantial racial minority is free from problems. Some societies are more tolerant than others, but tolerance is fragile. For most of us it is pleasanter to live segregated than to face the frictions of racially mixed housing. In the pure-white English society into which I was born, having at that time no Negroes to worry about, we developed our famous class system instead. As a middle-class child, I was unable to communicate with most of the children of my neighborhood, since they were "Oiks" and spoke a different dialect.

[11] A third fact of life is drugs. By this I mean not the harmless legal drugs like aspirin and penicillin, but the illegal ones, LSD, marijuana and so forth. Many people no doubt have more experience with these than I do, but at least I have not brought up a couple of teen-agers without realizing that drugs are an important part of the landscape. And it is clear to me that the existing drugs are only the first wave of an ever-increasing series of problems which may be included under the general heading of biological experimentation. As

biochemistry advances there will be more varied drugs, illegally available, offering strange adventures to reckless young people. To make these legal will never be acceptable to anxious parents and neighbors; to make them illegal will never effectively stop their abuse. Later on, when biology and genetics have advanced a little further, even more serious problems of medical experimentation will arise. Our young people may be able to induce dreams and hallucinations in each other, programmed to order, by gadgetry feeding directly into the brain. What reality would be able to compete with this dreamworld for their minds? Ultimately, perhaps a hundred years from now or perhaps sooner, humanity will be faced with the possibility of deliberate programming of the genetic make-up of children. Either a government using its paternalistic authority, or a group of individuals in defiance of authority, may cause children to be born differing radically from the norm in moral or intellectual power. Such experimentation may be of immense value from certain points of view. What a grand and terrible thing it would be to call into being a child with the endowments of Einstein or of Martin Luther King! And yet, which of our existing social institutions is strong enough to withstand the stresses that a generation of genetic experimentation would produce?

[12] I have listed three disagreeable facts that confront the human species, the facts of nationalism, racism, and biological engineering. Under the heading of biological engineering I include the whole range of problems of which LSD gives us a foretaste. These three facts are usually regarded as separate problems, each to be handled as best we can in its own context. I shall instead concentrate attention on the features common to all three, and see if there is perhaps some underlying pattern.

[13] I find the underlying pattern to be the propensity of human beings to function best in rather small groups. We are almost all familiar with the happiness that comes from a communal effort. Goethe has described it imperishably in the death scene of his "Faust." Our teen-agers are disoriented because they are no longer involved in the communal

activities of family and village, sowing and harvesting, hedging and ditching.

[14] Our pot-smoking teen-agers are unanimous in saying that the great thing about pot is not the drug itself but the comradeship which it creates. And to make the comradeship real, there must not only be a group of friends inside the circle but enemies outside, police and parents and authorities to be defied. Just as, in the old Yorkshire wool factory, the spirit among the workers was warm and intimate, not in spite of but because of their shared hostility to the mill-owner and his managers. This is human life the way it is: my son wearing his hair odiously long just because I dislike to be seen together with it in public, and we of the older generation fulfilling our duty as parents by keeping our hair short and marijuana illegal.

[15] I believe the strength of nationalism and racism derives ultimately from the same source as the tension between the generations. We all have a psychological need to feel identified with a group, preferably not too large a group, with a common purpose and a common enemy. Countries like the United States are already far too big to fulfill this need satisfactorily. Small countries like Holland and Switzerland can generally handle social problems better than big ones. Nationalism is most triumphantly successful in countries which are both small and threatened, such as Finland, Israel, North Vietnam and Biafra.

[16] It is easy to theorize, as many paleontologists have theorized, that the human species has built-in instincts of tribal exclusiveness, frozen into our inheritance during the hundreds of thousands of years which our ancestors spent roaming in small nomadic bands. Such a theory is plausible as an explanation of present-day nationalism, racism and teenage gang warfare, but I do not know whether it can ever be proved. For my purposes it is not important to decide whether exclusiveness is an inherited instinct or a culturally acquired characteristic. The important thing is that tribal exclusiveness exists in our species and has been essential to our rapid evolution.

[17] Rapid evolution in any species depends largely on a phenomenon known as "genetic drift." Genetic drift is the random drifting of the average genetic make-up in a small inbreeding, population. The speed of drift varies inversely with the square-root of the size of the breeding-group. The direction of drift is somewhat influenced by natural selection, but drift occurs even in the absence of selection. It seems to me incontestable that a group of apes could develop an aptitude for calculus, or symphonic music, or theological argument, only through genetic drift and not through natural selection. In fact all the things which we prize most in human culture, our appreciation of art, poetry, holiness and natural beauty, must be products of genetic drift.

[18] I believe, though this is pure speculation, that genetic drift has been of decisive importance to human progress even in historic times. When we make a list of the most creative periods in human history, confining ourselves to the Christian-European tradition with which I am familiar, we think immediately of eighth-century Jerusalem, fifth-century Athens, and fourteenth-century Florence. In each case we have a city, hardly more than a village by modern standards, producing out of a small population within a hundred years an astonishing concentration of intellectual achievement. In each case the outburst of genius followed a long period during which the city existed with an even smaller population, rather isolated from its neighbors and quarreling with them incessantly. It seems to me plausible that the best recipe for human cultural progress would read roughly as follows: Take a hundred city-states, each with population between ten and a hundred thousand; let each one hate its neighbors sufficiently to prevent substantial interbreeding; encourage priestly and aristocratic caste systems to reduce still further the size of breeding units; introduce an occasional major war or plague to keep the populations small; let the mixture simmer for a thousand years, and maybe one of your hundred cities will be the new Florence, the new Athens, or the new Jerusalem.

[19] So far I have presented the case for human divisiveness, for insularity, exclusiveness and intolerance. I want to make clear that these human qualities, however evil their con-

sequences in our present society, are not easily to be eradicated. Throughout the long centuries of our prehistory and even until quite recently, these qualities have been beneficial to our species. In the self-sacrifice of a soldier, the fury of a mob, the loyalty to his friends of a teen-ager, the same qualities are still with us. We still function best in small groups.

[20] Now we are all well aware that this is only half the story. We cannot go back to the Middle Ages or to classical Greece, even if we wished to. The idea of universal human brotherhood may still be remote for most of us. But against the historic forces of tribalism stand the three great forces of modern technology, the forces of weaponry, population growth, and pollution. We are in danger of exterminating ourselves with our hydrogen bombs and the still worse horrors with which biological engineering will soon provide us. We are in danger of exhausting our resources and ultimately reducing ourselves to a starvation diet through over-population. We are in danger of ruining all that is beautiful on this planet through our accumulation of poisonous mess. All three dangers demand that mankind unite. Each of them, and the problem of weapons above all, requires a world-wide authority to protect us from our own folly. Slowly and against stubborn resistance, practical necessities are driving us to forget our quarrels and accept peaceful coexistence with our enemies. For 24 years the nuclear physicists have been saying "One world, or none," and there is no reason to doubt that in the long run they are right. The Earth has grown too small for bickering tribes and city-states to exist on it. Our bombs are too big, our machines are too complicated, our smog and garbage are too pervasive to be left much longer in the hands of local authorities.

[21] As far into the future as anyone can see, the dangers of modern technology will continue to grow and will threaten mankind on this planet with the choice of political union or death. Political union will inevitably mean some degree of political oppression, government by remote bureaucracy, over-centralization. We will be lucky if we can succeed in organizing a world government which does not degenerate into a world police state. But I believe the forces of tribalism and nationalism will for a long time remain strong enough to

defeat attempts to impose world government. Men will prefer to live in filth with the threat of annihilation hanging over their heads, rather than allow foreigners to tax them.

[22] Unfortunately the unifying force of technology, while not yet powerful enough to bind us into a world-wide brotherhood, is already quite strong enough to destroy the historic benefits which we once derived from tribalism.

[23] Now I come at last to the hopeful part of my message. I have presented a gloomy view of our human predicament. On the one hand, we are historically attuned to living in small exclusive groups, and we carry in us a stubborn disinclination to treat all men as our brothers. On the other hand, we live on a shrinking and vulnerable planet which our lack of foresight is rapidly turning into a slum. Never again on this planet will there be unoccupied land, cultural isolation, freedom from bureaucracy, freedom for people to get lost and be on their own. Never again on this planet. But how about somewhere else?

[24] I believe in fact that space-travel does provide an answer to many of these grave human problems. The only question in my mind is "When?" Many of you may consider it ridiculous to think of space as a way out of our difficulties, when the existing space program, such as it is, is being rapidly cut down, precisely because it appears to have nothing to offer to the solution of social problems. It is of course true that the existing space program has nothing to offer. If one believes in space as a major factor in human affairs, one must take a very long view.

[25] To avoid misunderstanding, I would like to emphasize again that I am making a sharp distinction between human affairs and scientific affairs. The existing space program consists of two very unequal parts, the scientific program using unmanned vehicles and absorbing about one-tenth of the money, and the unscientific program including manned flights and taking nine-tenths of the money. The scientific program has already been of immense value to science. In the next two decades, if the economy axe has not chopped it to pieces, the scientific space program should be able to settle the question of the existence of life on Mars, and I cannot think

of any question in the whole of science more important than that. In the long run the discovery of alien life would undoubtedly have human as well as scientific consequences, but I do not include these in my discussion. I am looking for consequences of space travel that affect the mass of my fellow citizens and not merely my academic colleagues. The unscientific part of the existing space program affects the public more directly but only superficially. It is in essence an international sporting event with the whole world as spectators. I am a supporter of the manned space program for reasons which I will presently explain, but I do not pretend that it yet offers benefits commensurate with its cost, either to science or to the general public.

[26] How long it will take for space travel to become socially important is mainly a matter of economics, a field in which I have no competence. I will only put forward a few tentative remarks to suggest that the time should be measured in decades rather than in centuries. There is a prevalent view among the educated public that space travel is necessarily and permanently so expensive that it can never be made available to large masses of people. I believe this view to be incorrect. An interesting analysis of the economics of our existing space operations was made by Theodore Taylor ("Propulsion of Space Vehicles" in Marshak, "Perspectives in Modern Physics," Interscience, 1966). He calculated the cost of running a commercial jet-plane service from New York to Los Angeles under the following ground rules: (1) There shall be no more than one flight per month. (2) The airplane shall be thrown away after each flight. (3) The entire costs of Kennedy and Los Angeles airports shall be covered by the freight charges. Under these rules, which are the rules governing our present space program, the cost of freight between New York and Los Angeles is comparable to the cost of putting freight into orbit. The point of this calculation is that the economies of commercial airline operations are economies of scale and of efficient organization. There is no basic physical or engineering reason why it should be enormously cheaper to fly to Los Angeles than to fly into orbit.

[27] I will not go here into a technical discussion of

the problems of space propulsion. In order to make space travel cheap we need two things. The first is a reliable vehicle, preferably an air-breather, which can take off from an airport, fly itself directly into orbit, re-enter and land, and be ready to repeat the operation day after day. The second is a massive volume of traffic and a correspondingly massive sale of tickets. I believe the second of these requirements will be met automatically within a few decades after the first is achieved. There are formidable technical problems involved in producing the re-usable orbital vehicle, but I do not believe the problems are permanently insoluble. Few people in the existing space program have worked on these problems, because the policy has been to do things fast rather than cheaply. The present cut-back may in fact encourage more long-range work on cheaper vehicles. I hesitate to make numerical predictions, but it may help to make my remarks meaningful if I state my actual expectations for the time-scale of these developments. I expect that sometime between 50 and 100 years from now we will have space travel with a volume of traffic and a cost to the passengers comparable with our present intercontinental jet flights. This prediction has the great advantage that if the reality exceeds my hopes I may be here to enjoy it, whereas, if I am proved wrong the other way, I will never know it.

[28] I will not say more about the economic aspects of space travel. The technical problems can be solved only by long and hard work, not by philosophical discourse. I am here discussing the problems of goals and purpose. Why should so many people want to rush around in space? And what good will it all do?

[29] First I should like to make clear that I do not envisage emigration from Earth as solving the problem of the population explosion. Emigrants will always be a small minority, like the Spanish conquistadores rather than the Irish peasants of the Hungry Forties. Those who stay on Earth must solve their population problems, one way or another. Those who emigrate will have only postponed theirs.

[30] I conceive the expansion of mankind into space to confer benefits on us in three main respects. (I am still ignoring entirely the scientific benefits and speaking only of social

benefits.) The three benefits I will call garbage disposal, invulnerability and the open frontier, in what I consider to be increasing order of importance.

[31] If humanity were to be forever confined to Earth, the problem of pollution could hardly be solved without an enforced economic stagnation. Many industrial processes are inherently messy, and the sum-total of industrial processes threatens to heat the Earth's biosphere to an intolerable extent within a century or two at present rates of economic growth. If cheap space transportation were available, it would become socially desirable and probably economically advantageous to move many of the messier industries into space. The solar wind is a magnificent garbage-disposal system, sweeping any dispersed matter in the solar system into an outer darkness where it will never be seen again. Prime candidates for the move upstairs would be the nuclear reactor and processing industries with their very large radioactive waste and thermal pollution problems.

[32] The migration of industry into space need not be directed by a grandiose governmental plan. It would probably occur spontaneously as a result of economic pressures, if polluting industries were forced to pay for the privilege of remaining on Earth the actual cost of their pollutions. I foresee a time, a few centuries from now, when the bulk of heavy industry is space-borne, with the majority of mining operations perhaps transferred to the moon, and the Earth preserved for the enjoyment of its inhabitants as a green and pleasant land.

[33] If the problem of garbage disposal for an Earthbound humanity is difficult, the problem of invulnerability is essentially insoluble. How can we expect to go on living forever on this exposed planetary surface, armed with deadly weapons which year by year grow more numerous and more widely dispersed? The only way to make the Earth safe from these weapons would be to establish a supra-national monopoly of military force, and even such a monopoly would not give us permanent security. The guardians of the monopoly would be men with their own national loyalties, and there would always be danger that the monopoly would break up in ruin-

ous civil war, as happened on a smaller scale in 1861. We can hope to survive in a world bristling with hydrogen bombs for a few centuries, if we are lucky. But I believe we have small chance of surviving 10,000 years if we stay stuck to this planet. We are too many eggs in too small a basket.

[34] The emigration into distant parts of the solar system of a substantial number of people would make our species as a whole invulnerable. A nuclear holocaust on Earth would still be an unspeakable tragedy, and might still wipe out 99 per cent of our numbers. But the one per cent who had dispersed themselves could not be wiped out simultaneously by any man-made catastrophe, and they would remain to carry on the promise of our destiny. Perhaps some of them would also come back to repopulate the Earth, after the radioactivity had cooled off. I at least find it a consoling thought that the human race will one day be invulnerable, that we have only to survive this awkward period of a century or two between the discovery of nuclear weapons and the large-scale expansion of our habitat, and then we shall be masters of our fate, freed from the threat of permanent extinction.

[35] The third and to my mind deepest benefit which space offers to mankind is the recovery of an open frontier. At this point we come back to the question: Where will all these people go when they set out in their latter-day Mayflowers? It is conventional in science fiction to think of going to planets, to Mars in particular. But I do not think planets will play the major role in man's future. For one thing, they are mostly uninhabitable. For another thing, even if they are habitable they will not increase our living-space very much. If we succeed in colonizing Mars, Mars will soon resemble the Earth, complete with parking lots, income tax forms, and all the rest of it. It will not be possible to hide on Mars any more than on Earth.

[36] I believe the real future of man in space lies far away from planets, in isolated city-states floating in the void, perhaps attached to an inconspicuous asteroid or perhaps to a comet. Comets are especially important. It is believed that between a billion and 10 billion comets exist on the outer fringes of the solar system, loosely attached to the sun and

only very rarely passing close to it. Each of these comets is a mine of biologically useful materials, carbon, nitrogen and water. Together they provide a thousand times as much living space as the planets. Above all they provide an open frontier, a place to hide and to disappear without trace, beyond the reach of snooping policemen and bureaucrats.

[37] This vision of comet-hopping emigrants, streaming outward like the covered wagons on the Santa Fe Trail, is perhaps absurdly romantic or fanciful. Maybe it will never happen the way I imagine it. But I am convinced that something more or less along these lines will ultimately happen. Space is huge enough, so that somewhere in its vastness there will always be a place for rebels and outlaws. Near to the sun, space will belong to big governments and computerized industries. Outside, the open frontier will beckon as it has beckoned before, to persecuted minorities escaping from oppression, to religious fanatics escaping from their neighbors, to recalcitrant teen-agers escaping from their parents, to lovers of solitude escaping from crowds. Perhaps most important of all for man's future, there will be groups of people setting out to find a place where they can be safe from prying eyes, free to experiment undisturbed with the creation of radically new types of human beings, surpassing us in mental capacities as we surpass the apes.

[38] So I foresee that the ultimate benefit of space travel to man will be to make it possible for him once again to live as he lived throughout prehistoric time, in isolated small units. Once again his human qualities of clannish loyalty and exclusiveness will serve a constructive role, instead of being the chief dangers to his survival.

[39] Men's tribal instincts will move back from the destructive channels of nationalism, racism and youthful alienation, and find satisfaction in the dangerous life of a frontier society. Genetic drift and diversification will again become important factors in human progress. Only in this way, I believe, can the basic dilemmas of our age, arising from the discordance between our tribal loyalties and the necessities of a world-wide technological civilization, be resolved. And when the angry young men and rebels and racists have again a

frontier to which they can go, perhaps we timid and law-abiding citizens who choose to stay quietly down here on Earth will find it easier to live together in peace.

EXERCISES—*HUMAN CONSEQUENCES OF THE EXPLORATION OF SPACE*

Content

1. According to Dyson, why is nationalism on the increase throughout the world?
2. What are the three disagreeable facts that confront the human species, and what features are common to all three?
3. Why can small countries like Holland and Switzerland handle social problems better than the U.S.?
4. Define "genetic drift" as Dyson uses the term.
5. Explain the author's view of man's hope.
6. Who will the settlers of space be?

Style

1. Why did Dyson choose to write in first person? Could he have just as easily used a different point of view? Explain.
2. Who is Dyson's audience? Is then this essay formal, informal, or colloquial?
3. In paragraph (31), the author says, "Prime candidates for the move upstairs would be the nuclear reactor and processing industries with their very large radioactive waste and thermal pollution problems." What aspects of this sentence suggest the author's intended audience? Explain?
4. Does the author provide adequate definition of terms and clarification of ideas for the educated layman? Explain.
5. Briefly describe the author's organization of this essay. Explain your view of the effectiveness of his organization.
6. Examine the author's introductory paragraph. In regard to his audience, what has he intended to do in this paragraph?

Application of Stylistic Techniques

1. After you have decided on the stylistic level (formal, informal, colloquial) of this essay, rewrite the introductory paragraph to fit the other two levels.

2. Rewrite paragraph (3) in third person subjective, avoiding passive voice and the use of the impersonal pronoun "one."
3. Rewrite paragraph (32) by converting all passive voice verbs to active voice.
4. Explain the use of "we" in paragraph (20).
5. After having converted the point of view of paragraph (4) to the "editorial we," explain your reason for liking Dyson's use of "I" or your conversion to "we."
6. Explain the use of "you" in paragraph (24).
7. For what reason does Dyson close paragraph (24) with a sentence containing the impersonal "one"?

Suggestions for Writing

1. In an informal essay, writing from first-person-singular point of view, challenge Dyson's view of man's hope.
2. Select a topic and write an essay in first person singular.
   One World or None
   Two Many Eggs in One Small Basket
   The Force of a Common Cause
   Space: Man's Garbage Dump?
   The Pill: An End to the Urge to Kill?
   Man's Need for New Frontiers
   War on Exploration?
   Survival through Self-Preservation
   Conservation and Anti-Pollution Measures: A Waste of Time?
   Space and the Litter Bug

E. B. White was born in Mount Vernon, New York, on July 11, 1899. In 1922 he was graduated from Cornell. He is well known for his essays, short stories, and poems. He has held various jobs in journalism and has contributed regularly to *Harper's Magazine* and *The New Yorker*. He is still on the salaried staff of *The New Yorker,* working from his home in Maine. His books include *Quo Vadimus?, One Man's Meat, The Second Tree from the Corner,* and *The Points of My Compass*. He is also the author of two juvenile classics, *Charlotte's Web* and *Stuart Little,* for which he won the 1970 Laura Ingalls Wilder Award, which is presented by the Children's Services Division of the American Library Association every five years to an author of books that have, over a period of years, "made a substantial and lasting contribution to literature for children." In June, 1970, Mr. White's long awaited third book for children, *The Trumpet of the Swan,* was published. He edited and amplified *The Elements of Style* by William Strunk, Jr. In 1963 he received the Presidential Medal of Freedom.

The Age of Dust *(First Person Plural)*

E. B. WHITE

[1] On a sunny morning last week, we went out and put up a swing for a little girl, age three, under an apple tree—the tree being much older than the girl, the sky being blue, the clouds white. We pushed the little girl for a few minutes, then returned to the house and settled down to an article on death dust, or radiological warfare, in the July *Bulletin of the Atomic Scientists,* Volume VI, No. 7.

[2] The article ended on a note of disappointment. "The area that can be poisoned with the fission products available to us today is disappointingly small; it amounts to not more than two or three major cities per month." At first glance, the sentence sounded satirical, but a rereading convinced us that

From *The Second Tree from the Corner* (1954) by E. B. White. "The Age of Dust" originally appeared in *The New Yorker,* and is printed by permission of Harper & Row, Publishers, Inc.

the scientist's disappointment was real enough—that it had the purity of detachment. The world of the child in the swing (the trip to the blue sky and back again) seemed, as we studied the ABC of death dust, more and more a dream world with no true relation to things as they are or to the real world of discouragement over the slow rate of the disappearance of cities.

[3] Probably the scientist-author of the death-dust article, if he were revising his literary labors with a critical eye, would change the wording of that queer sentence. But the fact is, the sentence got written and published. The terror of the atom age is not the violence of the new power but the speed of man's adjustment to it—the speed of his acceptance. Already bombproofing is on approximately the same level as mothproofing. Two or three major cities per month isn't much of an area, but it is a start. To the purity of science (which hopes to enlarge the area) there seems to be no corresponding purity of political thought, never the same detachment. We sorely need, from a delegate in the Security Council, a statement as detached in its way as the statement of the scientist on death dust. This delegate (and it makes no difference what nation he draws his pay from) must be a man who has not adjusted to the age of dust. He must be a person who still dwells in the mysterious dream world of swings, and little girls in swings. He must be more than a good chess player studying the future; he must be a memoirist remembering the past.

[4] We couldn't seem to separate the little girl from radiological warfare—she seemed to belong with it, although inhabiting another sphere. The article kept getting back to her. "This is a novel type of warfare, in that it produces no destruction, except to life." The weapon, said the author, can be regarded as a horrid one, or, on the other hand, it "can be regarded as a remarkably humane one. In a sense, it gives each member of the target population [including each little girl] a choice of whether he will live or die." It turns out that the way to live—if that be your choice—is to leave the city as soon as the dust arrives, holding "a folded, dampened handkerchief" over your nose and mouth. We went outdoors

again to push the swing some more for the little girl, who is always forgetting her handkerchief. At lunch we watched her try to fold her napkin. It seemed to take forever.

[5] As we lay in bed that night, thinking of cities and target populations, we saw the child again. This time she was with the other little girls in the subway. When the train got to 242nd Street, which is as far as it goes into unreality, the children got off. They started to walk slowly north. Each child had a handkerchief, and every handkerchief was properly moistened and folded neatly—the way it said in the story.

EXERCISES—*THE AGE OF DUST*

Content

1. What does White say is the terror of the atomic age?
2. What is the author's attitude toward the "purity of science"?
3. In paragraph (4) explain the reason White says the folding of the little girl's handkerchief "seemed to take forever."
4. Explain the title *The Age of Dust.*

Style

1. In what person has the author written this essay? Explain his choice.
2. Having read the essay, would you say the author is a scientist? Explain.
3. Why does the author not use "we" in paragraph (2)?
4. Who is "we" in paragraph (4)?
5. What mood do you think the author was in when he wrote *The Age of Dust*?

Application of Stylistic Techniques

1. Rewrite paragraph (1) in first person singular.
2. Rewrite paragraph (1) in third person impersonal, using "one." Explain your reason for believing that "we" or "one" is more effective.
3. Rewrite paragraph (5) in the "imperative you." Does employment of the imperative make it necessary to change the verb tense? Explain.

4. Rewrite paragraph (1) as if you were writing for a group of scientists.

Suggestions for Writing

1. Attack E. B. White as a simpering sentimentalist, or support him as a man concerned about the future of mankind.
2. Compare and/or contrast Dyson's and White's mood toward man's hope for survival.
3. Select a topic and write an essay, using the editorial "we."
   What Good Is a Bomb Shelter?
   What Children Don't Know
   Scientists Have No Right to Be Objective!
   A Good Weapon Kills
   It'll Never Happen Here
   Who Pushes the Button?
   Objectivity vs. Subjectivity
   Man's Inability to Adjust to His World
   We Can Even Live with It!
   Over a Quarter of a Century after Hiroshima

William H. Whyte (1917–) received his B.A. from Princeton University in 1939. He was assistant managing editor for *Fortune Magazine* and contributed to *Harper's, Life,* and *Encounter.* His major works include *Is Anybody Listening, The Organization Man,* and *The Exploding Metropolis.*

You, Too, Can Write the Casual Style *(Second Person)*

WILLIAM H. WHYTE, JR.

[1] A revolution has taken place in American prose. No longer the short huffs and puffs, the unqualified word, the crude gusto of the declarative sentence. Today the fashion is to write casually.

[2] The Casual Style is not exactly new. Originated in the early Twenties, it has been refined and improved and refined again by a relatively small band of writers, principally for the *New Yorker,* until now their mannerisms have become standards of sophistication. Everybody is trying to join the club. Newspaper columnists have forsaken the beloved metaphors of the sports page for the Casual Style, and one of the quickest ways for an ad man to snag an award from other ad men is to give his copy the low-key, casual pitch; the copy shouldn't sing these days—it should whisper. Even Dr. Rudolf Flesch, who has been doing so much to teach people how to write like other people, is counseling his followers to use the Casual Style. Everywhere the ideal seems the same: be casual.

[3] But how? There is very little down-to-earth advice. We hear about the rapier-like handling of the bromide, the

keen eye for sham and pretension, the exquisite sense of nuance, the unerring ear for the vulgate. But not much about actual technique. The layman, as a consequence, is apt to look on the Casual Style as a mandarin dialect which he fears he may never master.

[4] Nonsense. The Casual Style is within everyone's grasp. It has now become so perfected by constant polishing that its devices may readily be identified, and they change so little that their use need be no more difficult for the novice than for the expert. (That's not quite all there is to it, of course. Some apparently casual writers, Thurber and E. B. White, among others, rarely use the devices.)

[5] The subject matter, in the first place, is not to be ignored. Generally speaking, the more uneventful it is, or the more pallid the writer's reaction to it, the better do form and content marry. Take, for example, the cocktail party at which the writer can show how bored everyone is with everyone else, and how utterly fatuous they all are anyhow. Since a non-casual statement—*e.g.*, "The party was a bore"—would destroy the reason for writing about it at all, the Casual Style here is not only desirable but mandatory.

[6] Whatever the subject, however, twelve devices are the rock on which all else is built. I will present them one by one, illustrating them with examples from such leading casual stylists as Wolcott Gibbs, John Crosby, John McCarten, and (on occasion) this magazine's "Mr. Harper." If the reader will digest what follows, he should be able to dash off a paragraph indistinguishable from the best casual writing being done today.

[7] *Heightened Understatement.* Where the old-style writer would say, "I don't like it," "It is not good," or something equally banal, the casual writer says it is "*something less than* good." He avoids direct statement and strong words —except, as we will note, where he is setting them up to have something to knock down. In any event, he qualifies. "Somewhat" and "rather," the bread-and-butter words of the casual writer, should become habitual with you; similarly with such phrases as "I suppose," "it seems to me," "I guess," or "I'm afraid." "Elusive" or "elude" are good, too, and if you see the

word "charm" in a casual sentence you can be pretty sure that "eludes me," or "I find elusive," will not be far behind.

[8] *The Multiple Hedge.* Set up an ostensibly strong statement, and then, with your qualifiers, shoot a series of alternately negative and positive charges into the sentence until finally you neutralize the whole thing. Lets take, for example, the clause, "certain names have a guaranteed nostalgic magic." Challenge enough here; the names not only have magic, they have guaranteed magic. A double hedge reverses the charge. "Names which have, *I suppose* [hedge 1], a guaranteed nostalgic magic, *though there are times that I doubt it* [hedge 2]. . . ."

[9] We didn't have to say they were guaranteed in the first place, of course, but without such straw phrases we wouldn't have anything to construct a hedge on and, frequently, nothing to write at all. The virtue of the hedge is that by its very negating effect it makes any sentence infinitely expansible. Even if you have so torn down your original statement with one or two hedges that you seem to have come to the end of the line, you have only to slip in an anti-hedge, a strengthening word (*e.g.*, "definitely," "unqualified," etc.), and begin the process all over again. Witness the following quadruple hedge: "I found Mr. Home entertaining *from time to time* [hedge 1] on the ground, *I guess* [hedge 2], that the singular idiom and unearthly detachment of the British upper classes have *always* [anti-hedge] seemed *reasonably* [hedge 3] droll to me, *at least in moderation* [hedge 4]." The art of plain talk, as has been pointed out, does not entail undue brevity.

[10] If you've pulled hedge on hedge and the effect still remains too vigorous, simply wipe the slate clean with a cancellation clause at the end. "It was all exactly as foolish as it sounds," says Wolcott Gibbs, winding up some 570 casual words on a subject, "and I wouldn't give it another thought."

[11] *Narcissizing Your Prose.* The casual style is nothing if not personal; indeed, you will usually find in it as many references to the writer as to what he's supposed to be talking about. For you do not talk about the subject; you talk about its impact on you. With the reader peering over your shoulder, you look into the mirror and observe your own re-

sponses as you run the entire range of the casual writer's emotions. You may reveal yourself as, in turn, listless ("the audience seemed not to share my boredom"); insouciant ("I was really quite happy with it"); irritated ("The whole thing left me tired and cross"); comparatively gracious ("Being in a comparatively gracious mood, I won't go into the details I didn't like"); or hesitant ("I wish I could say that I could accept his hypothesis").

[12] *Preparation for the Witticism.* When the casual writer hits upon a clever turn of phrase or a nice conceit, he uses this device to insure that his conceit will not pass unnoticed. Suppose, for example, you have thought of something to say that is pretty damn good if you say so yourself. The device, in effect, is to say so yourself. If you want to devastate a certain work as "a study of vulgarity in high places," don't say this flat out. Earlier in the sentence prepare the reader for the drollery ahead with something like "what I am tempted to call" or "what could best be described as" or "If it had to be defined in a sentence, it might well be called. . . ."

[13] Every writer his own claque.

[14] *Deciphered Notes Device; or Cute-Things-I-Have-Said.* In this one you are your own stooge as well. You feed yourself lines. By means of the slender fiction that you have written something on the back of an envelope or the margin of a program, you catch yourself good-humoredly trying to decipher these shrewd, if cryptic, little jottings. *Viz.*: "Their diagnoses are not nearly as crisp as those I find in my notes"; ". . . sounds like an inadequate description, but it's all I have in my notes, and it may conceivably be a very high compliment."

[15] *The Kicker.* An echo effect. "My reactions [included] an irritable feeling that eleven o'clock was past Miss Keim's bedtime,"—and now the Kicker—*"not to mention my own."* This type of thing practically writes itself. "She returns home. She should never have left home in the first place. ______ ________ _______ _____."*

[16] *Wit of Omission.* By calling attention to the fact that you are not going to say it, you suggest that here is

* "And neither should I."

something very funny you could say if only you wanted to. "A thought occurred to me at this point," you may say, when otherwise stymied, "but I think we had better not go into *that*."

[17] *The Planned Colloquialism.* The casual writer savors colloquialisms. This is not ordinary colloquial talk—nobody is more quickly provoked than the casual writer by ordinary usage. It is, rather, a playful descent into the vulgate. Phrases like "darn," "awfully," "as all getout," "mighty," and other folksy idioms are ideal. The less you would be likely to use the word normally yourself the more pointed the effect. Contrast is what you are after, for it is the facetious interplay of language levels—a blending, as it were, of the East Fifties and the Sticks—that gives the Casual Style its off-hand charm.

[18] *Feigned Forgetfulness.* Conversation gropes; it is full of "what I really meant was" and "maybe I should have added," backings and fillings and second thoughts of one kind or another. Writing is different; theoretically, ironing out second thoughts beforehand is one of the things writers are paid to do. In the Casual Style, however, it is exactly this exposure of the writer composing in public that makes it so casual. For the professional touch, then, ramble, rebuke yourself in print ("what I really meant, I guess"), and if you have something you feel you should have said earlier, don't say it earlier, but say later that you guess you should have said it earlier.

[19] *The Subject-Apologizer, or Pardon-Me-for-Living.* The Casual Stylist must always allow for the possibility that his subject is just as boring to the reader as it is to him. He may forestall this by seeming to have stumbled on it by accident, or by using phrases like: "If this is as much news to you as it is to me," or "This, in case you've been living in a cave lately, is. . . ."

[20] *The Omitted Word.* This all began modestly enough the day a *New Yorker* writer dropped the articles "the" and "a" from the initial sentence of an anecdote (*e.g.*, "Man we know told us"; "Fellow name of Brown"). Now even such resolutely lowbrow writers as Robert Ruark affect it, and they are applying it to any part of speech anywhere in the sentence. You can drop a pronoun ("Says they're shaped like

pyramids"); verb ("You been away from soap opera the last couple of weeks?"); or preposition ("Far as glamour goes...").

[21] *The Right Word.* In the lexicon of the casual writer there are a dozen or so adjectives which in any context have, to borrow a phrase, a guaranteed charm. Attrition is high—"brittle," "febrile," "confected," for example, are at the end of the run. Ten, however, defy obsolescence: *antic, arch, blurred, chaste, chill, crisp, churlish, disheveled, dim, disembodied.*

[22] They are good singly, but they are even better when used in tandem; *c.f.*, "In an arch, antic sort of way"; "In an arch, blurred sort of way;" "In an arch, crisp sort of way." And so on.

[23] Finally, the most multi-purpose word of them all: "altogether." Frequently it is the companion of "charming" and "delightful," and in this coupling is indispensable to any kind of drama criticism. It can also modify the writer himself (*e.g.*, "Altogether, I think . . ."). Used best, however, it just floats, unbeholden to any other part of the sentence.

[24] Once you have mastered these twelve devices, you too should be able to write as casually as all getout. At least it seems to me, though I may be wrong, that they convey an elusive archness which the crisp literary craftsman, in his own dim sort of way, should altogether cultivate these days. Come to think of it, the charm of the Casual Style is something less than clear to me, but we needn't go into *that.* Fellow I know from another magazine says this point of view best described as churlish. Not, of course, that it matters.

EXERCISES—*YOU, TOO, CAN WRITE THE CASUAL STYLE*

Content

1. In order to be effective, on what must the planned colloquialism rely?
2. Which of the twelve devices does the author consider most effective for achieving the casual style? Explain.
3. Why does Whyte say that the casual style is within anyone's grasp?

4. What are the "bread-and-butter" words of the casual writer?
5. How does a writer go about "narcissizing" his prose?

Style

1. Determine the point of view Whyte uses in each of the following paragraphs: (2), (3), (6). Explain Whyte's shifts in point of view within and among these paragraphs.
2. Explain the reason for saying that this essay is written in second person. Select several paragraphs that support your choice.
3. In paragraph (10), does Whyte use the indefinite "you" or the imperative "you"? Explain.
4. Determine whether you think the essay is written primarily in the indefinite "you" or the imperative "you" and explain your choice through specific references to the essay.
5. Determine Whyte's audience. Considering this audience, explain your view of Whyte's attitude toward his giving instruction in how to write the casual style.

Application of Stylistic Techniques

1. In paragraph (12), Whyte's first sentence is in third person. Write the balance of the paragraph in third person and briefly discuss which paragraph—Whyte's original or your totally third person version—is more effective.
2. Rewrite the first sentence of paragraph (10) in third person, avoiding the personal pronoun "one"; then in the editorial "we"; then in third person objective, using "one." Using passive voice, rewrite Whyte's original sentence.
3. By writing about some subject familiar to you, write a paragraph patterned after paragraph (5). Duplicate the point of view, punctuation, verb tense, voice, and word order of each sentence.
4. Rewrite paragraph (2) of Freeman Dyson's *Human Consequences of the Exploration of Space* in the casual style. Use as many of Whyte's twelve devices as you can.

Suggestions for Writing

1. Write an essay to tell someone how to do something (shoot a rabbit, punish a child, solve the racial problem, eliminate war, ride a motorcycle, eat an ice cream cone, etc.), using second person and maintaining the same attitude Whyte has toward his audience.

2. Writing in the indefinite "you," explain to your reader how to enjoy something (studying for an exam, a vacation without much money, a walk in the woods or along a beach, popular music, etc.).
3. Select a topic and write an essay, using second person.
   Writing Is Easy
   Anyone Can Write a 500-Word Theme
   The Value of "Cool" Prose
   The Snobbish Writer
   The Trend toward Subjectivity
   Hedging: A Way of Life
   What's Wrong with Narcissism?
   The Literary Wit
   The Vulgate: That's Where It's At
   Writing Is a Lot of Fun

John Jay Corson (1905–   ) received his B.S. from the University of Virginia in 1926; his M.S. in 1929, and his Ph.D. in 1933. He has been with the Social Security Board, the U.S. Employment Service, the Bureau of Old Age and Survivors Insurance, and Princeton University; he has been a professor of public and international affairs and a member of the Board of Sweetbriar College. He has contributed to *Atlantic Monthly, Nation's Business,* the *New York Times,* and *American Mercury.* His major works include *This Government, Manpower for Victory, Executives for the Federal Services, Economic Needs of Older People, The Government of Colleges and Universities,* and *Men Near the Top.*

Social Change and the University

(Third Person Subjective)

JOHN J. CORSON

[1] Student unrest, faculty disaffiliation, expanding enrollments, and similar phenomena are superficial irritants, not fundamental forces to which universities must adapt. Beneath these everyday events and conditions are several basic dilemmas that plague the entire society and that require fundamental changes in our major institutions.

[2] For example, our increased population and increased wealth have produced not just more rich people, but some basic changes in attitudes among many people. The social cement that holds together a democracy—a widely accepted value system—no longer exists.

[3] The young are demanding a reordering of national priorities. Not only is there a widely voiced discontent with

From *Saturday Review,* January 10, 1970.

the Vietnam war, there are vociferous complaints about the lack of housing, the conditions of the cities, the inadequacies of the welfare system, the high cost of medical care, and the persistence of inflation.

[4] These concerns are not superficial issues created by the young as vehicles for a venting of their spleen. They are the expressions of new expectations of our society created by its own success. As the industrial society succeeded the agricultural society, and was in turn succeeded by what has been described as the post-industrial society, a new and advanced civilization with different characteristics has been emerging. These characteristics are being hammered out in riots in the cities, in court battles over equal employment, in education, and in housing opportunities; they are an attempt to forge a modernized concept of human dignity. The war on poverty—not just the federal programs but society's acceptance of the necessity for the fight—is gradually building the expectation of a national minimum that provides not only income, but health and higher education as well.

[5] The smog over our cities, the Santa Barbara oil slick, the polluted rivers, the rising crime rates are all establishing other expectations of a livable environment. The frustration of consumers, who can't tell the relative merits of Fortrel versus Dacron, or the hazards in pesticides, cyclamates, or scores of other products, is substituting for the principle of "let the buyer beware" the expectation that government should protect the consumer.

[6] The importance to the university of those new expectations is that the university has been, should be, and increasingly will be the institution in our society concerned with the shaping of values. The university's philosophers, economists, sociologists, historians, political scientists, if they do their job, are not just passing on what earlier scholars had passed on to them. They are helping a vastly greater proportion of the upcoming generation to understand, to modify, and to extend the lore of the past to the problems of the present. And that brings them right squarely into the forces of today, into the changing characteristics of the society.

[7] The professors in our universities are stimulating

youths to question the precepts of parents, the pronouncements of press, TV, politicians, and business leaders, and the preachings of the church. That is as it has always been. The university cannot avoid being the staging ground for battle over social issues. It is essential that the university find the structures and the practices within which these battles may be fought with words and ideas rather than with stones and fists.

[8] Another fundamental factor is an increasing dependence on knowledge. New knowledge, whether it be about the irradiation of foods to insure a longer life for the sandwiches in vending machines or about miniaturization that permits the development of pneumatic tools for the most delicate cranial surgery, has become central to economic and social progress.

[9] Several consequences follow from this fact. The university must be expected to be called upon to do much of or most of the research for other segments of the society. The university will become closer, probably uncomfortably closer, to the centers of economic, military, and political decision-making, and such a situation must be faced squarely and decisively.

[10] Access to job opportunities now depends more than ever on the acquisition of a certain amount of this new knowledge, and this means that the university has become the gatekeeper to the workaday world. Because nearly 50 per cent of our young people are going on to college, it is rapidly taking on the status of a public utility, and, as it does, it must accept the obligations that go with that status.

[11] Another consequence of the new knowledge is its increasing specialization. As invention and discovery have expanded knowledge at an ever increasing rate, the individual's field of comprehension has been narrowed even as it has been enlarged in power. This development confronts both the society and the university with a perplexing dichotomy, because the codification of new knowledge requires increasing specialization, while the resolution of society's problems requires an ability to interrelate bits of knowledge from each of a variety of specialties, and from each of a variety of disciplines. The truly educated citizen, the effective parent, the

competent professional man, and the self-fulfilling individual must be broader than a mere specialist. Our colleges and universities are expected to breed broader values into the specialists they develop. This expectation poses problems of course content, of curriculum control, of departmental structure, and faculty selection and leadership.

[12] Another social dilemma impelling change in the university is the loss of autonomy. As the university marches, or is pushed, into an increasingly influential position in the resolution of public problems, as it becomes increasingly the gatekeeper governing entry into the job market, and as its share of the Gross National Product grows, it will be subjected inevitably to an ever more intensive surveillance by its several constituencies: students, alumni, faculties, donors, including corporations, federal and state governments, and the public generally.

[13] As this scrutiny increases, the mystique that has guaranteed autonomy for the college and university disappears. The logic has been inescapable: the state's scarce resources do not permit support of the duplication of public institutions or the duplicating of facilities within such institutions. This logic is being supplemented on private as well as public campuses by the reasoning that education is becoming too important and the costs too great to be left to the scholars. Regardless of whether that reasoning will be accepted, the moral of accumulating experience is that the university will not continue as an island unto itself.

[14] The erosion of authority throughout our society is another fundamental condition that is changing the university. Student revolts must be viewed in relation to other contemporaneous revolutionary action. Black communities have rebelled in more than a score of cities, a substantial minority of younger Catholic priests have challenged the hierarchy of their church, and even some members of the armed services have organized on a score of military bases to voice criticisms. The new relationship of the student to the university must be viewed within the context of these similar rebellions against authority.

[15] The obsolescence of much of the lore possessed by the older generation is one cause of this erosion of authority.

Coleridge said that experience is like the stern light on a ship, illuminating only the past. In a period of rapid technological change this is all the more true. Moreover, differing values that flow out of this obsolescence accelerate the erosion of authority.

[16] And the revolution in communication, not only in television, radio, and the press, but in communication between individuals at the supermarket, in the subway, and the like—the understanding generated by these experiences of urban living—has undermined the authority of the patriarch in American society, be he the teacher, dean, president, business executive, bishop, or even military commander.

[17] This general erosion of authority strikes at the heart of the university governance. The authority of the teacher has been eroded by the increasing maturity, real or superficial, of the student, and by the technological advances that tend to make obsolete many of the Ph.D.s who got their doctorates before World War II. The logic of fixing authority for education in the faculty has been strained by the apparent fact that a university does not have a faculty. It has a score of faculties made up of individuals, many of whom are more concerned with their status in their discipline than in their attachment to the university that pays their salary.

[18] The authority of the president in relation to the faculty, or faculties, was undermined when he became a fund-raiser and an administrator and lost his status as an educator. And the trustees have allowed the broad authority that they were endowed with by law and historical practice to atrophy by concentrating their attention on the financial, physical, and public relations problems of the university. For decades, they have not dared to make decisions as to faculty selection, curricular matters, and the very guts of the university operations.

[19] The function of the university will be expanded still further and changed. Its instruction function will be limited by the growth of the community colleges and expanded by the growth of graduate professional training. Its research and community service functions will be broadened markedly. Hence, new forms and process of government must be capable

of managing a collection of related laboratories, institutes, centers, clinics, and offices in relation to existing colleges and schools scattered over perhaps a dozen or more cities. The arrangements for governance of such a complex may be much more analogous to the structure of a holding company than to those of a body of scholars that we nostalgically look back to.

[20] The trustees of the universities, both public and private, need to reidentify the constituencies they serve, and redefine the authority they will exercise. The problem of constituency in the private university is probably more severe, because the trustees have accepted little obligation to any constituency other than the alumni. They are increasingly being held accountable by students, by the faculty, by the government that contributes the major portion of the resources on which they depend, as well as by the alumni and by the general public.

[21] These constituencies will likely demand a voice in the trustees' councils. And the boards of trustees may be forced to abandon self-perpetuation in whole, or in part, in favor of election or designation of representatives by one or more of these constituencies.

[22] The trustees of both public and private universities will be called upon to accept greater responsibility for educational, research, and public service functions. They may not be able to avoid accepting authority in these realms by the assertion that they are concerned only with broad policy, and that they have delegated authority to the president for education, research, and student relations.

[23] The president of a university must reclaim for himself and his principal administrators the authority to act. To achieve coordination within, to utilize effectively increasingly scarce resources, and to stimulate requisite change, the president and his deans need greater authority. That authority cannot be handed down by trustees, who, like the British Queen, have held it in abeyance so long in fact they no longer have the authority that is needed. It must be ceded by the faculties who possess it by virtue of their monopolistic control of the university's stock in trade—knowledge and the capacity to create and transmit knowledge. Faculties can be induced to

cede it, if appropriate mechanisms for consultations are established, maintained, and nurtured.

[24] One might still ask what kind of leadership is required in the president's office—educational, administrative? Both, of course, but what is needed above all in the president of a university, in an era of persistent and substantial change, is a man who makes it obvious that he knows where he wants to go and how to articulate and be persuasive in stating goals for his institution, and who has the rare combination of ability, skills, and energy needed to carry an administrative staff and a faculty along toward those goals.

[25] The faculty—or faculties—must be helped to see themselves as a legislative body, not as an executive body. That means the faculty should be made to assume responsibility for recommending broad educational policy to the trustees, and for determining the curriculum, for faculty selection and promotion policies, and for student affairs, and also help to discipline itself to keep its hands off the executive of such policy. But the reclaiming of authority, long exercised by a small minority of the whole faculty over such minutiae as student social behavior as well as the approval of faculty appointments and curriculum, will be difficult.

[26] The students are already being granted a larger voice in governance and will be granted a still larger voice. The problem is to determine what areas of governance students should be involved in, and then to devise ways of selecting students who have the time, the inclination, and the ability to cope with these matters in a responsible fashion.

[27] There are forces at work that will change the function of the university, that will substantially expand the university, and that will establish new demands on the university. In coping with that change, some of the most venerated concepts, practices, and traditions of an old, old institution will be altered or abandoned.

EXERCISES—*SOCIAL CHANGE AND THE UNIVERSITY*

Content

1. According to Corson, what new demands by society will change the role of the university?
2. What is one of the major reasons the university will not continue "as an island unto itself," as he puts it?
3. List the causes of erosion of the university's teachers' and president's authority.
4. Who should be made to assume responsibility for recommending educational policy, for determining curriculum, for selecting faculty, and for regulating student affairs?

Style

1. By what means does Corson avoid using the personal pronouns (I, we, you) and the impersonal "one" as his point of view? Give two examples from the essay.
2. For what reason does Corson use passive voice extensively, for example, in paragraph (19)?
3. What does the author's using third person achieve? Explain your answer in terms of his intended audience.

Application of Stylistic Techniques

1. Rewrite paragraph (19) using the impersonal "one" and change passive voice verbs to active.
2. Rewrite paragraph (19) substituting "we" for "one." Is the substitution likely to change a reader's attitude toward the writer? Explain.
3. Using the personal pronoun "you," rewrite paragraph (5).
4. Rewrite paragraph (3) of Dyson's essay *Human Consequences of the Exploration of Space* in third person subjective. Delete any words unnecessary for this point of view, i.e., "I do not believe that. . . ."

Suggestions for Writing

1. Using third person subjective, write an essay supporting or disputing Corson's conclusion that some of the most venerated concepts and traditions of the university will be altered or abandoned.

2. In third person subjective, write an essay defending some university tradition that Corson believes will be changed.
3. Select a topic and write an essay, using third person subjective.
   What Happened to the Ivy?
   Universities: Bastions of the Antique
   Who Runs the University?
   Militant Students and the Rights of Others
   Who Ought to Run the University?
   The University: Society's Governor?
   Academic Freedom and Responsibility
   The University as a Corporation
   The Value of Faculty Tenure
   Does a College Student Know What's Best for Him?

Ernest Sternglass (1923–   ) was born in Berlin, Germany; he resides in Pittsburgh, Pennsylvania, where he is Professor of Radiation Physics at the University of Pittsburgh. From 1946-1952, he was a physicist with U.S. Naval Ordinance Laboratory. He earned his B.A. degree at Cornell University; he received his Ph.D. in 1951.

The Death of All Children

(Third Person Objective)

ERNEST J. STERNGLASS

[1] Hopefully it is not too late to ask the members of Congress in their deliberations over the Administration's proposed Anti-Ballistic Missile system to pause and reflect on the nature and urgency of the matter they have been debating.

[2] In view of new evidence on the totally unexpected action of strontium 90 on human reproductive cells, it is apparent that Congress has not yet considered what may well be the most important factor affecting its decision to proceed or not to proceed with the first steps toward the A.B.M. shield. The fact is this: a full-scale A.B.M. system, protecting the United States against a Soviet first strike, could, if successful, cause the extinction of the human race. (Indeed, the scientific evidence indicates that *already* at least one of three children, who died before their first birthdays in America in the 1960's, may have died as a result of peacetime nuclear testing.) Such is the conclusion indicated by new information on the unanticipated genetic effect of strontium 90, presented at a recent meeting of the Health Physics Society.

From *Esquire,* September 1969. Reprinted by permission of the author.

[3] Proponents of the A.B.M. system argue that it is necessary to prevent the destruction of our deterrent forces by a massive first strike of Russian SS-9 missiles carrying thousands of multiple warheads. But the threat of such an attack loses all credibility against our present knowledge that the vast amounts of long-lived strontium 90 necessarily released into the world's rapidly circulating atmosphere could lead to the death of all Russian infants born in the next generation, thus ending the existence of the Russian people, together with that of all mankind.

[4] The unanticipated genetic effect of strontium 90 has become evident from an increase in the incidence of infant mortality along the path of the fallout cloud from the first atomic test in New Mexico in 1945, and from a detailed correlation of state-by-state infant mortality excesses with yearly changes of strontium 90 levels in milk.

[5] The computer-calculated change in infant mortality was found to have reached close to one excess death in the U.S. per one hundred live births due to the release of only 200 megatons of fission energy by 1963. This indicates that a release of some 20,000 megatons anywhere in the world, needed in offensive warheads for an effective first strike or in the thousands of defensive A.B.M. warheads required to insure interception, could lead to essentially no infants surviving to produce another generation.

[6] The specter of fallout has of course loomed before in the national anxiety over nuclear explosions. But the result of these studies comprises the first documented, long-range analysis showing direct quantitative correlations between strontium 90 and infant mortality. (They will be published later this year as recorded in the Proceedings of the 9th annual Hanford Biology Symposium.)

[7] The physicists who exploded the first atomic bomb at Alamogordo had expected radioactive materials of some kind and assumed that they would fall to earth downwind as far as fifty miles away. Accordingly, the test site had been located in an isolated area of southern New Mexico. When a subsequent series of tests was held in 1951, six years later, the scientists moved to the isolation of desert country in

southern Nevada. By now, however, and without the knowledge of the scientific community, the death rate of children *in states* downwind from Alamogordo had begun to rise.

[8] The infant mortality rates in the United States have been carefully collected for many years. From 1935 to 1950, the rate shows a steady decline, and mathematical models allow the rate to be extended to show, on the basis of previous experience, what the infant mortality rate for any time, consistent with the immediate past, ought to be. But while elsewhere (with one exception) in the U.S. the rate continued downward as expected; in the states downwind of Alamogordo it did not. There was no change in the infant death rate in 1946—the year after the Trinity test—but by 1950 the rate in Texas, Arkansas, Louisiana, Mississippi, Alabama, Georgia, and both Carolinas deviated upward from the normal expectancy. Increases in excess infant mortality of some twenty to thirty percent occurred some thousand to fifteen hundred miles away in Arkansas, Louisiana, and Alabama, where mortality rates were between 3 and 4.5 per hundred live births. Thus, as observed by our research group at the University of Pittsburgh, the Alamogordo blast appears to have been followed by the death, before reaching age one, of roughly one of one hundred children in the area downwind. No detectable increase in mortality rates relative to the computer-determined 1940-45 base line was observed in Florida, south of the path of the fallout cloud, or in the states to the north; and the mortality excesses became progressively less severe with increasing distance eastward, in a manner now understood to be characteristic of the activity along the path of a fallout cloud. Though the increase in infant mortality in these states was taking place during the years 1946-1950, it does not appear to have been associated with the Alamogordo fallout before our studies beginning in October, 1968.

[9] Meanwhile, the study of radiation effects proceeded elsewhere in the scientific community. It became known in the early 1950's that radioactive strontium was concentrated in cow's milk and transmitted, along with the calcium to which it bears a close chemical resemblance, to the rapidly growing bones of the fetus and the subsequent infant. Still, the radia-

tion from strontium 90, though long-lasting, was relatively small in degree; and it was a matter of record, from studies of young women employed in painting luminous watch dials, that very large amounts of radiation over long periods of time are required to produce bone cancer or leukemia in adults. Besides, the survivors of Hiroshima and Nagasaki and their offspring were carefully observed, without discovering any very serious long-term effects of radiation. A small number of leukemia cases turned up, and a very few detectable abnormalities among their children, but compared with the rest of Japan the difference was slight. The measurable effects of fallout, at the time, did not seem so ominous after all. So atmospheric nuclear weapons testing proceeded in Nevada until 1958, and continued in the Pacific until 1963 under the pressure of the Cold War. No obvious or clear-cut incidents of serious harm to anyone were reported outside the immediate area of testing.

[10] Still, there was concern among radiobiologists and geneticists over the possibility of radiation effects on the highly sensitive human reproductive cells, rapidly dividing and developing to form the human embryo during the first few weeks and months of gestation. Evidence from animal experiments, as well as from the observation of pregnant women who had been exposed to X-rays, suggested that ova and embryo might be from twenty to fifty times more sensitive to the development of leukemia than the mature adult. If so, the potential danger of even relatively small amounts of radiation would be greatly magnified.

[11] The evidence implicating X-rays in childhood leukemia had been discovered—quite unexpectedly—by Dr. Alice Stewart of Oxford University, in the course of a survey designed to uncover the causes of a disturbing rise in childhood leukemia among the children of England and Wales during the 1950's. Her study, published in 1958, showed that mothers who had received a series of three to five abdominal X-rays in the course of a pelvic examination gave birth to children who were almost twice as likely to die of leukemia or other cancers than the children of mothers who had not been X-rayed during pregnancy. Subsequent studies showed that only about six

percent of all childhood leukemia is related to X-rays, but Dr. Stewart's research remains significant, since before then no serious effects of ordinary diagnostic X-rays had ever been demonstrated, especially since a single abdominal X-ray gives the fetus a radiation dose not much larger than what each of us receives in the course of some three to five years from cosmic rays and the natural radiation in the rocks around us.

[12] It is true that leukemia and childhood cancer are relatively rare. Only about one child in one thousand is affected. Nevertheless, since leukemia and other cancers are the second greatest cause of death among children between five and fourteen (ranking only after accidents). Dr. Stewart's findings were regarded by physicians as startling, and efforts were made to check them. Perhaps the most definitive such examination was done by Dr. Brian MacMahon at the Harvard School of Public Health. Using a study population of close to 800,000 children born in large New England hospitals, where careful records of X-rays given to mothers were available, Dr. MacMahon confirmed Dr. Stewart's findings. He observed only about a forty percent increase in the cancer rate among exposed children, probably because of improvements in X-ray technology that allowed lower exposures.

[13] Meanwhile, in April, 1953, a sizable amount of nuclear debris from a test explosion in Nevada was wafted downwind some two thousand miles to the east and, thirty-six hours later, deposited by a rainstorm over the Albany-Troy region of New York State. Dr. Ralph Lapp, one of the first scientists to be concerned with the hazards of peacetime nuclear testing, drew attention to this heavy local fallout. Subsequent examination of the childhood leukemia pattern in this area showed that leukemia doubled over a period of some eight years after the fallout—and then decreased. Here, for the first time, was a documented case in which fallout appeared to produce serious effects at a rate consistent with what was expected from the study of children exposed to prenatal X-rays.

[14] Further examination of the leukemia rate for the entire State of New York revealed a pattern of increase and decrease following the sequence of individual test series in Nevada between 1951 and 1958, with a characteristic time

delay of about five years after each detonation. The rise and fall were particularly marked in the age group from five to fourteen years, the group most indicative of radiation-produced cases.

[15] More disturbing yet, the evidence showed that the arrival of the fallout was followed by a halt in the normal decline of the rate of stillbirths. For the previous fifteen years, from 1935 to 1950, the stillbirth rate had shown a regular and progressive decline. Within a year after testing began in Nevada in 1951, the rate began to deviate upward. Between 1957 and 1963 the fetal death rate, instead of steadily declining as it had from 1935 to 1950, leveled off completely at around twenty-three per thousand live births. In 1964, the fetal death rate rose to 27.3 per thousand, the first such leap since records had been kept in New York State. In 1965 and 1966, it declined slightly, as a gradual reduction of fallout in milk and food took place throughout the U.S. In contrast to New York, the fetal death rate for California—upwind of the Nevada test site, and therefore not affected by it—continued its steady decline, in line with the 1935-1950 figures from which New York so sharply deviated. Still, the rate of decrease began to slow down in California also—two to three years after the onset of hydrogen bomb tests in the Pacific in 1954.

[16] The implications of the fetal death rate could be considered much more serious for society than the incidence of childhood leukemia, since there are more than ten times as many fetal deaths reported than cases of childhood leukemia. Moreover, for every fetal death reported, an estimated five or six are not reported, yielding perhaps fifty or sixty fetal deaths for each case of leukemia. Consequently, the search for further evidence continued. More fallout seemed to be followed by more fetal deaths, but no precise statistical correlation had been drawn. Since the amount of strontium 90 deposited in the soil is easily measurable, the cumulative deposit of strontium 90 was plotted against the *excess* of fetal mortality over what the mortality *should* have been if the 1935-1950 decline had persisted. The finding: except for the first few years of testing in Nevada, when short-lived isotopes

rather than the long-lived strontium 90 were dominant, the fetal death rate in New York followed the same general pattern as the accumulated strontium 90 on the ground. Both curves showed the same decrease in rate of climb coincident with the temporary halt of nuclear testing from 1958 to 1961; both show a sharp rise beginning with the large Soviet test series in 1961. Two years after the test ban in 1963, both the fetal death rate and the radioactivity in the environment once again began to decline.

[17] A similar pattern in the fetal death rate exists in the data for the United States as a whole for all periods of gestation up to nine months. Again, there is a steady rate of decline until the Fifties, a leveling off in 1951-52, and an actual rise in 1954, corresponding to the onset of the Pacific H-bomb tests; and a second rise in 1961, corresponding to the Soviet test series.

[18] But perhaps the most disturbing evidence of all indicates that the rates of infant mortality in the United States and all over the world seem to have been affected by nuclear testing. The infant mortality rate is far more accurately known than the fetal death rate, since the death of a baby, unlike miscarriage or an abortion, rarely escapes notice in the advanced countries. Like fetal deaths, infant mortality had shown a steady decline in the period 1935-1950; but beginning with the Nevada tests in 1951 and continuing until just after the test ban in 1963, the rate suddenly leveled off in the U.S. This leveling off did not occur in such other advanced countries as Sweden, Holland and Norway, or in Southern Hemisphere countries like Chile and New Zealand, until late in the 1950's when hydrogen-bomb tests in the South Pacific and Siberia began to produce worldwide fallout on a much increased scale. Only after the major portion of the most violently radioactive material from the 1961-62 tests had disappeared did U.S. infant mortality begin to decline again in 1965, at a rate close to the previous 1935-1950 decline.

[19] The most serious effects appeared in the age group from one month to one year. Here, the rate of deaths per one thousand live births should have been, according to the 1935-1950 figures, about 2.7. Instead, the observed number was 5.4

per thousand, twice what it should have been and twice what it actually was in Sweden, where the rate had steadily declined to 2.6 per thousand.

[20] Not only was there a drastic change in overall infant mortality for the U.S. as compared to the rest of the advanced countries, but there were also disturbing patterns of change within the U.S. For example, the infant mortality rate started to level off sharply in the Eastern, Midwestern and Southern states within two years after the onset of atomic testing in Nevada in 1951, while it continued steadily downward in the dry Western states. But this is exactly the known pattern of accumulated radioactive strontium on the ground and in the diet, since strontium is most heavily deposited in states of high annual rainfall, especially in those to the east of Nevada.

[21] Serious difficulties remained, however, in establishing a casual connection between nuclear testing and these drastic changes in fetal and infant mortality. First, why should fallout, and in particular strontium 90, cause fetal and infant deaths, since it goes to the bones and should therefore cause, if anything, bone cancer and leukemia many years later? Second, there was no observed direct quantitative relation between different levels of strontium 90 in the body and mortality rates at any given age. Therefore it was difficult to see how the very small amounts of radiation resulting from peacetime testing could possibly have been the cause of the deviations in fetal death and infant mortality, especially since no significant genetic effects had been observed among the children of the Hiroshima and Nagasaki survivors.

[22] The causation puzzle now appears to be solved. In 1963, K. G. Luning and his co-workers in Sweden published their discovery that small amounts of strontium 90, injected into male mice three or four weeks prior to mating, produced an increase in fetal deaths among their offspring. No such increase appeared when corresponding amounts of chemically different radioactive cesium 137 were injected. More recently, evidence presented at an International Symposium on the Radiation Biology of the Fetal and Juvenile Mammal in May, 1969, has demonstrated severe chromosome damage, fetal

deaths and congenital malformations in the offspring of female mice injected with strontium 90 before and during pregnancy. Similar effects have now been observed for very small quantities of tritium, produced by both A-bombs and relatively "clean" hydrogen weapons.

[23] In the light of these studies, the absence of genetic effects in Hiroshima is understandable. In Hiroshima and Nagasaki, the bombs were detonated, not on the ground as in New Mexico, but at such an altitude that there was essentially no fallout in these two cities proper. The radiation exposure there resulted almost exclusively from the brief flash of X-rays, neutrons and gamma rays at the instant of explosion. Consequently no special effects related to strontium 90 appeared in the children of the survivors; but the rate of cancer deaths among children up to fourteen years in Japan as a whole jumped by more than two hundred percent between 1949 and 1951, four to six years after the bombs, when the fallout had had a chance to produce its effects throughout the southern parts of Japan—exactly the same delay observed after the fallout from Nevada arrived in Albany-Troy.

[24] But the problem remains of demonstrating a direct connection between the levels of strontium 90 in human fetuses and infants, on the one hand, and observed changes in fetal and infant mortality, on the other. Such a direct connection seems to emerge from the so-called "baby-tooth survey" carried out by the Dental School of Washington University in St. Louis, supported by the U.S. Public Health Service and directed by Dr. H. L. Rosenthal. Using the data from tooth-buds and mandibular bones of aborted fetuses and from baby teeth collected in the greater St. Louis area, Dr. Rosenthal's study showed that the concentration of strontium 90 in the teeth followed closely the measured concentrations in bone and milk. Measurement of the strontium 90 content of milk anywhere in the world permits a calculation of the concentration in the bones of infants and fetuses developing in the same areas. We have found a direct correlation between the yearly changes of strontium 90 contained in the teeth (and therefore the bones and bodies) of the developing human fetus and infant, and the changing excess mortality rates, going up and

down together as atmospheric tests began in 1951 and stopped in 1963.

[25] From our examinations of the infant mortality changes from a computer-fitted base line for 1935-1950, for various states in which the Public Health Service reported monthly values of the strontium 90 concentrations in the milk since 1957, there emerges a close correspondence between average strontium 90 levels and infant mortality changes. Wherever the strontium 90 rose to high values over a four-year period, as in Georgia, a large, parallel, year-by-year rise in infant mortality also took place; while in areas where there was little strontium 90 in the milk, as in Texas, the infant mortality remained at a correspondingly lower value. Other states such as Illinois, Missouri, New York and Utah also show a rise, peaking in the same 1962-1965 period at levels between these extreme cases, each according to their local annual rainfall and strontium 90 concentrations in their milk.

[26] For the United States as a whole, we found a detailed correspondence between and among: 1) the excess infant mortality relative to the 1935-1950 base line; 2) the total strontium 90 produced by nuclear weapons; 3) the strontium 90 thus produced actually reaching the ground; and 4) the four-year average concentration in U.S. milk from 1955, the year after the first large H-bomb tests; and 1965, the year when strontium 90 concentrations began to level off and started to decline once again.

[27] At the peak of this excess infant mortality, it was the District of Columbia that showed the largest excess in 1966—157 percent, compared with an average excess of 72 percent for the U.S. as a whole. The low value was found in dry New Mexico, minus-eleven percent—actually below the 1935-50 base line.

[28] To appreciate the magnitude of these effects, it must be recognized that in the 1950's about 2.5 to 3.0 infants out of every hundred born in the U.S. died before reaching the age of one year. The average excess infant mortality, therefore, represents close to one child out of one hundred born, or one of every 2.5 to 3.0 that died during the first year of life.

Since about four million children were born annually during this period, close to 40,000 infants one year old or less died in excess of normal expectations each year, totaling some 375,000 by the mid-Sixties and continuing at about 34,000 per year since the end of atmospheric testing by the U.S. and the U.S.S.R.

[29] It is no wonder, then, that infant mortality has been a major concern of our Public Health Service since this trend was first pointed out in 1960 by Dr. M. Moriyama of the National Center for Health Statistics.

[30] However, as Dr. Moriyama and his associates observed during an international conference devoted entirely to infant mortality in 1965, none of the factors so far considered —medical care, population movement, new drugs, pesticides, smoking or epidemics of infectious disease—suffices to explain the observed facts.

[31] That the recent excesses in infant mortality cannot readily be explained by medical and socioeconomic factors normally influencing mortality trends may be seen from an examination of the death rate in the various states following the Alamogordo blast. At the University of Pittsburgh, we have plotted the percentile infant mortality excesses or decrements relative to the computer-determined 1940-1945 base line for the first and fifth years after Alamogordo. In 1946, one year after the detonation, there was no sign of any excess infant mortality in the states downwind from New Mexico; but by 1950 a clear change toward excess infant mortality appeared in the states over which the fallout cloud had drifted, and only in those states. Furthermore, the excess mortalities are seen to be distributed in such a pattern as might be expected from nuclear fallout originating in New Mexico, since the effects are lowest in the dry area of western Texas, and largest in the areas of heavy rainfall first encountered by the cloud, namely Arkansas, Louisiana, Mississippi and Alabama, declining steadily thereafter toward the Atlantic.

[32] The only other area that showed a clear excess infant mortality greater than ten percent as compared to the 1940-1945 period was found to be North Dakota. There, subsequent measurements of strontium 90 in the milk, carried

out by the Health and Safety Laboratories of the Atomic Energy Commission, revealed the highest concentrations anywhere in the U.S. for which data is available prior to 1960. The causes of this "hot spot" are not yet fully understood, but they are quite possibly connected with known accidental discharges of radioactivity from the Hanford plant of the Manhattan Project, directly to the west, in the early years of its operation, where the fissionable plutonium for most of the nuclear weapons was produced beginning in 1944.

[33] Since no excess infant mortality was registered along the path of the New Mexico fallout cloud in the first year after the detonation, the deaths occurring downwind in later years could not have resulted from the direct effects of external radiation from fallout on the developing embryo. It becomes clear then that we are dealing with an effect on the reproductive cells of the parents, or a so-called genetic effect.

[34] The evidence available so far therefore suggests that radioactive strontium appears to be a far more serious hazard to man through its long-lasting action on the genetic material of the mammalian cell than had been expected on the basis of its well-known tendency to be incorporated into bone. The resultant effect appears to express itself most noticeably in excess fetal and infant mortality rates among the children born two or more years after a nuclear explosion. Presumably such factors as lowered birth weight and reduced ability to resist ordinary infectious diseases are involved, accounting for the greatest increase in infant mortality in the U.S. as compared to the advanced countries of Western Europe since the early 1950's. Children who receive adequate medical care are more likely to survive these factors than those who do not.

[35] What does all this imply for the debate over the deployment of new nuclear weapons systems, such as the A.B.M. or the M.I.R.V. (Multiple Independent Reentry Vehicle), carrying many nuclear warheads in a single missile? To appreciate the probable genetic effects of a large nuclear war, we can consider first the effect of small tactical-size nuclear weapons comparable to the 20 kiloton bombs detonated over Hiroshima, Nagasaki, and in the desert of Alamogordo. Since increases of some 20 to 30 percent excess infant mortal-

ity were observed from a thousand to fifteen hundred miles downwind in Arkansas, Alabama and Louisiana, where mortality rates were between 3 and 4.5 per hundred live births, the detonation of a single, small tactical-size nuclear weapon on the ground in the western United States appears to have led to one out of one hundred children born subsequently dying before reaching the age of one year. Therefore, the detonation of a hundred or so weapons of this size, amounting to the equivalent of only two megatons in the form of small warheads, would be expected to lead to essentially *no* children surviving to maturity in the states directly downwind.

[36] But according to former Defense Secretary Clark Clifford, speaking at a N.A.T.O. conference in the Fall of 1968, we have close to eight thousand tactical nuclear weapons in the kiloton range ready to be released in order to protect our European allies from a ground attack by Russia. Thus, we would probably achieve the protection of Western Europe at the cost of the biological end of these nations through the death of the children of the survivors, together with the likely death of most children subsequently born to the people of Eastern Europe, Russia and China as the radioactive clouds drift eastward around the world until they reach the United States. Thus, the use of the biologically most destructive small nuclear weapons in tactical warfare now appears to be at least as self-defeating as the release of large quantities of nerve gas, killing indiscriminately soldiers and civilians, friends and enemies alike.

[37] But, what about the use of large megaton warheads in a massive first strike or in A.B.M. missiles detonated high up in the stratosphere or outer space, as proposed for the Spartan missile that is to provide us with an impenetrable shield against a first strike attack by large Chinese or Russian missiles in the 1970's?

[38] According to the figures on infant mortality in the United States, based on the testing of large hydrogen weapons in the Pacific and Siberia, both in the atmosphere and outer space, close to one out of every one hundred children born are likely to have died as the result of only about 200 megatons worth of fission products into the world's atmosphere, under

conditions which were especially designed to minimize the possible effects on health.

[39] According to the testimony of Defense Secretary Melvin Laird in the Spring of 1969, the U.S.S.R. will have the capability of launching some 500 SS-9 missiles, each capable of carrying 25 megatons worth of bombs in the form of many multiple warheads, or a total of some 1500 to 2500 warheads. Together with comparable numbers launched by smaller missiles, the total megatonnage would therefore be of the order of 10 to 20,000 megatons needed in a first strike that attempts to destroy most of our thousands of missiles and bombers at the same time.

[40] Thus, the threat of a first strike by Russia loses all credibility since, in order to have any chance at all of preventing devastating retaliation, it would necessarily have to release so much radioactivity into the circulating atmosphere that it would lead to the death of most Russian infants born in the next generation, ending the existence of the Russian people together with that of all mankind.

[41] Since it takes at least three to five Anti-Ballistic Missiles launched to insure a high-probability of interception, the U.S. must be prepared to launch some 5000 to 15,000 A.B.M.'s in order to provide a meaningful "shield" against such a massive attack.

[42] We know that each Spartan missile must contain a warhead of at least 2 megatons to produce a sufficiently intense X-ray pulse to achieve interception, so that the use of this system to protect our own missiles and cities would require the detonation of some 10,000 to 30,000 megatons into the stratosphere, not counting any radioactivity from the Russian warheads, from our own counterstrike, or from the Russian A.B.M. missiles.

[43] Thus, even if anti-missile systems were to work with ideal perfection on both sides, preserving every home, every school, and every factory from destruction, the release of long-lived radioactive materials would produce more than a hundred times as much radioactive poison as during all the years of peacetime testing. Based on the excess mortality

observed during the period of testing, this would most likely be sufficient to insure that few if any children anywhere in the world would grow to maturity to give rise to another generation.

[44] Nor will it make much difference how high above the atmosphere the bombs are detonated, because the strontium 90 takes twenty-eight years to decay to half of its initial activity, long enough for most of it to return to earth well before another generation of children is born. And even if a perfectly "clean" weapon containing no fissionable material at all could ever be developed, the carbon 14 it produces would get into the genetic material controlling the life processes of all living cells, and it takes 5770 years before half of its radioactivity is exhausted.

[45] The implications of the warning mankind has received from the death of its infants during nuclear testing are therefore clear:

[46] Nuclear war, with or without anti-missiles or elaborate shelters, is no longer "thinkable" due to a fatal flaw in the assumptions of all our military war-gamers, namely the unexpectedly severe biological sensitivity of the mammalian reproductive system to genetically important by-products of nuclear weapons, which must now be regarded not merely as vastly destructive explosive and incendiary devices, but as the most powerful biological poison weapons that man has yet invented.

EXERCISES—*THE DEATH OF ALL CHILDREN*

Content

1. Specifically, to what does Sternglass attribute the increase in leukemia among children in New York State between 1951 and 1958?
2. Why does the author say the absence of genetic effects resulting from the A-bomb blasts in Hiroshima and Nagasaki is understandable?
3. What does the author hope to achieve by writing this essay?

4. Which death rate does Sternglass consider the most significant: fetal mortality, infant mortality, or mortality of children between the ages of five and fourteen? Why?
5. According to the author what constitutes genetic effect?

Style

1. Explain your reason for calling this essay formal or informal. Is the author successful in using language appropriate for his audience?
2. What bearing does the subject matter have upon the author's selection of a point of view from which to write?
3. What would be the effect of this essay if the author had used the impersonal "one"? Explain.
4. Could this essay be as effectively written using the personal "you"? Explain.
5. Explain your view of an author's writing this essay using the editorial "we."
6. Examine paragraph (46). Does the author demonstrate scientific objectivity here? Explain.
7. Why is the first sentence of paragraph (5) written in passive voice?

Application of Stylistic Techniques

1. Having selected a subject in which you have a particular interest, collect statistical information and arrange it in a paragraph as partial support of your opinion toward the subject without telling your opinion. Use paragraph (16) as a model.
2. Rewrite paragraph (43), using the indefinite "you."
3. Rewrite paragraph (43), using the editorial "we."
4. Briefly discuss your view of whether the indefinite "you" in question 2 or the editorial "we" in question 3 is more effective for the paragraph in which each occurs.
5. If you were to rewrite paragraph (46) in first person singular, explain what advantage—if any—there would be over the third person subjective.

Suggestions for Writing

1. Using third person, attack Sternglass as an alarmist who has used facts to frighten people.

2. Write an essay in third person to support Sternglass's use of factual material as a means to put across his concern for the future of mankind.
3. In third person, write an essay comparing and/or contrasting the effectiveness of Sternglass's essay with E. B. White's *Age of Dust.*
4. Select a topic and write an essay, using third person in the manner of Sternglass's essay.
   What Congress Did Today!
   The Crime against Our Progeny
   Who Determines What: Man or God?
   Atomic Weaponry: The Means to the End
   Who Said Man Is Rational?
   The Practicality of Being Prepared for A-Warfare
   Strontium 90 for Breakfast
   Children Won't Die!
   Humanitarianism vs. Self-Preservation
   Man Has to Have a Weapon
   Hiroshima at Home
   The Day I Saw a Child Love
   What If *They* Had a War and Nobody Showed?
   Mayday!
   Everybody Loves a Child

Edwin A. Joyce, Jr. (1937–) was born in Hampton, Virginia, and now resides in St. Petersburg, Florida. Having majored in marine biology, he conducts research at the Marine Research Laboratory, Florida Department of Natural Resources. He has contributed to *Sea Frontiers, Oceans Magazine*, and various departmental serials and scientific publications of the Marine Research Laboratory.

Commercial Shrimping

(Third Person Objective—Technical Report)

EDWIN A. JOYCE, JR.

[1] Commercial shrimping (that shrimping done in the offshore waters) has become seasonal in this area and is based primarily on the white shrimp *Penaeus setiferus* and the brown shrimp *P. aztecus*. The boats used on the grounds average about 60 feet in length and most are of the standard St. Augustine trawler design. During the peak seasons boats from North and South Carolina, Georgia, and Florida fish in this area. The off season finds only a few local shrimpers out of Fernandina, Mayport, St. Augustine, and Cape Canaveral still working the grounds.

[2] The better shrimping usually begins with the opening of the offshore grounds to night fishing on the first of June, to take advantage of the brown shrimp season which is from June through August. Throughout the rest of the year, night shrimping is illegal because the shrimpers believe that night trawling causes the white shrimp to scatter, thus decreasing the more productive day catch. The brown shrimp production usually reaches its peak in July. Production at this time is

Professional Paper Series, April 1965, Marine Research Laboratory, Florida Department of Natural Resources. Reprinted by permission.

not great in comparison to the catches during the white shrimp season. By August the brown shrimp production begins dropping and the first small white shrimp appear in the catch. These are the first of the new spawn to leave the nursery areas. By the time the grounds are again closed to night shrimping (August 31), the catches are usually running about half white shrimp and half brown shrimp. After September the brown shrimp are almost negligible (Figure 2).

[3] The white shrimp catches continue to increase through September, October, November, and December as the shrimp leave the rivers in increasingly large numbers. During these months production varies daily along the coast. The shrimpers state that it is possible to find schools of shrimp moving south along the coast and that these schools can be fished as far south as Cape Canaveral. The general method of relocating these schools is to check with the trynet at the place where fishing was terminated the previous day and if this tow is negative then further trynet tows are made to the south until the school is relocated. The estimate of distance traveled per day is from 6 to 12 miles.

[4] The peak white shrimp production is usually in December though it may fall in November or January. Bad weather at this time has a definite effect on production. After January at the latest, catches drop considerably but are still dominantly white shrimp (Figure 1). During February, March, April, and May most shrimpers turn to other means for their livelihood. Some boats are converted for snapper fishing while others continue to trawl but are more interested in the catches of fish. A few shrimp are caught inadvertently, but these seldom amount to more than a few pounds. In general, this situation continues until the night shrimping is again opened for the brown shrimp season.

[5] For the shrimper who trawls for a living the year round, production falls into three classes—the "off" season, the "brown shrimp" season, and the "white shrimp" season. During the "off" season, from approximately mid-January through May, it is difficult, and sometimes impossible, to make expenses even with the utilization of other species such as fish and crabs. The "brown shrimp" season is an improvement,

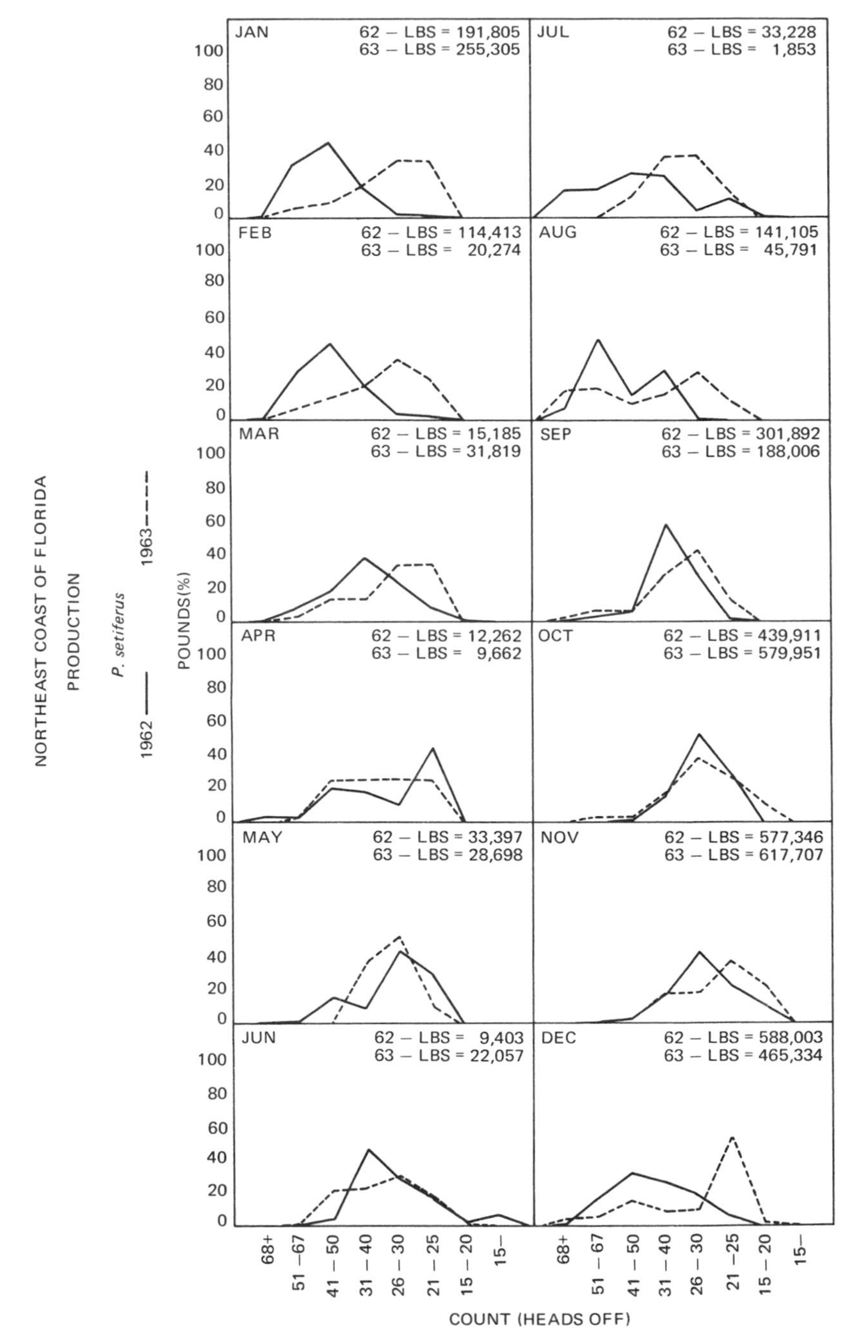

Figure 1. Commercial 1962–63 landings of *P. setiferus* from the northeast coast Florida.

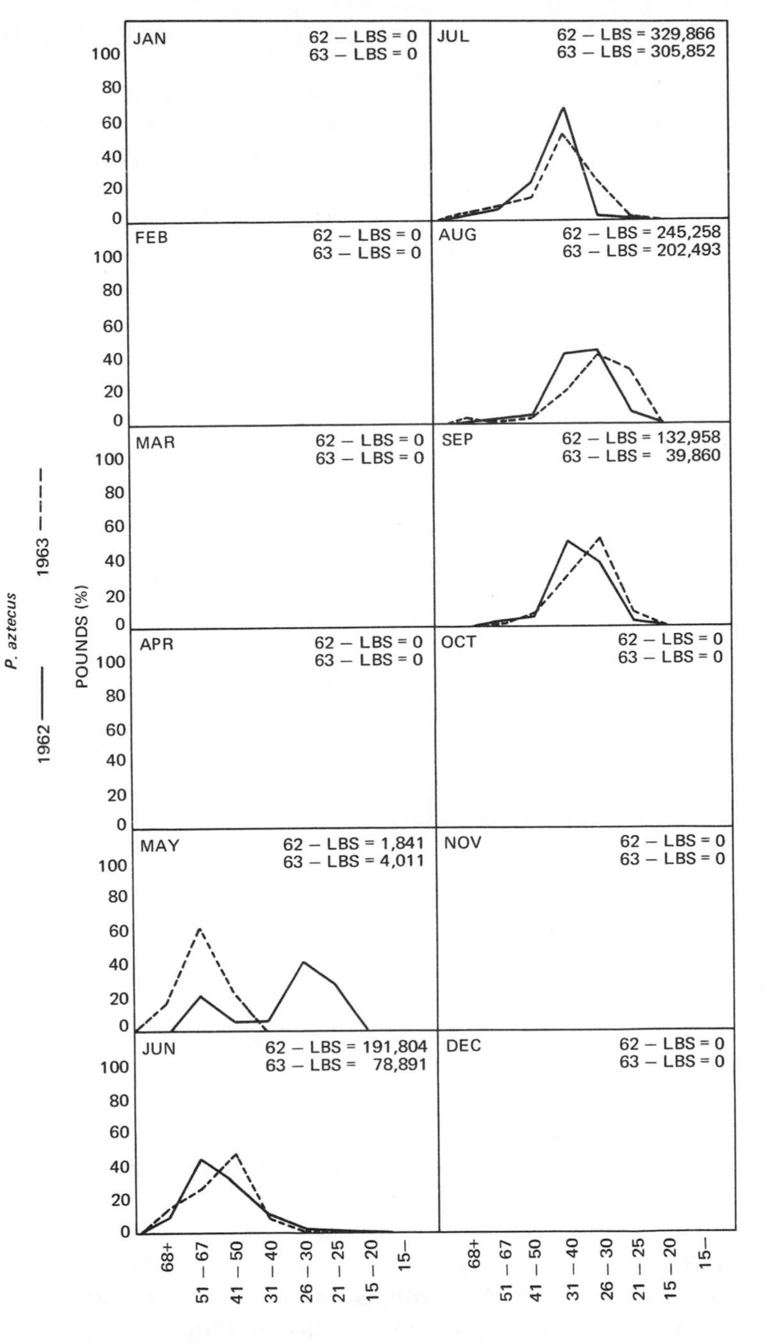

Figure 2. Commercial 1962–63 landings of *p. aztecus* from the northeast coast of Florida.

though the last few years have been disappointing. Production is usually sufficient to cover expenses and in most cases to provide a meager livelihood. Though it starts relatively slowly, the "white shrimp" season is the money crop for this area. It is during the last of October, November, December, and sometimes part of January that the shrimper makes the money that enables him to meet the expenses incurred during the previous "off" season. In good years a single day's catch may run as high as 15 to 20 boxes (100 lbs. per box) and prices vary from 60 to 85 cents per pound during the season. However, production also varies daily and catches usually average only 2 to 4 boxes per day's fishing.

[6] Weather plays an important part in the production of shrimp. Many days each year are lost to bad weather when the boats are unable to leave port. Occasional hurricanes during the late summer and fall and northeasters and northwesters during the winter and early spring make up most of the bad weather.

[7] As with all products, price varies indirectly with shrimp production. This variance tends to act as a buffer, for when the shrimp are scarce, price is up and vice versa. However, occasionally shrimp production may be very good in other areas (Texas, Louisiana, Campeche, and Tortugas) causing a lowering of prices. Then if catches in this area are poor, the fishermen are struck the double blow of poor catch and low price.

[8] Shrimp production varies from year to year. In some areas where there was a continual decline over a period of several years, fears were aroused concerning the possibility that over-fishing was the cause of the declines. In general, however, the bad years are followed by increased production sometimes even exceeding previous records, indicating that over-fishing was not the causative factor in the decline. An excellent example of this is Louisiana. An almost complete failure of the shrimp crop in 1961, St. Amant *et al* (1963), was followed by increased production in 1962 and a near record catch in 1963 (Commercial Fisheries Report, 1963). Such declines and increases in the catches in our area can be seen from Table 1. Value of the catch is also included to indicate price fluctuations.

[9] Any method of increasing the shrimp catch, especially during the "off" season, would be extremely beneficial to the shrimper. It must be remembered that during the off-season catches usually run from 10 to 25 pounds. If this could be increased to 50 or 75 pounds per day, then the shrimpers could at least meet expenses. Certain information gathered from this study indicates that this may indeed be possible.

[10] Probably the most important change that could be made would be reappraisal of the night fishing laws (Florida Board of Conservation Laws, 1961). As already mentioned, the shrimpers feel that night fishing causes a reduced daytime catch. Since the daytime catch (white shrimp) is the most productive, they feel that by limiting the night fishing strictly to that time when the nocturnal brown shrimp are in season, they will increase their catches. The basis of this law is virtually impossible to prove from a biological standpoint. If the shrimpers want this law for the reasons stated, they should have it. However, prohibiting night shrimping except during the white shrimp season would accomplish two things. It would stop night fishing during the time the shrimpers believe it is most likely to hurt daytime shrimping, and, it would allow complete freedom of fishing during the season when shrimping is poorest. Under this new interpretation the closed night shrimping season would run from mid-September to mid-January, the rest of the year would be open to night fishing. A further inducement to a longer period of open night fishing can be seen from our offshore statistics. More than 50 percent of our total offshore catch, including all species, was taken at night.

TABLE 1

Shrimp landings on the east coast of Florida 1956–1963

	No. lbs.	*Amount in $*
1956	5,702,465	2,178,265
1957	5,182,865	2,150,280
1958	5,512,433	2,208,934
1959	4,514,149	1,361,394
1960	6,809,053	2,167,984
1961	6,026,528	2,440,863
1962	5,187,980	2,542,951
*1963	3,939,990	1,736,399

*converted to heads on

[11] Still other factors became evident during this study which indicate the possibilities of larger catches. It appeared that the commercial species offshore have differing depth preferences and times of seasonal abundance. Some geographical differences also appeared between the species. *P. setiferus* was most abundant from September through January and seemed to prefer relatively shallow offshore waters. The Middle Area was the most productive, especially in December, January, February, and March. *P. aztecus* was most abundant from May through August and apparently preferred deeper offshore waters than *P. setiferus.* The Southern Area was proportionately the most productive. *P. duorarum* was most abundant in March, April, and May and appeared to prefer depths at least as great as *P. aztecus* and perhaps even deeper. The Middle and Southern Areas were the most productive for this species. To further illustrate this, Table 2 lists our production of the main species per month by area. The figures used are proportional so that each area represents the same number of stations.

[12] Most shrimping along the northeast coast of Florida is done in depths of less than 60 feet of water. Consequently, by changing the fishing depth and geographical location according to the time of year, it would seem that catches could be increased. This is especially true for *P. duorarum.* For the reasons previously discussed, it appears that the major adult grounds for *P. duorarum* probably lie offshore from the Mosquito Lagoon, Indian River Area. The peak catches of this species occur from March through May, during which time night shrimping is illegal. As a result, this species is only occasionally taken in any numbers. Mr. T. A. Smirch, working beyond the jurisdictional limit of the State of Florida, reports that he caught over 100 pounds of *P. duorarum* in one night. These shrimp were taken in late January from depths of 70 feet and over, offshore from Cape Canaveral. Mr. Smirch further stated that a few drags taken during the day had produced almost no "hoppers," while the night drags were relatively productive and seemed to get better as depth increased. Further night dragging done by Mr. Smirch in late spring also produced relatively good catches. Consequently,

indications are at least promising that there may be a small but fishable population in the deeper waters off the Mosquito Lagoon-Cape Canaveral region.

[13] It is also possible that the *P. aztecus* season might be extended if shrimping was done in deeper waters. Hildebrand (1954) indicates that the average depth of the brown shrimp grounds in Texas is 20 fathoms and that the season is at its peak from August through December or January. In our area the fishing depth seldom exceeds 11 fathoms and the main production is in July and August. Some exploratory shrimping at these depths, preferably at night, would be helpful.

[14] However, deeper waters are more vulnerable to bad weather. A great deal of fishing is done out of Cape Canaveral during the winter and early spring simply because the area is more protected against bad weather. To get to the above depths one must leave the protection afforded by the Cape. Therefore, even though these sources may be present, it is doubtful that they can be utilized to their full extent.

TABLE 2

Monthly proportional catches for commercial species in offshore areas

Offshore Area	June	July	Aug.	Sep.	Oct.	Nov.
Northern	616	979	1463	275	539	1122
Middle	651	1309	483	315	315	483
Southern	NS	960	312	276	NS	96

Offshore Area	Dec.	Jan.	Feb.	Mar.	Apr.	May	June
Northern	2574	682	770	88	66	330	NS
Middle	1386	1708	847	1407	371	1176	NS
Southern	492	720	108	552	504	1704	2100

NS = No samples taken

[15] A further means of increasing the income of the shrimper would be to utilize some other species of shrimp not now being exploited. The deep water royal red shrimp, *Hymenopeneus robustus* is a good example. However, this shrimp is only taken in depths of around 200 fathoms and requires larger boats and gear modifications than most of the local shrimpers cannot afford.

[16] In this locality there appears to be only one other species which might possibly be of commercial value and that is the rock shrimp, *Sicyonia brevirostris*. Bullis and Rathjen (1959) state that significant amounts were taken from several locations between Cape Canaveral and Cape Hatteras. They also state that their best production occurred in depths of 25 to 45 fathoms. Although our own catches were very limited, probably due to the shallow nature of our stations, Mr. T. A. Smirch caught large numbers of *S. brevirostris* off Cape Canaveral during January, February, and March in about 70 feet of water at night. These shrimp were of excellent taste and were marketable, although the price was below that received for the other species. Unfortunately, only a very few days were calm enough during these months to permit dragging at these depths.

[17] All of the above suggestions are possibilities for increased catches indicated primarily by the results from our own sampling. Much additional sampling should be done to determine the true potential, if any, of new shrimp sources.

EXERCISES—*COMMERCIAL SHRIMPING*

Content

1. What are the major reasons shrimpers suffer economic setbacks?
2. What does Joyce suggest is the most important change that could be made to help shrimpers?
3. What causes shrimpers to fish the Cape Canaveral (now Cape Kennedy) area during the winter and early spring?
4. When do the peak catches of the *P. duorarum* occur? Why?
5. By what means could the shrimping along the northeast coast be increased?

Style

1. What bearing does the subject matter have on determining whether Joyce's report is formal or informal? For what reason do you say this report is formal or informal?
2. Why does the author avoid using any personal pronouns (I, you, we)? Explain his avoidance of each of these pronouns.

3. Although this is a technical report, do you see any evidence of the author's opinion? If you do, refer to specific instances.
4. Of what value are tables and figures to this report?
5. Is the author primarily objective in this report? Explain.

Applications of Stylistic Techniques

1. Write an essay in third person objective point of view, in which you include tables and/or figures to support your thesis.
2. Rewrite paragraph (3) in the indefinite you. How effective is your version? Explain.
3. Explain what advantage there is, if any, in writing paragraphs (1) and (17) in first person.
4. Rewrite paragraph (6) in the editorial "we." Is it effective? Explain.
5. Rewrite paragraph (8) in totally active voice. Is Joyce's paragraph as effective?
6. Does Joyce rely heavily on passive voice? Explain.

Suggestions for Writing

The Elements and Commercial Fishing
Scientists Improve Our Lives
Commercial Fishing: A Necessity
Who Said Nobody Cares?
They're Good to Eat, But . . .
One Graph Is Worth a Thousand Words, At Least!
Conservation and the Fishing Industry
More Shrimp (or whatever), the Better
Fishing: The Fun Way to Riches!
Marine Culture and the Future

MOOD AND TONE

In communicating with your reader, you will find that point of view is closely linked with mood and tone: your emotional state and your *tone of voice.* Although some critics use the word "tone" to mean the same as mood, and others use it to mean tone and mood, it is perhaps best for you to make a distinction. For instance, you can think of your mood as *hostile* and your consequent tone as *sarcastic* (bitterly derisive). If you are *angry,* your tone might be *satiric* (wittily, and often humorously, denunciatory); if you are *disgusted,* it might be *ironic* (the opposite of what it *seems* to be saying); if you are *happy,* it might be *humorous* (comic, funny). In any case, mood and tone are closely related; and you can perceive a writer's mood through his tone.

Conciliatory tone:	I think he has halitosis. (mood: concern)
Condescending tone:	He has bad breath. (mood: disgust)
Invective tone:	His breath smells like an unemptied garbage can in the hot sun. (mood: bitterness)
Ironic tone:	Ah, his sweet breath would blind you to all else. (mood: disgust, opposite of what it *seems* to be saying)
Sarcastic tone:	Breath of life was his only weapon; it was all he needed. (mood: hostile)

Whatever tone you use, you must be careful to use it to make your attitude toward your subject clear. The person, for example, who attempts an ironic tone, must know his audience will recognize what he says as meaning just the opposite. And he had better not write, "The way to end strife is simply exterminate the minority races," unless he makes it clear he is ridiculing this kind of thinking. Otherwise, he is misunderstood and believed to be a wild-eyed racist, when he is in fact no such thing.

Irony, a figure of speech, and satire, a literary manner, are undoubtedly difficult to handle. If you feel happy, it is relatively easy to convey your mood through a joyful or humorous tone; if you are sad, it is relatively simple to show your mood through a somber or sentimental tone; if you are ill-humored, it is not too difficult to attack someone through a sarcastic tone. But irony and satire demand a clever combination of wit and humor.

When writing irony (a satiric method), you must often simultaneously maintain an element of humor and an air of personal detachment from the subject matter, even though your mood is both serious and passionate. And if you do not, you will likely end up writing invective or sarcasm. You must also say exactly the opposite of what you believe, but let the reader discover your true feelings indirectly through your wit, humor, and *appearance* of detachment.

Although irony and sarcasm, its near cousin, in extended use sometimes constitute literary manners of writing themselves, we generally consider them means, figures of speech, useful in writing satire. Others—which can also be extended into literary manners of writing—frequently employed in satire are invective, innuendo, parody and burlesque.

The two basic types of satire are Horatian satire and Juvenalian satire. Horatian pokes fun at the individual's and society's foibles—gently, humorously, and somewhat sympathetically prodding the target of the satire to be better. The Juvenalian, on the other hand, attacks men's evils with outraged moral indignation, pointing contemptuously to the perpetrators. The satirist, then, through wit, humor, and criticism, brings to light men's frailties. He subjects these weaknesses to public criticism and ridicule, but his intention is to encourage the improvement of mankind.

The writer striving to express his mood through sentimental tone finds a problem similar to that of writing irony and satire: the problem of just the right balance. The word "sentimental" suggests an undesirable quality to many people; many think of *sentimental* and *mawkish* as synonyms, calling any writing that is feebly emotional "sentimental." In fact, sentimentalism—not mawkishness—is a desirable human quality. Tender emotion and sensibility, even nostalgia, are surely nothing to be ashamed of. To abandon sentimentalism completely is to become totally dispassionate—completely devoid of personal feeling. However, the writer who reminisces and becomes nostalgic must avoid making his work mawkish, maudlin, overly sentimental. He must not cry in his beer, wallow miserably in his longing for the past. He needs balance: just enough tender emotion and sensibility to create a similar response in his readers, without making them sick to their stomachs.

Balance is the answer to many problems in style, especially when the scales tip toward excesses. Too much tender emotion, too much passive voice, too much adherence to one point of view—using, for example, third objective when personal experience demands first person—too much invective, too little attention to definition and clarification, all contribute to a weak style and an unsuccessful extension of the writer's personality.

MOOD AND TONE AND POETRY

We acknowledge the use of language to communicate information (i.e., a report), to persuade our audience (i.e., an advertisement), and to convey experience (i.e., the literary work) that might broaden our reader's understanding and awareness of all kinds of things in life. For these first two uses, language in the prose form generally suits us best; and if we want to make our feelings about the subject known, we do it partially through attention to our mood and tone. Also for the third use, the literary use, we employ prose, both fiction and non-fiction. However, we sometimes use poetry to heighten awareness and create understanding through the emotions. At times, our mood and tone dominate our expression. We care less about logically communicating our thoughts than we do about sharing our emotions; we are more concerned that the reader feels what we feel than that he acquires information or accepts our way of thinking.

Since poetry is the language of the emotions, and mood and tone stem primarily from our emotional condition, we cannot ignore the poet's extension of his personality through his mood and tone. The following three poems demonstrate a joyful tone, but the mood—the emotional condition—of each poet casts a different hue.

William Shakespeare (1564–1616) was born in Stratford-on-Avon, England. He was an actor, playwright, poet, and a partner in the Globe Theater and the Blackfriars Theater. He is best known for his plays. The most famous of these are *Romeo and Juliet* (ca. 1593), *A Midsummer Night's Dream* (ca. 1594), *Julius Caesar* (1599), *As You Like It* (ca. 1600), *Hamlet* (ca. 1602), *Othello* (ca. 1604), *King Lear* (1605?). His non-dramatic works are *Venus and Adonis* (1593), *The Rape of Lucrece* (1604), and *Sonnets* (1609).

Sonnet XXIX *(Joyful)*

WILLIAM SHAKESPEARE

When, in disgrace with Fortune and men's eyes,
I all alone beweep my outcast state,
And trouble deaf heaven with my bootless cries,
And look upon myself, and curse my fate,
Wishing me like to one more rich in hope,
Featured like him, like him with friends possest,
Desiring this man's art and that man's scope,
With what I most enjoy contented least;
Yet in these thoughts myself almost despising—
Haply I think on thee: and then my state,
Like to the Lark at break of day arising
From sullen earth, sings hymns at Heaven's gate;
For thy sweet love rememb'red such wealth brings
That then I scorn to change my state with Kings.

William Wordsworth (1770–1850) was born in Cockermouth in West Cumberland, on the northern fringe of the English Lake District. He was educated at Cambridge University and traveled abroad. One of the early leaders of Romanticism in England, he is well known for his nature worship and humanitarianism. In 1843, he was appointed Poet Laureate. The bulk of his best known poetry is contained in *Lyrical Ballads* (1798), which he published jointly with Samuel Taylor Coleridge. Other works include *Michael, Peter Bell, Ode on Intimations of Immortality,* the *Lucy* poems, *The World Is Too Much with Us,* and *Tintern Abbey.*

My Heart Leaps Up *(Joyful)*

WILLIAM WORDSWORTH

My heart leaps up when I behold
    A rainbow in the sky:
So was it when my life began;
So is it now I am a man;
So be it when I shall grow old,
    Or let me die!
The Child is the father of the Man;
And I could wish my days to be
Bound each to each by natural piety.

Emily Dickinson (1830–1886) was born in Amherst, Massachusetts, and was educated at Amherst Academy, South Hadley Female Seminary (Mount Holyoke) which she attended for less than one year. She led a brief and secluded life at home. Only two of her poems were printed during her lifetime, neither with her consent. Volumes so far published include *Poems* (1890), *Poems: Second Series* (1891), *Poems: Third Series* (1896), *The Single Hound* (1914), *Further Poems* (1929), *Unpublished Poems* (1936), *Poems: Centenary Edition* (1930), *Bolts of Melody* (1945).

I Taste a Liquor Never Brewed *(Joyful)*

EMILY DICKINSON

I taste a liquor never brewed—
From Tankards scooped in Pearl—
Not all the Frankfort Berries
Yield such an Alcohol!

Inebriate of Air—am I—
An Debauchee of Dew—
Reeling—thro endless summer days—
From inns of Molten Blue—

When "Landlords" turn the drunken Bee
Out of the Foxglove's door—
When Butterflies—renounce their "drams"—
I shall but drink the more!

Till Seraphs swing their snowy Hats—
And Saints—to windows run—
To see the little Tippler
From Manzanilla come!

EXERCISES—*WHEN IN DISGRACE WITH FORTUNE*
MY HEART LEAPS UP
I TASTE A LIQUOR NEVER BREWED

Content

1. What has inspired each poet to write his poem?
2. Explain the following lines.
   Shakespeare: With what I most enjoy contented least.
   Wordsworth: The Child is the father of the Man;
   Dickinson: To see the little tippler
   From Manzanilla come!

Style

1. Explain the relationship between each poet's mood and the resulting tone of the poem.
2. Which poem has the greatest number of poetic images that convey the poet's emotion? Explain.
3. Each poem differs from the other two in structure (rime scheme, meter, stanzaic form). Which poem's structure most successfully touches your emotions? Why?

Application of Stylistic Techniques

Maintaining as much of the poet's own language as you can, convert each poem into a prose paragraph. Explain your reasons for believing the prose is more effective or less effective—or just as effective—as the poetry. Deal specifically with mood and tone and the conveying of feeling.

Suggestions for Writing

1. Select a poem you especially like and write an essay describing the joy it relates to you.
2. In an essay discuss the merits of poetry over prose, or the converse.
3. Write a poem that is joyful in tone.
4. Select an aspect of one of the following often emotionally related topics and write an essay having a joyful tone.
   Nature

Freedom
Power
Love
Success
Beauty
Parenthood
Matrimony
God
Mankind

John Updike (1932–) was born in Pennsylvania. He was graduated from Harvard in 1954, and worked for the *New Yorker* from 1955–57. His major works include *Poorhouse Fair, Rabbit Run, The Centaur, Couples, Bech: A Book; Collections: The Same Door, Pigeon Feathers, The Carpentered Hen and Other Tame Creatures, Telephone Poles* (light verse), and *Assorted Prose.*

The Assassination *(Somber)*

JOHN UPDIKE *November 1963*

[1] It was as if we slept from Friday to Monday and dreamed an oppressive, unsearchably significant dream, which, we discovered on awaking, millions of others had dreamed also. Furniture, family, the streets, and the sky dissolved; only the dream on television was real. The faces of the world's great mingled with the faces of landladies who had happened to house an unhappy ex-Marine; cathedrals alternated with warehouses, temples of government with suburban garages; anonymous men tugged at a casket in a glaring airport; a murder was committed before our eyes; a Dallas strip-tease artist drawled amiably of her employer's quick temper; the heads of state of the Western world strode down a sunlit street like a grim village rabble; and Jacqueline Kennedy became Persephone, the Queen of Hades and the beautiful bride of grief. All human possibilities, of magnificence and courage, of meanness and confusion, seemed to find an image in this long montage, and a stack of cardboard boxes in Dallas, a tawdry movie house, a tiny rented room where some shaving cream still clung to the underside of a washbasin, a row of parking meters that had witnessed a panicked flight all acquired the opaque and dreadful importance that innocent objects acquire in nightmares.

[2] What did it mean? Can we hope for a meaning? "It's the fashion to hate people in the United States." This quotation might be from one of a hundred admonitory sermons delivered after President Kennedy's death. In actuality, it occurs in an interview granted in 1959 to a United Press reporter, Aline Mosby, by a young American defector then living in Moscow, Lee Harvey Oswald. The presumed assassin did not seem to be a violent man. "He was too quiet, too reserved," his ex-landlord told reporters. "He certainly had the intelligence and he looked like he could be efficient at doing almost anything." In his room, the police found a map on which was marked the precise path that three bullets in fact took. The mind that might have unlocked this puzzle of perfectly aimed, perfectly aimless murder has been itself forever sealed by murder. The second assassination augmented the first, expanded our sense of potential violence. In these cruel events, democracy seemed caricatured; a gun voted, and a drab Dallas neighborhood was hoisted into history. None of our country's four slain Presidents were victims of any distinct idea of opposition or hope of gain; they were sacrificed, rather, to the blind tides of criminality and insanity that make civilization precarious. Between Friday and Monday, three men died: a President, a policeman, and a prisoner. May their deaths be symbols, clues to our deep unease, and omens we heed.

December 1963

[3] Christmas this year has the air of a birthday party carried on despite a death in the family; the usual garishness that exhilarates and grates is absent, though not visibly so. In search of the invisible difference, we wandered out onto Fifth Avenue last week, and the first thing we saw was the large American flag on the Bank of New York which, because it was hung at half-mast, was beating itself aginst the windows and the limestone of the building. The flag was, in the brisk wind of that day, like a hapless tricolor bird trying to roost. All up and down the Avenue, the half-mast flags were gray from rubbing against sooty façades.

[4] We were led to notice, through observing the flags,

how Christmas tends to stop at the second story. With a few exceptions (the annual festoon at Lord & Taylor, the pipes and choirboys up at Saks), the wreaths and tinsel give out above the display windows, like sea wrack above the high-tide line. And we noticed, too, how little movement there is this year in the Christmas displays. We did see a papier mâché Santa, gift certificate in hand, revolving his torso in the window of the John B. Stetson Company; he seemed to be doing the hula, or the upper half of the Twist. Except for him, the windows were strangely still.

[5] Oh, we saw cheerful things: two nuns, themselves so immaculately packaged, carrying packages; the so-called Dog Bar at Wallachs (a little marble saucer set low to the pavement) splashing as self-importantly as a Neapolitan fountain; a harried lady doubling back to put a coin in a curbside Santa's pot. Saks was a glorious grotto, a super-Antarctica of white stalactites and frosty Spanish moss, where even the floorwalkers' white neckties had a polar primness, like the breasts of penguins. The women shopping were wonderful; this year's high heels do not jounce the face but wobble the ankles, so that women walking have the tremulous radiance of burning candles as, step by step, they quiver in and out of balance.

[6] But a sombre undercurrent persisted. Cartier's wore her strands of dull-gold tinsel like an old woman wearing a mourning shawl. The beards of the Santa Clauses along the street looked transparently false—shiny, ill-fitted appendages of nylon. In the old days, it seemed to us, the Santa Claus beards bristled like the coats of badgers and were as soft as the fleece of lambs. This year, they are palpably pretense; the party must go on. At Rockefeller Center, the tree is hung with two-dimensional balls, and the greenery in the center of the mall is confused with strange artifacts of white and silver wire—giant jack-in-the-boxes, outsize alphabet blocks, huge mock toys. The effect is not entirely fortunate. We kept seeing the green shrubbery through the wire constructions and wondering which we were meant to believe in—which was Christmas and which was Nature.

[7] We walked across the street to St. Patrick's Cathedral. It alone, on all the festive Avenue, seemed totally con-

vinced. We had never so closely observed the central doors, which are usually open or obscured by darkness. The six bronze figures on them we had assumed to be iconographically standard, indistinguishably Biblical. This was not so, and for those as inexcusably unobservant as we are, we will list them, left to right, top to bottom. On the doors of St. Patrick's Cathedral, in full-relief figures about a yard high, are St. Joseph, Patron of the Church; St. Patrick, Patron of This Church; St. Isaac Jogues, Martyr and First Priest in New York; St. Frances X. Cabrini, Mother of the Immigrant; Ven. Kateri Tekakwitha, Lily of the Mohawks; and Mother Elizabeth Seton, Daughter of New York. The Lily of the Mohawks, with her stoic face, her Indian headband, and her Christian cross, seemed peculiarly relevant to the gently forlorn metropolitan flux around us. We do not often enough, perhaps, think of ourselves as successors of the Indians—subsequent tenants, as it were, of a continuing mystery. We went inside the cathedral. A Mass was in progress, and it was well attended. At side altars, banks of candles glowed and wavered like crowds of female shoppers. At the front altar, the priest, the back of his white chasuble shining, seemed the lone passenger on a splendid, house-shaped boat afloat before our eyes. Bells rang. People knelt. Again bells rang. The kneelers rose; the noise of their rising merged with the shuffle and scrape of footsteps around us, in the rear of the cathedral.

[8] Outside on the street, Christmas did seem to have solidified. Cool sunlight was falling unruffled through the wind, and, looking at the crowds, we realized what the difference is this year. People are not determined to be jolly; they do not feel obligated to smile. From the sudden death of our young President, Americans may in time date a great physiognomic discovery: a human face may refuse, or fail, to smile and still be human.

EXERCISES—*THE ASSASSINATION*

Content

1. According to Updike, for what reason was President Kennedy killed?

2. What alone among all the festive preparations seems "totally convinced" about Christmas?
3. What is the "great physiognomic discovery" Updike writes about?

Style

1. List two phrases from each paragraph of this essay that demonstrate Updike's somber tone.
2. Judging from Updike's tone, how would you describe his mood?
3. In this essay, is Updike ever sentimental or mawkish or either? Explain.
4. Why does the author write in second person plural? Is he using an editorial "we"? Explain.

Application of Stylistic Techniques

1. Following Updike's heavy reliance upon description and metaphoric language, write a paragraph imitating his sentence patterns in paragraph (4).
2. Select some other festive time of year or celebrated day (Thanksgiving, Easter, Yom Kippur, Veteran's Day, Fourth of July, etc.) and develop a somber tone similar to Updike's in paragraph (3). Use contrasts similar to Updike's.
3. Rewrite paragraph (5) as objective reportage.
4. Rewrite paragraph (4) in second person. How does the use of "you" affect the tone?

Suggestions for Writing

1. Select some public occurrence that moved you emotionally and write an essay that through your somber tone discloses your feelings about the event.
2. Select a topic and write an essay having a somber tone.
   No Man Hath Greater Love
   The Children's Hospital
   Autumn
   An Unforgettable Moment
   The Day I Lost a Friend
   When Johnny Goes to War
   A Day at the Veteran's Hospital
   How Lucky We Are?
   The Time of the Storm
   What Good Is a Medal?

James Thurber (1894–1961), one of America's foremost humorists, was born in Columbus, Ohio, where he was educated at Ohio State University. He was on the staff of the *Columbus Dispatch, The Chicago Tribune* in Paris, and the *New Yorker.* His works include *Is Sex Necessary* (with E. B. White); *The Male Animal* (with Elliott Nugent); *The Thurber Carnival; Men, Women, and Dogs; The Owl in the Attic; My Life and Hard Times; Fables for Our Time; My World—and Welcome to It;* and *Thurber Country.*

University Days *(Humorous)*

JAMES THURBER

[1] I passed all the other courses that I took at my University, but I could never pass botany. This was because all botany students had to spend several hours a week in a laboratory looking through a microscope at plant cells, and I could never see through a microscope. I never once saw a cell through a microscope. This used to enrage my instructor. He would wander around the laboratory pleased with the progress all the students were making in drawing the involved and, so I am told, interesting structure of flower cells, until he came to me. I would just be standing there. "I can't see anything," I would say. He would begin patiently enough, explaining how anybody can see through a microscope, but he would always end up in a fury, claiming that I could *too* see through a microscope but just pretended that I couldn't. "It takes away from the beauty of flowers anyway," I used to tell him. "We are not concerned with beauty in this course," he would say. "We are concerned solely with what I may call the *mechanics* of flars." "Well," I'd say, "I can't see anything." "Try it just once again," he'd say, and I would put my eye to the micro-

scope and see nothing at all, except now and again a nebulous milky substance—a phenomenon of maladjustment. You were supposed to see a vivid, restless clockwork of sharply defined plant cells. "I see what looks like a lot of milk," I would tell him. This, he claimed, was the result of my not having adjusted the microscope properly, so he would readjust it for me, or rather, for himself. And I would look again and see milk.

[2] I finally took a deferred pass, as they called it, and waited a year and tried again. (You had to pass one of the biological sciences or you couldn't graduate.) The professor had come back from vacation brown as a berry, bright-eyed, and eager to explain cell-structure again to his classes. "Well," he said to me, cheerily, when we met in the first laboratory hour of the semester, "we're going to see cells this time, aren't we?" "Yes, sir," I said. Students to right of me and to left of me and in front of me were seeing cells; what's more, they were quietly drawing pictures of them in their notebooks. Of course, I didn't see anything.

"We'll try it," the professor said to me, grimly, "with every adjustment of the microscope known to man. As God is my witness, I'll arrange this glass so that you see cells through it or I'll give up teaching. In twenty-two years of botany, I—" He cut off abruptly for he was beginning to quiver all over, like Lionel Barrymore, and he genuinely wished to hold onto his temper; his scenes with me had taken a great deal out of him.

[3] So we tried it with every adjustment of the microscope known to man. With only one of them did I see anything but blackness or the familiar lacteal opacity, and that time I saw, to my pleasure and amazement, a variegated constellation of flecks, specks, and dots. These I hastily drew. The instructor, noting my activity, came back from an adjoining desk, a smile on his lips and his eyebrows high in hope. He looked at my cell drawing. "What's that?" he demanded, with a hint of a squeal in his voice. "That's what I saw," I said. "You didn't, you didn't, you *did*n't!" he screamed, losing control of his temper instantly, and he bent over and squinted into the microscope. His head snapped up. "That's your eye!" he shouted.

"You've fixed the lens so that it reflects! You've drawn your eye!"

[4] Another course that I didn't like, but somehow managed to pass, was economics. I went to that class straight from the botany class, which didn't help me any in understanding either subject. I used to get them mixed up. But not as mixed up as another student in my economics class who came there direct from a physics laboratory. He was a tackle on the football team, named Bolenciecwcz. At that time Ohio State University had one of the best football teams in the country, and Bolenciecwcz was one of its outstanding stars. In order to be eligible to play it was necessary for him to keep up in his studies, a very difficult matter, for while he was not dumber than an ox he was not any smarter. Most of his professors were lenient and helped him along. None gave him more hints, in answering questions, or asked him simpler ones than the economics professor, a thin, timid man named Bassum. One day when we were on the subject of transportation and distribution, it came Bolenciecwcz's turn to answer a question. "Name one means of transportation," the professor said to him. No light came into the big tackle's eyes. "Just any means of transportation," said the professor. Bolenciecwcz sat staring at him. "That is," pursued the professor, "any medium, agency, or method of going from one place to another." Bolenciecwcz had the look of a man who is being led into a trap. "You may choose among steam, horse-drawn, or electrically propelled vehicles," said the instructor. "I might suggest the one which we commonly take in making long journeys across land." There was a profound silence in which everybody stirred uneasily, including Bolenciecwcz and Mr. Bassum. Mr. Bassum abruptly broke this silence in an amazing manner. "Choo-choo-choo," he said, in a low voice, and turned instantly scarlet. He glanced appealingly around the room. All of us, of course, shared Mr. Bassum's desire that Bolenciecwcz should stay abreast of the class in economics, for the Illinois game, one of the hardest and most important of the season, was only a week off. "Toot, toot, too- tooooooot!" some student with a deep voice moaned, and we all looked encouragingly at Bolen-

ciecwcz. Somebody else gave a fine imitation of a locomotive letting off steam. Mr. Bassum himself rounded off the little show. "Ding, dong, ding, dong," he said, hopefully. Bolenciecwcz was staring at the floor now, trying to think, his great brow furrowed, his huge hands rubbing together, his face red.

[5] "How did you come to college this year, Mr. Bolenciecwcz?" asked the professor. "*Chuf*fa chuffa, *chuf*fa chuffa."

[6] "M'father sent me," said the football player.

[7] "What on?" asked Bassum.

[8] "I git an 'lowance," said the tackle, in a low, husky voice, obviously embarrassed.

[9] "No, no," said Bassum. "Name a means of transportation.

[10] What did you *ride* here on?"

[11] "Train," said Bolenciecwcz.

[12] "Quite right," said the professor. "Now, Mr. Nugent, will you tell us——"

[13] If I went through anguish in botany and economics —for different reasons—gymnasium work was even worse. I don't even like to think about it. They wouldn't let you play games or join in the exercises with your glasses on and I couldn't see with mine off. I bumped into professors, horizontal bars, agricultural students, and swinging iron rings. Not being able to see, I could take it but I couldn't dish it out. Also, in order to pass gymnasium (and you had to pass it to graduate) you had to learn to swim if you didn't know how. I didn't like the swimming pool, I didn't like swimming, and I didn't like the swimming instructor, and after all these years I still don't. I never swam but I passed my gymwork anyway, by having another student give my gymnasium number (978) and swim across the pool in my place. He was a quiet, amiable blonde youth, number 473, and he would have seen through a microscope for me if we could have got away with it, but we couldn't get away with it. Another thing I didn't like about gymnasium work was that they made you strip the day you registered. It is impossible for me to be happy when I am stripped and being asked a lot of questions. Still, I did better than a lanky agricultural student who was cross-examined just before I was. They asked each student what college he

was in—that is, whether Arts, Engineering, Commerce, or Agriculture. "What college are you in?" the instructor snapped at the youth in front of me. "Ohio State University," he said promptly.

[14] It wasn't that agricultural student but it was another a whole lot like him who decided to take up journalism, possibly on the ground that when farming went to hell he could fall back on newspaper work. He didn't realize, of course, that that would be very much like falling back full-length on a kit of carpenter's tools. Haskins didn't seem cut out for journalism, being too embarrassed to talk to anybody and unable to use a typewriter, but the editor of the college paper assigned him to the cow barns, the sheep house, the horse pavilion, and the animal husbandry department generally. This was a genuinely big "beat," for it took up five times as much ground and got ten times as great a legislative appropriation as the College of Liberal Arts. The agricultural student knew animals, but nevertheless his stories were dull and colorlessly written. He took all afternoon on each of them, on account of having to hunt for each letter on the typewriter. Once in a while he had to ask somebody to help him hunt. "C" and "L," in particular, were hard letters for him to find. His editor finally got pretty much annoyed at the farmer-journalist because his pieces were so uninteresting. "See here, Haskins," he snapped at him one day, "why is it we never have anything hot from you on the horse pavilion? Here we have two hundred head of horses on this campus—more than any other university in the Western Conference except Purdue—and yet you never get any real low down on them. Now shoot over to the horse barns and dig up something lively." Haskins shambled out and came back in about an hour; he said he had something. "Well, start it off snappily," said the editor. "Something people will read." Haskins set to work and in a couple of hours brought a sheet of typewritten paper to the desk; it was a two-hundred word story about some disease that had broken out among the horses. Is opening sentence was simple but arresting. It read: "Who has noticed the sores on the tops of the horses in the animal husbandry building?"

[15] Ohio State was a land grant university and there-

fore two years of military drill was compulsory. We drilled with old Springfield rifles and studied the tactics of the Civil War even though the World War was going on at the time. At 11 o'clock each morning thousands of freshmen and sophomores used to deploy over the campus, moodily creeping up on the old chemistry building. It was good training for the kind of warfare that was waged at Shiloh but it had no connection with what was going on in Europe. Some people used to think there was German money behind it, but they didn't dare say so or they would have been thrown in jail as German spies. It was a period of muddy thought and marked, I believe, the decline of higher education in the Middle West.

[16] As a soldier I was never any good at all. Most of the cadets were glumly indifferent soldiers, but I was no good at all. Once General Littlefield, who was commandant of the cadet corps, popped up in front of me during regimental drill and snapped,

[17] "You are the main trouble with this university!" I think he meant that my type was the main trouble with the university but he may have meant me individually. I was mediocre at drill, certainly—that is, until my senior year. By that time I had drilled longer than anybody else in the Western Conference, having failed at military at the end of each preceding year so that I had to do it all over again. I was the only senior still in uniform. The uniform which, when new, had made me look like an interurban railway conductor, now that it had become faded and too tight made me look like Bert Williams in his bellboy act. This had a definitely bad effect on my morale. Even so, I had become by sheer practise little short of wonderful at squad manoeuvres.

[18] One day General Littlefield picked our company out of the whole regiment and tried to get it mixed up by putting it through one movement after another as fast as we could execute them: squads right, squads left, squads on right into line, squads right about, squads left front into line etc. In about three minutes one hundred and nine men were marching in one direction and I was marching away from them at an angle of forty degrees, all alone. "Company, halt!" shouted General Littlefield, "That man is the only man who has it

right!" I was made a corporal for my achievement.

[19] The next day General Littlefield summoned me to his office. He was swatting flies when I went in. I was silent and he was silent too, for a long time. I don't think he remembered me or why he had sent for me, but he didn't want to admit it. He swatted some more flies, keeping his eye on them narrowly before he let go with the swatter. "Button up your coat!" he snapped. Looking back on it now I can see that he meant me although he was looking at a fly, but I just stood there. Another fly came to rest on a paper in front of the general and began rubbing its hind legs together. The general lifted the swatter cautiously. I moved restlessly and the fly flew away. "You startled him!" barked General Littlefield, looking at me severely. I said I was sorry. "That won't help the situation!" snapped the General, with cold military logic. I didn't see what I could do except offer to chase some more flies toward his desk, but I didn't say anything. He stared out the window at the faraway figures of co-eds crossing the campus toward the library. Finally, he told me I could go. So I went. He either didn't know which cadet I was or else he forgot what he wanted to see me about. It may have been that he wished to apologize for having called me the main trouble with the university; or maybe he had decided to compliment me on my brilliant drilling of the day before and then at the last minute decided not to. I don't know. I don't think about it much any more.

EXERCISES—*UNIVERSITY DAYS*

Content

1. Why does Thurber include his botany professor, his economics professor, the agricultural student, and the commandant of the cadet corps? Explain each one specifically.
2. Of all the persons mentioned, toward which one is the author most sympathetic? Explain.
3. Does the author seem apologetic about his having someone take his swimming test for him? Why or why not?
4. For what purpose is this essay written? Explain.

Style

1. In terms of his selection and treatment of the subject matter, explain who Thurber's intended audience is.
2. Would you classify this essay as informal or colloquial? Why?
3. Explain Thurber's choice of point of view.
4. Select a sentence from paragraph (4), one that demonstrates humor independent of the main topic of the paragraph. Why is this sentence humorous?
5. For what reason would you or would you not say that this essay smacks of Horatian satire? of Juvenalian satire?

Application of Stylistic Techniques

1. Rewrite the incident in paragraph (3) so that the narrator is treating the professor sarcastically; then, in another paragraph, satirically, either Horatian or Juvenalian.
2. Rewrite paragraph (19) in a somber tone.
3. Rewrite paragraph (16), using the impersonal "one," then the "we" of Updike's *Assassination* and E. B. White's *The Age of Dust.* Briefly discuss the merits of Thurber's "I" and your substitutions of "one" and "we."
4. Rewrite paragraph (15) in the style of a technical report, using passive voice and avoiding the impersonal "one" as well as the personal pronouns (I, we, you).

Suggestions for Writing

1. Write an essay in which you humorously treat some of your college experiences; write from first person point of view.
2. Select a topic and write an essay having a humorous tone. Be careful to avoid sarcasm and satirical methods.
   Colleges Have Changed
   Football Players Aren't Dumb
   The Militants and Me
   How to Dress for the College Occasion
   Biology Class and the Appetite
   Burning Down the Ad Building
   Fun at the Frat and Where It's Really At
   Sorority Girls!
   Today's Big Man on Campus
   College: The Happy Hunting Ground

Johnathan Swift (1667–1745) was born of English parents in Dublin, Ireland. He was educated at Kilkenny School and Trinity College, Dublin. Although an Anglican clergyman, he wrote satires on corruption in religion and learning. He was secretary of Sir William Temple in England and a political journalist. His major works include *A Tale of a Tub, The Battle of the Books, Gulliver's Travels,* and *The Journal to Stella.*

A Modest Proposal *(Ironic)*

JONATHAN SWIFT

[1] It is a melancholly Object to those, who walk through this great Town or travel in the Country, when they see the Streets, the Roads and Cabbin-doors crowded with Beggers of the Female Sex, followed by three, four, or six Children, all in Rags, and importuning every Passenger for an Alms. These Mothers instead of being able to work for their honest livelyhood, are forced to employ all their time in Stroling to beg Sustenance for their helpless Infants, who, as they grow up, either turn Thieves for want of Work, or leave their dear Native Country, to fight for the Pretender in Spain, or sell themselves to the Barbadoes.

[2] I think it is agreed by all Parties, that this prodigious number of Children in the Arms, or on the Backs, or at the Heels of their Mothers, and frequently of their Fathers, is in the present deplorable state of the Kingdom, a very great additional grievance; and therefore whoever could find out a fair, cheap and easy method of making these Children sound and useful Members of the Common-wealth, would deserve so well of the publick, as to have his Statue set up for a Preserver of the Nation.

[3] But my Intention is very far from being confined to provide only for the Children of professed Beggers, it is of a much greater Extent, and shall take in the whole Number

of Infants at a certain Age, who are born of Parents in effect as little able to support them, as those who demand our Charity in the Streets.

As to my own part, having turned my Thoughts, for many Years, upon this important Subject, and maturely weighed the several Schemes of other Projectors, I have always found them grossly mistaken in their computation. It is true, a Child just dropt from its Dam, may be supported by her Milk, for a Solar Year with little other Nourishment, at most not above the Value of two Shillings, which the Mother may certainly get, or the Value in Scraps, by her lawful Occupation of Begging; and it is exactly at one Year Old that I propose to provide for them in such a manner, as, instead of being a Charge upon their Parents, or the Parish, or wanting Food and Raiment for the rest of their Lives, they shall, on the Contrary, contribute to the Feeding and partly to the Cloathing of many Thousands.

[4] There is likewise another great Advantage in my Scheme, that it will prevent those voluntary Abortions, and that horrid practice of Women murdering their Bastard Children, alas! too frequent among us, Sacrificing the poor innocent Babes, I doubt, more to avoid the Expence than the Shame, which would move Tears and Pity in the most Savage and inhuman breast.

[5] The number of Souls in this Kingdom being usually reckoned one Million and a half, Of these I calculate there may be about two hundred thousand Couple whose Wives are Breeders; from which number I substract thirty Thousand Couples, who are able to maintain their own Children, although I apprehend there cannot be so many, under the present Distresses of the Kingdom; but this being granted, there will remain an hundred and seventy thousand Breeders. I again Substract fifty Thousand, for those Women who miscarry, or whose Children die by accident, or disease within the Year. There only remain an hundred and twenty thousand Children of poor Parents annually born: The question therefore is, How this number shall be reared, and provided for? which, as I have already said, under the present Situation of Affairs, is utterly impossible by all the Methods hitherto pro-

posed; for we can neither employ them in Handicraft or Agriculture; we neither build Houses, (I mean in the Country) nor cultivate Land: They can very seldom pick up a Livelihood by Stealing till they arrive at six years Old; except where they are of towardly parts; although, I confess, they learn the Rudiments much earlier; during which time they can however be properly looked upon only as Probationers; as I have been informed by a principal Gentleman in the County of Cavan, who protested to me, that he never knew above one or two instances under the Age of six, even in a part of the Kingdom so renowned for the quickest proficiency in that Art.

[6] I am assured by our Merchants, that a Boy or a Girl before twelve years Old, is no saleable Commodity, and even when they come to this Age, they will not yield above three Pounds, or three Pounds and half a Crown at most, on the Exchange; which cannot turn to Account either to the Parents or Kingdom, the Charge of Nutriment and Rags having been at least four times that Value.

[7] I shall now therefore humbly propose my own Thoughts, which I hope will not be liable to the least Objection.

[8] I have been assured by a very knowing American of my acquaintance in London, that a young healthy Child well Nursed is at a year Old a most delicious nourishing and wholesome Food, whether Stewed, Roasted, Baked, or Boiled; and I make no doubt that it will equally serve in a Fricasie, or a Ragoust.

[9] I do therefore humbly offer it to publick consideration, that of the Hundred and twenty thousand Children, already computed, twenty thousand may be reserved for Breed, whereof only one fourth part to be Males; which is more than we allow to Sheep, black Cattle, or Swine, and my Reason is, that these Children are seldom the Fruits of Marriage, a Circumstance not much regarded by our Savages, therefore, one Male will be sufficient to serve four Females. That the remaining Hundred thousand may at a year Old be offered in Sale to the Persons of Quality and Fortune, through the Kingdom, always advising the Mother to let them Suck plentifully in the last Month, so as to render them Plump, and Fat for a good

Table. A Child will make two Dishes at an Entertainment for Friends, and when the Family dines alone, the fore or hind Quarter will make a reasonable Dish, and seasoned with a little Pepper or Salt will be very good Boiled on the fourth Day, especially in Winter.

[10] I have reckoned upon a Medium, that a Child just born will weigh 12 pounds, and in a solar Year, if tolerably nursed, encreaseth to 28 Pounds.

[11] I grant this food will be somewhat dear, and therefore very proper for Landlords, who, as they have already devoured most of the Parents seem to have the best Title to the Children.

[12] Infant's flesh will be in Season throughout the Year, but more plentiful in March, and a little before and after; for we are told by a grave Author an eminent French Physician, that Fish being a prolifick Dyet, there are more Children born in Roman Catholick Countries about nine Months after Lent, than at any other Season; therefore reckoning a Year after Lent, the Markets will be more glutted than usual, because the Number of Popish Infants, is at least three to one in this Kingdom, and therefore it will have one other Collateral advantage, by lessening the Number of Papists among us.

[13] I have already computed the Charge of nursing a Begger's Child (in which List I reckon all Cottagers, Labourers, and four fifths of the Farmers) to be about two Shillings per Annum, Rags included; and I believe no Gentleman would repine to give Ten Shillings for the Carcass of a good fat Child, which, as I have said will make four Dishes of excellent Nutritive Meat, when he hath only some particular Friend, or his own Family to dine with him. Thus the Squire will learn to be a good Landlord, and grow popular among his Tenants, the Mother will have Eight Shillings neat Profit, and be fit for Work till she produces another Child.

[14] Those who are more thrifty (as I must confess the Times require) may flay the Carcass; the Skin of which, Artificially dressed, will make admirable Gloves for Ladies, and Summer Boots for fine Gentlemen.

[15] As to our City of Dublin, Shambles may be ap-

pointed for this purpose, in the most convenient parts of it, and Butchers we may be assured will not be wanting; although I rather recommend buying the Children alive, and dressing them hot from the Knife, as we do roasting Pigs.

[16] A very worthy Person, a true Lover of his Country, and whose Virtues I highly esteem, was lately pleased, in discoursing on this matter, to offer a refinement upon my Scheme. He said, that many Gentlemen of this Kingdom, having of late destroyed their Deer, he conceived that the Want of Venison might be well supply'd by the Bodies of young Lads and Maidens, not exceeding fourteen Years of Age, nor under twelve; so great a Number of both Sexes in every Country being now ready to Starve, for want of Work and Service: And these to be disposed of by their Parents if alive, or otherwise by their nearest Relations. But with due deference to so excellent a Friend, and so deserving a Patriot, I cannot be altogether in his Sentiments; for as to the Males, my American acquaintance assured me from frequent Experience, that their Flesh was generally Tough and Lean, like that of our Schoolboys, by continual exercise, and their Taste disagreeable, and to fatten them would not anwser the Charge. Then as to the Females, it would, I think with humble Submission, be a Loss to the Publick, because they soon would become Breeders themselves: And besides it is not improbable that some scrupulous People might be apt to Censure such a Practice, (although indeed very unjustly) as a little bordering upon Cruelty, which, I confess, hath always been with me the strongest Objection against any Project, how well soever intended.

[17] But in order to justify my Friend, he confessed, that this expedient was put into his Head by the famous Sallmanaazor, a Native of the Island Formosa, who came from thence to London, above twenty Years ago, and in Conversation told my Friend, that in his Country when any young Person happened to be put to Death, the Executioner sold the Carcass to Persons of Quality, as a prime Dainty, and that, in his Time, the Body of a plump Girl of fifteen, who was crucified for an attempt to poison the Emperor, was sold to his Imperial Majesty's prime Minister of State, and other great Mandarins of the Court, in Joints from the Gibbet, at four

hundred Crowns. Neither indeed can I deny, that if the same Use were made of several plump young Girls in this Town, who, without one single Groat to their Fortunes, cannot stir abroad without a Chair, and appear at a Play-house, and Assemblies in Foreign fineries, which they never will pay for; the Kingdom would not be the worse.

[18] Some Persons of a desponding Spirit are in great concern about that vast Number of poor People, who are Aged, Diseased, or Maimed, and I have been desired to imploy my Thoughts what Course may be taken, to ease the Nation of so grievous an Incumbrance. But I am not in the least Pain upon that matter, because it is very well known, that they are every Day dying, and rotting, by cold and famine, and filth, and vermin, as fast as can be reasonably expected. And as to the younger Labourers, they are now in almost as hopeful a Condition. They cannot get Work, and consequently pine away for want of Nourishment, to a degree, that if at any Time they are accidentally hired to common Labour, they have not Strength to perform it, and thus the Country and themselves are happily delivered from the Evils to come.

[19] I have too long digressed, and therefore shall return to my Subject. I think the Advantages by the Proposal which I have made are obvious and many, as well as of the highest Importance.

[20] For *First*, as I have already observed, it would greatly lessen the Number of Papists, with whom we are Yearly over-run, being the principal Breeders of the Nation, as well as our most dangerous Enemies, and who stay at home on purpose with a Design to deliver the Kingdom to the Pretender, hoping to take their Advantage by the Absence of so many good Protestants, who have chosen rather to leave their Country, than stay at home, and pay Tithes against their Conscience, to an Episcopal Curate.

[21] *Secondly*, The poorer Tenants will have something valuable of their own which by Law may be made lyable to Distress, and help to pay their Landlord's Rent, their Corn and Cattle being already seized, and Money a Thing unknown.

[22] *Thirdly*, Whereas the Maintenance of an hundred thousand Children, from two Years old, and upwards, can-

not be computed at less than Ten Shillings a Piece per Annum, the Nation's Stock will be thereby increased fifty thousand Pounds per Annum, besides the Profit of a new Dish, introduced to the Tables of all Gentlemen of Fortune in the Kingdom, who have any Refinement in Taste, and the will circulate among our Selves, the Goods being entirely of our own Growth and Manufacture.

[23] *Fourthly,* The constant Breeders, besides the gain of eight Shillings Sterling per Annum, by the Sale of their Children, will be rid of the Charge of maintaining them after the first Year.

[24] *Fifthly,* This Food would likewise bring great Custom to Taverns, where the Vintners will certainly be so prudent as to procure the best Receipts for dressing it to Perfection; and consequently have their Houses frequented by all the fine Gentlemen, who justly value themselves upon their Knowledge in good Eating; and a skilful Cook, who understands how to oblige his Guests, will contrive to make it as expensive as they please.

[25] *Sixthly,* This would be a great Inducement to Marriage, which all wise Nations have either encouraged by Rewards, or enforced by Laws and Penalties. It would encrease the Care and Tenderness of Mothers towards their Children, when they were sure of a Settlement for Life, to the poor Babes, provided in some Sort by the Publick, to their annual Profit instead of Expence; we should soon see an honest Emulation among the married Women, which of them could bring the fattest Child to the Market. Men would become as fond of their Wives, during the Time of their Pregnancy, as they are now of their Mares in Foal, their Cows in Calf, or Sows when they are ready to farrow, nor offer to beat or kick them (as is too frequent a Practice) for fear of a Miscarriage.

[26] Many other Advantages might be enumerated. For Instance, the Addition of some thousand Carcasses in our Exportation of Barrel'd Beef: The Propagation of Swine's Flesh, and Improvement in the Art of making good Bacon, so much wanted among us by the great Destruction of Pigs, too frequent at our Tables, which are no way comparable in Taste, or Magnificence to a well grown, fat yearling Child, which

roasted whole will make a considerable Figure at a Lord Mayor's Feast, or any other Publick Entertainment. But this, and many others, I omit, being studious of Brevity.

[27] Supposing that one thousand Families in this City, would be constant Customers for Infant's Flesh, besides others who might have it at merry Meetings, particularly at Weddings and Christenings, I compute that Dublin would take off Annually about twenty thousand Carcasses, and the rest of the Kingdom (where probably they will be sold somewhat cheaper) the remaining eighty Thousand.

[28] I can think of no one Objection, that will possibly be raised against this Proposal, unless it should be urged, that the Number of People will be thereby much lessened in the Kingdom. This I freely own, and 'twas indeed one principal Design in offering it to the World. I desire the Reader will observe, that I calculate my Remedy for this one individual Kingdom of Ireland, and for no Other that ever was, is, or, I think, ever can be upon Earth. Therefore let no man talk to me of other Expedients: Of taxing our Absentees at five Shillings a Pound: Of using neither Cloaths, nor Household Furniture, except what is of our own Growth and Manufacture: Of utterly rejecting the Materials and Instruments that promote Foreign Luxury: Of curing the Expensiveness of Pride, Vanity, Idleness, and Gaming in our Women: Of introducing a Vein of Parcimony, Prudence and Temperance: Of learning to love our Country, wherein we differ even from Laplanders, and the Inhabitants of Topinamboo: Of quitting our Animosities, and Factions, nor act any longer like the Jews, who were murdering one another at the very Moment their City was taken: Of being a little cautious not to sell our Country and Consciences for nothing: Of teaching Landlords to have at least one Degree of Mercy towards their Tenants. Lastly, Of putting a Spirit of Honesty, Industry, and Skill into our Shopkeepers, who, if a Resolution could now be taken to buy only our Native Goods, would immediately unite to cheat and exact upon us in the Price, the Measure, and the Goodness, nor could ever yet be brought to make one fair Proposal of just Dealing, though often and earnestly invited to it.

[29] Therefore I repeat, let no Man talk to me of these and the like Expedients, till he hath at least some Glimpse of Hope, that there will ever be some hearty and sincere Attempt to put them in Practice.

[30] But as to my self, having been wearied out for many Years with offering vain, idle, visionary Thoughts, and at length utterly despairing of Success, I fortunately fell upon this Proposal, which as it is wholly new, so it hath something Solid and Real, of no Expence and little Trouble, full in our own Power, and whereby we can incur no Danger in disobliging England. For this kind of Commodity will not bear Exportation, the Flesh being of too tender a Consistence, to admit a long Continuance in Salt, although perhaps I cou'd name a Country, which wou'd be glad to eat up our whole Nation without it.

[31] After all, I am not so violently bent upon my own Opinion, as to reject any Offer, proposed by wise Men, which shall be found equally Innocent, Cheap, Easy, and Effectual. But before something of that Kind shall be advanced in Contradiction to my Scheme, and offering a better, I desire the Author or Authors, will be pleased maturely to consider two Points. *First,* As Things now stand, how they will be able to find Food and Raiment for a hundred Thousand useless Mouths and Backs. And *Secondly,* There being a round Million of Creatures in Human Figure, throughout this Kingdom, whose whole Subsistence put into a common Stock, would leave them in Debt two Millions of Pounds Sterling, adding those, who are Beggers by Profession, to the Bulk of Farmers, Cottagers and Labourers, with their Wives and Children, who are Beggers in Effect; I desire those Politicians, who dislike my Overture, and may perhaps be so bold to attempt an Answer, that they will first ask the Parents of these Mortals, Whether they would not at this Day think it a great Happiness to have been sold for Food at a Year Old, in the manner I prescribe, and thereby have avoided such a perpetual Scene of Misfortunes, as they have since gone through, by the Oppression of Landlords, the Impossibility of paying Rent without Money or Trade, the Want of common Sustenance, with neither House

nor Cloaths to cover them from the Inclemencies of the Weather, and the most inevitable Prospect of intailing the like, or greater Miseries, upon their Breed for ever.

[32] I profess in the Sincerity of my Heart, that I have not the least Personal Interest in endeavouring to promote this necessary Work, having no other Motive than the Publick Good of my Country, by advancing our Trade, providing for Infants, relieving the Poor, and giving some Pleasure to the Rich. I have no Children, by which I can propose to get a single Penny; the youngest being nine Years Old, and my Wife past Child-bearing.

EXERCISES—*A MODEST PROPOSAL*

Content

1. What is Swift's purpose in writing this essay?
2. What circumstances in his country caused him to make his proposal?
3. What is Swift's attitude toward Americans? Support your conclusion by a quotation from his essay.
4. In paragraph (12), what does Swift's view of the Roman Catholics' observance of Lent disclose about his attitude toward the Roman Catholic religion?
5. If Swift's proposal were enacted, would you prefer to be born a male or female? Explain.

Style

1. Considering the time in which Swift lived and the educational level of people, who do you think was Swift's intended audience?
2. Is Swift ever sarcastic in this essay? Explain by identifying specific instances.
3. What purpose does paragraph (32) serve, aside from being the conclusion?
4. By pointing out specific examples in the essay, briefly support the reason for calling this essay an extended use of irony.
5. Judging from the manner in which Swift uses irony, what do you think his mood is?

Application of Stylistic Techniques

1. Write a paragraph intended to point out some foible of man; inform the reader, but avoid any use of irony. Then transform the paragraph to one of irony.
2. Rewrite paragraph (7), being literal and avoiding irony.
3. Rewrite paragraph (1), using the indefinite "you." Which is more effective, Swift's or the more personal "you"? Explain.
4. Rewrite paragraph (3) in a modern colloquial style.

Suggestions for Writing

1. In an essay of extended irony, propose a means of curing some social ill you feel results mainly from man's foolishness.
2. In an essay of extended irony support or denounce Swift's proposal.
3. Select a topic and write an essay of extended irony.
   The Means of Ending the War
   The Answer to Campus Unrest
   A Proposition for the Militants
   The Value of the Silent Majority
   Work: The Character Builder
   Adversity Builds Men
   The Solution to Racial Discrimination
   Industry—The Consumer's Protector
   How Politicians Help Us All
   Advertising Improves Our Lives

John Updike (1932–   ) was born in Pennsylvania. He was graduated from Harvard in 1954, and worked for the *New Yorker* from 1955–1957. His major works include *Poorhouse Fair, Rabbit Run, The Centaur, Couples, Bech: A Book, Collections: The Same Door, Pigeon Feathers, The Carpentered Hen and Other Tame Creatures, Telephone Poles* (light verse), and *Assorted Prose.*

No Dodo *(Satiric—Horatian)*

JOHN UPDIKE

[1] Lately, we've been pondering the pigeons in Bryant Park. It seemed to us that they showed a decided preference for the paving, and trod the grass gingerly and seldom. Only once did we see one roost in a tree. It was an awkward, touching performance, like that of a man tying the bow of an apron behind him. Why should the common pigeon be embarrassed in the presence of vegetation? Because, research showed, he is a descendant of the blue rock dove. *Columba livia* is a native of the cliffs and rocky islands of western Europe and northern Africa, with subspecies ranging from the Canary Islands to India and Japan. The American branch stems from some of the English colonists' domestic pigeons, who flew the coop, went wild, shed their fancy shapes (the shapes of domestic pigeons can be very fancy), reverted to the parent type, and headed for the cities. Pigeons, or doves, have never made much of a distinction between natural and man-made crannies. Song of Solomon 2:14 apostrophizes "my dove, that art in the clefts of the rock, in the secret places of the stairs." Homer speaks of "Messe's towers for silver doves renowned," and Juvenal describes "the tiled roof where the gentle pigeons leave their

eggs." Tibullus asks, "Why need I tell how the sacred white pigeon flutters unmolested about the numerous cities of Syrian Palestine?" No other bird has been widely revered. Disturbing their nests in the Mosque of Doves, Istanbul, is blasphemy. In 1925, the Bombay Stock Exchange was closed and riots were threatened because two European boys had ignorantly killed some street pigeons. Kama, the Hindu god of love (a minor diety), is sometimes depicted riding a dove. In Christian iconography, the dove represents the Holy Ghost. And, of course, there's Noah. The Arabian version of the Deluge contains a pretty touch. When the dove returned to the ark the second time, its feet were stained with red mud. Noah, realizing that this meant the waters were receding, prayed that the messenger's feet might remain that color. They have. There is a Filipino legend that, of all birds, only the dove understands the human tongue.

[2] Pigeons have been the most faithful of man's feathered friends. Records of the bird's domestication extend back to the Fifth Egyptian Dynasty, around 3000 B.C. Homing pigeons have been used as messengers through the centuries from Cyrus the Great, of Persia, to yesterday's bootleggers. How they home is still something of a mystery. Keen eyes and a good memory just don't quite explain it, and neither do theories about magnetic or electro-magnetic control, sensitivity to light rays, the effect of air currents on the nasal passages or the semicircular canals, or "celestial orientation." Ancient Romans and medieval monks bred pigeons. Mary Queen of Scots and Queen Victoria were fanciers. The hobby is conjectured to be of Indian or Persian origin, and the results are so elaborate that it took Darwin ninety-eight pages to prove that jacobins, satinettes, barbs (the ideal barb's head resembles a spool), turbits, dragoons, fantails (when the fantail strikes his favorite pose, he can't see over his chest), visors, pouters (the pouter looks like a tennis ball stuffed into a glove), long-faced tumblers, inside tumblers (the inside, or parlor, tumbler is prized for his inability to fly a few feet without taking a backwards somersault), priests, nuns, monks, archangels, etc., etc., were all artificial variations of one bird. The difference noticeable in the markings of street pigeons is

a vestige of their earlier domestication. Because their feather-color patterns provide an external record of hereditary influences, and because they are docile and hardy, pigeons are a favorite laboratory animal of modern geneticists.

[3] Pigeons are social, somewhat timid, strong, and monogamous. Once mated, they customarily stay so for life. The cock as well as the hen broods the eggs, the hen working all night, the cock relieving her around ten in the morning and mooching off at four in the afternoon. The same schedule applies to the feeding of the young; both sexes secrete "pigeon milk" in their crops. Before coition, at the bonbon stage of courtship, the male feeds a regurgitated substance to the female. Maeterlinck called *Columba livia* "the most sedentary, most homekeeping, most habit-ridden of bourgeois." Fire will not budge a brooding pigeon. If a female leaves her nest before an egg has been laid, the male marches behind her, pecking at her head, until she returns or faints. A male will fight to the death defending the sanctity of his hearth. The nests are simple affairs—flat arrangements of twigs, feathers, straw, any old thing. The Museum of Natural History once possessed one made of paper clips; it was found near Wall Street. Are pigeons stupid? It is true that they will inadvertently trample their young to death in the nest; they carry only one twig at a time, where the sparrow carries two or three; and a pigeon will make romantic overtures to a bit of broken glass. But, pigeon boosters reply, pigeons have big feet and small fledglings; the sparrow makes a sloppy nest; and what's wrong with looking in a mirror? Certainly the bird is very eager to survive, unlike his cousin, the passenger pigeon, and his great-uncle once removed, the dodo.

[4] New York City is a good town for pigeons. The health officials of London kill a third of the pigeon population each year. In 1945, Philadelphia started an anti-pigeon campaign, and it trapped twenty-six thousand birds before it admitted that pigeons are irrepressible. In 1930, the superintendent of the State Capitol in Albany poisoned a batch around the building, and the stirred legislators promptly passed the following law: "Pigeons shall not be killed within the limits of any city except for food purposes, or unless sick or injured

beyond recovery." The only major local violation of the statute occurred in 1937, when an unknown fiend, in two sessions (August 10th and November 17th), fed a hundred Broadway pigeons strychnine pellets. The uproar, including a *Times* editorial entitled "St. Francis Must Weep," was huge. Building owners wage cold war against pigeons with spikes, prongs, metal netting, and lye-strewn or electrified ledges. The absence of filigrees, cornices, and other nook-rich ornamentation from the newer buildings is partly an anti-nesting device, though the pigeon theory of modern architecture should not be pursued to the exclusion of Frank Lloyd Wright. The bird's main Manhattan enemy, strange to relate, is the duck hawk, who swoops from bridges and skyscrapers. When Dr. Harry Emerson Fosdick suggested that the predators nesting in the steeple of Riverside Church be wiped out, the city's falcon lovers raised a strenuous outcry. Not quite as strenuous, though, as that which greeted Magistrate Anthony Burke, who in the same month (July, 1936) handed down the opinion that people who feed pigeons are morons. This hit a lot of citizens, for upward of fifty thousand pigeons live in Manhattan on handouts plus garbage. Pigeons cannot vote, and only five are in the phone book—two Edwins, two Georges, and one Pete.

EXERCISE—*NO DODO*

Content

1. What role has the pigeon played in ancient religions? in domestic matters?
2. What do detractors of pigeons say about the intelligence of the pigeon?
3. What is the significance of the quotation from the *Times* editorial paragraph (4): "St. Francis must weep."?

Style

1. Explain your attitude toward Updike's use of "we" in this essay.
2. For what purpose does the author use the material in the parentheses?
3. What is the effect of the author's extensive explanation of pigeons as the "most faithful of man's feathered friends"?

4. As Horatian satire, this essay should be gently chiding man for some foible. For what foible does Updike chide man in this essay?
5. In paragraphs (3) and (4), how do the following lines contribute to the overall tone of the essay?
   ". . . , at the bonbon stage of courtship, the male feeds a regurgitated substance to the female."
   ". . . though the pigeon theory of modern architecture should not be pursued to the exclusion of Frank Lloyd Wright."

Application of Stylistic Techniques

1. Write a brief paragraph using the parentheses to establish tone in the manner Updike does.
2. Rewrite paragraph (4) in a somber tone, as if you are serious about the welfare of pigeons.

Suggestions for Writing

1. By overstating the importance of some relatively insignificant problem for man, point out a foolish aspect of man's behavior.
2. Select a topic and write an essay using Horatian satire.
   The Dog Leash Law
   The Diction of the T.V. Announcer
   T.V. Commercials
   Good Fences Make Good Neighbors
   A Sour Note
   Who Lives in a Trailer Park?
   A No-Hitter
   Man's Best Friend
   Guppies Need Care
   A Bird in a Gilded Cage

Arthur Buchwald (1925–) resides in Washington, D.C., where he is a syndicated columnist noted for his political satire. He was educated at the University of Southern California. He has been a correspondent for *Variety* in Paris and has contributed to the *New York Herald Tribune, Variety,* and *Harper's.* His major works include *The Brave Coward, A Gift from the Boys, Don't Forget to Write, Is It Safe to Drink the Water?, Sons of the Great Society,* and *The Establishment Is Alive and Well in Washington.*

The Trial of Jack the Ripper

(Satiric—Juvenalian)

ART BUCHWALD

[1] After reading the accounts of the trial in Hayneville, Alabama, where a jury found a socially prominent citizen "not guilty" of killing a civil rights seminary student, one wonders how Jack the Ripper would have fared if he had been a citizen of Alabama and had been caught and tried in Lowndes County.

[2] It might have gone something like this:

[3] First, the grand jury would indict him for manslaughter instead of murder on the grounds that, although he killed five women, it was done without malice.

[4] Then the trial takes place, An all-white jury made up of friends of the Ripper family is selected, and the judge, who is Jack's uncle, warns the prosecution to be brief and refrain from calling too many witnesses.

[5] The county prosecutor reluctantly charges that Jack killed five women by slitting their throats and spreading their innards about. The people in the courtroom chuckle and several

of Jack's cousins wave to him. The prosecutor produces the knife as evidence and then rests his case.

[6] The defense attorney for Jack does not deny the charges, which causes members of the KKK in the courtroom to applaud. But he maintains Jack was acting in self-defense.

[7] He calls his first witness. "Did you see the defendant stab his first victim?"

[8] "Yes, sir, I did. Rip was walking down the street late at night when this here woman pulls a switchblade on him, and he had no choice but to slash out at her first. It was quick thinking on his part, because that woman meant to do him harm."

[9] The second witness, Zeke Ripper, is called.

[10] "Zeke, eight days after Rip defended himself, he ran into another woman on the street. What was her name?"

[11] "Dark Annie Chapman."

[12] "Would you repeat that again?"

[13] "Dark Annie Chapman."

[14] "What happened, Zeke?"

[15] "Wal, Rip is just strolling along and suddenly Dark Annie comes up to him with a pistol in her hand like she's going to kill him, so Jack pulls out his knife and slits her throat."

[16] "Where's the pistol now, Zeke?"

[17] "Some nigra rushed up and took it away 'fore the police came."

[18] "Thank you, Zeke. Now, ladies and gentlemen of the jury, I'm not even going to call any witnesses in regards to the killings of 'Long Liz' Stride and Kate Edowes, because there is no need to. Jack saw both these women kissing nigras and he went up to them and told them to stop it and when they didn't Jack did what any Hayneville gentleman would do and stabbed them both in the abdomen.

[19] "As for the killing of Black Mary Kelly, I'd like to call Jefferson Lingo Ripper. Jefferson, what happened, in your own words?"

[20] "This here Black Mary, she comes up to Rip and she said something to him that I can't repeat here in court and poor Rip followed her to her room and cut her up. I've known

Rip since he was a boy and he wouldn't hurt a fly, but that woman provoked him something awful."

[21] Laughter from the court.

[22] "Are these Black Mary's clothes?"

[23] "Yes, sir."

[24] "Ladies and gentlemen of the jury, I ask, you, what kind of woman would wear clothes like this and bring shame and world-wide publicity to the good people of Lowndes County? No white man will be safe on the streets of Hayneville if you find Jack the Ripper guilty of defending himself. Put yourself in his place. Wouldn't you have done the same thing?"

[25] The judge asks the jury to file out and decide a verdict.

[26] The foreman says, "No need for that, judge. We find the defendant not guilty and we wish to take this opportunity to nominate Jack the Ripper for sheriff of this God-fearing community."

EXERCISES—*THE TRIAL OF JACK THE RIPPER*

Content

1. In paragraph (12), why does the defense attorney ask the witness to repeat the name?
2. Point out the ridiculous aspect of the incident in paragraph (15).
3. Why did Jack kill "Long Liz" Stride and Kate Edowes for "kissing nigras"?
4. Explain Buchwald's purpose in writing this essay.

Style

1. From what point of view does Buchwald write this essay? Explain.
2. Determine the author's mood and explain your choice.
3. Explain through several examples from the essay the reason for saying this essay is Juvenalian satire.
4. Are there any instances of irony in this essay? Explain your answer.

Application of Stylistic Techniques

1. Buchwald uses dialogue (direct discourse) in this essay to lend an air of authenticity to the speeches. Rewrite paragraphs (8) through (13) in one paragraph of indirect discourse.
2. Paragraph (20) is colloquial speech. Rewrite the paragraph in formal language—perhaps as a lawyer, a policeman, or coroner might write it.
3. Rewrite paragraph (1) in colloquial speech similar to Zeke Ripper's.
4. Rewrite paragraph (8) in the colloquial language of a native Brooklynite, a native New Englander, a native Southerner, or a native of an area with which you are familiar.

Suggestions for Writing

1. Using considerable dialogue, take some recent occurrence deserving of being satirized in the Juvenalian manner and write a piece similar to Buchwald's.
2. Select a topic and write an essay, using Juvenalian satire.
   Students Are Only Kids
   The Trial of the Black Panther
   Soul Music
   The Chicago Seven
   The Benefits of War
   Poverty Builds Character
   T.V., the Child's Best Teacher
   Garbage Collectors Are Overpaid
   Doctors Are Saints
   Airplanes Are Safest

Jack Richardson (1935–   ) resides in New York and has studied at the University of Paris and the University of Munich. He received his B.A. from Columbia University. He has contributed to *New World Writing, Review,* and *Harper's*. His major works include *The Prodigal, Gallows Humor,* and *The Prison Life of Harris Fillmore.*

Joe Namath and the Problem of Heroic Virtue

(Sarcastic—Individual)

JACK RICHARDSON

To begin with, a Jet is helpful, courteous, kind. . . .

[1] *Joe Namath cried!* The phrase didn't topple parliaments around the world, but in the quixotic land of American sports, where morals and manners still affect in public the uncomplicated sentimentality of Victorian melodrama, *Joe Namath cried!* became a sort of touchstone, an objective correlative to the ethical puzzle that had sportswriters and commentators, fans and players scattering about such words as "loyalty," "integrity," "obligation," and engaging in musings on morality as intricate and hazy as any medieval debate on a matter of theological punctilio. Asked by professional football's commissioner Pete Rozelle to divest himself of his interest in a New York restaurant because known gamblers were often found leaning against its bar, Namath's first choice was to divest himself of football instead. An unholy decision, it

would seem, had not the man who gave the American Football League a dignity equal to its National League rival claimed that what he was doing was a matter of principle and then gone on to display deep, lachrymose evidence that principled action is a painful, demanding experience.

[2] Now there are many ways of regarding this banishment from football of one of its most expensive possessions. The large, historical perspective might well be that there was a certain spiritual inevitability in the clash, that Namath and professional football were destined to quarrel because the latter is too involved with American myth to tolerate a Namath and must finally expel him in the manner of an organism instinctively rejecting an alien body, no matter how indispensable to the organism's life the intruder might prove to be. Boxing, after all, with a burst of righteous frenzy, reduced itself to moribundity by expelling Cassius Clay because of moral and social idiosyncrasies, so there is good reason to suspect that football, too, could have a collection of zealous antibodies which rush suicidally and compulsively to defend their system against any anomalous invader. Namath, although certainly an exciting adornment to the game, was still a nettlesome figure in the professional sports world, a world which, for all its venality, still wants to appear driven by altruistic yearnings to a public eager to believe it is not watching the corporate hustling, trading and hiring of a few hundred well-conditioned mercenaries. Along with this desire to keep the pursuit of money in the background, the makers of the game have a precious notion of image, a notion which tries to keep its heroes crew-cut, clear-eyed, happily married, politically antiseptic and, in all outward respects, examples of the American Way as it might be dreamed of by Senator Dirksen after a heavy, fried-chicken lunch. Thus, no matter how excellent and exciting Namath might have been as a player, it was still true that his unaccommodating ways gave rise to a great many suspicions that each pass he completed caused, somewhere in our land, another sideburn to sprout or another love-in to take place. For there was no doubt that if Namath stood for anything besides good football, it was hair and hedonism, qualities which cause pathological reactions among those

who want their sports heroes to be symbols of denial and models of indifference to any personal vanity that cannot be disguised under the respectable term "competitiveness."

[3] Yes, it could be that Namath and the American sports world were not meant to fuse and that the incident of sinister gamesters in his restaurant was simply something epiphenomenal to a deeper, more metaphysical rupture in our society. And yet, Namath wept! He did not turn his back on the pomposities of his profession and, with resignation, head off for the fleshspots and franchises of the world. No, he agonized, invoked principle and in every way presented a case as morally baroque as that of any Racine hero.

[4] Do not walk among gamblers and those who would cleave unto you so that they might advantage themselves on the point spread, said the Commissioner. And the Quarterback answered: You do not want me to live in this world, for there is in it no place where there are not those who seek an edge over their fellow men. Banish gamblers, and you banish all of life.

[5] Thus the moral battle lines. One man who weeps and sees the world as it is; another who makes laws based on a world as it might have been had the roses in Eden never faded. The philosopher against divine authority: it is no wonder that Namath left the public hearing and retired with his friends to sip, if not hemlock, at least a goodly portion of Johnny Walker Red and to talk of the Blessed Isles around Las Vegas where the truth of human nature is catered to and honored.

[6] Suppose then that this was the principle over which Namath wept. It is, after all, finally a question of reality, a question which someone of Namath's exuberance could easily turn into a moral battle, for he had never been tolerant of opinion, no matter how prevalent, which contradicted the facts as he knew them. Thus when the Baltimore Colts—a team of grim, collective excellence, whose symbol was the old, wounded hero, Johnny Unitas, a man who calls everybody "Sir"—became seventeen point favorites in the Super Bowl, Namath forcefully let it be known that reality was being abused.

[7] In that instance it was fairly simple to prove that

the establishment has miscalculated the truth of the matter, and Namath did just this by turning the Colts into a stunned, sulking, conquered people before millions of spectators. The confusion in the commissioner's office, however, would not be so easy to undo. How to convince him that in the great world beyond filled stadiums and pre-sold television rights there are pleasures almost as supreme as a goal-to-goal kickoff return? How to make clear that no matter what the generally accepted pieties may be, people *do* bet on football (I would guess that at least half the spectators at any game during the season have some sort of wager going) and to avoid all of them would mean a straight flight from the locker room to an underground cell guarded by Jesuits fanatical in their hatred of those who deal in the laws of probability.

[8] Also, since I have been known to gamble a bit myself, I would like to think that Namath was striking a blow for a more enlightened public attitude toward this way of life. For the most part, gamblers do not advocate the overthrow of the government, are indeed conservative and anti-Maoist in their politics, and at least when winning, make good companions and tolerant friends. They deserve a better fate than that of being marked as carriers of a moral typhus which forces restaurants to close and careers to end as soon as they make an appearance.*

[9] So then, what the Namath affair actually produced was two realities, two notions of the world that were fundamentally irreconcilable. Indeed, such an impasse does make for tears, for at such moments one discovers that there is no honorable way of maintaining a public and private self in this country without becoming either an outlaw or a politician. And so Namath honored a part of him that football's officialdom could not tolerate, and in so doing he made his point that athletes may be contractually indentured, but they are not bound to bow before the myths of public actuality. In the real world, people eat, drink, screw, gamble, wheel-and-deal, and

* I am here, of course, talking about honest gamblers, not bad, bad men who would try to fix a game. If the latter possibility with Namath is admitted, then, naturally, the whole affair escalates into moral absurdity.

that is the world Namath chose, without apology, to defend.

[10] What would Joe have done without the Jets? Probably nothing more spectacular than make a few bad movies and flit in and out of honest business investments. However, there were rumors about his opening a casino in Las Vegas, and that is where I should like to see him. Perhaps with those teammates who promised to defect with him working as pit bosses, dealers and bouncers. Namath could finally preside, like some heavy-lidded, brooding angel, over his notion of what the world is really about.

EXERCISES—*JOE NAMATH AND THE PROBLEM OF HEROIC VIRTUE*

Content

1. Why does Richardson refer to football players as "well-conditioned mercenaries"?
2. Why did football commissioner Rozelle order Namath "to divest himself of his interest in a New York restaurant"?
3. Define "realist" in the way Richardson uses it to describe Namath.
4. For what reasons does Namath cause a pathological reaction among many sports fans?
5. Why did the establishment miscalculate the result of the Jets-Colts Super Bowl game?
6. How would Richardson like to see Namath earn his living?

Style

1. Why does Richardson emphasize that "Joe Namath cried"?
2. For what stylistic purpose does the author include Cassius Clay, Senator Dirksen, and Johnny Unitas.
3. What kind of language is Richardson approximating in paragraph (4)? What is his purpose in using this kind of language at this point?
4. Analyze the tone of this essay and explain what you think Richardson's mood is.
5. List some statements that demonstrate sarcasm; then several that demonstrate irony.

6. How does the line "To begin with, a Jet is helpful, courteous, kind . . ." help set the tone of this essay?
7. Explain the reason for saying this essay treats Namath sarcastically.
8. Does the footnote to paragraph (8) add to or detract from the tone of the essay? Explain.
9. Examine the vocabulary of paragraphs (1) and (2) and determine for what audience the author intended this essay.

Application of Stylistic Techniques

1. Rewrite paragraph (4) in the same point of view and style as the rest of the essay.
2. Rewrite paragraph (3) in some colloquial style.
3. Rewrite the first two sentences of paragraph (2), as if you are writing it for an avid football fan who seldom ever reads more than the football program.
4. Rewrite the last sentence of paragraph (4), using a different metaphor.

Suggestions for Writing

1. Write sarcastically about some public figure, but refrain from just name-calling. Aim for the same kind of audience that Richardson does and use the same point of view.
2. Select a topic and write an essay, using a sarcastic tone. Choose an individual who might fit one of the topics.
   A Self-Righteous News Commentator
   An Honest Politician
   A Virtuous Educator
   A Self-Important Sports Figure
   An Expert
   A Talk-Show Host
   An Artist
   An Actor
   A Military Genius
   A Public Official

Earl Cameron Winchell is a pseudonym that suggests the subject matter and tone of this essay (*Earl* Wilson, John *Cameron* Swazey, and Walter *Winchell*). The author, in keeping with his sarcastic treatment of the topic, has chosen not to reveal his identity.

Acapulco Confidential
(Sarcastic—Group)

EARL CAMERON WINCHELL

[1] Last week the Duchess of Alabaster had a birthday, and the lovely talented, glamorous, charming, witty, vivacious international socialite celebrated the event with a series of fourteen luncheon and dinner parties in succession, all held at different "in" spots around lovely, tropical, funfilled, chic Acapulco (Mexico).

[2] A small, glittering group of two-hundred of the Duchess' most intimate friends met first at Sam's Roast Beef on the Costera, where Sam himself sang "Las Mañanitas" to the guest of honor and every sandwich was bedecked with a birthday candle. Meanwhile, Ziv's was preparing a sumptuous evening feast of hot gaspacho, Kool-Aid, prune salad, chili dogs, and a lifesize ice cream sculpture carved in the Duchess' exact tempting measurements. That naughty Ziv decorated the statue at strategic points with mint leaves flown in from Texas by Nan Filbert and cherries a la Cosa Nostra from the floating freezers of the Princess Sicilia.

[3] Next everyone walked (what fun!) to Big Boy, for a gala affair hosted by that unforgettable, never-to-be-forgetten, woman-to-be-remembered, what's-her-name from Hollywood, who was singing "Happy Birthday" as the guests arrived

From *The News* (Mexico City), vol. 20, no. 216 (February 8, 1970). Reprinted by permission.

(and was still singing it when all departed seven hours later.) Tadpole Stuftshirt, the octogenarian social sprinter who made millions in hotels in his youth (the scamp!) escorted South American chanteuse Clarissa Bravo to the bash, and the glitter got brighter with the arrival of Jaime Lasagna (of the world-renowned Restaurant Richochet) and his darling wife Windy.

[4] Later as everyone drifted into the luxurious patio of Tastee Freez, there was lovely, talented, charming, witty, etc. Gracie Mansions, perched high above the crowd on a plush red velvet swing tossing buckets of copa d'oro on the folks below and welcoming all with the dulcet tones of her famous voice calling "Beeen vuh-nee-dose ah Taystee Freez dee Ah-cuh-pooooool-co" Orlando Dishrag, the famed local resrateur, scooped out the pistachio-peanut ice cream for all, and the goodies were served to the eager well-wishers by the lovely, talented, charming, etc. Marusia Phallik, the stupendous Russian movie idol, political exile, and collector of priceless costume jewelry.

[5] Marusia was garbed beautifully for the occasion in her rhinestone tiara, a six-inch thick pearl collar, forty-two brass snakes coiling up each arm, seventeen rings, gypsy ear bobs, anklets of semi-precious glass beads, two jewelled garters, and a forty carat topaz in her naval. (The outfit was a creation of couturier designer Harpo Bizarre of the famed Boutique Unique.)

[6] Not to be outdone socially, Denny's served chocolate-covered tortillas for 24 hours in honor of the Duchess, each one adorned with a whipped cream cameo of the Duchess' profile, shaped by hand by that lovely, talented, etc., artist Sassy Butterfly in the gleaming stainless steel kitchen of the Acapulco jail. It was during the Denny's bash that the waitresses and busboys (all haute couture in their new uniforms from the Boutique Voyeur) suddenly passed out gauze masks to all the guests, switched the lights to No. 32 pink baby spots, and in swept that great beauty of the silver screen Pearl Woebegone, preceded by sixteen naked slaves who placed tiny pieces of fluffy oriental carpet in front of her tiny feet wherever she stepped. "Let's all go to my place," said Pearl, ever

the gracious hostess and the *entire* group of glittering jet-setters headed for the Pizza Palace via Urbanos de Acapulco (Primera classe).

[7] As always, Pearl's party was perfection. The place mats were designed especially for the party by that famous Mexican painter, sculptor, pottery artist, ceramic tiler, jewelry designer and silver-mine entrepreneur, Jose Carlos Alfredo Pepe Jorge Francisco Guillermo Jaime (Bob) Sánchez de Amarillo y Hamburgo S., and when Roy and Derby Rogers arrived with Janet and John Lennon, everyone knew the fiesta would be terrificissimo.

[8] What a surprise for the Duchess, whose ojos brimmed over with tears of joy, when she glanced out of the Venetian glass window of Hungry Herman's to catch sight of the impromptu bullfight El Cordobés stagged for her pleasure right in the middle of the Costero! That brilliant (and sexy) international matador presented the overwhelmed lady with the toro's tail, hoof, ears, etc. etc. etc. etc. which Alvin Pshaw is now gilding to make into a lovely charm bracelet for the Duchess' remembrance of her special day.

[9] The round of parties ended at Sanborns, where each and everyone of the celebrated guests was presented with a personal piñata containing an original oil painting on bark by Leonardo de Nearsight depicting the Duchess' family tree, and (surprise of surprises!) a pair of roller skates to get them to the next major social event of the season—the big anniversary celebration next week at Krakatoa 02, the super-chic luncheonette and night club high in the hills behind the new Estrella d'Oro bus station, which is celebrating its third-and-a-half week of operation on Friday . . . but we'll tell you all about THAT junket next week! (ED NOTE. We'll take the next trip with you. Stay in the saddle).

EXERCISES—*ACAPULCO CONFIDENTIAL*

Content

1. About whom is Winchell writing this essay: the Mexicans, the American tourists, the jet set, or the society-page journalists? Explain your choice.

2. What would someone do with a "personal piñata containing an oil painting" (paragraph (9))?

Style

1. What purpose do names such as "Tadpole Stuftshirt," "Pearl Woebegone," "Alvin Pshaw," and "Jaime Lasagna" serve in this essay?
2. Why does the author include phrases such as "to Big Boy, for a gala affair" and "into the luxurious patio of Tastee Freez"?
3. The first sentence in paragraph (1) is typical of the author's using a multitude of adjectives. Explain his reason for using so many. For what purpose does he use "etc."?
4. Why does he use parentheses so frequently?
5. From analyzing the tone of the essay, ascertain what you think caused Winchell to write this essay. What is his mood?
6. Has the author made use of irony, innuendo and/or invective? Explain.
7. For what reasons can you say this essay is sarcastic toward a group?
8. Who is the author's intended audience?
9. Explain the aptness of the title of this essay.

Application of Stylistic Techniques

1. Find an article on a newspaper society page that resembles the style that Winchell is mocking. Write a short description of similarities between Winchell's mocking style and your article's style.
2. Rewrite paragraph (1) reducing the number of adjectives by supplying more economical ones.
3. Imitate Cameron's style in paragraph (4), by writing a paragraph having the same sentence structure and basic idea. Make up your own incident and names.
4. Rewrite paragraph (3) as a policeman might do it in an observation report.

Suggestions for Writing

1. Write an essay about some social group that is frequently in the public's eye, using the same approach and style that Winchell does.

2. Select a topic and write an essay that is sarcastic toward a group.
   Athletes
   Policemen
   Students
   School Teachers
   Physicians
   Sex Symbols
   Do-Gooders
   Militant Feminists
   Minority Groups
   WASPS

Barry Farrell (1935–   ), a journalist, was born and reared in Seattle, Washington. He attended the University of Washington and worked as a reporter in Seattle and San Francisco. He has also been a speech writer. He joined *Time* in 1961 as a music critic and later worked as a correspondent in the Paris bureau. Now he lives in New York and is a regular contributor to *Life*. He thinks the best columns are "completely subversive" and adds: "There's very little point in praising what we all know deserves praise, or attacking the Ten Most Wanted men. The really good columnists all have the knack of seeing aspects of life that aren't moving smoothly with the flow. I think it's a mistake to write manifestos. Your opinion is the best and most personal thing you can offer, so why pretend that it doesn't consist of confusion and panic as well as whatever intelligence and solid instincts you might have."

Confessions of a Kite Hustler *(Sentimental—of Self)*

BARRY FARRELL

[1] I thought my display looked terrific spread out there on the grass, with everything sorted into pyramids and piles and a raven-black fighter swooping overhead. I'd even burned a few sticks of Glory of India incense, just to set the tone for my show. All the same, the carney people kept telling me that I should have made a sign.

RARE IMPORTED HAND-MADE
FIGHTER KITES FROM INDIA
SPECIAL $2 & $3 SPECIAL
HERE TODAY NOW

[2] Something like that might have brought on a buyers' stampede, and I suppose I would have put a sign up had I been selling kites for the sake of selling kites. But what I

intended selling was my own performance (my professional debut, in fact) and a signboard would have been as vulgar and distracting as a toe-shoe ad onstage at the Royal Ballet. Those who saw the kite and fell under its abiding spell would have to be trusted to have sense and eyesight keen enough to follow the kitestring earthward to me and my diffident display.

[3] The Rutland State Fair in Vermont seemed about my speed, a country fair with a midway and show, drawing about 15,000 visitors a day. Before setting up, I cased the grounds thoroughly, checking out the trees, the wires, the flow of the crowd. There was a tempting glade between the Maple Sugar House and the 4-H barn, but I figured the traffic in that zone would be a shade too apple-cheeked for my exotic wares. The Midway was less inviting still—against a skyline of Rock-o-Planes, Tempests and Scramblers, a kite would look as frail as a city sparrow. At last I discovered the perfect spot, an island of grass between the rack track and a gurgling Plexiglas tank where Skipper the Porpoise was swimming. Speed, the sea, the liquid sense of movement: this was where I'd find my people.

[4] I was 200 feet high and holding when the gates were opened and the first day's crowd came pushing in. The wind was a warming westerly, steady and soft, just right for an India fighter. A thumb-slur across the line was enough to bring me around for a dive, and I came swooning down past the tree-tops, past Skipper's tank and the Navy recruiters' bus, down until I was spinning a foot or less above the choppy river of approaching sunburned faces. Maiming hands reached up to snare me, but I was already vaulting away. With the raven safe in the altitudes, I tidied my stores of tails and reels and string, lighting another joss stick for good measure. The crowd, I knew, was transfixed—too stupefied to stop.

[5] As I waited for my first disciple customer to emerge from the timid masses, it struck me that for pure mental attitude, I was probably the best-trained pitchman at the fair. So maybe I didn't have a spiel, maybe I didn't have a sign. What did that matter when my kites were like sons to me? I

hadn't spent five years under the string for nothing. I had bought kites, built kites, flown kites in every weather, gathered in the breeze of the Atlantic, the Pacific, the Nile, the Seine. Could the Barca-Lounger man say as much?

[6] My weakness was in letting the birds mean too much to me. A simple fly at sunset wound up a recital, a lesson in aerodynamics, a consultation with a silent oracle. Selling a few kites might serve as a cure, I thought. I would reduce all these spiritualized complexities to the healthiest American equation: $2 for the little ones, $3 for the big.

[7] The wind turned fickle as the day grew warm and sticky, but a loudspeaker voice was summoning the crowd to Skipper's tank—the moment I'd been waiting for. Circus-style hot-doggery overcame me as the porpoise-fanciers assembled, and soon I was daring a corkscrew descent into the patchwork wind, circling close over the tank, risking everything. I could feel the weight of canny Vermont reckoning tied like a tail to my kite. Somewhere deep inside me, I sensed a sale coming on.

[8] Skipper's silly stunts were handsomely applauded—as mine might have been, given the porpoise's fancy signboard and MC. In an access of resentment, I sent the raven into a series of slips and glides, a wicked parody of the splashing flippered thing in the tank.

[9] "How much?"

[10] With a folklorically correct economy of words, a crag-faced Vermonter was asking the price of a bird. He stood near the display of tails, squinting up at the sky like an outdoorsman in a cigarette ad. I needed only a second to collect myself—"Two for the little ones, three for the big."

[11] Like many an amateur kite inspector, the Vermonter had trouble believing that the kite was in control. But the raven was on a maneuver of *haiku*-like perfection. I dove and climbed, turned and spun, calling my shots in advance. When at last I looked back with a forgiving smile, ready to do business, the Vermonter had wandered away.

[12] It wasn't until King Kovaz and the Auto Daredevils took to the track that my act finally got itself together. The screaming cars were skidding through dirt-track slaloms that

sent brown Sahara dust clouds billowing up across my grassy island, silting my tails, reels and birds, whirling the cloud up into the air. Every head turned to follow the rising pall —and there in the center, like a lunatic seagull, flew the raven. Suddenly, customers were jostling around my display. A kite? Of course. Two kites and a tail?

[13] I sold $69 worth of kites at the fair, which meant 21 Vermont apprentices and $69 worth of crowd acceptance for my act. My gratitude made it impossible to push very hard for sales, and by way of compensation for the business I was doing in birds, I found myself apologizing for the price of my string.

[14] Since my costs were the same as my prices, my profits were strictly emotional. Apart from the plain joy of flying, the fact of being part of a fair seemed to open conduits running 20 years back and more, to times when fairs stood like alps on my calendar. My heroes then were a clique of Filipino Yo-Yo merchants who worked the playground at my school, doing Dog-Bite-Me and Walka-De-Dog. Their medium was different from mine, of course, but their message was clearly the same: trouble will come to you only when you're not holding onto the string.

EXERCISES—*CONFESSIONS OF A KITE HUSTLER*

Content

1. In paragraph (3), what does the author mean when he says ". . . I figured the traffic would be a shade too apple-cheeked for my exotic wares"?
2. Explain the reason for saying this kite hustler's strength is also his weakness.
3. Why does the author look upon his customers as apprentices?
4. What kind of profit did the hustler make? Why?
5. In paragraph (11), why does the Vermonter wander away?

Style

1. Why does the author use the personal pronoun "I"?
2. What aspects of mawkishness, if any, do you find? Explain.

3. What does the author hope to achieve through phrases such as ". . . a kite would look as frail as a city sparrow" (paragraph (3)), ". . . and I came swooning down past the treetops . . ." (paragraph (4)), and ". . . consultation with a silent oracle" (paragraph (5))?
4. In paragraph (14), what effect does the mention of Yo-Yo merchants doing Dog-Bite-Me and Walka-De-Dog have on the tone of the essay?
5. Explain the reason for calling this essay sentimental about one's self.

Application of Stylistic Techniques

1. Rewrite paragraph (6) in a colloquial style.
2. Rewrite paragraph (4) in a report style that continues with the air-control-tower language of the following quotation: "I was 200 feet high and holding when . . .".
3. Rewrite paragraph (1) using the impersonal "one" and then the editorial "we." Explain for each one the problem of, or ease of, conveying the same tone this essay has.
4. Write an introductory paragraph of approximately 100 words, as if for a nostalgic essay.

Suggestions for Writing

1. Write an essay that is sentimental about some past experience of yours. Avoid mawkishness.
2. Select a topic and write an essay having a sentimental tone.
   Christmas 19______
   The First Car I Ever Owned
   Leaving Home
   A Quiet Place
   Confessions of a Shop Lifter (a Car Hop, a Life Guard, a Hunter, an Athlete, a Wall Flower, a Tough Guy, a Cheerleader, a Sissy, a Hot Rodder, etc.)
   A Day at the Fair (Circus, Carnival, Zoo, Festival, Museum, Car Races, Indian Reservation, Harbor, Hideout, Mountain Retreat, a New England Inn, etc.)
   The Longest (Shortest) Hike (Day, Night, Interview, etc.)
   The Big City
   The Home Place
   Play It Again

James Baldwin (1924–) lived in Paris for ten years. He was a minister for over three years; he has been a member of the advisory board of the Congress of Racial Equality and the National Committee for a Sane Nuclear Policy. He has contributed to *Harper's, The Nation, Esquire, Mademoiselle, New Yorker,* and *Liberator.* His major works include *Go Tell It on the Mountain, Notes of a Native Son, Giovanni's Room, Another Country, The Fire Next Time,* and *Blues for Mister Charlie.*

Sweet Lorraine

(Sentimental—of Others)

JAMES BALDWIN

[1] That's the way I always felt about her, and so I won't apologize for calling her that now. *She* understood it: in that far too brief a time when we walked and talked and laughed and drank together, sometimes in the streets and bars and restaurants of the Village, sometimes at her house, sometimes at my house, sometimes gracelessly fleeing the houses of others; and sometimes seeming, for anyone who didn't know us, to be having a knock-down, drag-out battle. We spent a lot of time arguing about history and tremendously related subjects in her Bleecker Street and, later, Waverly Place flats. And often, just when I was certain that she was about to throw me out, as being altogether too rowdy a type, she would stand up, her hands on her hips (for these down-home sessions she always wore slacks), and pick up my empty glass as though she intended to throw it at me. Then she would walk into the kitchen, saying, with a haughty toss of her head, "Really, Jimmy. You ain't *right,* child!" With which stern put-down, she would hand me another drink and launch into a brilliant analysis of just why I wasn't

First appeared in *Esquire,* November 1969. Reprinted by permission of Robert Lantz-Candida Donadio Literary Agency, Inc.

"right." I would often stagger down her stairs as the sun came up, usually in the middle of a paragraph and always in the middle of a laugh. That marvelous laugh. That marvelous face. I loved her, she was my sister and my comrade. Her going did not so much make me lonely as make me realize how lonely we were. We had that respect for each other which perhaps is only felt by people on the same side of the barricades, listening to the accumulating thunder of the hooves of horses and the treads of tanks.

[2] The first time I ever saw Lorraine was at the Actors' Studio, in the Winter of '58-'59. She was there as an observer of the Workshop Production of *Giovanni's Room*. She sat way up in the bleachers, taking on some of the biggest names in the American theatre because she had liked the play and they, in the main, hadn't. I was enormously grateful to her, she seemed to speak for me; and afterward she talked to me with a gentleness and generosity never to be forgotten. A small, shy, determined person, with that strength dictated by absolutely impersonal ambition: she was not trying to "make it"—she was trying to keep the faith.

[3] We really met, however, in Philadelphia, in 1959, when *A Raisin In The Sun* was at the beginning of its amazing career. Much has been written about this play; I personally feel that it will demand a far less guilty and constricted people than the present-day Americans to be able to assess it at all; as an historical achievement, anyway, no one can gainsay its importance. What is relevant here is that I had never in my life seen so many black people in the theatre. And the reason was that never in the history of the American theatre had so much of the truth of black people's lives been seen on the stage. Black people ignored the theatre because the theatre had always ignored them.

[4] But, in *Raisin*, black people recognized that house and all the people in it—the mother, the son, the daughter and the daughter-in-law—and supplied the play with an interpretative element which could not be present in the minds of white people: a kind of claustrophobic terror, created not only by their knowledge of the house but by their knowledge of the streets. And when the curtain came down, Lorraine and

I found ourselves in the backstage alley, where she was immediately mobbed. I produced a pen and Lorraine handed me her handbag and began signing autographs. "It only happens once," she said. I stood there and watched. I watched the people, who loved Lorraine for what she had brought to them; and watched Lorraine, who loved the people for what they brought to *her*. It was not, for her, a matter of being admired. She was being corroborated and confirmed. She was wise enough and honest enough to recognize that black American artists are in a very special case. One is not merely an artist and one is not judged merely as an artist: the black people crowding around Lorraine, whether or not they considered her an artist, assuredly considered her a witness. This country's concept of art and artists has the effect, scarcely worth mentioning by now, of isolating the artist from the people. One can see the effect of this in the irrelevance of so much of the work produced by celebrated white artists; but the effect of this isolation on a black artist is absolutely fatal. He *is*, already, as a black American citizen, isolated from most of his white countrymen. At the crucial hour, he can hardly look to his artistic peers for help, for they do not know enough about him to be able to correct him. To continue to grow, to remain in touch with himself, he needs the support of that community from which, however, all of the pressures of American life incessantly conspire to remove him. And when he is effectively removed, he falls silent—and the people have lost another hope.

[5] Much of the strain under which Lorraine worked was produced by her knowledge of this reality, and her determined refusal to be destroyed by it. She was a very young woman, with an overpowering vision, and fame had come to her early—she must certainly have wished, often enough, that fame had seen fit to drag its feet a little. For fame and recognition are not synonyms, especially not here, and her fame was to cause her to be criticized very harshly, very loudly, and very often by both black and white people who were unable to believe, apparently, that a really serious intention could be contained in so glamorous a frame. She took it all with a kind of astringent good humor, refusing, for

example, even to consider defending herself when she was being accused of being a "slum lord" because of her family's real-estate holdings in Chicago. I called her during that time, and all she said—with a wry laugh—was, "My God, Jimmy, do you realize you're only the second person who's called me today? And you know how my phone kept ringing *before!*" She was not surprised. She was devoted to the human race, but she was not romantic about it.

[6] When so bright a light goes out so early, when so gifted an artist goes so soon, we are left with a sorrow and wonder which speculation cannot assuage. One's filled for a long time with a sense of injustice as futile as it is powerful. And the vanished person fills the mind, in this or that attitude, doing this or that. Sometimes, very briefly, one hears the exact inflection of the voice, the exact timbre of the laugh—as I have, when watching the dramatic presentation, *To Be Young, Gifted and Black,* and in reading through these pages. But I do not have the heart to presume to assess her work, for all of it, for me, was suffused with the light which was Lorraine. It is possible, for example, that *The Sign In Sidney Brustein's Window* attempts to say too much; but it is also exceedingly probable that it makes so loud and uncomfortable a sound because of the surrounding silence; not many plays, presently, risk being accused of attempting to say too much! Again, *Brustein* is certainly a very *willed* play, unabashedly didactic: but it cannot, finally, be dismissed or categorized in this way because of the astonishing life of its people. It positively courts being dismissed as old-fashioned and banal and yet has the unmistakable power of turning the viewer's judgment in on himself. *Is all this true or not true?* the play rudely demands; and, unforgivably, leaves us squirming before this question. One cannot quite answer the question negatively, one risks being caught in a lie. But an affirmative answer imposes a new level of responsibility, both for one's conduct and for the fortunes of the American state, and one risks, therefore, the disagreeable necessity of becoming "an insurgent again." For Lorraine made no bones about asserting that art has a purpose, and that its purpose was

action; that it contained the "energy which could change things."

[7] It would be good, selfishly, to have her around now, that small, dark girl, with her wit, her wonder, and her eloquent compassion. I've only met one person Lorraine couldn't get through to, and that was the late Bobby Kennedy. And, as the years have passed since that stormy meeting—Lorraine talks about it in these pages, so I won't go into it here—I've very often pondered what she then tried to convey—that a holocaust is no respecter of persons; that what, today, seems merely humiliation and injustice for a few, can, unchecked, become Terror for the many, snuffing out white lives just as though they were black lives; that if the American state could not protect the lives of black citizens, then, presently, the entire State would find itself engulfed. And the horses and tanks are indeed upon us, and the end is not in sight. Perhaps it is just as well, after all, that she did not live to see with the outward eye what she saw so clearly with the inward one. And it is not at all farfetched to suspect that what she saw contributed to the strain which killed her, for the effort to which Lorraine was dedicated is more than enough to kill a man.

[8] I saw Lorraine in her hospital bed, as she was dying. She tried to speak, she couldn't. She did not seem frightened or sad, only exasperated that her body no longer obeyed her; she smiled and waved. But I prefer to remember her as she was the last time I saw her on her feet. We were at, of all places, the PEN Club, she was seated, talking, dressed all in black, wearing a very handsome wide, black hat, thin, and radiant. I knew she had been ill, but I didn't know, then, how seriously. I said, "Lorraine, baby, you look beautiful, how in the world do you do it?" She was leaving, I have the impression she was on a staircase, and she turned and smiled that smile and said, "It helps to develop a serious illness, Jimmy!" and waved and disappeared.

EXERCISES—*SWEET LORRAINE*

Content

1. What does Baldwin mean when he says "black American artists are in a very special case"?
2. What is it that "is absolutely fatal" to the black artist? Explain.
3. Explain the relationship between Lorraine Hansberry and James Baldwin.
4. What about Lorraine makes Baldwin call her "Sweet Lorraine"?
5. Explain Baldwin's view that Lorraine was "devoted to the human race, but she was not romantic about it."

Style

1. Is this essay mawkish? Explain.
2. What is the effect of the last sentence of paragraph (8) on the tone of this essay?
3. What is Baldwin trying to avoid by saying ". . . I won't apologize . . ." in the first sentence of paragraph (1)?
4. Explain the effect of the sentence structure and choice of words in the first sentence of paragraph (4).
5. Regarding tone, what does the last sentence of paragraph (7) do? How is Baldwin using "man"? Does he mean "human being" or the "male of the species"? Explain.
6. Explain Baldwin's shifting person in paragraph (6) from "we" to "one" to "I."

Application of Stylistic Techniques

1. Rewrite the first sentence of paragraph (4) in the language of a scientific report.
2. Rewrite paragraph (3) from the same point of view Baldwin uses in the last sentence of the paragraph.
3. Rewrite the following sentence of paragraph (6), as if you are aiming it for a very unsophisticated audience: "It positively courts being dismissed as old-fashioned and banal and yet has the unmistakable power of turning the viewer's judgment in on himself."
4. Imitating the exact sentence patterns of paragraph (8), describe your departure from someone for whom you had, or have, strong feelings.

Suggestions for Writing

1. Select a topic and write an essay having a sentimental view toward another person.
   The Prettiest (Sweetest, Richest, Poorest, Toughest, Ugliest, etc.) Girl (Boy) in the Sixth (Second, Ninth, etc.) Grade
   A First True Love
   The Girl (Boy) Next Door
   I Keep Remembering (Grandma, George, Alice, etc.)
   The Commander
   The Guy (Gal) Who Taught Me How to (Win, Lose, Fight, Throw a Ball, Kiss, Dance, Say Thank You, Grow Mushrooms, Ride a Horse, etc.)
   A Helping Hand
   The Fellow down the Street
   The Stranger
   He (She) Wasn't Black or White

DICTION

Another means the writer uses to extend his personality is diction. Diction, the foundation of style, is the careful use of words in speaking or writing. In the eighteenth century, writers inflated their diction for decoration and special effects, but today's writers usually strive for the precise use of vocabulary, avoiding pretentiousness. In speaking, diction implies the precise accent, inflection, intonation, and sound of words. In writing, it implies the precise choice of words, and the force, accuracy, and distinction with which words are used. A speaker has the aids of inflection, gesture, and facial expression to convey his meaning; but a writer has only the choice and arrangement of his words plus punctuation to impart what he intends. Thus, a careful writer selects every word to be accurate, appropriate, and effective in its position. He considers shades of meaning in both denotation and connotation. He realizes that although *big, large, huge, enormous,* and *gigantic* are synonyms, they are not interchangeable because they differ greatly in shades of meaning and suggestion.

Just as choices in other areas of style are often made subconsciously, so are word choices. Our use of language reflects our thinking patterns, and our thinking reflects the language we use. A native of Alabama thinks and says *"y'all";* a Brooklynite thinks and says *"youse guys."* The woman who says, "Let's have supper," thinks differently from the one who says, "Join me for dinner." The student of diction is aware of this influence of our culture and of our thinking upon language, and he endeavors to use words with regard to their exact implications, paying attention to associations of words and the attitudes words imply. If we think precisely, we can use language accurately and appropriately and communicate clearly.

Any writer concerned with diction must be concerned with denotation and connotation. Denotation is the general or dictionary meaning of a word, an unslanted meaning which most people ascribe to the word. Such a definition is composed of the class to which the referent of the word belongs and the characteristics that differentiate it from other members of the same class. Connotation is the implications and emotional overtones that words or phrases carry with them, what a word or phrase suggests as distinguished from what it says specifically. In short, connotation is whatever a person associates with a word beyond its simple referent. All words simultaneously have both denotative and connotative meaning, but in different degrees. For example, *collie* is primarily denotative, *mutt* is primarily connotative, and *dog* or *hound* can be primarily denotative or connotative according to the context and a person's past experiences and frame of reference.

To express yourself vividly, accurately, and clearly, you the writer must consider not only the fundamental idea behind the words you use (denotation), but also the shades of associated meanings they possess (connotation). Because a reader's connotation of a word may not be the same as yours, you should choose words likely to be similar in both denotation and connotation for most people. You should use specific words and examples, define abstract terms, and qualify concrete words in order to make clear and vivid.

A special way of evoking emotion and making writing connotative is through the use of figurative language. This type of language embodies one or more of the various figures of speech. The most common figures of speech are simile, metaphor, analogy, imagery, personification, hyperbole, and antithesis. Analogy (comparing something simple or known to something complex or unknown to explain the complex or the unknown) and imagery (appealing to the senses, especially to the visual) are often extended throughout an essay to provide unity and to intensify meaning. Figurative language imparts strength, freshness, and vividness to expression: Robert Burns's "O, my Luve is like a red, red rose,/ That's newly sprung in June" is more effective than "My Love is fresh and alive."

Scientific language is a special type of denotative language. The number of scientific terms used and the extent to which they are defined depends upon the audience. For example, the explanation of a rocket's trajectory to a group of junior high school students would be quite different from the explanation to a group of astronauts.

Your choices in diction reflect your personality. Your angle of vision and your purpose determine—consciously and subconsciously—your choices in diction. What matters most about language is its effectiveness in communicating ideas, and your attention to diction can increase your ability to communicate.

The following work was prepared by the Council for National Cooperation in Aquatics.

Artificial Respiration and Other First-Aid Measures

(Denotative Language)

[1] Drownings may be either active or passive. The person seized with a heart attack or other medical problems, rendered unconscious by fainting or by a blow, seized by a violent cramp or paralyzed by fear may simply slip beneath the surface without warning, in direct contrast to the easily recognized signs of distress. Increasing evidence that passive drownings exceed those of the active type means that a much keener, more alert vigilance by lifeguards is essential—"keep counting heads."

[2] The exhausted or panicky bather will usually continue to stay on the surface for a few moments and by his convulsive agitation, advertise the fact that he is drowning. His movements will be either violently or feebly unrelated to each other, depending on the amount of energy he possesses, causing him to bob up and down until finally, with tidal air depleted, he settles beneath the surface and starts downward.

[3] If the tidal air is lost on the first downward trip and he can make no move to rise again, he will not of his own volition reappear at the surface. On the other hand, if he manages to hold some tidal air on each downward trip and can still make frantic clawing efforts to return to the surface, the chances are he will reappear one or more times.

[4] Whatever the case, when enough tidal air escapes from the lungs to cause the specific gravity of the body to be greater than that of the water it displaces, the person starts downward. The rate at which the body descends is in exact proportion to its specific gravity but may be affected and deviated from the perpendicular by currents. As the body descends, the increasing pressure of the water on the chest walls forces out the remainder of the tidal air in a thin stream of bubbles. On occasion, the glottis may be in spasm, and when it is finally released, the remaining air may be lost in one great bubbling exhalation.

[5] Because "time" is such a vital factor in all cases of asphyxia, it is essential that an apparently drowned victim be given artificial respiration promptly. At most indoor and outdoor swimming pools this should not be a problem. At outdoor areas (lakes, rivers, bays, ocean) where rescues may involve greater distances from shore and possibly an underwater recovery of the victim, artificial respiration should be started as soon as the victim is brought to the surface, before and/or during the return to shore.

[6] The use of flotation devices as rescue equipment and minor adaptations of the mouth-to-mouth method of artificial respiration provide a practical, effective solution to this problem.

[7] Of the several known methods of artificial respiration, the three that are most often used include the mouth-to-mouth or mouth-to-nose method; the chest-pressure–arm-lift (Silvester) method; and the back-pressure–arm-lift (Holger-Nielsen) method.

MOUTH-TO-MOUTH (MOUTH-TO-NOSE) METHOD

[8] If there is foreign matter visible in the mouth, wipe it out quickly with your fingers or a cloth wrapped around your fingers.

1. Tilt the head back so the chin is pointing upward. Pull or push the jaw into a jutting position.

These maneuvers should relieve obstruction of the airway by moving the base of the tongue away from the back of the throat.

2. Open your mouth wide and place it tightly over the victim's mouth. At the same time pinch the victim's nostrils shut or close the nostrils with your cheek. Or close the victim's mouth and place your mouth over the nose. Blow into the victim's mouth or nose. (Air may be blown through the victim's teeth, even though they may be clenched.) The first blowing efforts should determine whether or not obstruction exists.
3. Remove your mouth, turn your head to the side and listen for the return rush of air that indicates air exchange. Repeat the blowing effort.
   For an adult, blow vigorously at the rate of about twelve breaths per minute. For a child, take relatively shallow breaths appropriate for the child's size, at the rate of about twenty per minute.
4. If you are not getting air exchange, recheck the head and jaw position. If you still do not get air exchange, quickly turn victim on his side and administer several sharp blows between the shoulder blades in the hope of dislodging foreign matter.
   Again sweep your fingers through the victim's mouth to remove foreign matter.
   Those who do not wish to come in contact with the person may hold a cloth over the victim's mouth or nose and breathe through it. The cloth does not greatly affect the exchange of air.

MOUTH-TO-MOUTH TECHNIQUE FOR INFANTS AND SMALL CHILDREN

[9] If foreign matter is visible in the mouth, clean it out quickly as described previously.

1. Place the child on his back and use the fingers of both hands to lift the lower jaw from beneath and behind, so that it juts out.

2. Place your mouth over the child's mouth *and* nose, making a relatively leakproof seal, and breathe into the child, using shallow puffs of air. The breathing rate should be about twenty breaths per minute.
   If you meet resistance in your blowing efforts, recheck the position of the jaw. If the air passages are still blocked, the child should be suspended momentarily by the ankles or inverted over one arm and given two or three sharp pats between the shoulder blades, in the hope of dislodging obstructing matter.

ADAPTATION OF MOUTH-TO-MOUTH TECHNIQUE

[10] Once the simple steps of mouth-to-mouth resuscitation are understood and practiced in the classroom or on the beach, they should be practiced in the following simulated situations.

1. *Victim and Rescuer in Water.* In deep water the rescuer treads water and supports the face-up, unconscious "victim" with one hand under the shoulder blades; with the other hand, pinch "victims" nostrils and tilt his head back. Rescuer executes a strong leg kick to raise his own head high enough to permit the rhythmic blowing action. In water of shoulder depth or less the same technique can be used while standing on the bottom.
2. *Boat and Single Rescuer.* The rescuer brings the "victim" to the side or stern of boat in a regular lifesaving carry; grasps the boat with one hand and supports "victim's" body in a face-up position on his thigh and knee. The free hand is used to pinch the "victim's" nostrils and tilt his head back.
3. *Boat, Surfboard or Canoe.* A single rescuer can quickly take a prone position across the boat, surfboard or canoe. With his head and arms over the side, the rescuer supports the "victim" behind the neck with one hand and pinches the nostrils and tilts the head back with the other hand.
4. *Single Rescuer With Torpedo Buoy.* In this simulated situation, the rescuer makes personal contact with the

"victim" and places him in the face-up position. The torpedo (or diamond) buoy is then brought into position *across* the "victim's" chest and his arm placed over the buoy. With the buoy now providing full support of the "victim," the rescuer can now perform mouth-to-mouth resuscitation as in Figure 55. *Note:* If a rescue tube is used, the rescuer can begin resuscitation as soon as the "victim" has been contacted and the tube is in position around the "victim's" body.

CHEST-PRESSURE–ARM LIFT (SILVESTER) METHOD

[11] If there is foreign matter visible in the mouth, wipe it out quickly with your fingers or a cloth wrapped around your fingers.

1. Place the victim in a face-up position; put something under his shoulders to raise them and allow the head to drop backward.
2. Kneel at the victim's head, grasp his arms at the wrists, cross them and press them over the lower chest. This should cause air to flow out.
3. Immediately release this pressure and pull the arms outward and upward over his head and backward as far as possible. This should cause air to rush in.
4. Repeat this cycle about twelve times per minute, checking the mouth frequently for obstructions.

[12] It is possible to perform this method in a boat or on a surfboard. On a boat, slide the victim's legs and hips under the midship seat. On a surfboard, the rescuer takes a straddle-seated position toward the front end (wider), facing the stern. When the victim is in a face-up position, there is always danger of aspiration of vomitus, blood or blood clots. This hazard can be reduced by keeping the head extended and turned to one side. If possible, the head should be a little lower than the trunk. If a second rescuer is available, have him hold the victim's head so that the jaw is jutting out. The helper should be alert to detect the presence of any stom-

ach contents in the mouth and keep the mouth as clean as possible at all times.

BACK-PRESSURE–ARM-LIFT (HOLGER-NIELSEN) METHOD

[13] If there is foreign matter visible in the mouth, wipe it out quickly with your fingers or a cloth wrapped around your fingers.

1. Place the victim face down, bend his elbows and place his hands one upon the other; turn his head slightly to one side and extend it as far as possible, making sure that the chin is jutting out.
2. Kneel at the head of the victim. Place your hand on the flat of the victim's back so that the palms lie just below an imaginary line running between the armpits.
3. Rock forward until the arms are approximately vertical and allow the weight of the upper part of your body to exert steady, even pressure downward upon the hands.
4. Immediately draw his arms upward and toward you, applying enough lift to feel resistance and tension at his shoulders. Then lower the arms to the ground. Repeat this cycle about twelve times per minute, checking the mouth frequently for obstruction.

[14] If a second rescuer is available, have him hold the victim's head so that the jaw continues to jut out. The helper should be alert to detect any stomach contents in the mouth and keep the mouth as clean as possible at all times.

[15] Practice in artificial respiration should be one of the key in-service training activities and should develop within the guards the desire to learn every detail of the lifesaving skill.

EXERCISES—*ARTIFICIAL RESPIRATION AND OTHER FIRST-AID MEASURES*

Content

1. What is the purpose of this article?
2. What is the difference in active and passive drowning?

3. Explain what happens when a person drowns.
4. What are the three most often used methods of artificial respiration? Briefly explain each.

Style

1. For what audience was this article written? Is it suitable for that audience?
2. What is the author's angle of vision?
3. How does the author avoid alienating his audience? In other words, how does he avoid being too authoritative or too condescending?
4. What paragraphs compose the introduction? How is the introduction related to the rest of the essay?
5. Throughout the essay the author shifts between third person point of view with passive voice verbs and second person imperative point of view. Why? For example, in paragraph (8), why does the author shift to second person point of view? Can the shift be justified? Or again, can the similar shift in paragraph (10) be justified?
6. In denotative writing all unfamiliar terms should be clarified in some way. Determine how the author explains the following terms within the text: a) active drowning (1); b) passive drowning (1); c) "keep counting heads" (1); d) tidal air (2–3); e) mouth-to-mouth method (7); f) Silvester method (7); g) Holger-Nielsen method (7); h) torpedo buoy (10). (The number after the phrase refers to the paragraph number.)
7. Diction should be precise in denotation and in connotation as well as appropriate to level, tone, and audience. With these points in mind, determine whether the following changes of wording are satisfactory: *vigilance* to *watch* (1); *depleted* to *gone* (2); *specific gravity* to *weight* (4); *forces out* to *disembogues* (4); *asphyxia* to *suffocation* (5); *maneuvers* to *movements* (8); *shallow breaths* to *small breaths* (8); *victim* to *individual* (8); *foreign matter* to *foreign particles* (8); *sweep* to *run* (8); *juts* to *sticks* (9); *shallow puffs* to *shallow exhalations* (9); *resuscitation* to *revival* (10); *tilt* to *lean* (10); *prone* to *supine* (10); *press* to *push* (11); *cycle* to *process* (11); *trunk* to *chest* (12); *rock* to *lean* (13).
8. Why does the author repeatedly remind the audience to remove any foreign matter from the victim's mouth?
9. In paragraph (10), why is "victim" enclosed in quotation marks?

10. Define by giving the class and the differentiae for five of the following: life guard, drowning, artificial respiration, glottis, exhalation, adult, child, simulated situations, knee surfboard, buoy, resuscitation, boat.

    Example

Genus		*Class*	*Differentiae*
Water	is	a liquid	which is colorless and transparent, is composed of two parts hydrogen to one part oxygen, and freezes at 32°F (0°C) and boils at 212°F (100°C).

Application of Stylistic Techniques

1. Rewrite paragraph (8) of this article in consistent third person singular objective point of view. Then rewrite it in consistent first person singular subjective point of view. Note and be prepared to discuss the differences in tone and purpose in the original and the two revisions.
2. In a novel, short story, or essay, find a paragraph which is highly connotative and rewrite it, using denotative language. Note and be prepared to discuss the differences in the two versions.
3. In a magazine or newspaper article, find a brief passage which is highly denotative. Change the key words to highly connotative synonyms. Be prepared to discuss the differences in meaning and tone.

Suggestions for Writing

1. Using denotative language, describe a tree, a flower, an automobile, a classroom, your bedroom, your backyard, or your Shangri-La.
2. Using denotative language, describe the stages of a rain storm or a snow storm.
3. In denotative language, explain how to change a tire, how to water ski, how to take an examination, or how to make a dress.

E. B. White was born in Mount Vernon, New York, on July 11, 1899. In 1921 he was graduated from Cornell. He is well known for his essays, short stories, and poems. He has held various jobs in journalism and has contributed regularly to *Harper's Magazine* and *The New Yorker*. He is still on the salaried staff of *The New Yorker*, working from his home in Maine. His books include *Quo Vadimus?, One Man's Meat, The Second Tree from the Corner,* and *The Points of My Compass.* He is also the author of two juvenile classics, *Charlotte's Web* and *Stuart Little,* for which he won the 1970 Laura Ingalls Wilder Award, which is presented by the Children's Services Division of the American Library Association every five years to an author of books that have, over a period of years, "made a substantial and lasting contribution to literature for children." In June, 1970, Mr. White's long awaited third book for children, *The Trumpet of the Swan,* was published. He edited and amplified *The Elements of Style* by William Strunk, Jr. In 1963 he received the Presidential Medal of Freedom.

Rediscovery *(Connotative Language)*

E. B. WHITE

[1] Coming in from the country, we put up at a hotel in midtown for a few days recently, to give the moths free rein in our apartment. Our hotel bedroom was on an air shaft, and whenever anyone took a shower bath the sissing sound could be heard clearly. People took showers frequently, because of the heat and because a shower is one of the ways you can kill time in a hotel. Somebody would come in at five in the afternoon and take a shower, then in the evening people would be taking showers around eight or nine, then after the theatre they would come back and take one, and then the late people—the playboys and the playgirls—would return at three in the morning and cool off in a shower. One morning we woke

From *The Second Tree from the Corner* (1954) by E. B. White. "Rediscovery" first appeared in *The New Yorker,* and is reprinted by permission of Harper & Row, Publishers, Inc.

at seven, or half woke, and lay in bed listening to the sissing. Everybody in the building seemed to be taking a shower. After a while we caught on. It was raining. Good for the crops at the bottom of the air shaft, probably.

[2] Sometimes our affection for New York becomes dulled by familiarity. No building seems high, no subway miraculous, no avenue enchanted—all, all commonplace. Then, in a moment of rediscovery, it is as though we were meeting the city again for the first time. This happened a couple of days ago when we dropped into our abandoned apartment to retrieve a book. It was a shut place—a stagnant tomb of camphor, drawn shades, and green memories. No air had entered or left, no tap had been turned, no picture gazed upon. The furniture, under dust covers, seemed poised to receive the dead. A fashion magazine lay open where it had been tossed, the fashionable ladies poised in summer dresses, waiting for fall. There was no mouse in the trap, no sherry in the decanter. Silent in the middle of turmoil, a cube of heat and expectancy, the place felt exciting and we were visited by a fresh sense of the surrounding city: the salt pressure of its tides, the perfect tragedy of each of its eight million inmates—so many destinations, so many arrivals and departures, and the fares being given and received, the promises given and received, the lights being switched on and off in the innumerable chambers, the flow of electricity and blood, the arrangements, the meetings, the purposeful engagements, and the people sealed tightly in phone booths dialing Weather, the calamities, the dead ends, the air drill poised ready to open the pavement, the dentist's drill poised ready to open the tooth, the conductor's baton poised ready, the critic's pencil poised ready, the ferry chain winding on the windlass, the thieves and vegetarians in the parks—we saw them all in dazzling clarity, as though the curtain had just lifted on New York. And when we quit the apartment and walked up the street, as though out upon a stage, we saw clearly the lady in black fishing in a trash can, and the sportive bachelor leaving his pointed shoes with the shoe-shine man at the corner, and we were spellbound at the majesty of ginkgoes and the courtesy

of hackmen. We hadn't had anything to drink, either. Just stopped in to get a book.

EXERCISES—*REDISCOVERY*

Content

1. What is the controlling idea of this essay? Is it stated or implied?
2. Why did E. B. White stay at a hotel in New York when he had an apartment there?
3. Why was White's apartment unoccupied at the time?
4. Why did people in the hotel take showers frequently?
5. Why did White go to his apartment? How did he feel while at his apartment? How did he feel when he left?

Style

1. What is the function of paragraph (1)? How is it related to paragraph (2)?
2. Why is paragraph (2) more connotative than paragraph (1)?
3. What techniques of development does E. B. White employ?
4. What is White's governing principle of organization in the essay?
5. Analyze the three-part structure of paragraph (2). Mark these parts and the transitions between parts in your book. Is the topic sentence of the paragraph stated or implied?
6. What is the tone of the essay?
7. From this brief essay what can you conclude about E. B. White's personality?
8. Why did White choose first person plural subjective point of view? How would the effect be different if he had used third person singular subjective point of view?
9. For what effects does White employ contrast? juxtaposition of opposites? repetition? parallelism?
10. For what purposes and effects does White use dashes? the colon?
11. Considering shades of meaning and appropriateness, comment on the following changes of wording: *free rein* to *freedom* (1); *kill time* to *spend time* (1); *cool off in* to *take* (1); *affection* to *disposition* (2); *dulled* to *deadened* (2); *rediscovery* to *discovery* (2); *meeting* to *seeing* (2); *retrieve* to *get* (2); *poised* to *waiting* (2); *tossed* to *placed* (2); *decanter* to *bottle* (2); *inmates* to *people* (2); *dazzling* to *brilliant* (2); *quit* to *left* (2); *fishing* to

rambling (2); *sportive* to *sporty* (2). (The number in parentheses refers to paragraph number.)

12. What are your connotations of the following words and phrases: *country* (1); *hotel* (1); *New York* (2); *subway* (2); *abandoned apartment* (2); *green memories* (2); *poised* (2); *summer* (2); *fall* (2); *the salt pressure of its tides* (2); *dead ends* (2); *ginkgoes* (2); *hackmen* (2)? Are your connotations the same as White's? As your classmates'? Can only one connotation be "right," or could White intend some of his words and phrases to be purposefully ambiguous? Would such ambiguity hinder or enrich communication? Explain.
13. Comment on the effect of the omission of the following passages: "and because a shower is one of the ways you can kill time in a hotel" (1); "after the theater" (1); "the playboys and the playgirls" (1); "or half woke" (1); "sealed tightly" (2); "as though the curtain had just lifted on New York" (2); "as though out upon a stage" (2).
14. What is the meaning of each of the following passages, and how does each contribute to the tone of the essay: "to give the moths free rein in our apartment" (1); "Good for the crops at the bottom of the air shaft, probably." (1); "We hadn't had anything to drink, either. Just stopped in to get a book." (2)?
15. Justify the use of the second person pronoun *you* in the third sentence of paragraph (1).
16. How does White employ variation in sentence length and type to vary his pace and his tone?
17. Find at least three figures of speech in the essay. Identify and explain the effects of each.

Application of Stylistic Techniques

1. Parse (analyze the grammatical parts and the functions and interrelationships of the parts) the tenth sentence of paragraph (2). Then try to write a sentence of your own by the same grammatical pattern.
2. In a news article or a history book, find a paragraph of description or narration which is primarily denotative. Rewrite the paragraph to make it primarily connotative. Explain the differences in meaning and tone.
3. Using the three-part structure, write a paragraph combining narration and description, similar to White's paragraph (2). Your paragraph might be on a return to the town or block where you

spent your childhood, or to a cabin on a lake, or to your high school.

Suggestions for Writing

1. Using connotative language, describe the same object or place you chose in question 1 under "Suggestions for Writing' following the essay *Artificial Respiration and Other First-Aid Measures:* a tree, a flower, an automobile, a classroom, your bedroom, your backyard, or your Shangri-La.
2. Write an impressionistic essay in which you use a predominance of connotative words in order to convey a specific mood, such as happiness, gaiety, joy, peacefulness, melancholy, nostalgia, pensiveness, etc.
3. Write an essay in which you recount how you "rediscovered" some place or person that had become "dulled by familiarity."

E. B. White was born in Mount Vernon, New York on July 11, 1899. In 1921 he was graduated from Cornell. He is well known for his essays, short stories, and poems. He has held various jobs in journalism and has contributed regularly to *Harper's Magazine* and *The New Yorker*. He is still on the salaried staff of *The New Yorker,* working from his home in Maine. His books include *Quo Vadimus?, One Man's Meat, The Second Tree from the Corner,* and *The Points of My Compass*. He is also the author of two juvenile classics, *Charlotte's Web* and *Stuart Little,* for which he won the 1970 Laura Ingalls Wilder Award, which is presented by the Children's Services Division of the American Library Association every five years to an author of books that have, over a period of years, "made a substantial and lasting contribution to literature for children." In June, 1970, Mr. White's long awaited third book for children, *The Trumpet of the Swan,* was published. He edited and amplified *The Elements of Style* by William Strunk, Jr. In 1963 he received the Presidential Medal of Freedom.

The Distant Music of the Hounds

(Figurative Language—Analogy)

E. B. WHITE

[1] To perceive Christmas through its wrapping becomes more difficult with every year. There was a little device we noticed in one of the sporting-goods stores—a trumpet that hunters hold to their ears so that they can hear the distant music of the hounds. Something of the sort is needed now to hear the incredibly distant sound of Christmas in these times, through the dark, material woods that surround it. "Silent Night," canned and distributed in thundering repetition in the department stores, has become one of the greatest of all

From *The Second Tree from the Corner* (1954) by E. B. White. "The Distant Music" originally appeared in *The New Yorker*, and is reprinted by permission of Harper & Row, Publishers, Inc.

noisemakers, almost like the rattles and whistles of Election Night. We rode down on an escalator the other morning through the silent-nighting of the loudspeakers, and the man just in front of us was singing, "I'm gonna wash this store right outa my hair, I'm gonna wash this store . . ."

[2] The miracle of Christmas is that, like the distant and very musical voice of the hound, it penetrates finally and becomes heard in the heart—over so many years, through so many cheap curtain-raisers. It is not destroyed even by all the arts and craftiness of the destroyers, having an essential simplicity that is everlasting and triumphant, at the end of confusion. We once went out at night with coon-hunters and we were aware that it was not so much the promise of the kill that took the men away from their warm homes and sent them through the cold shadowy woods, it was something more human, more mystical—something even simpler. It was the night, and the excitement of the note of the hound, first heard, then not heard. It was the natural world, seen at its best and most haunting, unlit except by stars, impenetrable except to the knowing and the sympathetic.

[3] Christmas in this year of crisis must compete as never before with the dazzling complexity of man, whose tangential desires and ingenuities have created a world that gives any simple thing the look of obsolescence—as though there were something inherently foolish in what is simple, or natural. The human brain is about to turn certain functions over to an efficient substitute, and we hear of a robot that is now capable of handling the tedious details of psychoanalysis, so that the patient no longer need confide in a living doctor but can take his problems to a machine, which sifts everything and whose "brain" has selective power and the power of imagination. One thing leads to another. The machine that is imaginative will, we don't doubt, be heir to the ills of the imagination; one can already predict that the machine itself may become sick emotionally, from strain and tension, and be compelled at last to consult a medical man, whether of flesh or of steel. We have tended to assume that the machine and the human brain are in conflict. Now the fear is that they are indistinguishable. Man not only is notably busy himself

but insists that the other animals follow his example. A new bee has been bred artificially, busier than the old bee.

[4] So this day and this century proceed toward the absolutes of convenience, of complexity, and of speed, only occasionally holding up the little trumpet (as at Christmas time) to be reminded of the simplicities, and to hear the distant music of the hound. Man's inventions, directed always onward and upward, have an odd way of leading back to man himself, as a rabbit track in snow leads eventually to the rabbit. It is one of his endearing qualities that man should think his tracks lead outward, toward something else, instead of back around the hill to where he has already been; and it is one of his persistent ambitions to leave earth entirely and travel by rocket into space, beyond the pull of gravity, and perhaps try another planet, as a pleasant change. He knows that the atomic age is capable of delivering a new package of energy; what he doesn't know is whether it will prove to be a blessing. This week, many will be reminded that no explosion of atoms generates so hopeful a light as the reflection of a star, seen appreciatively in a pasture pond. It is there we perceive Christmas—and the sheep quiet, and the world waiting.

EXERCISES—*THE DISTANT MUSIC OF THE HOUNDS*

Content

1. Why did E. B. White write this essay?
2. What is the main idea of the essay?
3. To what does the title of the essay refer?
4. What causes men to leave their warm homes to go out into a cold night for a coon hunt?
5. With what must Christmas now compete?
6. What aspects of modern society does White criticize?
7. In the next to last sentence, to what does "This week" refer?

Style

1. In this essay E. B. White uses a variety of figures of speech to convey and intensify his meaning, but the basic figure of speech is analogy. What is the basic analogy of this essay? In other words,

what two things have certain of their aspects compared? Trace the words and phrases White uses to sustain this analogy throughout the essay. Do you believe the analogy is valid? Discuss the multiple suggestions of this analogy.

2. Find examples of metaphor, simile, antithesis, personification, allusion, and imagery. Explain the literal meaning, the suggested meaning or meanings, and the effect of each.
3. Why did White use first person plural subjective point of view?
4. For what audience is this essay intended? Why?
5. From this essay, do you think White is optimistic or pessimistic? romantic or realistic? conservative or progressive? Horatian or Juvenalian? Why?
6. What are some of the ironic elements in this essay?
7. Diction involves not merely meanings of words, but shades of meanings of words. Also, connotation may be favorable or unfavorable. With these two comments in mind, first arrange the following groups of words on continuums with the least favorable on the left and the most favorable on the right; then choose the word in each group which best describes the tone of this essay. Be able to justify your placements on the continuums and your choice of words to describe White's essay.

   Group I: sardonic, ironic, satiric, sarcastic, bitter, acrid, derisive, mocking, taunting, ridiculing, jesting, maligning, caustic.

   Group II: sentimental, romantic, mawkish, maudlin, soppy, mushy, slushy, emotional, pathetic, passionate, nostalgic.
8. Is the connotation of each of the following favorable, unfavorable, or neutral: *wrapping* (1); *device* (1); *music* (1); *the dark material woods* (1); *canned* (1); *noisemakers* (1); *the silent-nighting of the loud speakers* (1); *miracle* (2); *heard in the heart* (2); *cheap curtain-raisers* (2); *warm homes* (2); *cold shadowy woods* (2); *dazzling* (3); *obsolescence* (3); *sifts* (3); *a medical man* (3); *absolutes* (4); *odd* (4); *appreciatively* (4); *perceive* (4)?
9. What rhetorical devices does White use to achieve unity and coherence in this essay?

Application of Stylistic Techniques

1. Rewrite paragraph (1) in first person singular. Then rewrite the same paragraph in third person singular. Is the original paragraph or Rewrite #1 or Rewrite #2 more effective for White's purposes? Why?

2. Write an example of each of the following types of figures of speech: 1) metaphor, 2) simile, 3) personification, 4) allusion, 5) antithesis, 6) imagery. Be as original as possible.
3. Express each of the following ideas in non-figurative language: 1) paragraph (1), sentence 3; paragraph (2), sentence 1; 3) paragraph (3), sentence 8; 4) paragraph (4), sentence 1.
4. Express each of the following ideas in figurative language:
   That girl is beautiful.
   My new car is fast.
   That test was difficult.
   The old house was frightening.
   The night was very dark.
   The clouds were lovely.

Suggestions for Writing

1. Write an essay in which you use a sustained analogy for clarity and vividness in exposition of an idea. You may choose one of the following basic comparisons, or you may use one of your own.
   Compare a city to a beehive or an ant hill.
   Compare war to a football game or other sport.
   Compare a child to a young tree.
   Compare life to a candle.
   Compare dead leaves to stagnant ideas.
   Compare the world to a stage.
   Compare life to a battle.
   Compare life to the sea.
   Compare a ripple on the water to an idea.
   Compare the human heart to a pump.
2. Write an essay in which you criticize some aspect of modern society, such as materialism, mechanization, pollution, poverty, prejudice, militarism, or cynicism.
3. Write an essay on the lessening of meaning in some holiday, custom, or tradition, such as the Fourth of July, Thanksgiving, Halloween, family reunions, birthday celebrations, or marriage.

John Updike (1932–   ) was born in Pennsylvania. He was graduated from Harvard in 1954, and worked for the *New Yorker* from 1955–1957. His major works include *Poorhouse Fair, Rabbit Run, The Centaur, Couples, Bech: A Book, Collections: The Same Door, Pigeon Feathers, The Carpentered Hen and Other Tame Creatures, Telephone Poles* (light verse), and *Assorted Prose.*

Central Park
(Figurative Language—Imagery)

JOHN UPDIKE

[1] On the afternoon of the first day of spring, when the gutters were still heaped high with Monday's snow but the sky itself was swept clean, we put on our galoshes and walked up the sunny side of Fifth Avenue to Central Park. There we saw:

[2] Great black rocks emerging from the melting drifts, their craggy skins glistening like the backs of resurrected brontosaurs.

[3] A pigeon on the half-frozen pond strutting to the edge of the ice and looking a duck in the face.

[4] A policeman getting his shoe wet testing the ice.

[5] Three elderly relatives trying to coax a little boy to accompany his father on a sled ride down a short but steep slope. After much balking, the boy did, and, sure enough, the sled tipped over and the father got his collar full of snow. Everybody laughed except the boy, who sniffled.

[6] Four boys in black leather jackets throwing snowballs at each other. (The snow was ideally soggy, and packed hard with one squeeze.)

[7] Seven men without hats.

[8] Twelve snowmen, none of them intact.

[9] Two men listening to the radio in a car parked outside the Zoo; Mel Allen was broadcasting the Yanks–Cardinals game from St. Petersburg.

[10] A tahr (*Hemitragus jemlaicus*) pleasantly squinting in the sunlight.

[11] An aoudad absently pawing the mud and chewing.

[12] A yak with its back turned.

[13] Empty cages labelled "Coati," "Orang-outang," "Ocelot."

[14] A father saying to his little boy, who was annoyed almost to tears by the inactivity of the seals, "Father (Father Seal, we assumed) is very tired; he worked hard all day."

[15] Most of the cafeteria's out-of-doors tables occupied.

[16] A pretty girl in black pants falling on them at the Wollman Memorial Rink.

[17] "BILL & DORIS" carved on a tree. "REX & RITA" written in the snow.

[18] Two old men playing, and six supervising, a checkers game.

[19] The Michael Friedsam Foundation Merry-Go-Round, nearly empty of children but overflowing with calliope music.

[20] A man on a bench near the carrousel reading, through sunglasses, a book on economics.

[21] Crews of shinglers repairing the roof of the Tavern-on-the-Green.

[22] A woman dropping a camera she was trying to load, the film unrolling in the slush and exposing itself.

[23] A little colored boy in aviator goggles rubbing his ears and saying, "He really hurt me." "No, he didn't," his nursemaid told him.

[24] The green head of Giuseppe Mazzini staring across the white softball field, unblinking, though the sun was in its eyes.

[25] Water murmuring down walks and rocks and steps. A grown man trying to block one rivulet with snow.

[26] Things like brown sticks nosing through a plot of cleared soil.

[27] A tire track in a piece of mud far removed from where any automobiles could be.

[28] Footprints around a KEEP OFF sign.

[29] Two pigeons feeding each other.

[30] Two showgirls, whose faces had not yet thawed the frost of their makeup, treading indignantly through the slush.

[31] A plump old man saying "Chick, chick, and feeding peanuts to squirrels.

[32] Many solitary men throwing snowballs at tree trunks.

[33] Many birds calling to each other about how little the Ramble has changed.

[34] One red mitten lying lost under a poplar tree.

[35] An airplane, very bright and distant, slowly moving through the branches of a sycamore.

EXERCISES—*CENTRAL PARK*

Content

1. When did Updike observe what he records in this essay?
2. Why did Updike choose so simple a title? Is it too simple to be eye-catching?
3. In paragraph (5), why did the boy sniffle?
4. What kind of snow is best for snowballs?
5. What is a tahr (paragraph (10))? an aoudad (paragraph (11))? a coati (paragraph (13))?
6. What is the purpose of the essay?

Style

1. What is the purpose of the colon at the end of paragraph (1)? Is this use of the colon orthodox? Is it effective?
2. Why didn't Updike write this essay as one long paragraph?
3. What is Updike's governing principal of organization? his principal of selection of details?
4. What rhetorical devices does Updike use to achieve unity in this essay?

5. Although the essay contains different tones in the varying sketches, there is one dominant tone throughout the essay. What is the dominant tone? What are some of the secondary tones?
6. Why are some of the sketches more detailed than others? Does this lack of proportion enhance or detract from the effectiveness of the essay?
7. Identify and discuss the effectiveness of each of the following figures of speech: "the sky itself was swept clean" (paragraph (1)); "their craggy skins glistening like the backs of resurrected brontosaurs" (2); "overflowing with calliope music" (19); "the film . . . exposing itself" (22); "The green head . . . staring" (24); "Water murmuring . . ." (25); "the frost of their makeup" (30).
8. Which of the senses—sight, sound, smell, touch, taste—do Updike's images appeal to most? Why?
9. Which of Updike's images are the most vivid? the most denotative? the most connotative? Which is your favorite image? Why?
10. From this essay what can you conclude about Updike's personality? Would he and E. B. White be likely to become friends? Why? Which man would you prefer to have as a friend? Why?

Application of Stylistic Techniques

1. Sit in a place of activity (such as the school cafeteria, the library, a classroom, a bench on campus, the parking lot of a shopping center, a party), and record at least fifteen brief figurative descriptions of what you perceive through your senses. (Updike uses thirty-five.) Be as vivid and precise as possible.
2. Compare E. B. White's method of description in *Rediscovery* to John Updike's method in this essay.

Suggestions for Writing

1. Using your sketches in question 1 under "Application of Stylistic Techniques" above, write a descriptive essay. You may pattern your essay after Updike's, or you may use other methods of organization and other types of sentences.
2. Write an essay in which you explain the joy or sadness of the change of seasons, e.g. summer to fall, or fall to winter, etc.
3. Use Updike's method of description to describe a person.

Albert Rosenfeld (1920–) was born in Philadelphia and now resides in New Rochelle, New York. He has a B.A. and an honorary Doctor of Letters from New Mexico State University. During World War II, he served in the European Theatre and received the Bronze Star. He has been a freelance writer and freelance correspondent for *Time, Life,* and *Fortune;* and the science and medicine editor for *Life.* He is now managing editor of *Family Health.* Among other magazines to which he has contributed are *Reader's Digest, Harper's Magazine, Commentary, New Mexico Quarterly*, and *Coronet.* He is also author of *Second Genesis* and *Irving Langmuir* (biography).

Beyond the Moon *(Scientific Language)*

ALBERT ROSENFELD

[1] As the astronauts were physically breaking the bonds of earth, the astronomers were, conceptually at least, pushing back the limits of the universe. Thus man, making his first giant leap into space, was reminded how trifling are the distances of mere moon journeys when measured on a cosmic scale.

[2] Not that 1968 produced any final solutions to the great cosmological riddles. Instead, the news from beyond pointed up for man how truly enigmatic the universe remains in the face of his exciting efforts to fathom it.

[3] In the detection instruments of orbiting satellites and in the computerized eyes of optical and radio telescopes, many unexpected astronomical objects turned up—among them the biggest stars yet discovered, a neighboring pair whose individual masses would make up 50 or 60 of our suns, and galaxies that radiate 100 times more energy than any previously known. Scientists remained baffled by the more

bizarre and discomforting presences that have turned up in the past few years: gamma-ray sources, X-ray stars and galaxies, ammonia molecules among the interstellar gases, ultraviolet and infrared emissions, neutron stars, quasars—and, newest and most tantalizing of all, pulsars.

[4] Even with some of the old phenomena, they kept running into new contradictions. For instance, attempting to compute the age of a distant star cluster known as NCG 188, they produced an answer that would have made NCG 188 older than the universe itself.

[5] Theorists struggling to construct a cosmology based on the equations of relativity know that the answers can lead either to a finite or to an infinite universe. Some favor the finite universe, but the assumption brought them to this paradoxical picture: a universe that continues to expand as it now appears to be doing until it reaches a certain maximum radius of billions of light-years, after which it starts contracting again, continuing to shrink until its radius equals zero—with no assurance that it will ever be able to expand again!

[6] One of the key concepts of relativity holds that the velocity of light is the speed limit of the universe. But this once-secured tenet is now being challenged. A few physicists have put forth the radical notion that, though it is impossible to accelerate a particle *past* the speed of light, there is nothing theoretically wrong with a particle moving faster than light *as long as it was already going that fast to begin with.* In that case it could never, ever move any *slower* than light. Such putative particles—Dr. Gerald Feinberg of Columbia named them "tachyons"—would, if they exist, be strange indeed. They would possess "imaginary mass" and "negative energy," and time for them would move backward. A search for tachyons is now under way.

[7] Meanwhile, the quasars, whose mystifying whatevers that are neither stars nor galaxies, continued to transmit, from billions of light-years away, outpourings of radio energy so prodigious that physicists have been hard put to account for them. Some scientists insisted that quasars *had* to be nearer to earth than originally calculated. Yet their

distances had been computed by the standard astronomical measuring stick, the celebrated "red shift"—that is, the shift of light toward the red end of the spectrum as the source moves away from us. Could there be something about quasars that made the red shift of *their* light mean something different?

[8] Studied closely, the light from a single quasar, PHL 938, seemed to be exhibiting four or five different and conflicting red shifts! This clearly meant that the red shift did *not* always mean the same thing throughout the universe. And if this could be true for quasars, it could be true for other celestial bodies. As a result, the red shift may have to be reappraised—and, with it, some cherished and long-standing notions about or expanding universe.

[9] The quasar puzzle, though still unsolved, led inadvertently to the discovery that caused the year's big excitement. In February, astronomers in Cambridge, England announced a new class of pulsating radio stars (pulsars). Their transmissions came with such fantastically precise regularity that scientists, at a loss to think how the signals could be produced by any natural object, were tempted to believe that these were at last the intelligent messages from Someone Out There. The notion was soon dropped, though some scientists are still wondering.

[10] By the end of 1968 some two dozen pulsars had been located by observatories around the world. In an effort to explain their emissions, early studies indicated that pulsars would have to be dense, compact objects—smaller in size than the earth, yet containing as much mass as the sun. Only two kinds of stars answered the description. One of them is known to exist—the "white dwarf," an old star which, as its thermonuclear fuel burns down, is gradually compressed by gravity into a dense mass of dull-glowing "degenerate matter."

[11] The other possibility, the so-called neutron star, is purely theoretical, dreamed up by astrophysicists in the 1930s but never detected in the real sky. How does a neutron star come about? When a sun-sized star grows old, it turns into a white dwarf. But if a star is much more massive than the sun, it reaches a critical state of instability and then flares

into a "supernova," spewing vast quantities of material out over vast distances. Meanwhile, at its inner core, "gravitational collapse" occurs, the explosive inward pressures creating a hard-packed mass of neutrons which, giving off little light, remain invisible (if they exist) to any present-day optical telescopes.

[12] A neutron star is, in its way, as astounding as a quasar or a tachyon. Its Alice-in-Wonderland material would be so superdense that some have called it a fifth state of matter—the fourth being the hot electrified gas known as "plasma." The matter that we perceive as solid on earth is mostly empty space. The particles are kept apart (and at the same time held together in delicate equilibrium) by a variety of nuclear, atomic and molecular forces. During the gravitational collapse of a supernova's core, all these forces are overwhelmed and the particles are jammed together, electrons and protons joining to form neutrons in a reversal of the normal process. The resulting mass, though much smaller than the earth (a neutron star may be but a few miles across), generates gravitational and magnetic fields so powerful (billions of times stronger than the earth's) as to require a new set of physical laws to deal with them. A matchboxful of matter from a neutron would weigh *billions* of earth *tons*.

[13] Several theories have been put forth which show how either a white dwarf or a neutron star might conceivably be a pulsar. But the most interesting, in the light of the latest evidence, was a theory proposed by Dr. Thomas Gold of Cornell. A pulsar, he suggested, might indeed be a neutron star (which among its other absurd characteristics, can spin at a rate of several hundred rpm) surrounded by an atmosphere of plasma. Though the star might be so tiny as to be lost in the vastness of the plasma clouds, its superpotent magnetic field could force the plasma to spin along with it. In this state of superspin the atoms and electrons on the outer edge of the atmosphere would be moving at almost the speed of light, emitting a lighthouselike beacon. According to Dr. Gold's theory, the plasma would exercise enough drag on the neutron star to slow its spin—and therefore the rate of its pulsations.

[14] As the year drew to a close, at least two pulsars were located in the midst of old supernovas—one of them the famous Crab Nebula—and a few of the pulsars were observed to be gradually slowing down as predicted. All this gave further credence to Dr. Gold's theory, and could turn out to be the first direct evidence that neutron stars do exist. But the evidence is still too tenuous for the conclusions to be anything but tentative. And the pulsar dilemma must be considered as unsettled as most of the other major mysteries of the universe.

[15] Man might well quail with humility and a sense of profound insignificance as he looks out at the unimaginable immensities of the cosmos. But he can take heart from the fact that he is both astronaut and astronomer—and that the entire universe as he knows it is after all a magnificent artifact of the creative human imagination.

EXERCISES—*BEYOND THE MOON*

Content

1. What is the main idea of this essay?
2. How is the title related to the main idea?
3. What is Rosenfeld's purpose in writing this essay?
4. What has been the effect of recent astronomical discoveries?
5. What are the more bizarre and discomforting presences detected in the outer reaches of the universe in the past few years?
6. What once-secure key concept of relativity is now being challenged?
7. What are some of the contradictions and paradoxes of modern astronomy?
8. What was the big discovery of 1967? What conclusion was drawn? Is this conclusion still accepted?
9. What two kinds of stars fit the description of pulsars?
10. What are the five states of matter?
11. What is the most interesting theory set forth to explain how either a white dwarf or a neutron star might conceivably be a pulsar? Who proposed this theory?
12. Is the pulsar dilemma now settled? Why?

Style

1. Define each of the following words in context: *conceptually* (paragraph (1)); *cosmic* (1); *enigmatic* (2); *neutron stars* (3); *quasars* (3); *pulsars* (3); *phenomena* (4); *radical* (6); *putative particles* (6); *prodigious* (7); *red shift* (7); *emissions* (10); *white dwarf* (10); *supernova* (11); *plasma* (12); *credence* (14); *tenuous* (14); *artifact* (15).
2. In this scientific essay Rosenfeld employs some scientific language to communicate his ideas. Does he explain all of these scientific terms in the essay, or does he just explain the least familiar? Why?
3. Is most of Rosenfeld's language denotative or connotative? Why?
4. For what audience is this essay written?
5. What is Rosenfeld's point of view?
6. Is this essay formal, informal, or colloquial?
7. Does Rösenfeld use primary facts or opinion to develop his essay?
8. Is the allusion to Alice in Wonderland in paragraph (12) appropriate?
9. What is the tone of paragraph (15)? the effect? Is such an ending appropriate in a scientific article?

Application of Stylistic Techniques

1. Using Rosenfeld's article, rewrite the introduction (paragraphs (1) and (2)) and conclusion (paragraph (15)) from a pessimistic position.
2. Rewrite Rosenfeld's introduction to make it suitable for a junior high school audience.
3. Choose a brief passage from a science textbook, and compare the style to Rosenfeld's style. Consider the following points: purpose, angle of vision, level, audience, point of view, tone, diction, effectiveness.

Suggestions for Writing

1. Using scientific language, write an essay explaining some scientific process, such as osmosis, reproduction of cells, photosynthesis, mutation, or evolution. Use your classmates as your audience.
2. Write an essay on the significance or the implications of Rosenfeld's article.

LANGUAGE PATTERNS

Another tool the writer uses to express his meaning and thus extend his personality is language patterns. As he chooses words, he arranges them in patterns to comunicate complete ideas. These patterns of language bring order to a conglomeration of unconnected words. Any language has certain established patterns the writer uses to arrange his words and communicate his intended meaning. When he uses variations from the normal word order—an established pattern—he achieves special effects, such as emphasizing certain ideas. The writer must choose the sentence patterns best suited to convey his meaning.

One choice the writer makes, either consciously or subconsciously, is the type of sentence structure to use. Manipulation of sentence structure enables the writer to show relationships between ideas through coordination and subordination. It is the writer's duty to connect ideas, to provide connectives (*when, which, who, that, and, or, but,* etc.) for the reader. The four types of sentences according to structure are simple (one and only one dependent clause), compound (two or more independent clauses), complex (one and only one indepedent clause plus one or more dependent clauses), and compound-complex (two or more independent clauses plus one or more dependent clauses). Examine the following sentences; dependent clauses are italicized.

Simple: Three boys were already in the classroom. (one independent clause)

Compound: Three boys were already in the classroom, and they began to whisper. (two independent clauses)

Complex: The three boys *who were already in the room* began to whisper. (one dependent clause and one independent clause)

OR

When the coed entered the classroom, three boys were already in the room.

(one dependent clause and one independent clause)

OR

When the coed entered the classroom, the three boys *who were already in the room* began to whisper. (two dependent clauses and one independent clause)

Compound-Complex: *When the coed entered the classroom,* three boys were already in the room, and they began to whisper. (one dependent clause and two independent clauses)

OR

When the coed entered the classroom, three boys were already in the room, and they began to whisper *because she was so beautiful.* (two dependent clauses and two independent clauses)

Thus, you can stress certain ideas by placing the more important ideas in independent clauses and by subordinating the restrictive elements or the less important ideas in dependent clauses. Phrases and single-word modifiers are also means you can use to subordinate. You need all of these means. But too much subordination is wordy and burdensome.

A predominance of short simple and compound sentences with a minimum of modifiers usually creates a brisk, straightforward style often used in narration, as in the following example from Hemingway's *Bull Fighting a Tragedy*:

> The bull went on without pausing to worry the picador lying on the ground. The next picador was sitting on his horse braced to receive the shock of the charge, his lance ready. The bull hit him sideways on, the horse and rider went up in the air in a kicking mass and fell across the bull's back. As they came down the bull charged into them. The dough-faced kid, Chicuelo, vaulted over the fence, ran toward the bull and flopped his cape into the bull's face. The bull charged the cape and Chicuelo dodged backwards and had the bull clear in the area.

But a predominance of long complex and compound-complex sentences with much subordination and modification creates a dense, intricate style such as in this passage from Faulkner's *On Privacy: The American Dream, What Happened To It?":*

> And if that was so, if the writer, a member of the craft he served, was victim too of that same force of which I was victim—that irresponsible use which is therefore misuse and which in its turn is betrayal, of that power called Freedom of the Press which is one of the most potent and priceless of the defenders and preservers of human dignity and rights—then the only defense left me was to refuse to co-operate, have anything to do with the project at all. Though by now I knew that would not save me, that nothing I could do would stop them.

Another way you can emphasize ideas is by variation in word order.

> The pretty coed walked across the campus.
> Pretty, the coed walked across the campus.
> Across the campus the pretty coed walked.
> Across the campus walked the pretty coed.

The first sentence above exemplifies normal word order in English: the subject followed by the predicate, with modifiers as close to the words modified as possible. The second sentence emphasizes "pretty" because it is not in its normal position next to the noun it modifies. The order of the other two sentences stresses the last word in each.

Another choice you must make is whether to use the normal, the parallel, or the periodic pattern. The normal pattern in English is subject followed by predicate with modifiers near the words modified. The parallel pattern employs balance of elements for clarity and emphasis, especially in comparison and contrast. The periodic pattern is one in which the main point of the sentence is withheld until the end for emphasis.

Normal: The spoiled child screamed when she didn't get her way.

Parallel: The spoiled child screamed, kicked, pulled her hair, and threw her toys around the playroom.

Periodic: When her father refused and she realized she would never get her way, the spoiled child screamed.

In the following example from the *Gettysburg Address,* Lincoln combined the parallel and the periodic patterns for rhetorical effects:

> It is rather for us to be here dedicated to the great task remaining before us—that from these honored dead we take increased devotion to that cause for which they gave the last full measure of devotion—that we here highly resolve that these dead shall not have died in vain—that this nation, under God, shall have a new birth of freedom and that government of the people, by the people, for the people, shall not perish from the Earth.

As you master English sentence structure, you master effective written communication in English. Your sentences should reflect and intensify your meaning; and as your meaning changes, your sentence patterns should change.

Ernest Hemingway (1899–1961) was born in Illinois. Famous novelist, short story writer, and journalist, he is noted for his terse style and action sentences. Early in his career, he worked as a reporter and foreign correspondent in Kansas City, Chicago, Toronto, Paris, the Near East, Germany, and Spain. His major novels include *The Sun Also Rises, A Farewell to Arms, For Whom the Bell Tolls,* and *The Old Man and the Sea*. His major short stories include "The Killers," "A Clean, Well-Lighted Place," and "The Snows of Kilimanjaro." His nonfiction works include *Death in the Afternoon,* a book on bullfighting, and *A Moveable Feast* (published posthumously), his memories of Paris among the expatriates in the early Twenties. He was awarded a Nobel Prize in 1954.

Bull Fighting a Tragedy

(Normal Word Order Sentences: Simple and Compound)

ERNEST HEMINGWAY

[1] It was spring in Paris and everything looked just a little too beautiful. Mike and I decided to go to Spain. Strater drew us a fine map of Spain on the back of a menu of the Strix restaurant. On the same menu he wrote the name of a restaurant in Madrid where the specialty is young suckling pig roasted, the name of a pension on the Via San Jerónimó where the bull fighters live, and sketched a plan showing where the Grecos are hung in the Prado.

[2] Fully equipped with this menu and our old clothes, we started for Spain. We had one objective—to see bull fights.

[3] We left Paris one morning and got off the train at Madrid the next noon. We saw our first bull fight at 4.30

that afternoon. It took about two hours to get tickets. We finally got them from scalpers for twenty-five pesetas apiece. The bull ring was entirely sold out. We had barrera seats. These the scalper explained in Spanish and broken French were the first row of the ringside, directly under the royal box, and immediately opposite where the bulls would come out.

[4] We asked him if he didn't have any less distinguished seats for somewhere around twelve pesetas, but he was sold out. So we paid the fifty pesetas for the two tickets, and with the tickets in our pockets sat out on the sidewalk in front of a big cafe near the Puerta del Sol. It was very exciting, sitting out in front of a cafe your first day in Spain with a ticket in your pocket that meant that rain or shine you were going to see a bull fight in an hour and a half. In fact, it was so exciting that we started out for the bull ring on the outskirts of the city in about half an hour.

[5] The bull ring or Plaza de Toros was a big, tawny brick amphitheatre standing at the end of a street in an open field. The yellow and red Spanish flag was floating over it. Carriages were driving up and people getting out of buses. There was a great crowd of beggars around the entrance. Men were selling water out of big terra cotta water bottles. Kids sold fans, canes, roasted salted almonds in paper spills, fruit and slabs of ice cream. The crowd was gay and cheerful but all intent on pushing toward the entrance. Mounted civil guards with patent leather cocked hats and carbines slung over their backs sat their horses like statues, and the crowd flowed through.

[6] Inside they all stood around in the bull ring, talking and looking up in the grandstand at the girls in the boxes. Some of the men had field glasses in order to look better. We found our seats and the crowd began to leave the ring and get into the rows of concrete seats. The ring was circular—that sounds foolish, but a boxing ring is square—with a sand floor. Around it was a red board fence—just high enough for a man to be able to vault over it. Between the board fence, which is called the barrera, and the first row of seats ran a narrow alley way. Then came the seats which were just like a foot-

ball stadium except that around the top ran a double circle of boxes.

[7] Every seat in the amphitheatre was full. The arena was cleared. Then on the far side of the arena out of the crowd, four heralds in medieval costume stood up and blew a blast on their trumpets. The band crashed out, and from the entrance on the far side of the ring four horsemen in black velvet with ruffs around their necks rode out into the white glare of the arena. The people on the sunny side were baking in the heat and fanning themselves. The whole sol side was a flicker of fans.

[8] Behind the four horsemen came the procession of the bull fighters. They had been all formed in ranks in the entrance way ready to march out, and as the music started they came. In the front rank walked the three espadas or toreros, who would have charge of the killing of the six bulls of the afternoon.

[9] They came walking out in heavily brocaded yellow and black costumes, the familiar "toreador" suit, heavy with gold embroidery, cape, jacket, shirt and collar, knee breeches, pink stockings, and low pumps. Always at bull fights afterwards the incongruity of those pink stockings used to strike me. Just behind the three principals—and after your first bull fight you do not look at their costumes but their faces—marched the teams or cuadrillas. They are dressed in the same way but not as gorgeously as the matadors.

[10] Back of the teams ride the picadors. Big, heavy, brown-faced men in wide flat hats, carrying lances like long window poles. They are astride horses that make Spark Plug look as trim and sleek as a King's Plate winner. Back of the pics come the gaily harnessed mule teams and the red-shirted monos or bull ring servants.

[11] The bull fighters march in across the sand to the president's box. They march with easy professional stride, swinging along, not in the least theatrical except for their clothes. They all have the easy grace and slight slouch of the professional athlete. From their faces they might be major league ball players. They salute the president's box and then spread out along the barrera, exchanging their heavy bro-

caded capes for the fighting capes that have been laid along the red fence by the attendants.

[12] We leaned forward over the barrera. Just below us the three matadors of the afternoon were leaning against the fence talking. One lighted a cigaret. He was a short, clear-skinned gypsy, Gitanillo, in a wonderful gold brocaded jacket, his short pigtail sticking out under his black cocked hat.

[13] "He's not very fancy," a young man in a straw hat, with obviously American shoes, who sat on my left, said.

[14] "But he sure knows bulls, that boy. He's a great killer."

[15] "You're an American, aren't you?" asked Mike.

[16] "Sure," the boy grinned. "But I know this gang. That's Gitanillo. You want to watch him. The kid with the chubby face is Chicuelo. They say he doesn't really like bull fighting, but the town's crazy about him. The next to him is Villalta. He's the great one."

[17] I had noticed Villalta. He was straight as a lance and walked like a young wolf. He was talking and smiling at a friend who leaned over the barrera. Upon his tanned cheek-bone was a big patch of gauze held on with adhesive tape.

[18] "He got gored last week at Malaga," said the American.

[19] The American, whom later we were to learn to know and love as the Gin Bottle King, because of a great feat of arms performed at an early hour of the morning with a container of Mr. Gordon's celebrated product as his sole weapon in one of the four most dangerous situations I have ever seen, said: "The show's going to begin."

[20] Out in the arena the picadors had galloped their decrepit horses around the ring, sitting straight and stiff in their rocking chair saddles. Now all but three had ridden out of the ring. These three were huddled against the red painted fence of the barrera. Their horses backed against the fence, one eye bandaged, their lances at rest.

[21] In rode two of the marshals in the velvet jackets and white ruffs. They galloped up to the president's box, swerved and saluted, doffing their hats and bowing low. From

the box an object came hurtling down. One of the marshals caught it in his plumed hat.

[22] "The key to the bull pen," said the Gin Bottle King.

[23] The two horsemen whirled and rode across the arena. One of them tossed the key to a man in torero costume, they both saluted with a wave of their plumed hats, and had gone from the ring. The big gate was shut and bolted. There was no more entrance. The ring was complete.

[24] The crowd had been shouting and yelling. Now it was dead silent. The man with the key stepped toward an iron barred, low, red door and unlocked the great sliding bar. He lifted it and stepped back. The door swung open. The man hid behind it. Inside it was dark.

[25] Then, ducking his head as he came up out of the dark pen, a bull came into the arena. He came out all in a rush, big, black and white, weighing over a ton and moving with a soft gallop. Just as he came out the sun seemed to dazzle him for an instant. He stood as though he were frozen, his great crest of muscle up, firmly planted, his eyes looking around, his horns pointed forward, black and white and sharp as porcupine quills. Then he charged. And as he charged I suddenly saw what bull fighting is all about.

[26] For the bull was absolutely unbelievable. He seemed like some great prehistoric animal, absolutely deadly and absolutely vicious. And he was silent. He charged silently and with a soft galloping rush. When he turned he turned on his four feet like a cat. When he charged the first thing that caught his eye was a picador on one of the wretched horses. The picador dug his spurs into the horse and they galloped away. The bull came on in his rush, refused to be shaken off, and in full gallop crashed into the animal from the side, ignored the horse, drove one of his horns high into the thigh of the picador, and tore him saddle and all, off the horse's back.

[27] The bull went on without pausing to worry the picador lying on the ground. The next picador was sitting on his horse braced to receive the shock of the charge, his lance

ready. The bull hit him sideways on, and horse and rider went high up in the air in a kicking mass and fell across the bull's back. As they came down the bull charged into them. The dough-faced kit, Chicuelo, vaulted over the fence, ran toward the bull and flopped his cape into the bull's face. The bull charged the cape and Chicuelo dodged backwards and had the bull clear in the arena.

[28] Without an instant's hesitation the bull charged Chicuelo. The kid stood his ground, simply swung back on his heels and floated his cape like a ballet dancer's skirt into the bull's face as he passed.

[29] "Olé!"—pronounced Oh-Lay!—roared the crowd.

[30] The bull whirled and charged again. Without moving Chicuelo repeated the performance. His legs rigid, just withdrawing his body from the rush of the bull's horns and floating the cape out with that beautiful swing.

[31] Again the crowd roared. The Kid did this seven times. Each time the bull missed him by inches. Each time he gave the bull a free shot at him. Each time the crowd roared. Then he flopped the cape once at the bull at the finish of a pass, swung it around behind him and walked away from the bull to the barrera.

[32] "He's the boy with the cape all right," said the Gin Bottle King. "That swing he did with the cape's called a Veronica."

[33] The chubby faced Kid who did not like bull fighting and had just done the seven wonderful Veronicas was standing against the fence just below us. His face glistened with sweat in the sun but was almost expressionless. His eyes were looking out across the arena where the bull was standing making up his mind to charge a picador. He was studying the bull because a few minutes later it would be his duty to kill him, and once he went out with his thin, red-hilted sword and his piece of red cloth to kill the bull in the final set it would be him or the bull. There are no drawn battles in bull fighting.

[34] I am not going to describe the rest of that afternoon in detail. It was the first bull fight I ever saw, but it was not the best. The best was in the little town of Pamplona high up in the hills of Navarre, and came weeks later. Up in Pam-

plona, where they have held six days of bull fighting each year since 1126 A.D., and where the bulls race through the streets of the town each morning at six o'clock with half the town running ahead of them. Pamplona, where every man and boy in town is an amateur bull fighter and where there is an amateur fight each morning that is attended by 20,000 people in which the amateur fighters are all unarmed and there is a casualty list at least equal to a Dublin election. But Pamplona, with the best bull fight and the wild tale of the amateur fights, comes in the second chapter.

[35] I am not going to apologize for bull fighting. It is a survival of the days of the Roman Coliseum. But it does need some explanation. Bull fighting is not a sport. It was never supposed to be. It is a tragedy. A very great tragedy. The tragedy is the death of the bull. It is played in three definite acts.

[36] The Gin Bottle King—who, by the way, does not drink gin—told us a lot of this that first night as we sat in the upstairs room of the little restaurant that made a specialty of roast young suckling pig, roasted on an oak plank and served with a mushroom tortilla and vino rojo. The rest we learned later at the bull fighters' pensione in the Via San Jeronimo, where one of the bull fighters had eyes exactly like a rattlesnake.

[37] Much of it we learned in the sixteen fights we saw in different parts of Spain from San Sebastian to Granada.

[38] At any rate bull fighting is not a sport. It is a tragedy, and it symbolizes the struggle between man and the beasts. There are usually six bulls to a fight. A fight is called a corrida de toros. Fighting bulls are bred like race horses, some of the oldest breeding establishments being several hundred years old. A good bull is worth about $2,000. They are bred for speed, strength and viciousness. In other words a good fighting bull is an absolutely incorrigible bad bull.

[39] Bull fighting is an exceedingly dangerous occupation. In sixteen fights I saw there were only two in which there was no one badly hurt. On the other hand it is very remunerative. A popular espada gets $5,000 for his after-

noon's work. An unpopular espada though may not get $500. Both run the same risks. It is a good deal like Grand Opera for the really great matadors except they run the chance of being killed every time they cannot hit high C.

[40] No one at any time in the fight can approach the bull at any time except directly from the front. That is where the danger comes. There are also all sorts of complicated passes that must be done with the cape, each requiring as much technique as a champion billiard player. And underneath it all is the necessity for playing the old tragedy in the absolutely custom bound, law-laid-down way. It must all be done gracefully, seemingly effortlessly and always with dignity. The worst criticism the Spaniards ever make of a bull fighter is that his work is "vulgar."

[41] The three absolute acts of the tragedy are first the entry of the bull when the picadors receive the shock of his attacks and attempt to protect their horses with their lances. Then the horses go out and the second act is the planting of the banderillos. This is one of the most interesting and difficult parts but among the easiest for a new bull fight fan to appreciate in technique. The banderillos are three-foot, gaily colored darts with a small fish hook prong in the end. The man who is going to plant them walks out into the arena alone with the bull. He lifts the banderillos at arm's length and points them toward the bull. Then he calls "Toro! Toro!" The bull charges and the banderillero rises to his toes, bends in a curve forward and just as the bull is about to hit him drops the darts into the bull's hump just back of his horns.

[42] They must go in evenly, one on each side. They must not be shoved, or thrown or stuck in from the side. This is the first time the bull has been completely baffled, there is the prick of the darts that he cannot escape and there are no horses for him to charge into. But he charges the man again and again and each time he gets a pair of the long banderillos that hang from his hump by their tiny barbs and flop like porcupine quills.

[43] Last is the death of the bull, which is in the hands of the matador who has had charge of the bull since his first attack. Each matador has two bulls in the afternoon. The

death of the bull is most formal and can only be brought about in one way, directly from the front by the matador who must receive the bull in full charge and kill him with a sword thrust between the shoulders just back of the neck and between the horns. Before killing the bull he must first do a series of passes with the muleta, a piece of red cloth he carries about the size of a large napkin. With the muleta the torero must show his complete mastery of the bull, must make the bull miss him again and again by inches, before he is allowed to kill him. It is in this phase that most of the fatal accidents occur.

[44] The word "toreador" is obsolete Spanish and is never used. The torero is usually called an espada or swordsman. He must be proficient in all three acts of the fight. In the first he uses the cape and does veronicas and protects the picadors by taking the bull out and away from them when they are spilled to the ground. In the second act he plants the banderillos. In the third act he masters the bull with the muleta and kills him.

[45] Few toreros excel in all three departments. Some, like young Chicuelo, are unapproachable in their cape work. Others like the late Joselito are wonderful banderilleros. Only a few are great killers. Most of the greatest killers are gypsies.

EXERCISES—*BULL FIGHTING A TRAGEDY*

Content

1. Why did Mike and the author go to Spain?
2. What is a barrera? a Veronica?
3. What incongruity always used to strike Hemingway at bull fights?
4. Of the three matadors of the afternoon, who was the greatest?
5. Why was the American that Hemingway met, called "the Gin Bottle King"? What is the irony of that nickname?
6. What is the meaning of the comment "It (bull fighting) is a survival of the days of the Roman Coliseum"?
7. Why does Hemingway call bull fighting a tragedy? What are the three acts of the tragedy?

Style

1. The sentences in Hemingway's essay are primarily simple and compound, normal-word-order sentences. Are such sentences appropriate and effective for Hemingway's purpose and subject? Why?
2. This essay is composed of two major divisions. Where does the first section end and the second section begin? Why?
3. What is the dominant tone of this essay?
4. Consider the following revision of paragraph (35):

   I am not going to apologize for bull fighting, a survival of the days of the Roman Coliseum; but it does need some explanation. Bull fighting is not a sport and was never supposed to be. It is a very great tragedy. This tragedy is the death of the bull which is played in three acts.

   What are the grammatical and structural differences in the two versions? Why is the original version more effective?
5. Answer the following questions about each of the sentences in paragraph (5): a) Is the sentence simple, compound, complex, or compound-complex? b) Is the sentence normal, balanced, or periodic? c) Are there any variations from normal English word order in the sentence? Choose another paragraph of at least five sentences, and analyze it by answering the same questions. What can you conclude about Hemingway's sentences?
6. Decide whether each of the following is a literal comparison or a figure of speech. If it is a figure of speech, identify it. Then decide how effective or ineffective you think each is.
   "like a football stadium" (paragraph (6))
   "like long window poles" (10)
   "Spark Plug" (10)
   "major league ball players" (11)
   "as a lance" (17)
   "like a young wolf" (17)
   "as porcupine quills" (25)
   "like some great prehistoric animal" (26)
   "like a cat" (26)
   "dough-faced" (27)
   "like a ballet dancer's skirt" (28)
   "a Dublin election" (34)
   "like a rattlesnake" (36)
   "like Grand Opera" (39)

7. Hemingway uses much coordination and parallelism to convey continuing action. Using the method illustrated below, indicate the parallel elements and their relationship to the rest of the sentence—for each of the listed sentences.

   Examples

   paragraph (4), sentence 2:

   we { paid pesetas . . . and sat . . .

   paragraph (5), sentence 2:

   yellow and red } Spanish flag was floating . . .

   paragraph (5), sentence 6
   paragraph (9), sentence 1
   paragraph (21), sentence 1
   paragraph (21), sentence 2
   paragraph (25), sentence 2
   paragraph (26), sentence 8
   paragraph (27), sentence 5
   paragraph (33), sentence 1
   paragraph (33), sentence 2
8. Find at least three examples of periodic sentences in this essay, and explain how and why Hemingway uses them.
9. What is the effect of the last sentence of the essay?
10. What can you conclude about Hemingway's personality from his style?

Application of Stylistic Techniques

1. Write an example of each of the following types of sentences: simple, compound, complex, compound-complex; normal, balanced, periodic.
2. Choose a paragraph from a favorite novel or short story and a paragraph from a textbook, and analyze each by answering the questions in #5 under "Questions on Style." How and why do they differ from Hemingway's writing?
3. By using more subordination and coordination, rewrite paragraph (17) to be just one sentence. How is the effect different from the effect of the original version?

Suggestions for Writing

1. Write an essay on the pomp and/or ritual of some sport or activity, such as football, baseball, or the circus.
2. Write an essay on your attitude toward some sport, such as: wrestling is a farce; boxing should be banned; basketball requires more dexterity than other sports. Choose any sport, but be honest and specific in explaining your attitude.
3. Write an essay in which you agree or disagree with Hemingway's opinion that bull fighting is a tragedy.

William Faulkner (1897–1962) worked briefly as a reporter in New Orleans, but later gained fame as a novelist and short story writer. He grew up in Oxford, Mississippi, the town upon which he based the "Jefferson" in his mythical Yoknapatawpha County in his novels. In this mythical area he traced several generations of the Sartoris and Snopes families in his various novels. He was awarded a Pulitzer Prize in 1954 for *A Fable* and again in 1962 for *The Reivers*. In 1950 he was awarded a Nobel Prize. His other major works include *The Bear, The Sound and the Fury, Light in August,* and *The Hamlet.*

On Privacy: The American Dream, What Happened to It?

(Subordination and Variation of Word Order in Sentences)

WILLIAM FAULKNER

[1] This was the American Dream: a sanctuary on the earth for individual man: a condition in which he could be free not only of the old established closed-corporation hierarchies of arbitrary power which had oppressed him as a mass, but free of that mass into which the hierarchies of church and state had compressed and held him individually thralled and individually impotent.

[2] A dream simultaneous among the separate individuals of men so asunder and scattered as to have no contact to match dreams and hopes among the old nations of the Old World which existed as nations not on citizenship but subject-

ship, which endured only on the premise of size and docility of the subject mass; the individual men and women who said as with one simultaneous voice: "We will establish a new land where man can assume that every individual man—not the mass of men but individual men—has the inalienable right to individual dignity and freedom within a fabric of individual courage and honorable work and mutual responsibility."

[3] Not just an idea, but a condition: a living human condition designed to be coeval with the birth of America itself, engendered, created, and simultaneous with the very air and word *America,* which at that one stroke, one instant, should cover the whole earth with one simultaneous suspiration like air or light. And it was, it did: radiating outward to cover even the old weary repudiated still-thralled nations, until individual men everywhere, who had no more than heard the name, let alone knew where America was, could respond to it, lifting up not only their hearts but the hopes too which until now they did not know—or anyway dared not remember—that they possessed.

[4] A condition in which every man would not only not be a king, he wouldn't even want to be one. He wouldn't even need to bother to need to be the equal to kings because now he was free of kings and all their similar congeries; free not only of the symbols but of the old arbitrary hierarchies themselves which the puppet-symbols represented—courts and cabinets and churches and schools—to which he had been valuable not as an individual but only as that integer, his value compounded in that immutable ratio to his sheer mindless numbers, that animal increase of his will-less and docile mass.

[5] The dream, the hope, the condition which our forefathers did not bequeath to us, their heirs and assigns, but rather bequeathed us, their successors, to the dream and the hope. We were not even given the chance then to accept or decline the dream, for the reason that the dream already owned and possessed us at birth. It was not our heritage because we were its, we ourselves heired in our successive generations to the dream by the idea of the dream. And not only

we, their sons born and bred in America, but men born and bred in the old alien repudiated lands, also felt that breath, that air, heard that promise, that proffer that there was such a thing as hope for individual man. And the old nations themselves, so old and so long-fixed in the old concepts of man as to have thought themselves beyond all hope of change, making oblation to that new dream of that new concept of man by gifts of monuments and devices to mark the portals of that inalienable right and hope:

[6] "There is room for you here from about the earth, for all ye individually homeless, individually oppressed, individually unindividualized."

[7] A free gift left to us by those who had mutually travailed and individually endured to create it; we, their successors, did not even have to earn, deserve it, let alone win it. We did not even need to nourish and feed it. We needed only to remember that, living, it was therefore perishable and must be defended in its crises. Some of us, most of us perhaps, could not have proved by definition that we knew exactly what it was. But then, we didn't need to: who no more needed to define it than we needed to define that air we breathed or that word, which, the two of them, simply by existing simultaneously—the breathing of the American air which made America—together that engendered and created the dream on that first day of America as air and motion created temperature and climaté on the first day of time.

[8] Because that dream was man's aspiration in the true meaning of the word *aspiration*. It was not merely the blind and voiceless hope of his heart: it was the actual inbreathe of his lungs, his lights, his living and unsleeping metabolism, so that we actually lived the Dream. We did not live *in* the dream: we lived the Dream itself, just as we do not merely live *in* air and climate, but we live Air and Climate; we ourselves individually representative of the Dream, the Dream itself actually audible in the strong uninhibited voices which were not afraid to speak clichés at the very top of them, giving to the cliché-avatars of "Give me liberty or give me death" or "This to be self-evident that all individual men were created

equal in one mutual right to freedom" which had never lacked for truth anyway, assuming that hope and dignity and truth, a validity and immediacy absolving them even of cliché.

[9] That was the Dream: not man created equal in the sense that he was created black or white or brown or yellow and hence doomed irrevocably to that for the remainder of his days—or rather, not doomed with equality but blessed with equality, himself lifting no hand but instead lying curled and drowsing in the warm and airless bath of it like the yet-wombed embryo; but liberty in which to have an equal start at equality with all other men, and freedom in which to defend and preserve that equality by means of the individual courage and the honorable work and the mutual responsibility. Then we lost it. It abandoned us, which had supported and protected and defended us while our new nation of new concepts of human existence got a firm enough foothold to stand erect among the nations of the earth, demanding nothing of us in return save to remember always that, being alive, it was therefore perishable and so must be held always in the unceasing responsibility and vigilance of courage and honor and pride and humility. It is gone now. We dozed, slept, and it abandoned us. And in that vacuum now there sound no longer the strong loud voices not merely unafraid but not even aware that fear existed, speaking in mutual unification of one mutual hope and will. Because now what we hear is a cacophony of terror and conciliation and compromise babbling only the mouth-sounds, the loud and empty words which we have emasculated of all meaning whatever—freedom, democracy, patriotism—with which, awakened at last, we try in desperation to hide from ourselves that loss.

[10] Something happened to the Dream. Many things did. This, I think, is a symptom of one of them.

[11] About ten years ago a well-known literary critic and essayist, a good friend of long standing, told me that a wealthy widely circulated weekly pictorial magazine had offered him a good price to write a piece about me—not about my work or works, but about me as a private citizen, an individual. I said No, and explained why: my belief that only a writer's works were in the public domain, to be discussed and

investigated and written about, the writer himself having put them there by submitting them for publication and accepting money for them; and therefore he not only would but must accept whatever the public wished to say or do about them from praise to burning. But that, until the writer committed a crime or ran for public office, his private life was his own; and not only had he the right to defend his privacy, but the public had the duty to do so since one man's liberty must stop at exactly the point where the next one's begins; and that I believed that anyone of taste and responsibility would agree with me.

[12] But the friend said No. He said: "You are wrong. If I do the piece, I will do it with taste and responsibility. But if you refuse me, sooner or later someone will do it who will not bother about taste or responsibility either, who will care nothing about you or your status as a writer, an artist, but only as a commodity: merchandise: to be sold, to increase circulation, to make a little money."

[13] "I don't believe it," I said. "Until I commit a crime or announce for office, they can't invade my privacy after I ask them not to."

[14] "They not only can," he said, "but once your European reputation gets back here and makes you financially worth it, they will. Wait and see."

[15] I did. I did both. Two years ago, by mere chance during a talk with an editor in the house which publishes my books, I learned that the same magazine had already set on foot the same project which I had declined eight years before; I don't know whether the publishers were formally notified or if they just heard about it by chance too, as I did. I said No again, recapitulating the same reasons which I still believed were not even arguable by anyone possessing the power of the public press, since the qualities of taste and responsibility would have to be inherent in that power for it to be valid and allowed to endure. The editor interrupted.

[16] "I agree with you," he said. "Besides, you don't need to give me reasons. The simple fact that you don't want it done is enough. Shall I attend to it for you?" So he did, or tried to. Because my critic friend was still right. Then I said:

[17] "Try them again. Say 'I ask you: please don't.'" Then I submitted the same *I ask you: please don't* to the writer who was to do the piece. I don't know whether he was a staff writer designated to the job, or whether he volunteered for it, or perhaps himself sold his employers on the idea. Though my recollection is that his answer implied, "I've got to, if I refuse they will fire me," which is probably correct, since I got the same answer from a staff member of another magazine on the same subject.

[18] And if that was so, if the writer, a member of the craft he served, was victim too of that same force of which I was victim—that irresponsible use which is therefore misuse and which in its turn is betrayal, of that power called Freedom of the Press which is one of the most potent and priceless of the defenders and preservers of human dignity and rights—then the only defense left me was to refuse to co-operate, have anything to do with the project at all. Though by now I knew that that would not save me, that nothing I could do would stop them.

[19] Perhaps they—the writer and his employer—didn't believe me, could not believe me. Perhaps they dared not believe me. Perhaps it is impossible now for any American to believe that anyone not hiding from the police could actually not want, as a free gift, his name and photograph in any printed organ, no matter how base or modest or circumscribed in circulation. Though perhaps the matter never reached this point: that both of them—the publisher and the writer—knew from the first, whether I did or not, that the three of us, the two of them and their victim, were all three victims of that fault (in the sense that the geologist uses the term) in our American culture which is saying to us daily: "Beware!" the three of us faced as one not with an idea, a principle of choice between good and bad taste or responsibility or lack of it, but with a fact, a condition in our American life before which all three of us were (at that moment) helpless, at that moment doomed.

[20] So the writer came with his group, force, crew, and got his material where and how he could and departed and published his article. But that's not the point. The writer is

not to be blamed since, empty-handed, he would (if my recollection is right) have been fired from the job which deprived him of the right to choose between good and bad taste. Nor the employer either, since to hold his (the employer's) precarious own in a craft can compel even him, head and chief of one of its integral components, to serve the mores of the hour in order to survive among his rival ones.

[21] It's not what the writer said, but that he said it. That he—they—published it, in a recognized organ which, to be and remain recognized, functions on the assumption of certain inflexible standards; published it not only over the subject's protests but with complete immunity to them; an immunity not merely assumed to itself by the organ but an immunity already granted in advance by the public to which it sold its wares for a profit. The terrifying (not shocking; we cannot be shocked by it since we permitted its birth and watched it grow and condoned and validated it and even use it individually for our own private ends at need) thing is that it could have happened at all under those conditions. That it could have happened at all with its subject not even notified in advance. And even when he, the victim, was warned by accident in advance, he was still completely helpless to prevent it. And even after it was done, the victim had no recourse whatever since, unlike sacrilege and obscenity, we have no laws against bad taste, perhaps because in a democracy the majority of the people who make the laws don't recognize bad taste when they see it, or perhaps because in our democracy bad taste has been converted into a marketable and therefore taxable and therefore lobbyable commodity by the merchandising federations which at the same simultaneous time create the market (not the appetite: that did not need creating: only pandering to) and the product to serve it, and bad taste by simple solvency was purified of bad taste and absolved. And even if there had been grounds for recourse, the matter would still have remained on the black side of the ledger since the publisher could charge the judgment and costs to operating loss and the increased sales from the publicity to capital investment.

[22] The point is that in America today any organization

or group, simply by functioning under a phrase like Freedom of the Press or National Security or League Against Subversion, can postulate to itself complete immunity to violate the individualness—the individual privacy lacking which he cannot be an individual and lacking which individuality he is not anything at all worth the having or keeping—of anyone who is not himself a member of some organization or group numerous enough or rich enough to frighten them off. That organization will not be of writers, artists, of course; being individuals, not even two artists could ever confederate, let alone enough of them. Besides, artists in America don't have to have privacy because they don't need to be artists as far as America is concerned. America doesn't need artists because they don't count in America; artists have no more place in American life than the employers of the weekly pictorial magazine staff writers have in the private life of a Mississippi novelist.

[23] But there are the other two occupations which are valuable to American life, which require, demand privacy in order to endure, live. These are science and the humanities, the scientists and the humanitarians: the pioneers in the science of endurance and mechanical craftsmanship and self-discipline and skill like Colonel Lindbergh who was compelled at last to repudiate it by the nation and culture one of whose mores was an inalienable right to violate his privacy instead of an inviolable duty to defend it, the nation which assumed an inalienable right to abrogate to itself the glory of his renown yet which had neither the power to protect his children nor the responsibility to shield his grief; the pioneers in the simple science of saving the nation like Dr. Oppenheimer who was harassed and impugned through those same mores until all privacy was stripped from him and there remained only the qualities of individualism whose possession we boast since they alone differ us from animals—gratitude for kindness, fidelity to friendship, chivalry toward women, and the capacity to love—before which even his officially vetted harassers were impotent, turning away themselves (one hopes) in shame, as though the whole business had had nothing whatever to do with loyalty or disloyalty or security or insecurity, but was simply to batter and strip him completely naked of the privacy lack-

ing which he could never have become one of that handful of individuals capable of serving the nation at a moment when apparently nobody else was, and so reduce him at last to one more identityless integer in that identityless anonymous unprivacied mass which seems to be our goal.

[24] And even that is only a point of departure. Because the sickness itself goes much further back. It goes back to that moment in our history when we decided that the old simple moral verities over which taste and responsibility were the arbiters and controls, were obsolete and to be discarded. It goes back to that moment when we repudiated the meaning which our fathers had stipulated for the words "liberty" and "freedom," on and by and to which they founded us as a nation and dedicated us as a people, ourselves in our time keeping only the mouth-sounds of them. It goes back to the moment when we substituted license in the place of liberty—license for any action which kept within the proscription of laws promulgated by confederations of the practitioners of the license and the harvesters of the material benefits. It goes back to that moment when in place of freedom we substituted immunity for any action to any recourse, provided merely that the act be performed beneath the aegis of the empty mouth-sound of freedom.

[25] At which instant truth vanished too. We didn't abolish truth; even we couldn't do that. It simply quit us, turned its back on us, not in scorn nor even contempt nor even (let us hope) despair. It just simply quit us, to return perhaps when whatever it will be—suffering, national disaster, maybe even (if nothing else will serve) military defeat—will have taught us to prize truth and pay any price, accept any sacrifice (oh yes, we are brave and tough too; we just intend to put off having to be as long as possible) to regain and hold it again as we should never have let it go: on its own compromiseless terms of taste and responsibility. Truth—that long clean clear simple undeviable unchallengeable straight and shining line, on one side of which black is black and on the other white is white, has now become an angle, a point of view having nothing to do with truth nor even with fact, but depending solely on where you are standing when you look at it.

Or rather—better—where you can contrive to have him standing whom you are trying to fool or obfuscate when he looks at it.

[26] Across the board in fact, a parlay, a daily triple: truth and freedom and liberty. The American sky which was once the topless empyrean of freedom, the American air which was once the living breath of liberty, are now become one vast down-crowding pressure to abolish them both, by destroying man's individuality as a man by (in that turn) destroying the last vestige of privacy without which man cannot be an individual. Our very architecture itself has warned us. Time was when you could see neither from inside nor from outside through the walls of our houses. Time is when you can see from inside out though still not from outside in through the walls. Time will be when you can do both. Then privacy will indeed be gone; he who is individual enough to want it even to change his shirt or bathe in, will be cursed by one universal American voice as subversive to the American way of life and the American flag.

[27] If (by that time) walls themselves, opaque or not, can still stand before that furious blast, that force, that power rearing like a thunderclap into the American zenith, multiple-faced yet mutually conjunctived, bellowing the words and phrases which we have long since emasculated of any significance or meaning other than as tools, implements, for the further harassment of the private individual human spirit, by their furious and immunized high priests: "Security." "Subversion." "Anti-Communism." "Christianity." "Prosperity." "The American Way." "The Flag."

[28] With odds at balance (plus a little fast footwork now and then of course) one individual can defend himself from another individual's liberty. But when powerful federations and organizations and amalgamations like publishing corporations and religious sects and political parties and legislative committees can absolve even one of their working units of the restrictions of moral responsibility by means of such catch-phrases as "Freedom" and "Salvation" and "Security" and "Democracy," beneath which blanket absolution the individual salaried practitioners are themselves freed of individual

responsibility and restraint, then let us beware. Then even people like Dr. Oppenheimer and Colonel Lindbergh and me (the weekly magazine staff writer too if he really was compelled to choose between good taste and starvation) will have to confederate in our turn to preserve that privacy in which alone the artist and scientist and humanitarian can function.

[29] Or to preserve life itself, breathing; not just artists and scientists and humanitarians, but the parents by law or biology of doctors of osteopathy too. I am thinking of course of the Cleveland doctor convicted recently of the brutal slaying of his wife, three of whose parents—his wife's father and his own father and mother—with one exception did not even outlive that trial regarding which the Press itself, which kept the sorry business on most of the nation's front pages up to the very end, is now on record as declaring that it was overcovered far beyond its value and importance.

[30] I am thinking of the three victims. Not the convicted man: he will doubtless live a long time yet; but of the three parents, two of whom died—one of them anyway—because, to quote the Press itself, "he was wearied of life," and the third one, the mother, by her own hand, as though she had said, *I can bear no more of this.*

[31] Perhaps they died solely because of the crime, though one wonders why the coincidence of their deaths was not with the commission of the murder but with the publicity of the trial. And if it was not solely because of the tragedy itself that one of the victims was "wearied of life" and another obviously said, *I can bear no more*—if they had more than that one reason to relinquish and even repudiate life, and the man was guilty as the jury said he was, just what medieval witchhunt did that power called Freedom of the Press, which in any civilized culture must be accepted as that dedicated paladin through whose inflexible rectitude truth shall prevail and justice and mercy be done, condone and abet that the criminal's very progenitors be eliminated from the earth in expiation of his crime? And if he was innocent as he said he was, what crime did that champion of the weak and the oppressed itself participate in? Or (to repeat) not the artist. America has not yet found any place for him who deals only in things of the

human spirit except to use his notoriety to sell soap or cigarettes or fountain pens or to advertise automobiles and cruises and resort hotels, or (if he can be taught to contort fast enough to meet the standards) in radio or moving pictures where he can produce enough income tax to be worth attention. But the scientists and the humanitarian, yes: the humanitarian in science and the scientist in the humanity of man, who might yet save that civilization which the professionals at saving it—the publishers who condone their own battening on man's lust and folly, the politicians who condone their own trafficking in his stupidity and greed, and the churchmen who condone their own trading on his fear and superstition—seem to be proving that they can't.

EXERCISES—*ON PRIVACY: THE AMERICAN DREAM, WHAT HAPPENED TO IT?*

Content

1. According to Faulkner, what was the American dream? Why does he use past tense when referring to the American dream? What has happened to this dream?
2. Why would Faulkner not agree to have a piece written about him as an individual?
3. What two groups of people have forfeited their right to individual privacy?
4. Why do we have no laws against bad taste?
5. What is the main idea of the essay? Where does Faulkner state this point?
6. What three occupations demand privacy in order to endure?
7. Who might yet save our civilization?

Style

1. What is the tone of this essay?
2. Is this essay formal, informal, or colloquial? Support your conclusion.
3. For what audience is this essay suitable? In answering this question, consider the subject, the purpose, diction, sentence structure, and structure of the essay.
4. The first nine paragraphs of this essay comprise an extended

definition of the American dream. Why does Faulkner develop this definition so specifically?

5. What is the purpose of the anecdote about magazine articles (paragraph (11)–(21)? of the reference to Colonel Lindburgh (23)? of the reference to Dr. Oppenheimer (23)? of the reference to the Cleveland doctor—Sam Shepherd—and his family (29)–(31)?
6. Paragraphs (2), (3), (4), (5), (7), and (8) all begin with fragments. How can this use of fragments be justified? What is the rhetorical effect of this parallelism?
7. Find and mark in your textbook margin two examples of each of the following: simple sentence, complex sentence, compound sentence, compound-complex sentence, fragment, normal sentence, balanced sentence, periodic sentence, variation from normal word order. What is the effect of each?
8. Analyze Faulkner's use of punctuation to clarify and intensify his meaning. Notice especially his use of colons, semicolons, and dashes.
9. Throughout the essay Faulkner suggests that America has a disease or sickness. Circle the words and phrases in the essay which convey this idea. Then decide what America's sickness is.
10. Count the number of words in each sentence in paragraph (9). What is the effect of the variation in length?
11. From this essay, what can you conclude about Faulkner's personality?

Application of Stylistic Techniques

1. Compare and contrast Hemingway's style to Faulkner's style. Is each suited to its purpose, method, and subject?
2. Write a paragraph emulating Hemingway's style, and then write a paragraph emulating Faulkner's style. In your paragraphs, pay particular attention to sentence structure. Which style—if either—is easier to write effectively?
3. Choose either sentence 1 of paragraph (22) or sentence 5 of paragraph (31), parse it (analyze it grammatically and structurally), and then write an original sentence by the same pattern.

Suggestions for Writing

1. Write an essay in which you agree or disagree with one of Faulkner's ideas.

2. In an essay, write an extended definition of an abstract term, such as freedom, honesty, love, friendship, education, infatuation, beauty, liberty, or religion. Use plenty of examples to define. Avoid the superficial and the hackneyed.
3. Write an essay in which you criticize some aspect of modern society. You might write on dehumanization, urbanization, pollution, escapism, greed, conformity, violence, etc.
4. Write an essay in which you explain your concept of the American dream, what you think America should be.

Laurence A. Jolidon II (1938–   ) was born in Tulsa, Oklahoma, received his degree in English and American literature from Baldwin-Wallace College, and is now news editor of the *St. Petersburg Times.* Before coming to Florida in 1968, he worked as a reporter on various newspapers in Ohio and New York and was a Professional Journalism Fellow at Stanford University in 1967.

Decade of Destiny

(Emphasis in Sentences)

LAURENCE A. JOLIDON

[1] In the Space Needle, a carillon of more than 500 bells plays in the clouds 600 feet above Seattle. They toll for linear man, he that is non-McLuhan.

[2] It is April 21, 1962, the hot dang down and out start of the Golden Era, gang. Listenup.

[3] The golden telegraph key used by 7 presidents to inaugurate earlier events in bygone eras sits warming under a Palm Beach sun.

[4] The sun glints on the PT-109 tie clasp on the President's shirt, and a breeze catches a shock of brown hair. One hand is in his two-button suit pocket.

[5] With the other he presses the telegraph key, and his touch starts machinery that focuses an antenna in Andover, Maine, on the star Cassiopeia, 10,000 light years away. The antenna picks up a radio wave that left the star 10,000 years earlier. The resulting signal is sent to Seattle by cable and microwave radio where it rings in the Century 21 exposition.

[6] It is less than a step from that telegraph key to the moon, where man sends his electronic and human emissaries to dissipate the mysterious forces that have held his wide-angle lens to the ground.

From *St. Petersburg Times*, December 28, 1969. Reprinted by permission.

[7] He must know the sky, dodge the meteorites, see the strobe lights of interstellar space so that he may control his destiny, aim his rocketships, still his nerves.

[8] For in the global village at his feet, the new life is begun, the new freedom is won.

[9] Here is Hiroshima's child, dancing somewhere between nudity and mere nakedness, bringing the new thing all back home, yeah.

[10] Bringing the new permissiveness, the birth control pill in the changepurse, abortions on the installment plan, see-through, cut-out, switched-on micro-mini ju-jus to the discount rack.

[11] (Sex education, dear, is on the school board agenda, you don't want to miss the double feature.)

[12] Bringing the new culture, the drug culture, the dragged-out cülture, the uptight culture, the zonked, zapped, stoned, gone culture of the psychedelic, oversonic, bossa-nova-groovy-love-rock peace thing, huh. Yeah.

[13] Bringing new careers for the newly awakened, the New Leftists to the chartered plane to Hanoi-Haiphong, to the Mississippi Delta for some bloody voter registration, the Young Americans for Freedom to the mimeograph machine, the young, mustachioed and sometimes bearded lawyers and doctors to the poverty pockets, the architects of the new analysis to the underground, unpaid press. Dig.

[14] Bringing new entertainment for the newly hip, the light show on the dance hall wall, the wriggling, shaking, stomping in the audience, the Italian western where every cow-poke dies, the husband-wife, real-life drama starring the Anouk Aimees, the Yves Montands, the Richard Burtons, or the Paul Newmans, the nude scene and the Grand Prix, the novel no one wouldn't dare to print, babe, Lady Chatterly and Mary McCarthy.

[15] (If you hurry you can catch the last chorus line at the Copa, the dousing of the lights at Lindy's, the end of an ego at Arthur's, the last lick at the Peppermint Lounge.)

[16] Bringing the new morality, bringing Vanessa Redgrave (don't tell me, "Blow-Up") and Mia Farrow (oh, yeah, "Rosemary's Baby") out in the public and pregnant out of wed-

lock, bringing 14 television "quiz show" winners (no hints please, for $64,000 . . .) who know all the answers as well as the questions, bringing more than 100 Air Force cadets who know all the answers before seeing the questions, bringing CIA money to the National Student Association. Wow.

[17] Bringing the new social consciousness, students who snap at Gen. Lewis Hershey's heels, burn a draft card for peace, hold a rally for decency, live in Peru for the Peace Corps, scout an Indian reservation for VISTA, shout "Kill a Commie for Christ!" Boss.

[18] Bringing the human form mixed in a new chemistry, a classic appreciation of form and movement wired to uninhibited electrodes of honesty and compassion.

[19] Bringing the new feminism, the female executive, the female militant, the "liberated" woman, the death of the "sex symbol," Ayn Rand and Raquel Welch, Margaret Mead and Barbarella.

[20] Bringing the new youth movement, millionaires under 30 who run record empires, geniuses under 30 who make scientific breakthroughs, bright bureaucrats under 30 in the White House and Congress, solid activities under 30 for McCarthy, for Humphrey, for Nixon. Yes, for Nixon.

[21] But it is not all Aquarius out of Haight-Ashbury, foaled in the East Village. It is not all hallucination, hair to there, dashikis and lovebeads, civil war infantry coats, chest medals, freakouts and James Brown on stage, motorcycles, funny smoke and bells on hightop moccasins.

[22] Within the Golden Era there is a quieter time, a more peaceful place. There are White House weddings and Lawrence Welk in living color in a million living rooms, Aristotle Onassis sharing his millions with a president's widow, Elizabeth Taylor getting the Cartier diamond from Dick. There is high style, there is cool living, there is beauty, there is taste.

[23] There is romance and fascination.

[24] Where Princess Margaret marries a photographer, where Bishop James Pike talks to his dead son, and writes a book about it. Where the lifestyle of the criminal grows grand enough to imagine the Star of India, a British mail train worth $7-million, the ransom for a Frank Sinatra Jr. Funky.

[25] The Golden Era finds the living mathematics of the star Cassiopeia, and the lights now blinking up there have long since gone. The reflection is in our head, and the gleam is in our eye.

[26] That is what the Golden Era teaches us. Take your head apart and put your own thing together.

[27] Life is a linear feat to be lived in cubic inches.

[28] And impossible to measure.

EXERCISES—*DECADE OF DESTINY*

Content

1. What is "non-McLuhan" man?
2. What is the "global village"?
3. What are the causes of the "new life"?
4. What are the characteristics of the "new life"?
5. What does the "Golden Era" teach us?

Style

1. What specific devices does Jolidon use to emphasize ideas?
2. In what specific ways does he vary the pace or speed of movement of his ideas?
3. What is the purpose and the effect of beginning paragraphs (10), (12), (13), (14), (16), (17), (18), (19), and (20) with the word *beginning*? Why does Jolidon break this pattern in paragraph (21)?
4. Is the diction of this essay primarily denotative or connotative? formal, informal, or colloquial? Why?
5. What is the tone of the essay? Explain.
6. What is Jolidon's angle of vision?
7. Three of Jolidon's major rhetorical devices are allusion, irony, and juxtaposition of opposites. In your textbook, mark several examples of each. Be prepared to discuss the effect of each.
8. Why did Jolidon use parentheses to enclose paragraphs (11) and (15)?
9. Why are paragraph (23), (27), and (28) such brief paragraphs?
10. Does Jolidon use more coordination or subordination in sentence structure? Why?
11. What is the effect of ending paragraphs with single words, such as "Yeah" (12), "Dig" (13), "Wow" (16), and "Boss" (17)?

Application of Stylistic Techniques

1. Emulating the style of Jolidon, briefly explain a movement, custom, change, or tradition.
2. Although every author's style reflects his personality, determine whether Jolidon's style is more similar to that of Hemingway or Faulkner, and why.
3. Parse or analyze sentence 2 of paragraph (21). Then write an original sentence of the same pattern and tone.

Suggestions for Writing

1. In an essay, explain how you think the Seventies are different from the Sixties.
2. In an essay, explain what you consider to be the major causes of our present cultural patterns.
3. In an essay, describe a scene or an event, stressing the irony and contrasts of the situation. You might, for example, describe a parade, a march, a church service, a rock concert, or a traffic jam.

PART THREE

Method and Style

When you write, you begin with an experience or an idea which you want to communicate to others. You may want to capture and share the beauty of the beach at sunset, to express the importance of your first lengthy visit away from home, to explain that folk-rock lyrics provide the poetry of youth today, or to support your contention that abortion laws should be liberalized now. In order to communicate these ideas successfully, you must choose from the four basic methods of communication—description, narration, exposition, and argument—the method or combination of methods by which you can best accomplish your purpose. You will virtually never use any one mode to the simultaneous exclusion of all the others. You will, for example, usually use description and narration as aids to exposition and argument. Your purpose should determine the dominant method.

DESCRIPTION

To fulfill the purpose of capturing a beach scene at sunset, you would choose description as your dominant method. Description means giving the characteristics or qualities of something—a place, a person, or an object, even a process or an event. For effective description you should limit the description to a certain time and provide plenty of specific details to recreate the scene or object in the reader's mind. To organize these details, you would probably arrange them by spatial order; for the beach scene you would likely move from the sand to the surf to the sea to the horizon to the sky.

Description may be objective or subjective. Both types are based on fact, but the factual details included are selected according to purpose, audience, and importance. In objective description your purpose is to present information briefly, clearly, completely, and impersonally, in order to enable your reader to understand that information. Your aim is to communicate the essential facts in their simplest denotative and most unequivocal language. The appeal of objective description is to the intellect of your reader. Usually objective description is used for technical and scientific reports, and is written for a limited audience. For example, an ecologist might describe the beach scientifically in order to help the city council understand the necessity of providing funds for erosion control.

On the other hand, your purpose in subjective description is to evoke feeling or arouse emotion in any audience, and your appeal is to the emotions rather than to the intellect. This type of description goes beyond mere information-giving and, through a personalized treatment of the information, through connotative language, and through sensory appeals, adds vividness and evokes mood. A young woman might write a subjective description of the beach in a letter to her boyfriend, in order to convey her feelings of isolation and loneliness without him; or an author might use such a description to set the mood for an event in his short story or novel. To avoid undue mawkishness or gushiness, any writer of subjective description must exercise special control in his selection of details and diction.

NARRATION

To relate the events of your first extended period away from home at college, or in the service, or on a trip, you would choose narration, the method used to tell a story or to relate a series of events chronologically. The basic types of narration are fiction, based on imagination, and nonfiction, based on fact or experience. For our purposes in studying and developing style, we are primarily concerned with nonfiction; however, writers use similar techniques in both types of narration.

Familiarity with the kinds of nonfiction narration will help you choose the one appropriate for your purpose. Historical narration recounts an event in history based on fact. You read it in history books and newspapers. The "Warren Report" on the assassination of John F. Kennedy and the "Walker Report" on the events surrounding the 1968 Democratic Convention in Chicago are contemporary historical documents, as are the news accounts of the latest developments in Indochina or of the recent university demonstrations. Such narration is impersonal and attempts to be exhaustive. A second type of narration is speculative narration, which relates a possible event in history as it might have happened. Using historical characters, the writer creates an event that did not happen, but plausibly could have happened. Based on speculation as to what might have been, this type of narration is midway between nonfiction and fiction. Different writers might present an event in the life of Aristotle or of Queen Elizabeth I as historical narration, as speculative narration, or as historical fiction. All three writers would base their accounts on historical research, but treat the information differently.

Another type is experiential narration, retelling a personal experience simply for the purpose of sharing that experience—one the writer considers significant—with the reader. A fourth type is reminiscent narration, also based on personal experience, but written to capture and evoke emotion. Whereas historical narration is objective, experiential and reminiscent narration are subjective.

To communicate without becoming mawkish in these latter two types of narration, you must exercise the same control as you do in subjective description. To narrate your experience, you could select either the experiential or reminiscent type. If you want simply to relate the excitement of your first college basketball game or the interesting aspects of a trip to San Francisco, you would use experiential; but if you want to capture the nostalgia of youth lost while at college or in the service, you would use reminiscent.

EXPOSITION

The third basic method of communication is exposition. To explain an idea or a process, exposition is the method we use. Because all of us have many ideas or opinions to share with others, exposition is the dominant form of prose. It appeals primarily to the understanding; and in order to explain ideas clearly, a writer must clarify and support his generalizations with specific details. In exposition he can use a variety of means for development, such as examples, illustrations, analysis, classification, comparison, contrast, cause to effect, and definition. He must also consider the structure of his material. The structure of exposition may be either tight (careful attention to the meshing of incidents and details through logical organization and transition, i.e., James Baker's *Alienation*) or loose (use of one element, such as a person or a place, to unify incidents and details that might otherwise seem unrelated, i.e., George Frazier's *John Steinbeck! John Steinbeck! How Still We See Thee Lie*). A special type of exposition is process, explaining how to do something, such as how to scuba dive safely, or how something happens, such as how a storm develops. The level of process may be formal or informal.

Once you have chosen exposition as the method best suited to your purpose, you must choose the best means, structure, and level for clear communication to your specific audience. For example, if you want to explain to your classmates that folk-rock lyrics provide the significant poetry for youth today, you might use loose structure, colloquial level, and illustrations for development.

ARGUMENT

Argument, the fourth method of nonfiction prose, attempts by logical or sometimes emotional means to convince the readers of the truth or falsity of a proposition. For our purposes we classify argument into four basic types. First is the formal argument of hypothesis in which the specific purpose is to convince the readers to accept the writer's belief or proposition. An example might be your attempt through logical means to convince your friends to accept the idea that abortion laws are archaic and unjustified. On the other hand is the formal argument of policy in which the purpose is to bring about change. An example is a logical argument to persuade your classmates to encourage their legislators to change the abortion laws. A third type, emotional argument, now widespread in advertising and politics, also attempts to incite action, but employs devious techniques to appeal to the emotions and the subconscious. Typical of emotional argument is a radical conservative's denunciation of the morality of long-haired youth. Thinking people are aware of these techniques and reject such irrational attempts at persuasion. The fourth type, informal argument, employs a conversational tone and informal style to establish a close relationship with general readers and thus to convince them to agree with the writer's observations. When writing argument, you must be very careful to avoid alienating your readers, to avoid fallacies, and to avoid mere emotional burping. Valid, effective argument is one of the most difficult types of writing.

Thus, you first determine your purpose, then choose the method or combination of methods by which you can best accomplish your purpose. Your purpose, method, and audience govern and liberate your style: in keeping with these rhetorical elements, you determine the level, point of view, mood and tone, diction, and language patterns. This process of composition reflects your personality.

Thomas Henry Huxley (1825–1895), British scientist, educator, and essayist, influenced English thought not only by his writings, but also by his lectures on scientific, philosophical, and religious thought, directing his comments toward the layman in science and logic. His purpose was to promote the understanding of science as a method of thought useful to all people; he described science as "trained and organized common sense." His major ideas are expressed in *On the Advisableness of Improving Natural Knowledge, A Liberal Education, Science and Culture,* and *Evolution and Ethics.*

A Piece of Chalk

(Objective Description)

THOMAS HENRY HUXLEY

[1] The language of the chalk is not hard to learn, not nearly so hard as Latin, if you only want to get at the broad features of the story it has to tell; and I propose that we now set to work to spell that story out together.

[2] We all know that if we "burn" chalk the result is quick-lime. Chalk, in fact, is a compound of carbonic acid gas, and lime, and when you make it very hot the carbonic acid flies away and the lime is left. By this method of procedure we see the lime, but we do not see the carbonic acid. If, on the other hand, you were to powder a little chalk and drop it into a good deal of strong vinegar, there would be a great bubbling and fizzing, and, finally, a clear liquid, in which no sign of chalk would appear. Here you see the carbonic acid in the bubbles; the lime, dissolved in the vinegar, vanishes from sight. There are a great many other ways of showing that chalk is essentially nothing but carbonic acid and quick-lime. Chemists enunciate the result of all the experiments which prove this, by stating that chalk is almost wholly composed of "carbonate of lime."

[3] It is desirable for us to start from the knowledge of this fact, though it may not seem to help us very far towards

what we seek. For carbonate of lime is a widely-spread substance, and is met with under very various conditions. All sorts of limestones are composed of more or less pure carbonate of lime. The crust which is often deposited by waters which have drained through limestone rocks, in the form of what are called stalagmites and stalactites, is carbonate of lime. Or, to take a more familiar example, the fur on the inside of a tea-kettle is carbonate of lime; and, for anything chemistry tells us to the contrary, the chalk might be a kind of gigantic fur upon the bottom of the earth-kettle, which is kept pretty hot below.

[4] Let us try another method of making the chalk tell us its own history. To the unassisted eye chalk looks simply like a very loose and open kind of stone. But it is possible to grind a slice of chalk down so thin that you can see through it —until it is thin enough, in fact, to be examined with any magnifying power that may be thought desirable. A thin slice of the fur of a kettle might be made in the same way. If it were examined microscopically, it would show itself to be a more or less distinctly laminated mineral substance, and nothing more.

[5] But the slice of chalk presents a totally different appearance when placed under the microscope. The general mass of it is made up of very minute granules; but, imbedded in this matrix, are innumerable bodies, some smaller and some larger, but, on a rough average, not more than a hundredth of an inch in diameter, having a well-defined shape and structure. A cubic inch of some specimens of chalk may contain hundreds of thousands of these bodies, compacted together with incalculable millions of the granules.

[6] The examination of a transparent slice gives a good notion of the manner in which the components of the chalk are arranged, and of their relative proportions. But, by rubbing up some chalk with a brush in water and then pouring off the milky fluid, so as to obtain sediments of different degrees of fineness, the granules and the minute rounded bodies may be pretty well separated from one another, and submitted to microscopic examination, either as opaque or as transparent objects. By combining the views obtained in these various methods, each of the rounded bodies may be proved to be a beautifully-

constructed calcareous fabric, made up of a number of chambers, communicating freely with one another. The chambered bodies are of various forms. One of the commonest is something like a badly-grown raspberry, being formed of a number of nearly globular chambers of different sizes congregated together. It is called *Globigerina,* and some specimens of chalk consist of little else than *Globigerinæ* and granules. Let us fix our attention upon the *Globigerina.* It is the spoor of the game we are tracking. If we can learn what it is and what are the conditions of its existence, we shall see our way to the origin and past history of the chalk.

[7] A suggestion which may naturally enough present itself is, that these curious bodies are the result of some process of aggregation which has taken place in the carbonate of lime; that, just as in winter, the rime on our windows simulates the most delicate and elegantly arborescent foliage—proving that the mere mineral water may, under certain conditions, assume the outward form of organic bodies—so this mineral substance, carbonate of lime, hidden away in the bowels of the earth, has taken the shape of these chambered bodies. I am not raising a merely fanciful and unreal objection. Very learned men, in former days, have even entertained the notion that all the formed things found in rocks are of this nature; and if no such conception is at present held to be admissable, it is because long and varied experience has now shown that mineral matter never does assume the form and structure we find in fossils. If any one were to try to persuade you that an oystershell (which is also chiefly composed of carbonate of lime) had crystallized out of sea-water I suppose you would laugh at the absurdity. Your laughter would be justified by the fact that all experience tends to show that oyster-shells are formed by the agency of oysters, and in no other way. And if there were no better reasons, we should be justified, on like grounds, in believing that *Globigerina* is not the product of anything but vital activity.

[8] Happily, however, better evidence in proof of the organic nature of the *Globigerinæ* than that of analogy is forthcoming. It so happens that calcareous skeletons, exactly similar to the *Globigerinæ* of the chalk, are being formed, at

the present moment, by minute living creatures, which flourish in multitudes, literally more numerous than the sands of the sea-shore, over a large extent of that part of the earth's surface which is covered by the ocean.

EXERCISES—*A PIECE OF CHALK*

Content

1. Why is quick-lime the result when we burn chalk?
2. Of what is chalk composed?
3. What does a slice of chalk look like under a microscope?
4. What is *Globigerina*?

Style

1. Is Huxley's diction primarily denotative or connotative? Why?
2. Although this essay deals with a scientific subject, Huxley uses relatively few scientific terms. Why?
3. Huxley uses various techniques to clarify his ideas. Point out an example of each: contrast, comparison, analogy, example, definition, simile, metaphor.
4. Why does Huxley shift between first person, third person, and second person in this essay?
5. Is this essay formal, informal, or colloquial?

Application of Stylistic Techniques

1. Rewrite paragraph (2) in consistently third person plural objective point of view. Compare and contrast this version to Huxley's version.
2. Compare and contrast Huxley's style to the style in a modern science textbook.
3. Compare and contrast Huxley's style to the style of Rosenfeld in *Beyond the Moon.*

Suggestions for Writing

1. Using some of Huxley's techniques, write an essay on the language of the sea, the language of the stars, the language of the moon rocks, the language of fossils, the language of rock strata, the language of the genes, or another similar subject.
2. Explain a complex scientific process through the use of analogy.

John Updike (1932–) was born in Pennsylvania. He was graduated from Harvard in 1954, and worked for the *New Yorker* from 1955–1957. His major works include *Poorhouse Fair, Rabbit Run, The Centaur, Couples, Bech: A Book, Collections: The Same Door, Pigeon Feathers, The Carpentered Hen and Other Tame Creatures, Telephone Poles* (light verse), and *Assorted Prose.*

Spring Rain

(Subjective Description of a Place)

JOHN UPDIKE

[1] As the sky is pushed farther and farther away by the stiff-arms of this and that new steel frame, we sometimes wonder if what is reaching us is really weather at all. Whenever we have looked down at the street this spring, the perpetually rain-coated figures have appeared to be marching, jerkily foreshortened and steadfastly downstaring, under a kind of sooty fluorescence bearing little relation to the expansive and variable light of outdoors. The other day, as if at the repeated invitation of all those raincoats, it *did* rain, and we ventured outdoors ourself; that is to say, we made our way down several corridors and shafts and into a broader corridor called Forty-fourth Street, whose ceiling, if one bothered to look, consisted of that vaguely tonic, vaporish semi-opacity old-fashionedly termed the Firmament. On this day, the Firmament, which showed as a little, ragged strip wedged between the upper edges of the buildings, seemed in a heavy temper. Water was being silently inserted in the slots between the building tops, and a snappy little secondary rain was dripping from marquees, overhead signs, fire escapes, and ledges. On the street itself, whose asphalt had emerged from the blanket

of winter as creased and bumpy as a slept-on sheet, the water was conducting with itself an extravagantly complicated debate or ripple and counter-ripple, flow and anti-flow. It looked black but not dirty, and we thought, in that decisive syntactical way we reserve for such occasions, how all water is in passage from purity to purity. Puddles, gutters, sewers are incidental disguises: the casual avatars of perpetually reincarnated cloud droplets; momentary embarrassments, having nothing to do with the ineluctable poise of H_2O. Throw her on the street, mix her with candy wrappers, splash her with taxi wheels, she remains a virgin and a lady.

[2] The breeze caught its breath, the rain slackened, and the crowds that had been clustered in entranceways and under overhangs shattered and scattered like drying pods. We went over to Fifth Avenue; the buildings there, steeped in humidity, seemed to be a kind of print of their own images, a slightly too inky impression of an etching entitled "Fifth Avenue, Manhattan, c. 1962."

[3] No matter how long we live among rectangular stones, we still listen, in the pauses of a rain, for the sound of birds chirping as they shake themselves. No birds chirped, but the cars and buses squawked in deeper, openly humorous voices, and a trash can and a mailbox broke into conversation. CAST YOUR BALLOT HERE FOR A CLEANER NEW YORK, the trash can said, and MAIL EARLY IN THE DAY IT'S THE BETTER WAY, the mailbox beside it quickly responded. Both seemed to be rejoicing in the knowledge of their own inner snugness—of all the paper, folded or crumpled, addressed or discarded, that they had kept dry through the shower.

[4] The façades of the buildings darkened in tint, the lights within windows seemed not merely to burn but to blaze, and abruptly the rain was upon us again. In the instant before it fell, the air felt full of soft circular motions and a silent cry of "Hurry!" Pedestrians hustled for shelter. The search converted Fifth Avenue into a romantic and primitive setting for adventure. Pelted, we gained the cave of Finchley's Tudor arcade, with its patio-red floor and plastic orange tree and California sports jackets. The next instant, we ran on into the green glade of the Olivetti entrance, with its typewriter-

tipped stalagmite. Finally, we lodged in the narrow but deep shelter of Brentano's leafy *allée* of best-sellers, and from there we observed how the rain, a gusty downpour now, had the effect of exquisitely pressing the city down into itself. Everything—taxi roofs, umbrellas, cellophane-skinned hats, even squinting eyebrows—conveyed a sharp impression of shelter. Just as in a Miró painting the ovals and ellipses and lima beans of color sail across the canvas, so the city seemed a mobile conglomerate of dabs of dryness swimming through a fabric of wet. The rain intensified yet one more notch; the Fred F. French Building developed a positively livid stain along its bricks and the scene seemed squeezed so tight that it yielded the essence of granite, the very idea of a city. In a younger century, we might have wept for joy.

[5] And when the rain stopped at last, a supernaturally well-staged effect was produced in the north. Owing to the arrangement of the slabs of Rockefeller Center, the low, westward-moving sun had laid an exclusive shaft of light upon the face of St. Patrick's Cathedral. Like two elegant conical bottles, the steeples were brimful of a mildly creamy glow. We hastened toward the omen, but by the time we reached the site the sunshine had faded. Yet, looking up through the skeleton globe upheld here by the grimacing Atlas, we saw beyond the metal framework what was, patchy blue and scudding gray, indisputably sky.

EXERCISES—*SPRING RAIN*

Content

1. What is pushing the sky farther and farther away from us?
2. What invited the rain?
3. What did Updike think when he looked at the water in the street?
4. What did the trash can and the mailbox say to each other?
5. What was the effect of the gusty downpour of rain?
6. What happened when the rain stopped?

Style

1. What mood does the essay evoke?
2. Why does Updike use first person plural subjective point of view?

3. In Updike's essay, is the connotation of each of the following words favorable or unfavorable: *fluorescence* (1); *corridor* (1); *blanket* (1); *avatars* (1); *ineluctable* (1); *steeped* (2); *squawked* (3); *façades* (4); *primitive* (4); *cave* (4); *glade* (4); *stalagmite* (4); *stain* (4); *slabs* (5); *omen* (5)?
4. Mark in your textbook an example of each of the following: personification, simile, metaphor, allusion.
5. Analyze and explain how Updike combines chronological and spatial organization.
6. Of all of Updike's images, which do you consider most effective? Why?

Application of Stylistic Techniques

1. Compare and contrast Updike's and Huxley's essays. Consider the following points: method, tone, purpose, audience, level, angle of vision, diction, sentence structure.
2. Rewrite the first paragraph of Updike's essay from third person singular subjective point of view. How does the effect differ from that of the original version?
3. Rewrite paragraph (5) in an objective manner instead of Updike's subjective manner. How does the effect of your version differ from that of Updike's version?

Suggestions for Writing

1. Choose a phenomenon of nature, such as a rainstorm, a snowstorm, sunrise, or sunset. Write a short essay describing it objectively. Then write a short essay describing it subjectively.
2. Write an essay in which you convey the mood of a place, such as a busy city street, a mountain top, a party room, a classroom, or a church.

Deems Taylor (1885–1966), New York composer and critic, entered journalism after his graduation from New York University. He was a war correspondent and later a music critic. As a composer he is mainly self-taught. His best known work is *Through the Looking Glass,* an impressionistic suite for orchestra based on Lewis Carroll's fantasy. He also composed two operas, a suite for string quartet, incidental music for several Broadway plays, and many songs. *Of Men and Music* and *The Well-Tempered Listener* are books of criticism collected from his radio talks as the intermission speaker on the Sunday afternoon broadcasts of the New York Philharmonic Symphony from 1936–1943.

The Monster

(Subjective Description of a Person)

DEEMS TAYLOR

[1] He was an undersized little man, with a head too big for his body—a sickly little man. His nerves were bad. He had skin trouble. It was agony for him to wear anything next to his skin coarser than silk. And he had delusions of grandeur.

[2] He was a monster of conceit. Never for one minute did he look at the world or at people, except in relation to himself. He was not only the most important person in the world, to himself; in his own eyes he was the only person who existed. He believed himself to be one of the greatest dramatists in the world, one of the greatest thinkers, and one of the greatest composers. To hear him talk he was Shakespeare, and Beethoven, and Plato, rolled into one. And you would have had no difficulty in hearing him talk. He was one of the most exhausting conversationalists that ever lived. An evening with him was an evening spent in listening to a monologue. Some-

times he was brilliant; sometimes he was maddeningly tiresome. But whether he was being brilliant or dull, he had one sole topic of conversation: himself. What *he* thought and what *he* did.

[3] He had a mania for being in the right. The slightest hint of disagreement, from anyone, on the most trivial point, was enough to set him off on a harangue that might last for hours, in which he proved himself right in so many ways, and with such exhausting volubility, that in the end his hearer, stunned and deafened, would agree with him, for the sake of peace.

[4] It never occurred to him that he and his doing were not of the most intense and fascinating interest to anyone with whom he came in contact. He had theories about almost any subject under the sun, including vegetarianism, the drama, politics, and music; and in support of these theories he wrote pamphlets, letters, books . . . thousands upon thousands of words, hundreds and hundreds of pages. He not only wrote these things, and published them—usually at somebody else's expense—but he would sit and read them aloud, for hours, to his friends and his family.

[5] He wrote operas; and no sooner did he have the synopsis of a story, but he would invite—or rather summon—a crowd of his friends to his house and read it aloud to them. Not for criticism. For applause. When the complete poem was written, the friends had to come again, and hear *that* read aloud. Then he would publish the poem, sometimes years before the music that went with it was written. He played the piano like a composer, in the worst sense of what that implies, and he would sit down at the piano before parties that included some of the finest pianists of his time, and play for them, by the hour, his own music, needless to say. He had a composer's voice. And he would invite eminent vocalists to his house, and sing them his operas, taking all the parts.

[6] He had the emotional stability of a six-year-old child. When he felt out of sort, he would rave and stamp, or sink into suicidal gloom and talk darkly of going to the East to end his days as a Buddhist monk. Ten minutes later, when something pleased him, he would rush out of doors and run

around the garden, or jump up and down on the sofa, or stand on his head. He could be grief-stricken over the death of a pet dog, and he could be callous and heartless to a degree that would have made a Roman emperor shudder.

[7] He was almost innocent of any sense of responsibility. Not only did he seem incapable of supporting himself, but it never occurred to him that he was under any obligation to do so. He was convinced that the world owed him a living. In support of this belief, he borrowed money from everybody who was good for a loan—men, women, friends, or strangers. He wrote begging letters by the score, sometimes groveling without shame, at others loftily offering his intended benefactor the privilege of contributing to his support, and being mortally offended if the recipient declined the honor. I have found no record of his ever paying or repaying money to anyone who did not have a legal claim upon it.

[8] What money he could lay his hands on he spent like an Indian rajah. The mere prospect of a performance of one of his operas was enough to set him running up bills amounting to ten times the amount of his prospective royalties. On an income that would reduce a more scrupulous man to doing his own laundry, he would keep two servants. Without enough money in his pocket to pay his rent, he would have the walls and ceiling of his study lined with pink silk. No one will ever know—certainly he never knew—how much money he owed. We do know that his greatest benefactor gave him 6,000 dollars to pay the most pressing of his debts in one city, and a year later had to give him 16,000 dollars to enable him to live in another city without being thrown into jail for debt.

[9] He was equally unscrupulous in other ways. An endless procession of women marches through his life. His first wife spent twenty years enduring and forgiving his infidelities. His second wife had been the wife of his most devoted friend and admirer, from whom he stole her. And even while he was trying to persuade her to leave her first husband he was writing to a friend to inquire whether he could suggest some wealthy woman—*any* wealthy woman—whom he could marry for her money.

[10] He was completely selfish in his other personal

relationships. His liking for his friends was measured solely by the completeness of their devotion to him, or by their usefulness to him, whether financial or artistic. The minute they failed him—even by so much as refusing a dinner invitation—or began to lessen in usefulness, he cast them off without a second thought. At the end of his life he had exactly one friend left whom he had known even in middle age.

[11] He had a genius for making enemies. He would insult a man who disagreed with him about the weather. He would pull endless wires in order to meet some man who admired his work, and was able and anxious to be of use to him—and would proceed to make a mortal enemy of him with some idiotic and wholly uncalled-for exhibition of arrogance and bad manners. A character in one of his operas was a caricature of one of the most powerful music critics of his day. Not content with burlesquing him, he invited the critic to his house and read him the libretto aloud in front of his friends.

[12] The name of this monster was Richard Wagner. Everything that I have said about him you can find on record —in newspapers, in police reports, in the testimony of people who knew him, in his own letters, between the lines of his autobiography. And the curious thing about this record is that it doesn't matter in the least.

[13] Because this undersized, sickly, disagreeable, fascinating little man was right all the time. The joke was on us. He *was* one of the world's great dramatists; he *was* a great thinker; he *was* one of the most stupendous musical geniuses that, up to now, the world has ever seen. The world did owe him a living. People couldn't know those things at the time, I suppose; and yet to us, who know his music, it does seem as though they should have known. What if he did talk about himself all the time? If he talked about himself for twenty-four hours every day for the span of his life he would not have uttered half the number of words that other men have spoken and written about him since his death.

[14] When you consider what he wrote—thirteen operas and music dramas, eleven of them still holding the stage, eight of them unquestionably worth ranking among the world's

great musico-dramatic masterpieces—when you listen to what he wrote, the debts and heartaches that people had to endure from him don't seem much of a price. Eduard Hanslick, the critic whom he caricatured in *Die Meistersinger* and who hated him ever after, now lives only because he was caricatured in *Die Meistersinger*. The women whose hearts he broke are long since dead: and the man who could never love anyone but himself has made them deathless atonement, I think, with *Tristan und Isolde*. Think of the luxury with which for a time, at least, fate rewarded Napoleon, the man who ruined France and looted Europe; and then perhaps you will agree that a few thousand dollars' worth of debts were not too heavy a price to pay for the *Ring* trilogy.

[15] What if he was faithless to his friends and to his wives? He had one mistress to whom he was faithful to the day of his death: music. Not for a single moment did he ever compromise with what he believed, with what he dreamed. There is not a line of his music that could have been conceived by a little mind. Even when he is dull, or downright bad, he is dull in the grand manner. There is a greatness about his worst mistakes. Listening to his music, one does not forgive him for what he may or may not have been. It is not a matter of forgiveness. It is a matter of being dumb with wonder that his poor brain and body didn't burst under the torment of the demon of creative energy that lived inside him, struggling, clawing, scratching to be released; tearing, shrieking at him to write the music that was in him. The miracle is that what he did in the little space of seventy years could have been done at all, even by a great genius. Is it any wonder that he had no time to be a man?

EXERCISES—*THE MONSTER*

Content

1. Who was "the monster"? Is the title appropriate to describe him?
2. Why doesn't it matter that he was a monster?
3. What is the irony of Eduard Hanslick being caricatured in *Die Meistersinger*?

4. To what one mistress was "the monster" faithful?
5. Why didn't "the monster" have any time to be a man?
6. What is the main idea of this essay?

Style

1. What is Taylor's attitude toward the man he calls "the monster"? How does he reveal this attitude?
2. Why does Taylor devote so little space to physical description?
3. Why does Taylor wait until paragraph (12) to reveal the identity of "the monster"? What effect does the withholding of the identity have?
4. This essay is composed of two parts. What paragraph functions as transition between these parts?
5. Is Taylor's diction primarily denotative or connotative?
6. How does Taylor use parallelism in this essay?
7. What is the effect of Taylor's ending the essay with a question?
8. Why did Taylor use third person singular subjective point of view?
9. What is Taylor's purpose in this essay?
10. Why does Taylor use general to specific order instead of specific to general order in most of his paragraphs?

Application of Stylistic Techniques

1. Taylor develops most of his paragraphs by using details and examples to support clear topic sentences. Use one of his topic sentences as the first sentence of a paragraph of your own. Develop your paragraph by at least five details concerning a person you know.
2. Rewrite paragraph (5) in an objective manner.

Suggestions for Writing

1. Using plenty of details, write a character analysis of someone you know well. Be subjective, but not mawkish.
2. In an essay, agree or disagree with Taylor's attitude toward geniuses. Support your position with plenty of examples.

Edward Gibbon (1737–1794), English historian, born at Putney-on-Thames, England, attended Westminster and Magdalen College, Oxford, but received his most valuable education through extensive, independent reading. He settled in London and from 1774–1783 served in Parliament, which he considered "a school of civil prudence." In 1772 he began work on his monumental work *The History of the Decline and Fall of the Roman Empire;* the first volume was published in 1776, and the sixth and last volume in 1788. This historical masterpiece is considered the greatest historical work in the English language.

Rome Besieged

(Historical Narration)

EDWARD GIBBON

[1] We may fairly estimate the inhabitants of Rome at twelve hundred thousand—a number which cannot be thought excessive for the capital of a mighty empire, though it exceeds the populousness of the greatest cities of modern Europe.

[2] Such was the state of Rome under the reign of Honorius, at the time when the Gothic army formed the siege, or rather the blockade, of the city. By a skillful disposition of his numerous forces, who impatiently watched the moment of an assault, Alaric encompassed the walls, commanded the twelve principal gates, intercepted all communication with the adjacent country, and vigilantly guarded the navigation of the Tiber, from which the Romans derived the surest and most plentiful supply of provisions. The first emotions of the nobles and of the people were those of surprise and indignation that a vile barbarian should dare to insult the capital of the world; but their arrogance was soon humbled by misfortune; and their unmanly rage, instead of being directed against an enemy in arms, was meanly exercised on a defenceless and innocent victim. Perhaps in the person of Serena the Romans might

have respected the niece of Theodosius, the aunt, nay even the adoptive mother, of the reigning emperor; they abhorred the widow of Stilicho, and they listened with credulous passion to the tale of calumny which accused her of maintaining a secret and criminal correspondence with the Gothic invader. Actuated or overawed by the same popular frenzy, the senate, without requiring any evidence of her guilt, pronounced the sentence of her death. Serena was ignominiously strangled; and the infatuated multitude were astonished to find that this cruel act of injustice did not immediately produce the retreat of the barbarians and the deliverance of the city.

[3] That unfortunate city gradually experienced the distress of scarcity and at length the horrid calamities of famine. The daily allowance of three pounds of bread was reduced to one-half, to one third, to nothing; and the price of corn still continued to rise in a rapid and extravagant proportion. The poorer citizens, who were unable to purchase the necessaries of life, solicited the precarious charity of the rich; and for a while the public misery was alleviated by the humanity of Læta, the widow of the emperor Gratian, who had fixed her residence at Rome and consecrated to the use of the indigent the princely revenue which she annually received from the grateful successors of her husband. But these private and temporary donatives were insufficient to appease the hunger of a numerous people, and the progress of famine invaded the marble palaces of the senators themselves. The persons of both sexes who had been educated in the enjoyment of ease and luxury discovered how little is requisite to supply the demands of nature and lavished their unavailing treasures of gold and silver to obtain the coarse and scanty sustenance which they would formerly have rejected with disdain. The food, the most repugnant to sense or imagination, the ailments the most unwholesome and pernicious to the constitution, were eagerly devoured and fiercely disputed by the rage of hunger. A dark suspicion was entertained that some desperate wretches fed on the bodies of their fellow-creatures whom they had secretly murdered; and even mothers (such was the horrid conflict of the two most powerful instincts implanted by nature in the human breast), even mothers are said to have tasted the

flesh of their slaughtered infants! Many thousands of the inhabitants of Rome expired in their houses or in the streets for want of sustenance; and as the public sepulchres without the walls were in the power of the enemy, the stench which arose from so many putrid and unburied carcasses infected the air, and the miseries of famine were succeeded and aggravated by the contagion of a pestilential disease.

[4] The assurances of speedy and effectual relief, which were repeatedly transmitted from the court of Ravenna, supported for some time the fainting resolution of the Romans, till at length the despair of any human aid tempted them to accept the offers of a preternatural deliverance. Pompeianus, præfect of the city, had been persuaded, by the art of fanaticism of some Tuscan diviners, that by the mysterious force of spells and sacrifices they could extract the lightning from the clouds and point those celestial fires against the camp of the barbarians. The important secret was communicated to Innocent, the bishop of Rome; and the successor of St. Peter is accused, perhaps without foundation, of preferring the safety of the republic to the rigid severity of the Christian worship. But when the question was agitated in the senate, when it was proposed as an essential condition that those sacrifices should be performed in the Capitol by the authority and in the presence of the magistrates, the majority of that respectable assembly, apprehensive either of the Divine or of the Imperial displeasure, refused to join in an act which appeared almost equivalent to the public restoration of paganism.

[5] The last resource of the Romans was in the clemency, or at least in the moderation, of the king of the Goths. The senate, who in this emergency assumed the supreme powers of government, appointed two ambassadors to negotiate with the enemy. This important trust was delegated to Basilius, a senator of Spanish extraction already conspicuous in the administration of provinces, and to John, the first tribune of the notaries, who was peculiarly qualified by his dexterity in business as well as by his former intimacy with the Gothic prince. When they were introduced into his presence they declared, perhaps in a more lofty style than became

their abject condition, that the Romans were resolved to maintain their dignity either in peace or war, and that if Alaric refused them a fair and honourable capitulation he might sound his trumpets and prepare to give battle to an innumerable people exercised in arms and animated by despair. "The thicker the hay, the easier it is mowed," was the concise reply of the barbarian; and the rustic metaphor was accompanied by a loud and insulting laugh, expressive of his contempt for the menaces of an unwarlike populace enervated by luxury before they were emaciated by famine.

[6] He then condescended to fix the ransom which he would accept as the price of his retreat from the walls of Rome: *all* the gold and silver in the city, whether it were the property of the state or of individuals; *all* the rich and precious movables; and *all* the slaves who could prove their title to the name of *barbarians.* The ministers of the senate presumed to ask, in a modest and suppliant tone, "If such, O king! are your demands, what do you intend to leave us?" "YOUR LIVES," replied the haughty conqueror; they trembled and retired. Yet before they retired a short suspension of arms was granted, which allowed some time for a more temperate negotiation. The stern features of Alaric were insensibly relaxed; he abated much of the rigour of his terms, and at length consented to raise the siege on the immediate payment of five thousand pounds of gold, of thirty thousand pounds of silver, of four thousand robes of silk, of three thousand pieces of fine scarlet cloth, and of three thousand pounds weight of pepper. But the public treasury was exhausted; the annual rents of the great estates in Italy and the provinces were intercepted by the calamities of war; the gold and gems had been exchanged, during the famine, for the vilest sustenance; the hoards of secret wealth were still concealed by the obstinacy of avarice; and some remains of consecrated spoils afforded the only resource that could avert the impending ruin of the city. As soon as the Romans had satisfied the rapacious demands of Alaric they were restored in some measure to the enjoyment of peace and plenty. Several of the gates were cautiously opened; the importation of provisions from the river and the adjacent country was no longer obstructed

by the Goths; the citizens resorted in crowds to the free market which was held during three days in the suburbs; and while the merchants who undertook this gainful trade made a considerable profit, the future subsistence of the city was secured by the ample magazines which were deposited in the public and private granaries.

[7] A more regular discipline than could have been expected was maintained in the camp of Alaric; and the wise barbarian justified his regard for the faith of treaties by the just severity with which he chastised a party of licentious Goths who had insulted some Roman citizens on the road to Ostia. His army, enriched by the contributions of the capital, slowly advanced into the fair and fruitful province of Tuscany, where he proposed to establish his winter-quarters; and the Gothic standard became the refuge of forty thousand barbarian slaves who had broken their chains and aspired, under the command of their great deliverer, to revenge the injuries and the disgrace of their cruel servitude. About the same time he received a more honourable reinforcement of Goths and Huns, whom Adolphus, the brother of his wife, had conducted at his pressing invitation from the banks of the Danube to those of the Tiber, and who had cut their way, with some difficulty and loss, through the superior numbers of the Imperial troops. A victorious leader, who united the daring spirit of a barbarian with the art and discipline of a Roman general, was at the head of an hundred thousand fighting men; and Italy pronounced with terror and respect the formidable name of Alaric.

EXERCISES—*ROME BESIEGED*

Content

1. How did Alaric blockade Rome?
2. Why was Serena sentenced to death?
3. How did the scarcity of food affect the city?
4. Why was the Tuscans' plan for deliverance rejected?
5. What were the original terms of Alaric's ransom which he would accept as the price of his retreat from the walls of the city? What did he finally settle for?

Style

1. Is this excerpt formal, informal, or colloquial?
2. What is the tone of the essay?
3. Historians usually try to be as objective and denotative as possible. Can Gibbon's use of the following words be justified: *skillful disposition* (2) *vile barbarian* (2); *unfortunate city* (3); *horrid calamities* (3); *precarious charity* (3); *peculiarly qualified* (5); *perhaps in a more lofty style than became their abject condition* (5); *this rustic metaphor* (5); *the haughty conqueror* (6); *rapacious demands* (6)?
4. Note two examples of each of the following: normal sentence, balanced sentence, and periodic sentence.
5. Is Gibbon's dense style (much coordination and subordination) appropriate for his subject?

Application of Stylistic Techniques

1. Rewrite paragraph (3) in first person singular subjective point of view, as an eye witness might relate the events.
2. Compare and contrast Gibbon's style with that of an article in a newspaper or news magazine. How can you account for the differences? Which do you prefer? Why?

Suggestions for Writing

1. Using paragraph (3) as a pattern, write an objective explanation of how water pollution, air pollution, water shortage, or the announcement of an approaching storm affects the people of an area.
2. Using the same topic as in number 1 above, write a subjective account of the effects upon the people.

Thomas Carlyle (1795–1881), born of Scottish parents, grew up in an atmosphere of Puritanism and was educated at Edinburgh University where he became interested in science and philosophy. He wrote religious, philosophical, and historical essays; his style is marked by passionate bursts of persuasion and strong confidence in his message. His works include *Sartor Resartus,* a semi-autobiography; *Heroes and Hero-Worship,* biographical essays of famous world leaders; and *History of the French Revolution,* a stirring account of the French struggle for liberty.

The Fall of the Bastille
(Speculative Narration)

THOMAS CARLYLE

[1] The Bastille is besieged!

[2] On, then, all Frenchmen that have hearts in your bodies! Roar with all your throats of cartilage and metal, ye sons of liberty; stir spasmodically whatsoever of utmost faculty is in you, soul, body, or spirit, for it is the hour! Smite thou, Louis Tournay, cartwright of the Marais, old soldier of the Régiment Dauphiné; smite at that outer drawbridge chain, though the fiery hail whistles around thee! Never, over nave or felloe, did thy ax strike such a stroke. Down with it, man; down with it to Orcus; let the whole accursed edifice sink thither, and tyranny be swallowed up forever! Mounted, some say, on the roof of the guardroom, some "on bayonets stuck into joints of the wall," Louis Tournay smites, brave Aubin Bonnemère (also an old soldier) seconding him. The chain yields, breaks; the huge drawbridge slams down, thundering. Glorious! and yet, alas! it is still but the outworks. The eight grim towers with their invalide musketry, their paving stones and cannon mouths, still soar aloft intact; ditch yawning impassable, stone-faced; the inner drawbridge with its *back* toward us; the Bastille is still to take! . . .

[3] Paris, wholly, has got to the acme of its frenzy, whirled all ways by panic madness. At every street barricade there whirls, simmering, a minor whirlpool, strengthening the barricade, since God knows what is coming; and all minor whirlpools play distractedly into that grand fire maelstrom which is lashing round the Bastille.

[4] And so it lashes and roars. Cholat, the wine merchant, has become an impromptu cannoneer. See Georget, of the marine service, fresh from Brest, play the King of Siam's cannon. Singular (if we were not used to the like). Georget lay last night taking his ease at his inn; the King of Siam's cannon also lay, knowing nothing of *him* for a hundred years; yet now, at the right instant, they have got together, and discourse eloquent music; for, hearing what was toward, Georget sprang from the Brest diligence, and ran. Gardes Françaises, also, will be here with real artillery. Were not the walls so thick! Upward from the esplanade, horizontally from all neighboring roofs and windows, flashes one irregular deluge of musketry, without effect. The invalides lie flat, firing comparatively at their ease from behind stone; hardly through portholes show the tip of a nose. We fall, shot, and make no impression!

[5] Let conflagration rage of whatsoever is combustible! Guardrooms are burnt, invalides messrooms. A distracted "peruke maker with two fiery torches" is for burning "the saltpeters of the arsenal," had not a woman run screaming, had not a patriot, with some tincture of natural philosophy, instantly struck the wind out of him (butt of musket on pit of stomach), overturned barrels, and stayed the devouring element. A young, beautiful lady seized, escaping, in these outer courts, and thought, falsely, to be De Launay's daughter, shall be burnt in De Launay's sight; she lies, swooned, on a paillasse; but, again, a patriot—it is brave Aubin Bonnemère, the old soldier—dashes in, and rescues her. Straw is burnt; three cartloads of it, hauled hither, go up in white smoke, almost to the choking of patriotism itself; so that Elie had, with singed brows, to drag back one cart, and Réole, the "gigantic haberdasher," another. Smoke as of Tophet, confusion as of Babel, noise as of the crack of doom!

[6] Blood flows, the aliment of new madness. The wounded are carried into houses of the Rue Cerisaie; the dying leave their last mandate not to yield till the accursed stronghold fall. And yet, alas! how fall? The walls are so thick! Deputations, three in number, arrive from the Hôtel-de-Ville. These wave their town flag in the arched gateway, and stand, rolling their drum, but to no purpose. In such crack of doom De Launay cannot hear them, dare not believe them; they return, with justified rage, the whew of lead still singing in their ears. What to do? The firemen are here, squirting with their fire pumps on the invalides cannon to wet the touch-holes; they unfortunately cannot squirt so high, but produce only clouds of spray. Individuals of classical knowledge propose *catapults*. Santerre, the sonorous brewer of the suburb Saint-Antoine, advises rather that the place be fired by "a mixture of phosphorous and oil of turpentine spouted up through forcing pumps." O Spinola-Santerre, hast thou the mixture *ready?* Every man his own engineer! And still the fire deluge abates not: even women are firing, and Turks—at least one woman (with her sweetheart) and one Turk. Gardes Françaises have come: real cannon, real cannoneers. Usher Maillard is busy; half-pay Elie, half-pay Hulin, rage in the midst of thousands.

[7] How the great Bastille clock ticks (inaudible) in its inner court, there, at its ease, hour after hour; as if nothing special, for it or the world, were passing! It toiled one when the firing began, and is now pointing toward five, and still the firing slakes not. Far down in their vaults, the seven prisoners hear muffled din as of earthquakes; their turnkeys answer vaguely.

[8] Woe to thee, De Launay, with thy poor hundred invalides! . . .

[9] What shall De Launay do? One thing only De Launay could have done—what he said he would do. Fancy him sitting, from the first, with lighted taper, within arm's length of the powder magazine; motionless, like an old Roman senator, or bronze lamp holder; coldly apprising Thuriot, and all men, by a slight motion of his eye, what his resolution was.

Harmless he sat there, while unharmed; but the king's fortress, meanwhile, could, might, would, or should in nowise be surrendered, save to the king's messengers; one old man's life is worthless, so it be lost with honor; but think, ye brawling *canaille*, how will it be when a whole Bastille springs skyward? In such statuesque, taper-holding attitude, one fancies De Launay might have left Thuriot, the red clerks of the Basoche, curé of St. Stephen, and all the tagrag and bobtail of the world, to work their will.

[10] And yet, withal, he could not do it. . . . Distracted he hovers between two—hopes in the middle of despair; surrenders not his fortress; declares that he will blow it up, seizes torches to blow it up, and does not blow it. Unhappy old De Launay, it is the death agony of the Bastille and thee! Jail, jailoring, and jailor, all three, such as they may have been, must finish.

[11] For four hours now has the world bedlam roared; call it the world chimera, blowing fire! The poor invalides have sunk under their battlements, or rise only with reversed muskets; they have made a white flag of napkins, go beating the chamade, or seeming to beat, for one can hear nothing. The very Swiss at the portcullis look weary of firing, disheartened in the fire deluge; a porthole at the drawbridge is opened, as by one that would speak. See Huissier Maillard, the shifty man! On his plank, swinging over the abyss of that stoned ditch, plank resting on parapet, balanced by weight of patriots, he hovers perilous—such a dove toward such an ark! Deftly, thou shifty usher; one man already fell and lies smashed, far down there against the masonry! Usher Maillard falls not; deftly, unerringly, he walks, with outspread palm. The Swiss holds a paper through the porthole; the shifty usher snatches it and returns. Terms of surrender: Pardon, immunity to all! Are they accepted? *"Foi d'officier* [on the word of an officer]," answers half-pay Hulin, or half-pay Elie—for men do not agree on it—"they are!" Sinks the drawbridge, Usher Maillard bolting it when down; rushes in the living deluge; the Bastille is fallen!

[12] *Victoire! La Bastille est prise!*

EXERCISES—*THE FALL OF THE BASTILLE*

Content

1. Why wasn't the arsenal burned?
2. Explain the meaning of this sentence: "Every man his own engineer!" (paragraph (6))
3. What is De Launoy's dilemma?
4. What act of bravery did Maillord perform?
5. What were the terms of surrender?

Style

1. Although the fall of the Bastille occurred before Carlyle was born, he relates these events as vividly as an eye witness would. What techniques does he employ to achieve this sense of immediacy and realism?
2. What is Carlyle's purpose in this excerpt?
3. What is Carlyle's tone? Explain.
4. What is Carlyle's angle of vision? Explain.
5. How does Carlyle evoke emotion in the reader? What emotions do you feel as you read this piece?
6. Is Carlyle's diction primarily denotative or connotative?
7. What is the effect of Carlyle's great variety in sentence length? For what purposes does he use short sentences? long sentences?
8. Why does Carlyle use so many exclamatory sentences?
9. Why does Carlyle use second person imperative in paragraph (2)?
10. Why are the first and last paragraphs so brief?

Application of Stylistic Techniques

1. Compare and contrast Carlyle's style to Gibbon's style in historical narration.
2. Rewrite the first five sentences of paragraph (2), eliminating the second person imperative point of view.
3. Rewrite paragraph (11) from an objective position instead of the subjective.

Suggestions for Writing

1. Choose an event in history, and using Carlyle's speculative method, write a vivid, subjective account of it. Use your imagination to achieve the emotional effect of an eye witness account.
2. Using a common event (such as taking an examination, eating a meal, or driving to school), write a parody burlesquing or imitating Carlyle's essay.

John Keats (1920–   ) is a contemporary American freelance writer and social critic whose major interest lies in education. He was a child during Prohibition, an adolescent during the Depression and the New Deal of the 1930's, and a soldier in World War II. In *The New Romans* he points out the tragic difference between America as it is and America as it could be, and in *The Sheepskin Psychosis* he examines the effects of higher education on the masses in America. Also, he has contributed to *Holiday, Life,* and *Saturday Evening Post,* and has written *Schools Without Scholars* and *They Fought Alone.*

On Running Away

(Experiential Narration)

JOHN KEATS

[1] Ralph and I considered the possibility of police pursuit. We briefly debated the advisability of disguises. We decided that the wisest course was to try to postpone pursuit. To that end, we would tell our parents that we had each been invited by the other boy's family to spend the summer in Michigan. We made our secret plans, and one afternoon, shortly after high-school graduation, we uttered our little lies and headed for the railroad yards. That evening, while our families were no doubt discovering that neither owned a summer camp in Michigan, we were already far from our comfortable New Jersey suburb, rattling west across America. Our object was to get to China to join the American Volunteer Group in its aerial combat against the Japanese.

[2] Two weeks later America was still rattling past, but now there was not a tree or house in sight. We slid the boxcar door wide open at dawn to see a vast prairie, pale gold in the east, dark in the west. Mountaintops shone above the shadows as they caught the first light. We were lonely, stiff

from sleeping on a jittering wooden floor, cold, and tired of eating canned dog food. I have a clear memory of that morning in the morning of my life, now more than a quarter century ago. I can see in mind's eye those empty distances, and feel again that emptiness inside me. I am certain that Ralph was as fearful as I that day, but we did not admit our misgivings to each other. That would have been as much an admission of failure as returning home.

[3] As we sat in the open doorway, watching the day brighten and the Rockies draw slowly nearer, I reflected on the recent past. No small part of the charm of running away from home lay in the presumption that the world was full of dangers. Naturally, we were eager to encounter them. Nothing was more pleasant than to imagine returning home as bronzed soldiers of fortune, bearing interesting scars and laden with the gifts of a grateful Chinese government. En route to the wars we would, of course, slay the usual number of local dragons. We were not running away from life but into it. We were sure that what we had left behind was lifeless. Our New Jersey suburb was pudgy with Buicks and Packards; a thing of clean linen, toothbrushes, electric razors, the once-a-week sound of the maid running the vacuum cleaner, and the empty conversations of soft-bellied people who worked in offices and played bridge and went to Bermuda in the spring.

[4] Our view of ourselves, now that we rode boxcars and rolled our own cigarettes, was that we were tough. We wore blue denims, and soot from the coal-burning trains was ground into our clothing and our skin. Our adolescent stubble always seemed to be three days old. The men we now met were, for the most part, illiterates. The only woman we had seen on the trains had been a moron who was the chattel of a man who offered her to us for a dime each. One of the boys we had met was a male prostitute bound for Los Angeles. Two of the men in the gondola ahead of us looked to be thieves. There was no question about it: we were seeing Life. Unfortunately, it only too closely resembled the one we had left.

[5] I could not help thinking, as we clacked along, that we knew of two thieves at home. One was a member of Rotary; the other, a minister's son. How was the man with the moron

different from the parents who haunted summer hotels in perpetual hope of selling their unattractive daughters into matrimony? One of our high-school classmates had been established in a New York apartment by a successful businessman. The difference between that boy and the one headed for Los Angeles was that one moved in wealthier—I almost said better—circles. I have said that Ralph and I were inwardly fearful, but I should make clear that what was secretly feared was that life would prove not challenging but merely dull. In fact, we were finding it not only dull but dirty.

[6] There were perils, but they were largely mechanical. For instance, one of our fellow passengers, an elderly nondescript, had made the mistake of dozing in the sunlight near the forward edge of a boxcar roof. When the cars banged together as the fast freight began to brake, clattering down the long hill into Cheyenne, the first sudden lurch tossed him forward, off the roof and under the wheels, which instantly bisected him. One night when Ralph and I sheltered from the rain in a sort of cave formed by overhanging boards piled on a flatcar, we narrowly escaped a similar fate when the load shifted as we rounded a curve. Stupidity, we realized, was lethal. But where were the unknown dangers with which the world was supposedly replete? Specifically, where were the toughs and murderers who, in the public mind, so thickly populated the hobo jungles and the Hoovervilles?

[7] We met none. The well-fed burghers of our hometown, to whom the Depression was more of a nuisance than a catastrophe, regarded the scarecrows of the Hoovervilles as dubiously as a French marquis might have looked on a Parisian mob in 1790, but they were wrong. At least in the West, the hobo jungles were merely unofficial public campsites tenanted by a slowly changing population of migrants down on their luck. Feeling a need for government, these men formed their own. Many were veterans of World War I, and in camp after camp a former sergeant was elected or appointed leader. He greeted new arrivals, assigned them huts or sleeping space and explained the rules: *No fighting, thieves get beat up, you keep your place clean. And remember, try to bring back something for chow. Everybody brings something for chow.*

[8] In the America of those days everyone understood everyone else's problem, because it was also his own. If a man could not find work in one town, he tried another. Having no money to spend for transportation, he thumbed rides (which those who had cars were glad to offer), or he hopped a freight (while brakemen looked the other way). The people on the road were not derelicts. The derelicts, then as now, lived in the Skid Rows of our cities. All the men and boys on the road, however modest their activities and backgrounds, were looking for work. Some were bindle stiffs who had known nothing all their lives except stoop labor, moving forever from harvest to harvest. Others were genuine hobos—men who could work at nearly any trade, but whose free choice it was to hold no job long. All hobos said they intended to settle down someday, but not just yet. There was still a lot of country they wanted to see first. With rare exceptions, we met none but friends. Perhaps it is true that in good times no one takes to the road but the bad, but in our bad times we met virtually none but the good.

[9] Ralph and I had looked for jobs wherever the trains stopped on our way through the Midwest, and while we found none, there were always housewives who would put their cares aside to consider ours. They would give us make-work so that we should not seem beggars. We would wash the windows, or whitewash the henhouse, or clean the yard or the rain gutters, and while we puttered, the woman would prepare us a meal. Often as not they would also give us a package of food to take to the train. In small towns everyone knew the train schedules, and sometimes we would be told, "Gracious, there *is* some work I do want done, but you boys won't have time for it before the train leaves, so why don't you just sit down and I'll try to find something in the icebox."

[10] It was disappointing to be welcomed everywhere, when it was so important to us to learn whether we could make our unaided way through a violent world. Of course, we heard that the railroad detectives were the sadistic enemies of the tramp. We heard they loved nothing more than to beat a defenseless man insensible and toss his body on an outbound freight. The most famous of these detectives was one Green

River Slim. Alas, we never saw a yard detective, and Green River Slim turned out to be just as imaginary, and as ubiquitous, as that other great American whose name was also found chalked upon a thousand boxcars (and who later would go to war)—Kilroy.

[11] In retrospect it is clear to me that Ralph and I were the only people of our acquaintance on the road who were dangerous. We were looking for trouble; everyone else was looking for work. Our ambition was to kill Japanese for fun and money, and meanwhile prove to the world how tough we were. Nobody seemed to view us in just this light except, perhaps, a toothless old wreck, with breath like a vulture's, who accosted us outside a Skid Row bar in Chicago.

[12] "Want to see how hard you can hit?" he asked us. "Gimme a quarter, I'll let you hit me. See can you knock me out."

[13] He followed us for nearly a block, pleading, promising not to hit back, flattering us, and finally, when he saw it was no use, cursing. Looking back on it, I think we fled from him.

[14] Novelty, rather than true discovery, entertained us to the foothills of the Rockies. It would be years before we learned the truth of Montaigne's remark that the traveler must take himself wherever he goes. Yet I do remember that our first sight of those mountains seemed a mockery; I remember the feeling of emptiness they created inside me. In themselves they were an enormous fact, and consideration of one fact led to a consideration of others. One was that no one wanted us to do anything for him except leave town; people were glad to help us on our way. Another was that we had nothing to offer anyone except manual labor, which was not in demand, or our money, which was. We had left home with two hundred dollars between us, all saved from the unearned money our families had allowed us. It had cost us thirty dollars to purchase blankets, denims, work shoes and sufficient dog food to carry us to South Dakota. Canned dog food recommended itself to us as the cheapest comestible to be had. It constituted a balanced diet, and was rather tasty—at first. The meals donated by housewives were occasional banquets,

but as the trains rolled farther west and the towns thinned out, dog food became our staple, and it seemed that we might have to consume another one hundred and seventy dollars' worth of it if we could not immediately find a ship for China. I now suspect that what caused my feeling of emptiness was a premonition that one could not live without money, but that no one could earn money save at the loss of one's freedom. The world seemed a jail.

[15] In the high Rockies, two boys our age boarded the train. They were Louis Wang, a Chinese-American of Fresno, and Phillip Benoff, a Russian-American from Los Angeles. They had gone adventuring to the East Coast and now were returning to California; Phil to join the Army and Louis to join a gambling house where he would run a dice table. We told them of our plans, and they decided to come along with us instead. In that moment we became an army, and the world brightened considerably. Changed by the alchemy of a dream, the mountains' vast sterility was transformed into a magnificence. We would sort the facts of life to suit ourselves. Crossing the Pacific would be no problem. Everyone knew that boys could get jobs as wipers to work a passage. Boys had been running away to sea for centuries. We had only to find a ship that needed four wipers.

[16] Before it was over, we must have walked the docks of every port on the West Coast—including those of minor fishing towns. *Were we members of the union?* No. *Let's see your identification paper.* We had none.

[17] *Do you have passports?* Passports?

[18] We went to the union offices. *Buddy, we got 3,000 guys on the beach, and every single one of them is an Able Seaman.*

[19] Ralph and I, blue-eyed and blond, went to Scandinavian shipping companies, saying, "Ay ban Swade. Ay yust want ship home." And they laughed and said they were sorry.

[20] We persisted until someone finally told us the truth about the American Volunteer Group. It seemed that the volunteers had been carefully selected by the United States Government from its ranks of Army, Navy and Marine Corps pilots. We went to the recruiting offices, only to be told

that we would need at least two years of college credits to qualify for the aviation-cadet programs. At this point, we all went to Fresno with Louis to think things over.

[21] College was out of the question for Louis and Phil, but Ralph and I had only to ask to go, and our parents would send us. In Fresno I began to see the fallacy of our position: our confidence in ourselves had all along been based on the assumption that we were different from all other men: not on the slightest feeling of identity with mankind. This could not be helped; we were what our first eighteen years had made us. At any moment we could have walked out of the shacks of the hobo jungle to the nearest Western Union office, and hours later been dressed in decent clothes, sitting down to the best dinner in the best hotel of whatever town it was, while a hotel clerk booked reservations for us on the next Pullman headed for Newark, New Jersey. The difference between us and all others was, as Smollett would say, wholly matter-money. In the back of our minds we had always known this, and it was the source of our strength and the source of our great weakness; it made us hold something back in our relationships with others; we were never identifying with them; thus a barrier, built of dollars, shut us off from the kindness of Midwestern housewives, and from Louis and Phil. We and the other people on the road were of different tribes.

[22] I do not mean to say that I worked all this out in so many words at age eighteen, sitting at the bar of a tacky one-story gambling house in Fresno, watching Chinese playing fan-tan and Americans shooting craps. I simply mean that I was then dimly but uneasily aware of what I am now saying. I remember that we did wonder aloud whether going back home to college would not be an admission of defeat, but that we rationalized our way to the view that the *only* path to war in the Chinese skies led through two years of college followed by an aviation-cadet program. This decided, we broke what had been a summer-long silence and wrote our first letters home.

[23] The immediate answer was a large check, which we expected, and the utterly demoralizing news—which we had not expected at all—that our parents, confident that we

would get over our silliness, had already entered us in college for the fall term. In those days not many colleges demanded College Entrance Examination Board test scores, but all of them had vacancies and most were willing to pretend that the customer was always bright.

[24] Our parents' casual certainty about us was infuriating. We therefore determined upon one final gesture that would restore to us something of our romantic view of ourselves as hard, tough men. Louis Wang had a motorcycle. If he would let us borrow it, we would ride it east and send it back to him. Ralph's father owned a manufacturing concern (Ralph showed Louis the company letterhead) and Ralph would have the shipping department crate the motorcycle and send it back.

[25] Oddly enough, Louis agreed. Perhaps he was intrigued by our idea of trying to drive across the continent without stopping except for gasoline. We all wondered if anyone had done this before; if it really could be done; if so, in how little time. So Louis showed us how to start and stop the thing, and we bought a pillow in a five-and-ten-cent store to wire onto the back fender to form a seat for the one who would not be driving. It would not take us long to learn how to drive it, Louis said. We shook hands and went blasting out of Fresno forever.

[26] We raced furiously to Sacramento; scuttered over the mountains and into Reno with our backsides beginning to turn black and blue. We sped across the salt flats; paused for gasoline, coffee and a bottle of whiskey at a Wyoming town where all three were sold at the town's one store. Our headlights, at ninety miles an hour, suddenly illuminated white-faced Herefords wandering across an open range in Montana, and we went off the road to avoid them, shouting and scattering gravel and cattle; somehow wobbled back onto the road again and out of the herd. We gradually drew closer to what we believed to be the lights of a town, shining far ahead in the clear Western distances, only to realize at last that, in our grogginess, we were creeping nearer and nearer to the tailgate of an enormous, brightly lighted trailer truck. We drank black coffee at the next gas pump; coffee laced with

whiskey. We also fell asleep while rounding a curve in Iowa. I remember seeing a shower of sparks, and eventually realizing they were caused by the foot peg grinding along the pavement while centrifugal force and an unbanked curve were keeping us alive. I shouted to Ralph to stop trying to show off, and he woke up suddenly, caught himself, and swerved back to our own side of the road.

[27] Eighty hours after leaving Fresno we were streaking along the new Pennsylvania Turnpike at night, chased by police. They did not arrest us. They merely wanted to tell us the road was not yet open; that a thousand yards ahead was a place where the first bridge would be, when it was built. When we reached New Jersey we slept for two days, and it was some days later before the swelling left our hands and arms and the bruises faded from our buttocks.

[28] Then, having nothing better to do, we went to college. We hated that. The boys and girls who went to college were nothing but tame kids who would unquestioningly evolve into the bridge players who made nonconversation. They joined fraternities, cheered at the games, did their homework, earned their grades, went to the dances and swung and swayed with Sammy Kaye; while we, in our arrogant innocence, looked derisively upon all this from an outside world. We were different. We were 6,000 miles by boxcar and motorcycle apart from them. We knew it, and they did too. Just to be sure they knew, we always rolled our own cigarettes on campus and dressed in our own sooty denim pants.

[29] Looking back on it now, it seems odd to say we felt such a difference between ourselves and the college children, particularly when I have already said that we, in a formless way, had begun to suspect that the artificial differences between one man and another are inconsequential when compared to the real similarities that unite them. Moreover, Ralph and I were now back among our own kind. Why, then, the studied insolence of the Bull Durham and the dirty Levi's?

[30] I suppose, now, that the pose and the costume were our own way of saying to other colleagians, *You know nothing about it.* We would sit in economics class, and the others would brightly chatter with the young doctoral student

who was our instructor, and I would slump back in my chair with my hands in my pockets, angry and silent, hearing nothing of this footless patter of cyclical depressions. Instead, I would see in my mind's eye a filling-station door open, and the woman in the man's coat and hat emerge, a scarf wrapped around her nose and mouth to keep out the driving dust; she would wad another protective rag around the nozzle of the hose and the opening of the gas tank to put two dollars' worth of gasoline into a wretched jalopy crowded with an empty-faced family of spindly children and bearing on its roof rug-wrapped bundles and the flat steel web of a cheap double bed, and hear the man ask whether, instead of paying the money, he could stay and work for two days.

[31] An *ad hominem* approach to Economics 201A was not a certain path to success in the subject, but I cared nothing for the course and less for the grade. The feeling grew on me that no one in college, including the smug young instructors with the Phi Beta Kappa keys, knew what the devil he was talking about; that they were all playing at an intellectual game that insulted the dignity of experience.

[32] This was not a feeling I could put into words at that time. I had only the unexpressed knowledge, sitting silent inside me, that there was no place for me then, or perhaps ever, in any world I did not make for myself. Indeed, in retrospect, this seems to have been the cardinal lesson of our summer's trip. It will be seen that Ralph and I failed to make our dream come true; that our first young research for the stuff of life proved only that we were not at home in either the suburban or the proletarian worlds. Nor were we at home in the academic world. In fact, we would never be at home in any patterned world. No one ever is. No matter how much we share with all mankind, each of us is bitterly alone. Our true distance from our neighbor begins to yawn when we at length discover the unexplored darkness within ourselves, and begin to understand that he who travels farthest and fastest into this darkness must travel alone; and that the ultimate destination of every traveler is always himself.

[33] It was just this sense of the void within us that our trip had given us; it was our first, urgent command to get

to work and fill the void; our summer trip provided us with our first inkling that our claims to identity would be entirely determined by our experience of ourselves.

[34] In this sense, I can say that some part of me, now and forever, answers to the sounds of a train whistling lonely in the night, and to the deep tones of foghorns in the mists of the Northwestern coast. Some part of me is still a boy sweating at unloading watermelons from a truck in Portland; I am still shivering atop a cattle car in the winds driving through the snow-covered high passes. There is still in whoever I am the wink of campfires and the sight of the drunken man jumping across a fire and someone hitting him with a railroad spike and him falling into the fire. I can still see the lights of San Francisco and of Alcatraz from Coit Tower, and the delicate faces of the Chinese girls that Louis found for us. I have a memory of walking the docks in the rain in Seattle, and of sleepless nights in the fumigated cots of flophouses run by the Gospel Mission; of the Western wastelands creeping past and a hawk swooping on a gopher. Most clearly, I can see the faces of hopeful men who would never know anything other than disappointment, and the burst of spray against the rocks and among the tidal pools of Monterey. I remember lying on rattling floorboards at night, wondering whether I would wind up in jail, or whether any girl would ever want to marry me, and if I would ever see my family again. I have many memories, and if I am not sure yet what all of them mean, I am nonetheless certain that whoever I am is whatever my memories have made me; that I am becoming whatever I can find out about myself.

[35] Nagging at my mind is Churchill's remark that "without a measureless and perpetual uncertainty, the drama of human life would be destroyed." I suppose that each of us, in his own way and at his own time, ventures as far as he chooses to dare in search of himself. Amy Lowell wondered, "Christ! What are patterns for?" They are largely for the timid; for those who find them comfortable. It seems to me that an adventure must be defined as an undertaking whose end it is impossible to know.

[36] That is why I applaud the youthful dramatist, the would-be adventurer, who breaks the pattern, who with mounting excitement writes the farewell note and slips out the window at dead of night to set off afoot for the railroad yards to board a freight bound for California. I believe I know how he feels. More important, I know that he is not running away from something so much as he is running toward something: toward life; toward himself; toward an end that cannot be known.

[37] I wish him well. His chances of finding what he seeks are never good, but they are at least better than the chances of those who stay at home, placidly accepting patterns they never made, or chose.

EXERCISES—*ON RUNNING AWAY*

Content

1. Why did Ralph and the author not admit their early misgivings to each other?
2. In what ways was running away romantic to the boys?
3. Why did they feel they were running into life, not away from it?
4. What were some of the ironies of their journey?
5. What did Keats decide was the fallacy of their position?
6. Why did they decide to return home?
7. What is the main idea of this essay—the "cardinal lesson" Keats learned from his trip?

Style

1. Why did Keats use first person subjective for his essay?
2. The account of the journey is composed of three sections. What are they? Which paragraphs make up each part?
3. The journey ends in paragraph (27). Why did Keats include paragraphs (28)–(37)? How are the comments in these paragraphs foreshadowed in the first part of the essay?
4. What is Keats' angle of vision? Explain.
5. What is the tone of the essay? Explain.
6. Is the essay formal, informal, or colloquial? Explain.
7. Who is Keats' audience?

8. Why does Keats withhold his main point until near the end of the essay? Why doesn't he express it in an expository paragraph?
9. What can you conclude about Keats' personality from this essay?

Application of Stylistic Techniques

1. Rewrite paragraph (1) in third person singular subjective point of view.
2. Compare and contrast the pace of Keats' essay to Carlyle's.

Suggestions for Writing

1. Write an essay of expository narration, telling of an event through which you gained insight into yourself, other human beings, or society. Be sure you make your interpretation of the event explicitly clear.
2. Write an essay on the ironies of life.
3. Write an essay, explaining or agreeing or disagreeing with one of the following statements from Keats' essay:
   "In good times no one takes to the road but the bad." (paragraph (8))
   "The traveler must take himself wherever he goes." (paragraph (14))
   "No one can live without money, but no one can earn money save at the loss of one's freedom." (paragraph (14))
   "The artificial differences between one man and another are inconsequential when compared to the real similarities that unite them." (paragraph (29))
   "No one is ever at home in a patterned world." (paragraph (32))
   "The ultimate destination of every traveler is always himself." (paragraph (32))
   "Our claims to identity would be entirely determined by our experience of ourselves." (paragraph (33))

John Updike (1932–   ) was born in Pennsylvania. He was graduated from Harvard in 1954, and worked for the *New Yorker* from 1955–1957. His major works include *Poorhouse Fair, Rabbit Run, The Centaur, Couples, Bech: A Book, Collections: The Same Door, Pigeon Feathers, The Carpentered Hen and Other Tame Creatures, Telephone Poles* (light verse), and *Assorted Prose.*

The Lucid Eye in Silver Town

(Reminiscent Narration)

JOHN UPDIKE

[1] The first time I visited New York City, I was thirteen and went with my father. I went to meet my Uncle Quin and to buy a book about Vermeer. The Vermeer book was my idea, and my mother's; meeting Uncle Quin was my father's. A generation ago, my uncle had vanished in the direction of Chicago and become, apparently, rich; in the last week he had come east on business and I had graduated from the eighth grade with high marks. My father claimed that I and his brother were the smartest people he had ever met—"go-getters," he called us, with perhaps more irony than at the time I gave him credit for—and in his visionary way he suddenly, irresistibly felt that now was the time for us to meet. New York in those days was seven dollars away; we measured everything, distance and time, in money then. World War II was over but we were still living in the Depression. My father and I set off with the return tickets and a five-dollar bill in his pocket. The five dollars was for the book.

[2] My mother, on the railway platform, suddenly ex-

claimed, "I *hate the Augusts.*" This surprised me, because we were all Augusts—I was an August, my father was an August, Uncle Quincy was an August, and she, I had thought, was an August.

[3] My father gazed serenely over her head and said, "You have every reason to. I wouldn't blame you if you took a gun and shot us all. Except for Quin and your son. They're the only ones of us ever had any get up and git." Nothing was more infuriating about my father than his way of agreeing.

[4] Uncle Quin didn't meet us at Pennsylvania Station. If my father was disappointed, he didn't reveal it to me. It was after one o'clock and all we had for lunch were two candy bars. By walking what seemed to me a very long way to pavements only a little broader than those of my home town, and not so clean, we reached the hotel, which sprouted somehow from the caramel-colored tunnels under Grand Central Station. The lobby smelled of perfume. After the clerk had phoned Quincy August that a man who said he was his brother was at the desk, an elevator took us to the twentieth floor. Inside the room sat three men, each in a gray or blue suit with freshly pressed pants and garters peeping from under the cuffs when they crossed their legs. The men were not quite interchangeable. One had a caterpillar-shaped mustache, one had tangled blond eyebrows like my father's, and the third had a drink in his hand—the others had drinks, too, but were not gripping them so tightly.

[5] "Gentlemen, I'd like you to meet my brother Marty and his young son," Uncle Quin said.

[6] "The kid's name is Jay," my father added, shaking hands with each of the two men, staring them in the eye. I imitated my father, and the mustached man, not expecting my firm handshake and stare, said, "Why, hello there, Jay!"

[7] "Marty, would you and the boy like to freshen up? The facilities are through the door and to the left."

[8] "Thank you, Quin. I believe we will. Excuse me, gentlemen."

[9] "Certainly."

[10] "Certainly."

[11] My father and I went into the bedroom of the

suite. The furniture was square and new and all the same shade of maroon. On the bed was an opened suitcase, also new. The clean, expensive smells of leather and lotion were beautiful to me. Uncle Quin's underwear looked silk and was full of fleurs-de-lis. When I was through in the lavatory, I made for the living room, to rejoin Uncle Quin and his friends.

[12] "Hold it," my father said. "Let's wait in here."

[13] "Won't that look rude?"

[14] "No. It's what Quin wants."

[15] "Now, Daddy, don't be ridiculous. He'll think we've died in here."

[16] "No he won't, not my brother. He's working some deal. He doesn't want to be bothered. I know how my brother works; he got us in here so we'd stay in here."

[17] "*Really*, Pop. You're such a schemer." But I did not want to go in there without him. I looked around the room for something to read. There was nothing, not even a newspaper, except a shiny little phamphlet about the hotel itself. I wondered when we would get a chance to look for the Vermeer book, and what the men in the next room were talking about. I wondered why Uncle Quin was so short, when my father was so tall. By leaning out of the window, I could see taxicabs maneuvering like windup toys.

[18] My father came and stood beside me. "Don't lean out too far."

[19] I edged out inches farther and took a big bite of the high cold air spiced by the distant street noises. "Look at the green cab cut in front of the yellow," I said. "Should they be making U-turns on that street?"

[20] "In New York it's O.K. Survival of the fittest is the only law here."

[21] "Isn't that the Chrysler Building?"

[22] "Yes, isn't it graceful though? It always reminds me of the queen of the chessboard."

[23] "What's the one beside it?"

[24] "I don't know. Some big gravestone. The one deep in back, from this window, is the Woolworth Building. For years it was the tallest building in the world."

[25] As, side by side at the window, we talked, I was

surprised that my father could answer so many of my questions. As a young man, before I was born, he had travelled, looking for work; this was not *his* first trip to New York. Excited by my new respect, I longed to say something to remold that calm, beaten face.

[26] "Do you really think he meant for us to stay out here?" I asked.

[27] "Quin is a go-getter," he said, gazing over my head. "I admire him. Anything he wanted, from little on up, he went after it. Slam. Bang. His thinking is miles ahead of mine—just like your mother's. You can feel them pull out ahead of you." He moved his hands, palms down, like two taxis, the left quickly pulling ahead of the right. "You're the same way."

[28] "Sure, sure." My impatience was not merely embarrassment at being praised; I was irritated that he considered Uncle Quin as smart as myself. At that point in my life I was sure that only stupid people took an interest in money.

[29] When Uncle Quin finally entered the bedroom, he said, "Martin, I hoped you and the boy would come out and join us."

[30] "Hell, I didn't want to butt in. You and those men were talking business."

[31] "Lucas and Roebuck and I? Now, Marty, it was nothing that my own brother couldn't hear. Just a minor matter of adjustment. Both those men are fine men. Very important in their own fields. I'm disappointed that you couldn't see more of them. Believe me, I hadn't meant for you to hide in here. Now what kind of drink would you like?"

[32] "I don't care. I drink very little any more."

[33] "Scotch-and-water, Marty?"

[34] "Swell."

[35] "And the boy? What about some ginger ale, young man? Or would you like milk?"

[36] "The ginger ale," I said.

[37] "There was a day, you know, when your father could drink any two men under the table."

[38] As I remember it, a waiter brought the drinks to

the room, and while we were drinking them I asked if we were going to spend all afternoon in this room. Uncle Quin didn't seem to hear, but five minutes later he suggested that the boy might like to take a look around the city—Gotham, he called it. Baghdad-on-the-Subway. My father said that that would be a once-in-a-life-time treat for the kid. He always called me "the kid" when I was sick or had lost at something or was angry—when he felt sorry for me, in short. The three of us went down in the elevator and took a taxi ride down Broadway, or up Broadway—I wasn't sure. "This is what they call the Great White Way," Uncle Quin said several times. Once he apologized. "In daytime it's just another street." The trip didn't seem so much designed for sight-seeing as for getting Uncle Quin to the Pickernut Club, a little restaurant set in a block of similar canopied places. I remember we stepped down into it and it was dark inside. A piano was playing "There's a Small Hotel."

[39] "He shouldn't do that," Uncle Quin said. Then he waved to the man behind the piano. "How are you, Freddie? How are the kids?"

[40] "Fine, Mr. August, fine," Freddie said, bobbing his head and smiling and not missing a note.

[41] "That's Quin's song," my father said to me as we wriggled our way into a slippery curved seat at a round table.

[42] I didn't say anything, but Uncle Quin, overhearing some disapproval in my silence, said, "Freddie's a first-rate man. He has a boy going to Colgate this autumn."

[43] I asked, "Is that really your song?"

[44] Uncle Quin grinned and put his warm broad hand on my shoulder; I hated, at that age, being touched. "I let them think it is," he said, oddly purring. "To me, songs are like young girls. They're all pretty."

[45] A waiter in a red coat scurried up. "Mr. August! Back from the West? How are you, Mr. August?"

[46] "Getting by, Jerome, getting by. Jerome, I'd like you to meet my kid brother, Martin."

[47] "How do you do, Mr. Martin. Are you paying New York a visit? Or do you live here?"

[48] My father quickly shook hands with Jerome, some-

what to Jerome's surprise. "I'm just up for the afternoon, thank you. I live in a hick town in Pennsylvania you never heard of."

[49] "I see, sir. A quick visit."

[50] "This is the first time in six years that I've had a chance to see my brother."

[51] "Yes, we've seen very little of him these past years. He's a man we can never see too much of, isn't that right?"

[52] Uncle Quin interrupted. "This is my nephew Jay."

[53] "How do you like the big city, Jay?"

[54] "Fine." I didn't duplicate my father's mistake of offering to shake hands.

[55] "Why, Jerome," Uncle Quin said, "my brother and I would like to have a Scotch-on-the-rocks. The boy would like a ginger ale."

[56] "No, wait," I said. "What kinds of ice cream do you have?"

[57] "Vanilla and chocolate, sir."

[58] I hesitated. I could scarcely believe it, when the cheap drugstore at home had fifteen flavors.

[59] "I'm afraid it's not a very big selection," Jerome said.

[60] "I guess vanilla."

[61] "Yes, sir. One plate of vanilla."

[62] When my ice cream came it was a golf ball in a flat silver dish; it kept spinning away as I dug at it with my spoon. Uncle Quin watched me and asked, "Is there anything especially you'd like to do?"

[63] "The kid'd like to get into a bookstore," my father said.

[64] "A bookstore. What sort of book, Jay?"

[65] I said, "I'd like to look for a good book of Vermeer."

[66] "Vermeer," Uncle Quin pronounced slowly, relishing the r's, pretending to give the matter thought. "Dutch school."

[67] "He's Dutch, yes."

[68] "For my own money, Jay, the French are the people to beat. We have four Degas ballet dancers in our living room

in Chicago, and I could sit and look at one of them for hours. I think it's wonderful, the feeling for balance the man had."

[69] "Yeah, but don't Degas' paintings always remind you of colored drawings? For actually *looking* at things in terms of paint, for the lucid eye, I think Vermeer makes Degas look sick."

[70] Uncle Quin said nothing, and my father, after an anxious glance across the table, said, "That's the way he and his mother talk all the time. It's all beyond me. I can't understand a thing they say."

[71] "Your mother is encouraging you to be a painter, is she, Jay?" Uncle Quin's smile was very wide and his cheeks were pushed out as if each held a candy.

[72] "Sure, I suppose she is."

[73] "Your mother is a very wonderful woman, Jay," Uncle Quin said.

[74] It was such an embarrassing remark, and so much depended upon your definition of "wonderful," that I dug at my ice cream, and my father asked Uncle Quin about his own wife, Tessie. When we left, Uncle Quin signed the check with his name and the name of some company. It was close to five o'clock.

[75] My uncle didn't know much about the location of bookstores in New York—his last twenty years had been spent in Chicago—but he thought that if we went to Forty-second Street and Sixth Avenue we should find something. The cab driver let us out beside a park that acted as kind of a backyard for the Public Library. It looked so inviting, so agreeably dusty, with the pigeons and the men nodding on the benches and the office girls in their taut summer dresses, that, without thinking, I led the two men into it. Shimmering buildings arrowed upward and glinted through the treetops. This was New York, I told myself: the silver town. Towers of ambition rose, crystalline, within me. "If you stand here," my father said, "you can see the Empire State." I went and stood beneath my father's arm and followed with my eyes the direction of it. Something sharp and hard fell into my eye. I ducked my head and blinked; it was painful.

[76] "What's the trouble?" Uncle Quin's voice asked.

[77] My father said, "The poor kid's got something into his eye. He has the worst luck that way of anybody I ever knew."

[78] The thing seemed to have life. It bit. "Ow," I said, angry enough to cry.

[79] "If we can get him out of the wind," my father's voice said, "maybe I can see it."

[80] "No, now, Marty, use your head. Never fool with the eyes or ears. The hotel is within two blocks. Can you walk two blocks, Jay?"

[81] "I'm blind, not lame," I snapped.

[82] "He has a ready wit," Uncle Quin said.

[83] Between the two men, shielding my eye with a hand, I walked to the hotel. From time to time, one of them would take my other hand, or put one of theirs on my shoulder, but I would walk faster, and the hands would drop away. I hoped our entrance into the hotel lobby would not be too conspicuous; I took my hand from my eye and walked erect, defying the impulse to stoop. Except for the one lid being shut and possibly my face being red, I imagined I looked passably suave. However, my guardians lost no time betraying me. Not only did they walk at my heels, as if I might topple any instant, but my father told one old bum sitting in the lobby, "Poor kid got something in his eye," and Uncle Quin, passing the desk, called, "Send up a doctor to Twenty-eleven."

[84] "You shouldn't have done that, Quin," my father said in the elevator. "I can get it out, now that he's out of the wind. This is happening all the time. The kid's eyes are too far front."

[85] "Never fool with the eyes, Martin. They are your most precious tool in life."

[86] "It'll work out," I said, though I didn't believe it would. It felt like a steel chip, deeply embedded.

[87] Up in the room, Uncle Quin made me lie down on the bed. My father, a handkerchief wadded in his hand so that one corner stuck out, approached me, but it hurt so much to open the eye that I repulsed him. "Don't torment me," I said,

twisting my face away. "What good does it do? The doctor'll be up."

[88] Regretfully my father put the handkerchief back into his pocket.

[89] The doctor was a soft-handed man with little to say to anybody; he wasn't pretending to be the family doctor. He rolled my lower eyelid on a thin stick, jabbed with a Q-tip, and showed me, on the end of the Q-tip, an eyelash. He dropped three drops of yellow fluid into the eye to remove any chance of infection. The fluid stung, and I shut my eyes, leaning back into the pillow, glad it was over. When I opened them, my father was passing a bill into the doctor's hand. The doctor thanked him, winked at me, and left. Uncle Quin came out of the bathroom.

[90] "Well, young man, how are you feeling now?" he asked.

[91] "Fine."

[92] "It was just an eyelash," my father said.

[93] "*Just* an eyelash! Well I know how an eyelash can feel like a razor blade in there. But, now that the young invalid is recovered, we can think of dinner."

[94] "No, I really appreciate your kindness, Quin, but we must be getting back to the sticks. I have an eight-o'clock meeting I should be at."

[95] "I'm extremely sorry to hear that. What sort of meeting, Marty?"

[96] "A church council."

[97] "So you're still doing church work. Well, God bless you for it."

[98] "Grace wanted me to ask you if you couldn't possibly come over some day. We'll put you up overnight. It would be a real treat for her to see you again."

[99] Uncle Quin reached up and put his arm around his younger brother's shoulders. "Martin, I'd like that better than anything in the world. But I am solid with appointments, and I must head west this Thursday. They don't let me have a minute's repose. Nothing would please my heart better than to share a quiet day with you and Grace in your home. Please give

her my love, and tell her what a wonderful boy she is raising. The two of you are raising."

[100] My father promised, "I'll do that." And, after a little more fuss, we left.

[101] "The child better?" the old man in the lobby called to us on the way out.

[102] "It was just an eyelash, thank you, sir," my father said.

[103] When we got outside, I wondered if there were any bookstores still open.

[104] "We have no money."

[105] "None at all?"

[106] "The doctor charged five dollars. That's how much it costs in New York to get something in your eye."

[107] "I didn't do it on purpose. Do you think I pulled out the eyelash and stuck it in there myself? I didn't tell you to call the doctor."

[108] "I know that."

[109] "Couldn't we just go into a bookstore and look a minute?"

[110] "We haven't time, Jay."

[111] But when we reached Pennsylvania Station, it was over thirty minutes until the next train left. As we sat on a bench, my father smiled reminiscently. "Boy, he's smart, isn't he? His thinking is sixty light-years ahead of mine."

[112] "Whose?"

[113] "My brother. Notice the way he hid in the bathroom until the doctor was gone? That's how to make money. The rich man collects dollar bills like the stamp collector collects stamps. I knew he'd do it. I knew it when he told the clerk to send up a doctor that I'd have to pay for it."

[114] "Well, why *should* he pay for it? *You* were the person to pay for it."

[115] "That's right. Why should he?" My father settled back, his eyes forward, his hands crossed and limp in his lap. The skin beneath his chin was loose; his temples seemed concave. The liquor was probably disagreeing with him. "That's why he's where he is now, and that's why I am where I am."

[116] The seed of my anger seemed to be a desire to recall him to himself, to scold him out of being old and tired. "Well, why'd you bring along only five dollars? You might have known something would happen."

[117] "You're right, Jay. I should have brought more."

[118] "Look. Right over there is an open bookstore. Now if you had brought *ten* dollars—"

[119] "Is it open? I don't think so. They just left the lights in the window on."

[120] "What if it isn't? What does it matter to us? Anyway, what kind of art book can you get for five dollars? Color plates cost money. How much do you think a decent book of Vermeer costs? It'd be cheap at fifteen dollars, even secondhand, with the pages all crummy and full of spilled coffee." I kept on, shrilly flailing the passive and infuriating figure of my father, until we left the city. Once we were on the homeward train, my tantrum ended; it had been a kind of ritual, for both of us, and he had endured my screams complacently, nodding assent, like a midwife assisting at the birth of family pride. Years passed before I needed to go to New York again.

EXERCISES—*THE LUCID EYE IN SILVER TOWN*

Content

1. Why did Updike go to New York? Why was it to be such an exciting trip for him? Why was he disappointed in the visit?
2. When did Updike's father call him "the kid"?
3. How did Updike's father, Jay, differ from his brother, Quin? Which man would you prefer to know?
4. What is the meaning of the title?
5. What does the last paragraph mean?

Style

1. Updike's purpose in this essay is more to convey an emotion than to express an idea. What is that emotion? What techniques does he use to achieve his purpose?
2. What is the function of paragraph (2)?

3. Why, stylistically speaking, can't the last two sentences of the essay be omitted?
4. What are the purposes of dialogue in this essay? Is the dialogue realistic?
5. What methods of characterization does Updike use?
6. What is Updike's point of view?
7. What is Updike's angle of vision?
8. Is Updike's language primarily denotative or connotative? Why?

Application of Stylistic Techniques

1. Rewrite paragraph (1) in third person singular subjective.
2. Rewrite paragraph (45)–(61), changing the dialogue to indirect quotations.
3. Compare Updike's techniques of narration with those of Keats. Explain the reasons for the differences.
4. To practice the use of dialogue, record—as accurately as possible—a conversation which you overhear.

Suggestions for Writing

1. Write an essay of personal reminiscence of an incident in childhood. Choose, arrange, and express your details to convey a specific mood.
2. In an essay, use dialogue to characterize an individual.

James Baker (1940–   ), born in Clarksville, Texas, resides in Bowling Green, Kentucky, where he is an assistant professor of humanities at Western Kentucky University. He has written *Thomas Merton: Silent Cistercian as Social Critic* and has contributed articles to *Catholic World, Continuum, Religion in Life,* and *The Baptist Faculty Paper.*

Alienation: Sign of Sickness or Symbol of Health?

(Tight Exposition)

JAMES BAKER

[1] Politicians, parents, university administrators, and television commentators have tried to persuade their audiences that the word "alienation" is much overused today. They say we should ignore the insignificant few who are claiming more public attention than their number merits.

[2] No one who reads about or views firsthand the happenings in this country can deny that the word "alienation" is in vogue today. But the thousands of editorials, news bulletins, and adult conversations which spotlight events in Berkeley, Columbia, and Chicago have led many intelligent interpreters to confess that the word is not really used in excess of its reality. The small but vocal minority of young people, most of them college students, who are alienated from the morality of contemporary society, from the Establishment ruled by older people, or from organized religion with all its activities, is very much on everyone's mind, and their alienation has become a problem for modern man to talk about, to worry about, and perhaps to do something about.

[3] In order to understand the problem of alienation

From *The Baptist Faculty Paper*, Fall, 1969. Reprinted by permission of the author.

better, I recently began a study of its causes, its dynamics, and its results. One part of my study involved a class of honor students whom I asked to write papers on the subject of alienation, particularly emphasizing and analyzing the alienation they detected in themselves and in their fellow students. They were asked to define alienation, to list the objects from which they and their friends felt alienated, and to suggest reasons for such widespread alienation. Their observations were most enlightening. They seemed to define alienation as a loss of faith in certain things, and they said that college students are alienated from parents, arbitrary social and moral codes, American political life, the "American dream," organized religion, God, and even themselves. They thought that today's college student has lost faith because he has been taught ideals and then forbidden to practice them. He has been taught that killing another human being is wrong, but he is forced to kill other human beings in Vietnam. He has been taught that the American political system is flexible and can be reformed by concerned citizens, but he is defeated and then turned from the door of the Democratic convention. He has been taught that the church is Christ's instrument of redemption in the world, but he sees it politely avoiding all the issues involved in redeeming modern society. My students felt that young people have a greater sense of right and wrong than their elders and that their one vice is an intolerance of old people's hypocrisy.

[4] Some of our leading writers and artists have sensed this spirit of alienation and have presented it with a clarity that inevitably provokes the reader or viewer to respond with sympathy or anger. Such contemporary novelists as Bernard Malamud (*The Fixer*) and Saul Bellow (*Herzog*) and such film makers as Mike Nichols (*The Graduate*) and Ingmar Bergman (*The Virgin Spring* and *The Silence*) have created the theme of alienation with power and sagacity. Perhaps the most explicit description of alienation among these is to be found in Bergman's *Silence* when a young woman leaves her sister to die in a strange city.

[5] This alienation, this loss of faith, this breakdown in communication, this sound of silence that is so typical of our

society is born of the idealist's disillusionment. The person who prides himself on being a hardheaded realist cannot be disillusioned for he never gives himself in faith to anyone or anything. Only the person who has ideals, whose faith in certain people and things leads him to fall in love with them, can be so disillusioned as to be alienated from those things he admires.

[6] There are four different levels of alienation; the first three are found among the officially "alienated," the fourth among those whom society calls well-adjusted. The first is the level of silent alienation, the level of the sigh. The young person whose educational background and personality do not permit him to make his alienation known suffers in silence. He is a member of the large number of students who seem to be well-adjusted but quiet, lonely, brooding.

[7] W. Somerset Maugham, in his short story *Mirage*, tells of a young medical student in London, who, because of too much night life, found himself in academic and legal trouble and was forced to emigrate to China. For more than twenty years he worked as a cargo inspector, saving his money and dreaming of the day when he would return to England and resume his life of play. When he finally did return to London, he was too old and the town had changed too much for him to pick up the pieces of his life. He soon began to dream of returning to the good old days of hard work in China. Stopping off in Haiphong on his way back to China, he began to fear that he would be as disappointed in China as he had been in London, and so he lived out his days almost within sight of China, disillusioned by one mirage and afraid to test another.

[8] Many young people are like this man. They once believed in parents, American ideals, the church, and even God. But they have been disillusioned, and their disillusionment has turned to sorrowful alienation. They never protest openly, but they are afraid ever to trust again.

[9] A second level of alienation is filled by young people who are disillusioned but refuse to believe that their alienation cannot be overcome. They will not accept their alienation in silence. They want to believe, even though they have been disappointed. They want to overcome their alienation by bringing

their grief into the open, by forcing others to listen, by re-establishing lines of communication. They protest their alienation, and their protest is basically a plea for help.

[10] A good example of this rejection of alienation was the protest marches of Martin Luther King. He and his people were largely alienated from American life, yet they retained a deep faith in the basic goodness of the constitution of the United States and in the decency of white Americans. Dr. King quoted the Declaration of Independence as well as the New Testament when he called for laws that would make all men as equal before the law as they are before God. He rejected his alienation, and his protests were among the few healthy signs of life in America from 1955 to 1968.

[11] Another example of the rejection of alienation was the effort of college students all through the spring and summer of 1968 to nominate Senator Eugene McCarthy for President of the United States on the Democratic ticket. These students refused to keep silent after being disillusioned by the failure of their party to answer the domestic needs of the American people and to end the war in Vietnam. Their hard work reaped large dividends as McCarthy pulled huge percentages of the popular vote in a number of primaries. Their work was a protest against the alienation they felt, and it was one of the few healthy signs of life in the election year.

[12] Many adults and comfortable citizens belittle such protests. It is true that some young people protest out of hatred and some because it is the "in" thing to do, but for a multitude of young people it is the only authentic reaction to alienation. Protest, when it is peaceful in purpose and non-violent in practice, can be the tactic of the intelligent person who knows he is alienated and wants to remedy the situation. It may be his last attempt to regain his faith.

[13] A third level of alienation, however, is achieved when this protest is ignored—when no one responds and when communication and faith are not re-established. When all hope is gone, the silent person will turn his face to the wall and simply refuse to look upon the scene. But the protester, the one who still is attracted to the object from which he is alienated, will respond with an emotional outburst. The comfortable

white man may move to a hut in the wilderness; the hungry, rejected black man may burn his rat-infested block.

[14] The sincerely bereaved Negro who broke store windows when Dr. King was shot and the young white student who pushed the jittery Chicago police into a bloody confrontation are examples of this radical stage in alienation. When all faith is gone, when the idealist's disillusionment is deepest, then perhaps violence is understandable; regrettable but understandable.

[15] Some young people silently accept their alienation from the leaders of society, from the electoral process, from religion, from God, and from their fellowmen. Some seek to grab society's, religion's, or God's lapels and force them to listen. Some strike out passionately at the object of their unrequited love and disillusionment. But a fourth type of young person, in another level altogether, is alienated without knowing it. His is the most tragic alienation of all, even more tragic than the alienation that leads to violence. This type person feels that all is well. He looks forward to buying a home in the suburbs, a station wagon for the family—and a small import for himself, and a color television set for his living room. He thinks that the Saturday football game and the Sunday afternoon gin party with friends are the end and goal of man. He does not feel alienated and his society does not think he is alienated. He fits into society as a worker, a player, and a fully adjusted participant.

[16] This young person who does not know or care about the problems of life is the most alienated of all men for he is alienated from the very meaning of life. He is never disillusioned because he never believed in higher values. He does not realize that he cannot communicate with his fellowman for he never knew such communication. He is the whited sepulchre, filled with dead men's bones, and his puny activities are the odor fumes of decay.

[17] While the disillusioned idealist who rejects his alienation by protesting it openly is often thought by society to be sick and the person who is blithely unaware of his alienation from the meaning of life is considered healthy, the opposite is true. Protest is actually the natural response of the

healthy personality while the self-satisfied smile of the unconsciously alienated betrays his illness. Marriage and the bearing of children are protests against solitude. Reading books and attending college are protests against ignorance. Prayer and worship are protests against alienation from God. While silence, unconsciousness, and violence each in its own way reveals illness, positive protest against alienation reveals life and health.

EXERCISES—*ALIENATION: SIGN OF SICKNESS OR SYMBOL OF HEALTH?*

Content

1. How did Baker's students define alienation? What did they consider to be the cause of the alienation of today's college student?
2. Why can't a realist be disillusioned?
3. What are the four levels of alienation? Which is the most tragic type of alienation? Why?
4. What does Baker mean when he says that protest is a healthy sign of life in America?
5. What is Baker's main idea? Where does he state that idea?

Style

1. What is Baker's purpose in this essay? Explain.
2. Is the essay formal, informal, or colloquial? Explain.
3. Who is Baker's audience? Explain.
4. What is Baker's point of view? Explain.
5. Which paragraphs compose the introduction? the body? the conclusion?
6. What specific devices for coherence does Baker use? Give examples.
7. What specific methods of development does Baker use to make his ideas clear and specific? Give examples.
8. Why does Baker use specific to general instead of general to specific organization?
9. Why are Baker's sentence patterns suitable to his subject and method?

Application of Stylistic Techniques

1. In paragraph (3) Baker uses his students' ideas to define alienation by examples. Using this same technique of definition by examples, define an abstract term such as honesty, tolerance, bigotry, conservatism, or liberalism.
2. Using paragraph (7) as a pattern, write a brief synopsis of a short story.

Suggestions for Writing

1. Using one of the following topics or your own, write an expository essay in which you *refute* what you consider to be a myth of our society, such as:
   Everybody should go to college.
   Young people are irresponsible.
   Man is inherently a selfish creature.
2. Using classification into types, levels, or stages, in an essay explain some abstract idea, such as conformity, love, maturity, hypocrisy, or disillusionment. Develop your essay by examples.

George Frazier (1911–) was born in Boston and now lives in Boston and New York City. He is a columnist for *The Boston Globe* and has contributed to *Esquire* and many other national magazines. He has also written *The One with the Mustache Is Costello.*

John Steinbeck! John Steinbeck! How Still We See Thee Lie

(Loose Exposition)

GEORGE FRAZIER

[1] He ridiculed the Nobel Prize, claiming that it was no prize to be proud of if somebody like Pearl Buck could win it. He made a practice of reading Hemingway's dialogue in a monotone in an effort to belittle his better; he rarely told an anecdote the same way twice; he mentioned darkly having killed a man with his fists; he was a terrible liar; he beat his dog. Yet, for all his flaws, he was a fun person and now that he is in the ground, God knows we have few enough of his like left. In the Forties I was with him almost daily over a two-and-a-half-year stretch and I can testify that he was never a bore.

[2] I met him of a midnight when each of us was walking his sheepdog on First Avenue, he, a large, heavy man with a flat, web-footed walk, coming down the avenue and I heading up it. We were tugged toward each other by our suddenly sniffing dogs. For almost a minute neither of us spoke and then he said, "We should get together. The dogs would like it. My name's Steinbeck."

[3] "Are you in the book?"

[4] He took out a pen and pad and scribbled something. "Call me."

[5] And then he was gone. When I reached the corner I stopped under the streetlight and read what he had written—John Steinbeck. *The* John Steinbeck—*In Dubious Battle* and *Of Mice and Men, Tortilla Flat* and *The Grapes of Wrath*—John Steinbeck. One of the two or three writers I'd want to call up on the phone, the way Holden Caulfield wanted to call Isak Dinesen up. And now—tomorrow—I was going to call John Steinbeck up, because he had *asked* me to.

[6] It is odd about the great—or if not the great exactly, then at least the esteemed or successful or renowned; odd how so often they feel they aren't esteemed or successful or renowned enough; odd, too, how they must further prove themselves by inventing harmless little fictions about their not generally recognized gifts, odd how it is not enough that they are good writers or painters or tap dancers, like Hemingway that day in his Havana *finca* challenging Brooklyn Dodgers' pitcher Hugh Casey to a boxing match and then, when he was soundly whipped, demanding that he and Casey duel with swords. I've never known an abundantly talented person more tormented by misgivings than John Steinbeck.

[7] When, for example, he learned that I'd gone to Harvard, he suddenly became insecure and spiteful in my presence and it was months before I was able to convince him that the prevalent image of a Harvard man exists only among people who never went to Harvard. "My God, John, you should see some of them," I told him, and he gave that great roar of a laugh, and from then on there was never any uneasiness between us. But he had a whole slew of sources of discontent, not the least of which during the time we were close was the glamour surrounding Hemingway.

[8] In the evening, sitting in the paneled living room of his garden apartment on East Fifty-first Street, he would suddenly put down the bowl of onions he was peeling for the great chili he used to make. "Hemingway," he'd sneer, although nobody had mentioned Hemingway, and he would get up and go over and take *The Sun Also Rises* from a bookshelf.

Then, sighing with satisfaction, he would read aloud, intoning the celebrated dialogue in a deliberately flat voice, without cadence, without caesura, and naturally it sounded awful. Then, pursing his lips and nodding, he would close the book and slap it against his knee. "God damn it, I don't understand why people think Hemingway can write dialogue." And for a little while he would be very happy.

[9] But then, as if suddenly stabbed by the remembrance of Hemingway's reputation as a fist fighter, he would give us a confidential look. "I killed a man once," he'd say. "I don't trust myself any more. I avoid fights. I have a savage temper."

[10] And his wife, Gwynn, an exceptionally pretty, shapely girl who became godmother to my older son, would wink at my wife and me and give a quick, amused shrug. But he did have a savage temper, which, in the time I knew him well, was directed almost exclusively toward Willie, his sheepdog. This was not the same man who was afterwards to travel across the country in the company of Charley. In those moments of his impatience with Willie he was maniacal. Willie would be stretched out in front of the door leading onto the garden when Steinbeck would suddenly command him to come to him. If the dog failed to do so promptly, John would take a long, stout stick from the coffee table, go over and seize Willie by the collar, and smash at him so furiously that the rest of us cringed.

[11] "They have to know who's boss," he'd say. "That's why dogs love me. They know who the master is." And he would relate some story about some dog he had once had, naturally never telling it the same way twice. It annoyed him that my sheepdog was obedient and affectionate. "God damn it, you're not tough enough with him," he'd tell me. "The damn dog has no spirit."

[12] But that was the dark side of him. Mostly he was warm and generous and kind, although often an endearing fraud—like, for instance, his claiming to cherish his privacy and the anonymity of his person. Actually, he was fascinated by fame, his own as well as others', and he was constantly pumping me for information about the show-business people I used to meet in my capacity as Entertainment Editor of *Life*.

He would listen like a wide-eyed child when I would tell him how, only that afternoon, Gary Cooper had fallen asleep while looking at some pictures in my office, or that, at lunch a few days earlier, Sluggy, the then-Mrs. Humphrey Bogart, had turned on me when I tried to intervene in a violent squabble between her and her husband during lunch at "21."

[13] And afterwards, when my wife and I began to go our own ways, he used to beg me to tell him what had happened on the dates I had with Marie McDonald, a move actress known, and with ample reason, as The Body. And inevitably, when he and I would be with friends, he would repeat what little I had told him, except that his version was highly embellished, and it was he, not I, who had been out with The Body.

[14] But what seemd to delight him most was appropriating my experiences with Bogart, with whom I was spending a good deal of time in preparation for a *Life* piece I was doing on him. Every day I would leave my office around noon, meet Bogart at "21," and by five we would be smashed. During the course of the afternoon he would besiege me with questions: Where was I born? Where did I go to college? When the hell was I going to get my raincoat cleaned? When I would beg him to be serious he would become indignant, pick up the table telephone, and dictate a wire to *Life*.

[15] VERY DIFFICULT TO DO PIECE ON FRAZIER, it would read. HE HAS NO COLOR. STRONGLY SUGGEST YOU FORGET THIS ASSIGNMENT AND GIVE ME ANOTHER ONE. REGARDS, BOGART.

[16] Later, I would gape in disbelief as John regaled people with my odyssey, but now it would be he who had gotten stoned with Bogie.

[17] One day, when Steinbeck discovered that Bogart and I were going to Madison Square Garden to see the fight between somebody whose name escapes me and Lew Jenkins, a tough Texan known as The Sweet Swatter from Sweetwater, he said that he sure as hell would like to see that fight. I was able to get him a ticket and, as things turned out, he and Bogart got along beautifully, Steinbeck telling how he had once killed a man with his fists, and the actor allowing as how only sheer willpower had kept him from killing Jack Warner. After the fight, Bogart insisted that the three of us go to Jenkins'

dressing room. When I tried to demur, he said, "Look, the guy fought lousy. I want to give him a few pointers."

[18] And he did, but the trouble was that Jenkins didn't receive them very graciously. He listened impatiently to Bogart for a few minutes, then began to scowl. "For Christ's sake, what the hell *is* this?" he said, and, grabbing the actor around the waist and by the collar of his trench coat, he lugged him over to the shower, turned it on, and held him under it. A few nights later, Steinbeck was telling some people at Manny Wolf's, one of his favorite restaurants, about the Jenkins fight. "Jenkins is a tough son of a bitch all right, but tough guys can be taken," he said. "In his dressing room after the fight he started to insult Bogie and I had to push him under the shower to cool him off. I didn't want to have to hit him."

[19] When I first knew Steinbeck, he used to ridicule my partiality for the Cub Room of the Stork Club, a privileged preserve which, for all the gossamer goings-on, was an assembly place for the talented and the interesting. But one night I finally prevailed upon him to join me and from that point on he was hooked, forever inventing one pretext or another for me to take him there. And as time went on he took his place in the pantheon that was present night after night. But then he grew a beard in order, he claimed, to avoid being recognized. Not long afterward he phoned me around two o'clock one morning.

[20] "For Christ's sake," he grumbled.

[21] "What the hell's the trouble?"

[22] "God damn it, they won't let me in the Stork. They say they don't know me. They claim John Steinbeck doesn't have a beard."

[23] "Listen, you silly son of a bitch. You grow a beard so you won't be recognized and now you're raising hell because somebody doesn't know you. Okay, let me talk to Gregory."

[24] But if he could be deeply and bitterly hurt when his presence was unacknowledged, he would almost blubber with gratitude at a word of admiring recognition. We were in the Cub Room one night when Spencer Tracy came in and sat at a table almost directly opposite to us. John glanced shyly at the actor a few times, but Tracy, who was talking to somebody at

the next table, did not notice him. Finally Steinbeck said, "A damn good actor, but an awful jerk."

[25] "Who's that?"

[26] "Tracy. I've met him a few times, but I guess he's like all the rest of the Hollywood crowd."

[27] Just then Tracy looked across the room. "John!" he said, getting up and coming over to our table. And for the next half hour he talked about *In Dubious Battle,* which he had just reread. Steinbeck fairly glowed with gratitude and afterward, as the two of us walked home, it was as if he had never uttered a word against Tracy, who by then had become, to John, one of nature's noblemen.

[28] Steinbeck was touched by being a celebrity even in the little enclave where we both lived, I on Beekman Place and he three blocks away. Though it was a tight little island populated mostly by the rich and the beautiful, the talented and the famed—Irving Berlin and Billy Rose, Huntington Hartford and William Shirer and some devastatingly beautiful models —it had the chummy air of a small town, with our country store the Gristede's on First Avenue, our playing fields the swimming pool and squash court at One Beekman, our coffeehouse a saloon called Billy's. John delighted in little acknowledgements of his talent and he would grin happily when he would be recognized as he browsed in the bookstore on the corner of First Avenue and Fifty-first Street, a lovely, lovely place owned by a literate and compassionate man who spent most of his profits tiding over indigent writers who lived in the neighborhood. It was his practice whenever one of his customers had a book published to make a window display of it and to put up a large sign reading "LOCAL BOY MAKES GOOD." He had done it for Russell Maloney and William Shirer and a lot of others, a courtesy that impressed Steinbeck greatly when I told him about it. One day I decided to ask the owner to put the sign up amid a windowful of John's books. The next afternoon, when I knew that it had been done, I phoned Steinbeck and suggested a walk. When we reached the bookstore I stopped and feigned astonishment. "John! Look!"

[29] He studied the display for a moment and then began to blush. "God damn nonsense. I don't go for that stuff."

[30] "Yes, I know," I said. "He should know that. I'll tell you what I'll do. You can't do it because it would seem ungracious, but I'll get him to take it out of the window."

[31] He looked at me with something like terror. "Good God, no." He shook his head emphatically. "You can't do that. It'd hurt his feelings." And for weeks thereafter he would take anyone who dropped by his apartment over to the bookstore window to point out how no one could have any privacy in New York.

[32] He was a mass of contradictions—on the one hand, absolutely without prejudice toward race or color or creed, and, on the other, catty about whomever or whatever with which he was unacquainted; now professing to be utterly indifferent to clothes and yet, a moment later, letting you know he was custom-tailored by telling of the fitter who, patting him cozily, inquired whether he dressed on the right or left side. Nor was his ignorance ever any deterrent to his arrogance, his air of authority. The fact that he had no interest in sports did not stop him from hinting that had he remained at Stanford, which he always referred to as "the university," he would undoubtedly have become an All-American fullback.

[33] "The Nobel Prize, for Christ's sake," he said one evening, although it had not been mentioned until then. "What the hell prestige does it have when it goes to somebody like Pearl Buck?" Naturally, as I discovered later, he had never read a line by Miss Buck.

[34] But if he belittled those whom he didn't know, he was almost fanatically loyal to old friends like Nunnally Johnson; Jed Harris; Pat Covici, his editor at Viking Press; Tim Costello, the saloonkeeper; Leonard Lyons; Juan Negrin, the eminent neurologist, and his wife, Mexican actress Rosita Diaz; Burl Ives; Ed Ricketts, the marine biologist with whom he had collaborated on *Sea of Cortez;* Frank Loesser; Harold Guinzburg, his publisher; Henry Fonda; and Annie Laurie Williams, the wisp of a woman who was his agent for dramatic and motion-picture rights. These were among the few persons with whom he, basically a very shy man, felt completely at ease. With strangers he was likely to be standoffish, even a little cranky, and frequently something of a sham. If, for instance,

some new acquaintance unwittingly paraded a certain erudition, Steinbeck would try to display his own scholarship by bringing up the Arthurian legend and the Gregorian chant, about both of which he had little learning indeed. He was rather less well-read than he claimed. One evening, when we were discussing an essay for which I'd won a Bowdoin Prize at college (an essay that, though he'd never read it, annoyed the hell out of him because it was a study of the Attic influences in Hemingway), he asked me who selected the Bowdoin winner.

[35] "All I know is that the year I won, Professor Howard Maynadier was the head judge."

[36] "Maynadier?" He pursed his lips. "Hmmm." And then, shaking his head dismissively, "I never heard of him."

[37] Nor did I feel cruel enough to inform him that Howard Maynadier, good God, was perhaps the outstanding authority on the Arthurian legend, about which he, Steinbeck, pretended to know so damn much. But, on subsequent occasions, the bitch in me would prevail and I would quote something in Middle English about Arthur just to see his blank reaction. Still, for all his pretensions to intellectuality, he turned down every honorary degree offered him.

[38] We were sitting in his living room one evening when he suddenly looked up from the onions he seemed to be perpetually peeling to announce that he had an idea for a musical comedy and that he would like me to collaborate with him. I couldn't have been more flattered and, after thinking it over that night, I phoned him the next morning to say that I was so eager to work with him that I'd quit *Life*. The plot concerned a medicine man who traveled the countryside performing feats of magic and selling snake oil, and it seemed promising enough to Frank Loesser for him to agree to provide the words and music. One of the two producers was to be Stewart Chaney, the brilliant stage designer, and the other a young public-relations man named Alfred Katz. At John's suggestion I hired a maid's room in my apartment building so that we could work without interruption.

[39] Around eleven in the morning a week later, Steinbeck showed up with a tape recorder. After plugging it in, he

began testing it, but instead of uttering the sort of thing said on such investigative occasions, he proceeded to do an imitation of Bing Crosby, singing *Where The Blue Of The Night Meets The Gold Of The Day* in a dreadful monotone punctuated by the patented Crosby boo-boo-boos. This went on for three or four minutes. "Okay," he said. "That seems all right." And then he paused, rubbing his lips with his fingertip meditatively. I waited expectantly. "You know," he said finally, "if I weren't a writer, I think I'd like to be an impersonator. That Crosby wasn't bad you know." And he reached for the microphone and began to imitate Crosby's *Down The Old Ox Road.*

[40] By one-thirty in the afternoon we had dictated maybe a hundred words that had anything to do with *The Wizard of Maine,* which was the working title of the musical. "Well," he said, rubbing his hands in satisfaction, "we got the show on the road. I think it's time for us to go out for a couple of drinks and some lunch." And that was the way it went week after week. In the meantime, however, Steinbeck, ordinarily taciturn about any work in progress, had told a number of people about *The Wizard of Maine.*

[41] We were having dinner at "21" one evening when an M-G-M executive approached our table. Steinbeck, who had met him on the Coast, invited him to sit down.

[42] "I hear you have something exciting going for you," said the man. "A musical comedy."

[43] Steinbeck nodded. "Yes, and it looks damn good. George and I are doing it together."

[44] "Good. Then I can make you an offer. I talked to the Coast office today and when I told them about what you're working on, they authorized me to offer you $100,00 as an advance. If the thing turns out like we think it will, you'll get a hell of a lot more, and if it doesn't, well you've got the hundred grand."

[45] "I see," said Steinbeck. "I'll tell you what. Let George and me talk about it and I'll phone you tomorrow."

[46] When the man had gone, I slapped Steinbeck on the shoulder. "John, we've got fifty grand apiece."

[47] "Maybe."

[48] "What the hell do you mean 'maybe'?"

[49] "I've got to think about it."

[50] "Oh, for Christ's sake."

[51] "Don't worry, I'll call him tomorrow. As a matter of fact, I want you to be there when I do. Come by my place around eleven."

[52] The next morning I was at Steinbeck's by a quarter to eleven. We had a couple of beers and then he said that he would make the call. Everything seemed, at least from his part of the conversation, to be going well. Finally he said, "Okay, then, it's a deal," and was about to hang up when something occurred to him. "Oh, look, one more thing," he said. "When you draw up the contract I want it specified that Judy Garland won't appear in the movie."

[53] I heard an outburst of anger from the other end of the phone. "That's the way it's got to be," Steinbeck said finally, and then, after the M-G-M executive had replied, he sighed. "Look, don't make me repeat myself. Either you agree Garland won't be in it or the hell with it." Then there was a pause while the other man spoke. Steinbeck nodded. "Okay, then. The hell with it." And he slammed the receiver down.

[54] I was staring at him in disbelief. "John! What the hell have you done? My God, a hundred thousand out the window."

[55] "I'm sorry, but that's the way it has to be."

[56] "But what have you got against Judy Garland?"

[57] "I have plenty against Judy Garland."

[58] "Do you know her?"

[59] "Never met her in my life."

[60] "Well, you don't like her in pictures then?"

[61] "Hell, I have better things to do than to watch Judy Garland movies. I've never seen one of her damn pictures."

[62] "But you insisted that she couldn't be in *The Wizard of Maine*. And you've never seen her on the screen!"

[63] "What the hell has that got to do with it?" he said, getting up and going over to pour us each a beer.

EXERCISES—*JOHN STEINBECK! JOHN STEINBECK! HOW STILL WE SEE THEE LIE*

Content

1. How did Frazier meet John Steinbeck?
2. Why was Steinbeck constantly peeling onions?
3. What made Steinbeck change his attitude toward Spencer Tracy?
4. Why didn't Steinbeck make the deal with MGM for the $100,000 advance on his musical comedy *The Wizard of Maine?*
5. What is Frazier's main idea in this expository essay?

Style

1. Although this essay is loosely structured exposition, it is unified. What unifies the essay?
2. Could the order of anecdotes be changed without changing the effect and meaning of the essay?
3. What devices does Frazier use to characterize Steinbeck?
4. Is this essay formal, informal, or colloquial? Explain.
5. What is the tone of the essay? Explain.
6. What is the effect of the ending? How does it give a note of finality to the essay?
7. How does Frazier avoid making his essay maudlin?

Application of Stylistic Techniques

1. Using paragraph (1) as a pattern, write a capsule characterization of someone you know well.
2. Write a sentence structured like Sentence 1 of paragraph (6).
3. Compare and contrast Frazier's techniques of loose exposition for characterization with Taylor's techniques of description for characterization in *The Monster.*

Suggestions for Writing

1. Use one of the following generalizations by Frazier about Steinbeck as the main idea for exposition of a character you know. Develop that idea by a series of anecdotes.
   "He is never a bore."

"Although he is an abundantly talented person, he is tormented by misgivings."
"He is a mass of contradictions."
"He is almost fanatically loyal to old friends."
"He has a savage temper."
"He is really a shy person."

2. Analyze the character of someone you know well by alternating expository passages and anecdotes.
3. Write an eulogy for someone you knew well and loved or respected highly. Let your sentiment be genuine and honest; do not become maudlin.

Laurence C. Blenheim (1917–) resides in Glenside, Pennsylvania, where he is an associate professor of broadcasting and communication at Temple University. He has had twenty years experience as a professional broadcaster. Now he is Director of Education of the International Educational Television Workshop at Temple and is involved in continuing research, experimentation, and writing on learning by television. He has contributed to *Av Communication Review.*

Television Teaching by Professional Performers? *(Formal Process)*

LAURENCE C. BLENHEIM

[1] It has occurred to the writer that possibly an invalid assumption is made when an experienced teacher is asked to leave his classroom (where he has proved his capability), is put into a new environment (a television studio), and is told, in effect, "Now, be an excellent teacher on television just as you are in your classroom."

[2] The assumption in such a situation seems to be that a good classroom teacher makes a good television teacher—probably better than would anybody else. But, as far as could be determined, no one had ever experimentally proved or disproved it. A pilot study, therefore, was conducted in an effort to determine the validity of the concept. The basic design, findings, and conclusions of the study are reported here in very brief fashion.

From *AV Communication Review*, vol. 17, no. 3, Fall 1969. Reprinted by permission of the author and publisher.

[3] The fundamental question, decided upon for this investigation at the college level, was whether experienced teachers can induce as much factual retention in students by means of televisioned lectures as can experienced television performers.

The problem was to test the hypothesis that there is no significant difference between the achievement registered by a control group (students taught by experienced teachers) and an experimental group (taught by experienced communicators) as indicated by a comparison of the means of the test scores of the two groups when both groups receive instruction by means of television lectures.

[4] A review of the literature revealed some opposing points of view in regard to the kind of background television teachers ought to have. Costello and Gordon, for example, in their book, *Teach with Television* (1961, p. 92), cast doubt on the belief that good classroom teachers necessarily make good television teachers. McBride agrees (1965, p. 5). It is the belief of such writers that when there are differences in teaching situations, differences in teacher requirements may need to be considered.

[5] Carpenter (1960, p. 87) spelled out a reminder that in actual practice educators generally tend to emphasize knowledge of subject matter in their selection of television teachers. In addition, Arden (1964, p. 15) and Fritz (1962, p. 142) concur that subject matter expertise is of greater significance to good teaching than "performance" factors.

[6] Such divergent viewpoints focus on the question of who makes the better television teacher, the academic specialist or the professional communicator?

This experiment, involving three teachers and three professional communicators, was conducted during the fall, 1967, term at Temple University. The 241 subjects, all in basic sociology, were contained in six randomly selected sections of about 40 each. Each experimental section had its own instructor for the three class sessions included in the study. Each of the academics had at least seven years of college teaching experience, an advanced degree in sociology, and a recognized competency among his fellow sociologists. Each teacher prepared and delivered three television lectures, and while the content of the lectures centered on 15 basic points, every teacher was free to develop those points as he wished.

[7] The professional communicators had no particular training in sociology, but each had at least 15 years' experience as broadcast announcers and actors. Each was rated by his associates as particularly competent in his field.

[8] Every communicator-taught section was paired with an academic-taught section, and every communicator was asked to read, verbatim, the lectures of the academic with whom he was paired. Thus, three section pairs were established. Following the series of three lectures, a multiple-choice test was administered. The results were examined within each set of sections to compare levels of retention within respective academic-taught and communicator-taught classes. Mean test scores and analysis of variance at the .05 level of significance were utilized in testing the study's basic hypothesis.

Upon examining the results of this matched-pair experiment involving academic-taught and communicator-taught sections, the following were found:

1. Comparing overall scores, students in academic-taught sections were significantly more retentive than those in communicator-taught sections.
2. In only one of the three matched pairs of sections was there a significant difference in the level of student retention.
3. The mean scores for five of the six sections studied were not significantly different, regardless of instructor type.
4. One academic-taught section differed significantly from all the other sections in the experiment.

Additional analysis of the findings was undertaken to determine why one academic-taught section performed differently from all other sections. Two possibilities that had to be considered were 1) section effect, that the one high-scoring section was in some way "better" than the other sections, and 2) teacher effect, that the teacher was more effective in teaching by television than any other instructor of either type.

[9] Regarding the first possibility, it was found that the high scoring section averaged nearly 14 points lower on the College Board Verbal Scholastic Aptitude Test than the grand

mean for all participating sections. Upon further inspection of test scores, it was determined that women scored significantly higher than men. The high-scoring class contained the highest woman-to-man ratio of any section in the study. However, the data also indicated that both male and female students in this section attained higher mean scores than that for males and females in any of the other five sections.

[10] When considerng teacher effect, it was the opinion of teaching and television personnel observing the lectures given by the teacher of the deviant academic-taught section that the instructor appeared to be the least effective television lecturer, and that the teacher's speech pattern included more "verbal tics" than that of any other television instructor. For example, this teacher frequently ended sentences with the phrase "and so on" and began the following sentence with "Now. . . ."

An item analysis was made of test answers given by both the high-scoring experienced teacher group and the experienced communicator class with which this academic-taught section was paired. It was found that the teacher class outperformed the communicator-taught section on nearly 77 percent of questions (or 24 out of 30) utilized in the test instrument.

When comparing the high level of performance by the deviant academic-taught section with the lack of smooth delivery on the part of the class' instructor, it is apparent that in this study the two do not appear to be related. "Verbal tics," for example, did not appear to impede the achievement level of this section. Also, when considering the results among the five other sections studied, it is apparent that 1) experienced communicators performed about as well as experienced teachers; and 2) in this classroom experiment, experienced teachers performed as well as or better than experienced communicators.

This study tends to support the view that the academic-type is at least as effective as the communicator-type in the televised college lecture situation, and, therefore, the experienced teacher appears to be slightly preferable to the experienced communicator as a television lecturer. However, considerably more research must be undertaken before any firm conclusions are reached.

Among the areas to be considered in such research are the following:

1. The subject areas where communicator-type television lecturers might be best utilized.

2. The male-female ratio and instructor sex as factors in student achievement.

3. The use of a "manuscript bank" of television lectures for course units, written by outstanding subject matter specialists, delivered by experienced teachers and by professional communicators.

4. The effect upon student achievement of lectures written by pairs of teachers and communicators, with content determined by academics and writing style by communicators.

5. The specific combination of communication and/or personal qualities of television instructors that are meaningful contributors to student achievement.

REFERENCES

Arden, E. Great scholar, great teacher. *Journal of Higher Education,* 1964, *35* (3), 150–153.

Carpenter, C. R. Approaches to promising areas of research in the field of instructional television. *New teaching aids for the American classroom.* Stanford, Calif.: Institute of Communication Research, 1960.

Costello, L., & Gordon, G. N. *Teach with television.* New York: Hastings House, 1961.

Fritz, M. F., et al. *Survey of television utilization in Army training.* Human Engineering Report, Special Devices Center, S301-01–1, December 31, 1962.

McBride, J. Twenty elements of instructional television. *Monograph Service,* I, L. Washington, D.C.: National Association of Educational Broadcasters, Instructional Division, September 1965.

EXERCISES—*TELEVISION TEACHING BY PROFESSIONAL PERFORMERS?*

Content

1. What is the assumption on which most educational television is

based? Did the experiment at Temple University prove this assumption to be valid or invalid?

2. How was the experiment on television teaching at Temple University set up?
3. What were the findings of the experiment?

Style

1. Is this essay tightly or loosely structured?
2. Who is Blenheim's audience?
3. This essay is an example of formal process. What stylistic techniques make it formal?
4. What is Blenheim's angle of vision?
5. Why did Blenheim avoid first person in this essay?
6. Is Blenheim's language primarily denotative or connotative? Why?
7. How does Blenheim organize his essay? Mark the sections of the essay in your text.
8. What is the purpose of paragraphs (4), (5), and (6)?
9. Is Blenheim subjective or objective?
10. What do the references at the end add to the essay?

Application of Stylistic Techniques

1. Rewrite paragraph (1), using first person and eliminating all passive voice verbs. How do the tones of the two versions differ? Why is Blenheim's version more appropriate for his purposes?
2. Compare Blenheim's style to the style used to explain a process or experiment in one of your social science or natural science textbooks.

Suggestions for Writing

1. Write an essay in which you explain the process of a laboratory experiment in one of your science courses. Be sure to include the hypothesis, the methodology for testing that hypothesis, and the results of the experiment.
2. Write an essay on one of the following topics suggested by Blenheim's essay:

   The Effectiveness of Teaching by Television
   How to Improve Teaching by Television
   Why I Prefer (or Don't Prefer) Television Lectures to Traditional Lectures
   The Effective Use of Machines in Education
   How to Improve the Quality of Education

This essay was prepared by the staff *of Changing Times: The Kiplinger Magazine.*

How to Hunt for Bargains *(Informal Process)*

[1] In a time of inflation what is so welcome as a bargain that really does save money? Opportunities that look like good buys are plentiful, but the trick is to be able to distinguish between the phony come-on and the real McCoy.

[2] The best way to be sure you get a bargain when you go after one is to know the ins and outs of the bargain-hunting game: curb the yen to buy on impulse . . . acquire the knack of reading newspaper ads . . . become suspicious of stores that omit vital information from their ads . . . plan for seasonal bargains . . . study bargain-basement principles . . . decide when to buy high quality and when not to . . . compute in advance what hidden charges can do to your purchase price.

[3] All this takes a certain amount of head scratching, pencil figuring, leg work and restraint. It also requires that you examine the style in which you live and decide whether you need or want to change any part of it.

[4] *Work out your strategy.* Many bargains can be marked off in advance on your calendar and, equally important, anticipated in your budget. The housewife who plans to stock up on sheets and pillowcases during the white sales is out of luck if she discovers there's not enough spare cash, particularly after Christmas, to take full advantage of the bargains offered.

[5] The same principle holds for many other items. You may have a coat that will do for this winter but will look worn

by next year. You can plan on buying one for next year at the February clearances, at savings of up to 50% on the original price. If you think holiday bills may have you down, you can buy your winter clothing in August and September, when many stores hold advance sales of their new season's stock. Although price reductions aren't as great—around 15% frequently—you still are making a saving and you do get the pick of the offerings as well as the bonus of the latest styles.

[6] Some of your summer clothing can be bought at its cheapest after the Fourth of July. With a careful eye for standard fashions, you can store away cheaply such hard-worked items as bathing suits, shorts, jerseys, summer shirts, suits and dresses.

[7] Stocks of big appliances, such as washers, dryers and television sets, generally go on sale after new models come out in the fall. If you don't need the very newest in push buttons and dials, you can save substantially by waiting for the price reductions on current models.

[8] The big furniture sales usually come twice a year, in January and midsummer, but the spectacular price cuts invariably are on the stuff nobody wanted because it was badly made or garish or uncomfortable. Good prices on good furniture are available, though, especially on standard couches, beds and chairs that have been in stock for a year to 18 months. (For a calendar of store sales see the box.)

[9] Food accounts for a huge chunk of the weekly expenses, but there are ways to cut the bill without scrimping on portions or quality. If you live within easy range of several supermarkets, you can shop at each of them for their week's specials, taking advantage of the low prices without running up a large gasoline bill.

[10] A surer way to save is to prepare complete shopping lists from menus you have worked up in advance. The menus help you plan proper use of leftovers; the shopping lists keep you from picking up the impulse items set out so temptingly by the store.

[11] When a bargain in canned goods comes up, buy more than you need. You can always tuck those cans of corn, stewed tomatoes or corned beef away for the time when you want

them and prices are dear. If you own a large home freezer, the fall specials on frozen foods offer good opportunities to bank your food savings. And by waiting to buy fresh produce until each variety is in full season, you won't have to pay hot house prices that inflate your bill even more. (For a list of storage times for frozen foods see the box.)

[12] Two other shopping suggestions: Never shop on an empty stomach and never let the man of the house shop alone. Either way, you end up with too many expensive or needless goodies.

[13] *Understand the ads.* You must know what the ads in the newspaper are telling you before you can determine whether they are touting real bargains. Stores that want to preserve their good reputation are careful of what they say about their prices and goods. Here are explanations of what they usually mean.

[14] *Sale:* All or most of the wares listed were bought specifically for this event, such as a glassware or fall clothing sale. The store plans ahead to buy large quantities of the sale items and to sell at lower than usual prices. Often a major manufacturer will produce irons, toasters and the like designed especially to sell at attractive prices. The appliances have fewer special features than usual but can represent a good buy nonetheless.

[15] *Clearance:* This is aimed at clearing out goods already in stock. Sometimes it involves items from all over the store, sometimes only certain merchandise, such as home furnishings, sportswear or millinery. Stores must do this to make way for new merchandise that has been ordered previously, and the result can be big price reductions. Some stores have a policy requiring a cut of at least 25% before goods can be advertised this way, and many price reductions are greater.

[16] *Special purchase* or *manufacturer's closeout:* In a special-purchase sale, the store probably has bought a large order of some items at an advantageous price, which it is passing on to you. A closeout means that a manufacturer wants to get rid of that line of stock and is selling out at a lower than usual price, with the store again passing the benefit on.

[17] *"Regularly," "usually"* and *"formerly":* These

A CALENDAR FULL OF GOOD BUYS

Here is the schedule that stores usually follow in planning their sales, promotions, clearances and special events. Naturally, not every store includes every item in its plans. (Source: National Retail Merchants Assn.)

	Jan	Feb	Mar	Apr	May	Jun	July	Aug	Sept	Oct	Nov	Dec
Appliances (major)										X	X	
Bedding	X					X		X				
China and glassware			X						X		X	
Christmas toys											X	
Drugs and cosmetics	X											
Evening wear										X		
Fabrics				X			X					
Floor coverings	X					X						
Foundations and lingerie	X			X		X						
Furniture	X					X	X	X		X		
Furs	X						X	X				
Garden supplies			X									
Gourmet food											X	
Home furnishings	X				X					X		
Hosiery				X		X						
Housewares		X	X									
Jewelry					X							
Ladies' shoes				X		X						
Luggage					X							
Men's and boys' wear						X			X			
Outdoor furniture					X							
Outerwear										X		
Resort and cruise wear	X											X
Silverware											X	
Skiing supplies										X		
Sleepwear				X		X						
Sporting goods									X			
White goods	X				X			X			X	

Special sales: storewide clearances in Jan.-Feb. and July-Aug., Valentine's Day, Lincoln's birthday, Washington's birthday, St. Patrick's Day, pre-Easter, Mother's Day, Memorial Day, graduation, Father's Day, pre- and Fourth of July, back-to-school needs, Labor Day, Columbus Day, Election Day, Veteran's Day, Thanksgiving, Christmas promotions, post-Christmas.

words are used by reputable stores to indicate previous bona fide prices. Not all stores are equally conscientious, however, so you should find out what a store's reputation is before you take its word as truth.

[18] *"Comparable value":* This is a more complex representation and, unfortunately, can mean a variety of things. If you know how to judge value, then you can tell whether a suit selling for $47 really has a comparable value of $65. If you don't know, you may be paying $47 for a $35 suit.

[19] Despite repeated crackdowns by the Federal Trade Commission and other agencies, "bait" ads are still with us. Those are the ads for such items as appliances, sewing machines, carpets and cars that list startlingly low prices to get you inside the door. But often there's only one of the items on hand and, as they say in the trade, it is "nailed to the floor." The idea is to switch you to a far more expensive item. At the first indication of this, walk out. One thing you're not going to get is a bargain.

[20] Special holiday sales, such as those held on George Washington's birthday in many cities, offer such improbable buys as 99-cent typewriters and $3 fur coats. By standing in line all night, you may be able to get a deal like that. And if you can brave the crowds, you may find many other items at substantially reduced prices. But don't get carried away and lug home some of the overpriced junk that the merchants try to fob off.

[21] *Watch the basement.* The wares that stock bargain basements often come from famous stores, and some of the basements, such as Filene's in Boston, are famous in their own right. Generally, the system works this way. Goods that don't sell within a certain time in a store are marked down perhaps 10% and moved to a "sale" rack in the same department. If they still don't sell, they descend to the basement for a series of markdowns. Canny shoppers with plenty of time can sometimes follow an item through the entire sequence and buy just before the price goes so low that someone else gets it first.

[22] Some goods come from other stores. Filene's, for example, has merchandise from many stores, even outside the Boston area. Gimbels in New York City takes the women's

shoes that haven't been sold by Saks Fifth Avenue, its high-priced subsidiary.

[23] Smart shoppers make a specialty of choosing stand-

KEEPING FROZEN FOOD

Stocking your freezer with food bought on "specials" is a good way to cut costs. Just be sure you don't go overboard and buy more than you can really use. The U.S. Department of Agriculture recommends that foods be stored no longer than the following limits at 0° F. Beyond these periods deterioration of quality tends to be noticeable. (The figures apply to fresh and commercially frozen items. Since it is often impossible to know how long the latter have been frozen before you buy them, these figures should be considered outside limits for commercially frozen foods. Home-frozen items, on the other hand, would keep somewhat longer than the times shown.)

food	*storage limit (in months)*
bakery products:	
white bread, plain rolls	3
cakes:	
angel, chiffon	2
chocolate layer	4
pound, yellow	6
fruit	12
doughnuts	3
pies (unbaked):	
apple, boysenberry, cherry, peach	8
fruit:	
cherries, peaches, raspberries, strawberries	12
fruit juice concentrates:	
apple, grape, orange	12
ice cream, sherbet	1
meat:	
beef:	
roasts, steaks	12
ground beef	3
lamb:	
roasts	12
patties	3
pork (fresh):	
roasts	8
sausage	2
pork (cured)	2
veal:	
roasts	8
chops, cutlets	4
cooked meats:	
meat dinners, meat pies, swiss steaks	3
poultry:	
chicken:	
whole	12
cut-up	9
livers	3
turkey:	
whole	12
cut-up	6
duck, goose (whole)	6
cooked chicken and turkey:	
sliced meat and gravy	6
pies	12
fried chicken	4
vegetables:	
asparagus, beans, peas, cauliflower, corn, spinach	8

ard shirts, sweaters and other goods from among the counters of soiled clothing, seconds and irregulars. As long as the spot will clean out and the irregularity is not obvious, there's a big saving.

[24] You may run into goods that are more expensive than those on the upper floors. That's usually because the manager of the basement is pushing a special purchase that happens to be of better quality than a similar line upstairs.

[25] *Check the discount stores.* Their ads list attractive buys in profusion, but it often takes extensive checking to determine whether you can do better there than elsewhere on that color television set, radio or electric can opener. For an accurate fix you must develop your skills as a comparison shopper. You may find, for example, that some department stores have been forced by competition to set discount prices on some items.

[26] You should shop by make and model so that accurate comparisons are possible. That "brand-new, factory-carton" television set may be a two-year-old model. Don't settle for a floor sample, unless the price is so right that you can't refuse. And be leery of a brand you've never heard of; it may prove totally unreliable.

[27] Even among discount stores, prices can vary greatly, so check as many as you can before you buy. Just as important as price is the question of guarantees and service. You should think twice about the purchase if you would be required to travel to the other side of town for warranty work on an appliance.

[28] *Decide on quality.* You can save by buying furniture and rugs on sale, but there's no sense in overdoing the thrift. These typically are items that must last a good while and a $98 couch may not stand up long under the wear and tear an active family can give.

[29] If you don't have the money to pay for high-priced quality, investigate secondhand stores. Some top-quality furniture ends up there at reasonable prices. And you might pick up a badly scratched table for very little and refinish it with one of the easy-finish kits.

[30] Cheap clothing that must take a lot of wear isn't always a good buy either. A more expensive suit or dress will often last far longer comparatively and look better all the while. Some cities have thrift shops where wealthy women dispose of their expensive gowns and dresses, often worn only once.

[31] Sometimes cheaper quality does make good sense. For many meat dishes, USDA Good grade is as satisfactory as Choice or Prime, and you actually get more meat because there is less marbling. Those streaks of fat add tenderness you don't need if you braise the meat.

[32] *Don't wipe out your bargain.* You can save a few dollars on a purchase only to pay more in the long run through extra charges. The bill tacked on for installation of a washer or dryer can eat up every dollar you saved by careful shopping, so get a definite figure on what that is going to cost before making a final decision.

[33] If you put your bargain purchases on a revolving charge account, the 1½% interest charge on the unpaid balance can transform your low-priced find into a high-priced luxury. It's best to calculate in advance how those charges will affect the total price you pay. You may decide that it's better to wait until you can pay cash.

[34] Auto dealers offer plenty of "bargains," most of them illusory. You can find huge discounts on new luxury cars loaded with options toward the end of the model year. Remember that service and maintenance expenses often are immense on such machines. Hard bargaining and trips to several dealers are still the best ways to find the best price.

[35] If you're buying a used car, you can check the average prices in the *Official Used Car Guide* of the National Automobile Dealers Association, which is carried by most banks that make auto loans. Also, have the car inspected, either by a trusted mechanic or at an auto diagnostic center. A car that looks good may be a terrible bargain mechanically.

[36] The cheapest way to pay is cash and the most expensive almost always is through dealer financing. You can get a variety of cheaper loans from a bank—a straight auto loan, a

passbook loan if you have enough savings to pledge against the loan, or a demand note that's secured by good-quality stock certificates.

[37] It all sums up this way: To get a bargain, you've got to plan, save, wait and shop around plenty. Then when these bargains appear, you can step in, snap them up and sit back feeling justifiably pleased with yourself.

EXERCISES—*HOW TO HUNT FOR BARGAINS*

Content

1. What are the six major steps in the process of hunting for bargains? Briefly explain each. What are some of the other suggestions for bargain hunting mentioned in the essay?
2. What does each of the following ads mean: sale (paragraph (14)); clearance (paragraph (15)); special purchase (paragraph (16)); manufacturer's closeout (paragraph (16)); "regularly," "usually," and "formerly" (paragraph (17)); "comparable value" (paragraph (18))?
3. Why should you find out a store's reputation before you believe its ads?
4. What is a "bait" ad?
5. When are cosmetics usually on sale? fabrics? luggage? sporting goods? home furnishings?
6. How are bargain basements generally stocked?
7. What is the recommendation of the U.S. Department of Agriculture for frozen storage of each of the following: cooked, sliced turkey; ice cream; orange juice concentrate; fruit cake; corn?
8. Why should you be leery of a brand of which you have never heard?
9. What is "marbling"?
10. What is the cheapest way to buy a car? the most expensive way almost always?

Style

1. Who is the intended audience of this essay? Explain.
2. Why does the essay employ second person imperative point of view? Is this point of view effective? Explain.

3. This essay is an example of informal process exposition. What specific stylistic techniques make it informal? Refer to specific words and passages in the essay which exemplify these techniques.
4. Is the essay objective or subjective? Explain.
5. Is the rhetorical question at the beginning of the essay effective? Explain.
6. Can you discern any reason or pattern for the order of the six major steps in the process of bargain hunting? Explain.
7. Does the essay contain sufficient specific detail for adequate development? Explain by referring to specific passages in the essay. What methods of development are used? Again explain by referring to the essay.
8. Is the concluding paragraph effective? Explain.
9. Why was the information in the boxed charts not included in the text proper? Explain.

Application of Stylistic Techniques

1. Compare and contrast the style in this essay of process with the style of Blenheim's essay. Be specific.
2. Rewrite paragraph (1) in formal style. Which version do you prefer? Why?
3. Rewrite paragraph (2) in third person singular objective point of view. Then rewrite paragraph (2) in first person singular subjective point of view. Which of the three versions is more effective for the intended purpose? Why?

Suggestions for Writing

1. In an essay, agree or disagree with one of the recommended steps in bargain hunting, supporting your position with specific narrative illustration—either a sustained illustration or a series of brief illustrations.
2. Write an essay on the disadvantages of bargain hunting. Be sure to include plenty of specific examples and illustrations.
3. Write an essay of informal process. Remember that your purpose is to explain and inform, but make your essay as interesting as possible to your intended audience. Suitable subjects include how to study, play bridge, swim, surf, ski, fish, play the guitar, read, take a test, cook a favorite dish, buy a secondhand car, repair an automobile, drive safely, etc.

C. Vann Woodward (1908–) received his education from Emory University, Columbia University, and the University of North Carolina. He now is Sterling Professor of History at Yale and president of the American Historical Association. His publications include *The Battle for Leyte Gulf, Reunion and Reaction, Origins of the New South,* and *The Strange Career of Jim Crow.*

American History (White Man's Version) Needs an Infusion of Soul *(Formal Argument of Process)*

C. VANN WOODWARD

[1] All who write or teach American history are aware by now of the demand for more attention to the part that Negro people have played. It may come quietly from a distressed college dean, or it may come peremptorily and noisily from militant student protest. In any case the demand is insistent that we move over and make room. With whatever grace they can muster and whatever resources they command, historians as teachers are responding one way or another. New colleagues are recruited (black if humanly possible), new courses listed ("Black" or "Afro" in the title), new textbooks written, new lectures prepared. Or in a pinch, old colleagues may have to be pressured and reconditioned and old lectures hastily revised. The adjustment is often awkward and some-

times rather frantic, but American academic institutions are responding, each after its own style and fashion—clumsily, belatedly, heartily, or half-heartedly, as the case may be.

[2] We are concerned here, however, not with the institutional response and its problems nor even primarily with the social purpose and the overdue ends of justice sought, as important as these things unquestionably are. Rather we are concerned for the moment with the professional problems the movement poses, particularly with the impact, good, bad, or indifferent, it will have—is having, has had—upon the writing and reinterpretation of American history. Will it warp as much as it will correct? Will it substitute a new racism for an old? Will historians be able to absorb and control the outraged moral passions released and bend to the social purposes dictated without losing balance and betraying principle? Or will the historian's moral engagement compromise the integrity of his craft? Granting inevitable losses in detachment, will the gains in moral insight outbalance the losses?

[3] On the positive side, certain corrective influences may be scored up as incremental gain immediately apparent. One consequence of having Negro critics or colleagues looking over one's shoulder or having more Negro historians is that embarrassing white-supremacy and ethnocentric *gaffes* are likely to become much rarer in the pages of respected historians. This is not to say that the profession will thus be purged of moral obtuseness and intellectual irresponsibility. These shortcomings are likely to remain constants in the historical profession as in other parts of the human community. But they are likely to find different forms of expression.

[4] Negro history seems destined to remain the moral storm center of American historiography. It is hard to see how it could very well be otherwise, at least for some time to come. Slavery was, after all, the basic moral paradox of American history. It was what Dr. Samuel Johnson had in mind when he asked, "How is it that we hear the loudest *yelps* for liberty among the drivers of Negroes?" But the paradox is older and deeper than the temporary embarrassments of 1776, of slaveholders yelping for liberty, writing the Declaration of Independence, and fighting for the natural rights of man.

[5] Back of that were the European dreamers of America as an idyllic Arcadia, the New Jerusalem, the Promised Land, the world's new hope of rebirth, fulfillment and redemption. Before the dreamers came the discoverer of America, who returned from one of his voyages with a cargo of Indian slaves. After him came the explorers and colonizers who competed in the lucrative African slave trade and brought millions of slaves to the New World. It is, in fact, difficult to see how Europeans could have colonized America and exploited its resources otherwise.

[6] David B. Davis, in his book "The Problem of Slavery in Western Culture," has phrased the paradox perfectly: "How was one to reconcile the brute fact that slavery was an intrinsic part of the American experience with the image of the New World as uncorrupted nature, as a source of redemption from the burdens of history, as a paradise which promised fulfillment of man's highest aspirations?"

[7] One way of dealing with the problem was that of Hector St. John De Crèvecoeur, who wrote the classic statement of the American idyll of democratic fulfillment. "What then is the American, this new man?" was his famous question. And his answer was: "He is either an European, or the descendant of an European. . . ." Crèvecoeur simply defined the Negro out of American identity. It is significant that the tacit exclusion went unnoticed for nearly two centuries. Crèvecoeur's precedent was widely followed in the writing of American history. It might be called the "invisible man" solution.

[8] Another way of dealing with Davis's problem of brute fact and idyllic image was to recognize the Negro's existence all right, but either to ignore moral conflicts and paradoxes in moral values forced by his existence and status, or to attempt to reduce them to other and morally neutral categories of explanation. This might be called the moral-neutrality approach.

[9] Neither the invisible-man solution nor the moral-neutrality approach is any longer acceptable. Moral engagement ranging upward to total commitment now predominates. This approach divides into overlapping, though distinguish-

able, categories. One of them is embraced in the general class of paternalistic historiography but divides broadly into Northern and Southern schools. Northern-type paternalism is usually the more self-conscious. One representative of this school assures the Brother in Black that "Negroes are, after all, only white men with black skins, nothing more, nothing less," endowed with all the putative white attributes of courage, manhood, rebelliousness, and love of liberty. Another concedes the deplorable reality of the "Sambo personality," but attributes it to the potency of the plantation master as white father image and other misfortunes.

[10] The modern Southern paternalist, falling back on his regional heritage, takes to the role more naturally and with less self-consciousness. He disavows the concept of the benevolent plantation school for Africans, but proceeds as if the school actually worked admirably, with some exceptions, and turned out graduates fully prepared for freedom and equality. Any shortcomings or failings on the part of the blacks are attributed to delinquencies of the "responsible" whites, the paternalists. These assumptions result in a charitable picture of the freedom during emancipation and Reconstruction and the era following. Instead of a "white man with a black skin," the Negro is elected an honorary Southerner by paternalists below the Potomac.

[11] Moral preoccupations and problems shape the character of much that is written about the Negro and race relations by modern white historians, but they are predominantly the preoccupations and problems of the white man. His conscience burdened with guilt over his own people's record of injustice and brutality toward the black man, the white historian often writes in a mood of contrition and remorse as if in expiation of racial guilt or flagellation of the guilty.

[12] This is not to deny to the historian the role of moral critic nor to dismiss what has been written out of deep concern for moral values. The history of the Negro people and race relations has profited more from the insights and challenges of this type of writing in the last two decades than from the scholarship of the preceding and much longer era of moral neutrality and obtuseness.

[13] Granting the value of the part white historians have played in this field, the Negro still has understandable causes for dissatisfaction. For however sympathetic they may be, white historians with few exceptions are primarily concerned with the moral, social, political and economic problems of white men and their past. They are prone to present to the Negro as *his* history the record of what the white man believed, thought, legislated, did and did not do *about* the Negro. The Negro is a passive element, the man to whom things happen. He is the object rather than the subject of this kind of history. It is filled with the infamies and the philanthropies, the brutalities and the charities, the laws, customs, prejudices, policies, politics, crusades and wars of whites *about* blacks.

[14] "Racial attitudes" or "American attitudes" in a title mean white attitudes. "The Negro image" means the image in white minds. In this type of history, abolitionists, radical Republicans and carpetbaggers are all of the same pale pigmentation. Not until the civil-rights workers of the nineteen-sixties do the prime movers and shakers of Negro history take on a darker hue in the history books, and not in all of them at that.

[15] Negro history in this tradition—and many Negro historians themselves followed the tradition, virtually the only one available in university seminars—was an enclave, a cause or a result, a commentary or an elaboration of white history. Black history *was* white history. Denied a past of his own, the Negro was given to understand that whatever history and culture he possessed was supplied by his association with the dominant race in the New World and its European background. Thoroughly Europocentric in outlook, American whites subscribed completely to the myth that European culture, *their* culture, was so overwhelmingly superior that no other could survive under exposure to it. They also shared the European stereotypes, built up by three centuries of slave traders and elaborated by 19th- and 20th-century European imperialists, of an Africa of darkness, savagery, bestiality, and degradation. Not only was the African stripped of this degrading heritage on American shores and left cultureless, a Black Adam in a new garden, but he was seen to be doubly fortunate in being

rescued from naked barbarism and simultaneously clothed with a superior culture. The "myth of the Negro past" was that he had no past.

[16] So compelling was this myth, so lacking any persuasive evidence to the contrary, so universally prevalent the stereotypes of Africa in their American world that until very recently Negroes adopted them unquestioningly themselves. W. E. B. Du Bois wrote of N.A.A.C.P. members with a "fierce repugnance toward anything African . . . Beyond this they felt themselves Americans, not Africans. They resented and feared any coupling with Africa."

[17] White friends of the Negro defended him against any slurs associating him with Africa as if against insult. And Negroes commonly used the words "African" and "black" as epithets of an opprobrious sort. They were *Americans* with nothing to do with Africa or its blackness, nakedness and savagery. Africa, like slavery, was something to be forgotten, denied, suppressed. With an older American pedigree and a far better claim than first and second generation immigrants of other ethnic groups, Negroes could protest the remoteness of their foreign origins and the exclusiveness of their American identity. "Once for all," wrote Du Bois in 1919, "let us realize that we are Americans, that we were brought here with the earliest settlers, and that the very sort of civilization from which we came made the complete adoption of Western modes and customs imperative if we were to survive at all. In brief, there is nothing so indigenous, so completely 'made in America' as we."

[18] A few years ago a French writer used the word *"décolonisation"* in the title of a book on the contemporary movement for Negro rights in America. While the analogy that this word suggests is misleading in important respects, it does call attention to the wider environment of the national experience. The dismantling of white supremacy since World War II has been a worldwide phenomenon. The adjustment of European powers to this revolution has appropriately been called decolonization, since this is the political effect it had on their many possessions in Asia, Africa and the Caribbean. The outward trappings, the political symbols, the pomp and ceremony

of decolonization doubtless contained a considerable amount of collective ego gratification for the ethnic groups concerned.

[19] But even more gratifying perhaps was the physical as well as symbolic withdrawal of the dominant whites, together with the debasement of their authority and the destruction of the hated paraphernalia of exclusiveness and discrimination. (We know from the writings of Frantz Fanon and others how much of the colonial syndrome of dependency, inferiority and self-hatred lingered behind the new facade of national sovereignty and how little the life of the masses was affected. But the gratifications were there, too, and for the ruling-class élites these were no doubt considerable.)

[20] The dismantling of white supremacy was simultaneously taking place in the United States, but the process was accompanied by no such pomp and circumstance and no such debasement of white authority and power. What did take place in America was far less dramatic. It came in the form of judicial decisions, legislative acts and executive orders by duly constituted authority that remained unshaken in the possession of power. It came with "all deliberate speed," a speed so deliberate as to appear glacial or illusory.

[21] The outward manifestations were the gradual disappearance of the little signs, "White" and "Colored," and the gradual appearance of token black faces in clubs, schools, universities and boards of directors. Some of the tokens were more impressive: a Cabinet portfolio, a Supreme Court appointment, a seat in the Senate, the office of Mayor. By comparison with the immediately preceding era in America these developments were striking indeed. But by contrast with the rituals and symbols of decolonization in Africa and the Caribbean, they took on a much paler cast.

[22] American Negro attitudes toward the ancestral homeland changed profoundly. The traditional indifference or repugnance for things African, the shame and abhorrence of association with Africa, gave way to fascinated interest, pride and a sense of identification. The art, folklore, music, dance, even the speech and clothing of Africa have taken on a new glamour and emotional significance for people who have never seen that continent and will never set foot on it. Instead of con-

cealing marks of African identification, many young people increasingly emphasize, invent or exaggerate them in dress, speech or hair style.

[23] We are destined to hear a great deal more about Africa from Afro-Americans as time goes on. This will find its way into historical writing and some manifestations may seem rather bizarre. Before we assume a posture of outrage or ridicule, it might be well to put this phenomenon into historical perspective.

[24] The assimilation of European ethnic groups in America throughout the history of immigration has not only been a story of deculturation and acculturation—the shedding of foreign ways and the adoption of new values—it has also been a story of fierce struggles to assert and maintain ethnic interests and identity. One key element in that struggle has been the group's sense of its past. Each immigrant group of any size established its historical societies and journals in which filiopietism has free rein. Not only the Norwegians but the Irish and the Jews have contested with Italians the claim to the discovery of America.

[25] These assertions of group pride in a common past, mythic or real, have accompanied a strong urge for assimilation and integration in American society. In the opinion of the anthropologist Melville J. Herskovits "[to] the extent to which the past of a people is regarded as praiseworthy, their own self-esteem will be high and the opinion of others will be favorable."

[26] Denied a praiseworthy past or for that matter a past of any sort that is peculiarly their own, Negro Americans have consequently been denied such defenses and self-esteem as these resources have provided other and less vulnerable American groups. Now that they are seeking to build defenses of their own and a past of their own, they are likely to repeat many of the ventures in myth-making and filiopietism in which other minorities have indulged.

[27] One of their temptations will be to follow the example of their brothers in Africa now in search of national identity for brand-new nation states. Nationalists have always invoked history in their cause and abused it for their purposes.

No nations have been so prone to this use of history as new nations. Unable to rely on habituation of custom by which old states claim legitimacy and the loyalty of their citizens, new-born nations (our own, for example) invoke history to justify their revolutions and the legitimacy of new rulers.

[28] Like their American kin, the Africans had also been denied a past of their own, for European historians of the imperialist countries held that the continent, at least the sub-Saharan part, had no history before the coming of the white man. Historians of the new African states have not been backward in laying counterclaims and asserting the antiquity of their history and its importance, even its centrality in the human adventure.

[29] Inevitably some black patriots have been carried away by their theme. One Ghanaian historian, for example, goes so far as to assert that Moses and Buddha were Egyptian Negroes, that Christianity sprang from Sudanic tribes, and that Nietzsche, Bergson, Marx and the Existentialists were all reflections of Bantu philosophy. How much of this overwrought nationalism of the emergent African states will take root in American soil remains to be seen. Already something like it has found expression in cults of black nationalism and is seeking lodgement in the academies.

[30] It seems possible that the new pride in Africa's achievements, identification with its people and their history, and the discovery of ancestral roots in its culture could contribute richly to the self-discovery and positive group identity of a great American minority. What had been suppressed or regarded with shame in this American sub-culture could now be openly expressed with confidence and pride.

[31] The extent of African survivals in Negro-American culture has been debated for a generation by anthropologists. No doubt such survivals have been exaggerated and admittedly there are fewer in the United States than in Latin America and the West Indies. But the acknowledged or imagined African survivals in religious and marital practices, in motor habits, in speaking, walking, burden carrying and dancing have gained new sanction and a swinging momentum.

[32] It seems to me that the reclaimed African heritage

could give a third dimension to the tragically two-dimensional man of the Du Bois metaphor. "One ever feels his two-ness," he wrote, "an American, a Negro; two souls, two thoughts, two unreconciled strivings; two warring ideals in one dark body. . . ." Du Bois thought that "the history of the American Negro is the history of this strife," and that "this double-consciousness, this sense of always looking at one's self through the eyes of others" was his tragedy. The recovery of an African past and a third dimension of identity might have a healing effect on the schizoid "two-ness," the "two-soul" cleavage of the Negro mind.

[33] There are, unhappily, less desirable consequences conceivable for the preoccupation with Africa as a clue to racial identity. For in the hands of nationalist cults it can readily become a *mystique* of skin color and exclusiveness of alienation and withdrawal. It can foster a new separatism, an inverted segregation, a black apartheid. It can seek group solidarity and identity by the rejection of the White Devil and all his works simply because of white association. This is part of what Erik Erikson meant by "negative identity," the affirmation of identity by what one is not. With reference to that concept, he remarked on "the unpleasant fact that our Godgiven identities often live off the degradation of others." It would be one of the most appalling ironies of American history if the victims of this system of human debasement should in their own quest for identity become its imitators.

[34] One manifestation of black nationalism in academic life is the cry that only blacks are truly qualified to write or to interpret or to teach the black experience. In the special sense that, other things being equal, those who have undergone an experience are best qualified to understand it, there is some truth in this claim.

[35] American history, the white man's version, could profit from an infusion of "soul." It could be an essential corrective in line with the tradition of countervailing forces in American historiography. It was in that tradition that new immigrant historians revised first-family and old-stock history, that Jewish scholars challenged WASP interpretations, that Western challengers confronted New England complacencies,

Yankee heretics upset Southern orthodoxies, Southern skeptics attacked Yankee myths, and since the beginning the younger generation assaulted the authority of the old. Negro historians have an opportunity and a duty in the same tradition.

[36] An obligation to be a corrective influence is one thing, but a mandate for the exclusive pre-emption of a subject by reason of racial qualification is quite another. They cannot have it both ways. Either black history is an essential part of American history and must be included by all American historians, or else it is unessential and can be segregated and left to black historians.

[37] But Negro history is too important to be left entirely to Negro historians. To disqualify historians from writing Negro history on the grounds of race is to subscribe to an extreme brand of racism. It is to ignore not only the substantial corrective and revisionary contributions to Negro history made by white Americans, but also those of foreign white scholars such as Gilberto Freyre of Brazil, Fernando Ortiz of Cuba, Charles Verlinden of Belgium and Gunnar Myrdal of Sweden. To export this idea of racial qualifications for writing history to Latin America is to expose its narrow parochialism. The United States is unique, so far as I know, in drawing an arbitrary line that classifies everyone as either black or white and calls all people with any apparent African intermixture "Negroes." The current usage of "black" as it is applied to a people, their culture, and their history in this country, is the unconscious adoption by "black" nationalists of a white myth peculiar to the United States.

[38] The fact is that there are few countries left in the New World that are not multiracial in population. In many of them racial intermixture and intermarriage are prevalent. To impose the rule of racial qualification for historians of such multiracial societies as those of Trinidad, Cuba, Jamaica, Brazil or Hawaii would be to leave them without a history. What passes for racial history is often the history of the relations between races—master and slave, imperialist and colonist exploiter, and exploited, and all the political, economic, sexual and cultural relations and their infinitely varied intermixtures.

[39] To leave all the history of these relations in the hands of the masters, the imperialists or the exploiters would result in biased history. But to segregate historical subjects along racial lines and pair them with racially qualified historians would result in fantastically abstract history. This is all the more true since it is the relations, attitudes and interactions between races that are the most controversial and perhaps the most significant aspects of racial history.

[40] Some would maintain that the essential qualification is not racial but cultural, and that membership in the Afro-American subculture is essential to the understanding and interpretation of the subtleties of speech, cuisine, song, dance, folklore and music composing it. There may be truth in this. I am not about to suggest that the Caucasian is a black man with a white skin, for he is something less and something more than that. I am prepared to maintain, however, that so far as their culture is concerned, all Americans are part Negro. Some are more so than others, of course, but the essential qualification is not color or race. When I said "all Americans," unlike Crèvecoeur, I included Afro-Americans. They are part Negro too, but only part. So far as their culture is concerned they are more American than Afro and far more alien in Africa than they are at home, as virtually all pilgrims to Africa have discovered.

[41] Many old black families of Philadelphia and Boston are less African in culture than many whites of the South. The Southern white "acculturation" began long ago and may be traced in the lamentations of planters that their children talked like Negroes, sang Negro songs, preferred Negro music at their dances and danced like Negroes. It was observed by travelers like Frederick L. Olmsted, who was "struck with the close cohabitation and association of black and white . . . black and white faces constantly thrust out of doors to see the train go by.

[42] It is still a moot question whether white revivalist behavior—shouts, jerks, "unknown tongues," possession and the rest—is a reflex of Africanism or vice versa. Even the sophisticated Mary Boykin Chestnut, on attending a Negro church at her plantation, admitted that she "wept bitterly"

and added that "I would very much have liked to shout, too." But, as Herskovits says in his book "The Myth of the Negro Past," "Whether Negroes borrowed from whites or whites from Negroes, in this or any other aspect of culture, it must always be remembered that the borrowing was never achieved without resultant change in whatever was borrowed." If there was a "black experience" and a "white experience," there was also a "gray experience."

[43] Modern white parents have a complaint that differs from that of the antebellum planters but resembles it. For where the old planters' children took on their African acculturation unconsciously by a process of osmosis, the contemporary collegiate swinger, protester and rebel is a deliberate, assiduous, and often egregiously servile imitator. It was Langston Hughes's lament that "you've taken my blues and gone . . . " and he was probably justified in his complaint in the same poem that ". . . you fixed 'em/So they don't sound like me. . . ." But if so it was certainly for no lack of effort on the part of the young white imitator, "The White Negro." He is but the latest contribution to the "gray experience."

[44] Whether the revision of Negro history is undertaken by black historians or white historians, or preferably by both, they will be mindful of the need for correcting ancient indignities, ethnocentric slights and paternalistic patronizing, not to mention calculated insults, callous indifference and blind ignorance. They will want to see full justice done at long last to Negro achievements and contributions, to black leaders and heroes, black slaves and freedmen, black poets and preachers.

[45] As for white historians, I doubt that their contribution to this revision would best be guided by impulses of compensatory exaggeration. The genuine achievements of Negro Americans throughout our history are substantial enough in view of the terrible handicaps under which they labored. They should receive the credit that they have been denied. But during the greater part of the struggle for power and place and frame that make up so much of history, black men were kept in chains and illiteracy and subject thereafter to crippling debasement and deprivation. The number of landmarks and

monuments they were able to leave on the history of their country was necessarily limited.

[46] It is a misguided form of white philanthropy and paternalism that would attempt to compensate by exaggerating or by the celebration of even more obscure and deservedly neglected figures of the past. Equally misguided are impulses of self-flagellation and guilt that encourage the deprecation of all things European or white in our civilization and turn its history into a chorus of *mea culpas*. The demagoguery, the cant and the charlatanry of historians in the service of a fashionable cause can at times rival that of politicians.

[47] The Negro historian in present circumstances labors under a special set of pressures and temptations. One that will require moral fiber to resist is the temptation to gratify the white liberal's masochistic cravings, his servile yearnings to be punished. This is indeed a tempting market, but historians would do well to leave it to the theater of the absurd.

[48] Another temptation is to give uninhibited voice to such sentiments as Du Bois expressed in his declaration: "I believe in the Negro race, in the beauty of its genius, the sweetness of its soul. . . ." A sincere sentiment, no doubt, but before releasing such pronouncements for publication it might be advisable to substitute the word "white" for the word "Negro" and play it back for sound: "I believe in the *white* race, in the beauty of its genius, the sweetness of its soul. . . ." At present, the celebratory impulse runs powerfully through the historiography of this field. "Let us now praise famous men," saith Ecclesiasticus.

[49] Now is a time to do honor to heroes, justice to the obscure and to demonstrate beyond doubt that the downtrodden seethed constantly with resistance to oppression and hostility to their oppressors. The demand for such history is understandable. But the historian will keep in mind that the stage of history was never peopled exclusively by heroes, villains and oppressed innocents, that scamps and time servers and antiheroes have always played their parts. He might be reminded also that the charlatans and knaves and rakehells of Malcolm X's Harlem were probably as numerous as their

white counterparts and represent a neglected field of Negro history.

[50] It is to be hoped that white as well as black historians will reserve some place for irony as well as for humor. If so they will risk the charge of heresy by pointing out in passing that Haiti, the first Negro republic of modern history, though born of a slave rebellion, promptly established and for a long time maintained an oppressive system of forced labor remarkably similar to state slavery; that Liberia, the second Negro republic, named for liberty, dedicated to freedom and ruled by ex-slaves from the United States, established a flourishing African slave trade; that one sequel to the liberation of the black mutineers of the slave ship "Amistad" in 1841 with the aid of John Quincy Adams was that Cliqué, the leader of the liberated, returned to Africa and became a slave trader himself.

[51] These instances are not adduced to alleviate the guilt of the white man, who rightfully bears the greater burden. In all the annals of Africa there could scarcely be a more ironic myth of history than that of the New World republic which reconciled human slavery with natural rights and equality and on the backs of black slaves set up as the New Jerusalem, the world's best hope for freedom. The mythic African counterparts look pale alongside the American example. They do serve, however, as reminders that the victims as well as the victors of the historical process are caught in the human predicament.

[52] Joseph Conrad once remarked that women, children and revolutionaries have no taste for irony. These are certainly not the most propitious times for the cultivation of that taste. Not only is it an abomination to revolutionaries, but mixed motives, ambivalence, paradox and complexity in any department are equally suspect.

[53] In times like these the historian will be hard put to it to maintain his creed that the righteousness of a cause is not a license for arrogance, that the passion for justice is not a substitute for reason, that race and color are neither a qualification nor a disqualification for historians, that myths, however therapeutic, are not to be confused with history, and

that it is possible to be perfectly serious without being oppressively solemn. To defend this position under the circumstances will require a certain amount of what some call "cool" and others grace—grace under pressure, which was Hemingway's definition of courage.

EXERCISES—*AMERICAN HISTORY (WHITE MAN'S VERSION) NEEDS AN INFUSION OF SOUL*

Content

1. What is Woodward's primary concern in this essay?
2. According to David B. Davis, what is the paradox of American history? What is Crèvecoeur's "invisible man" solution to this paradox? What is the moral-neutrality approach to the paradox? Why is neither approach any longer acceptable?
3. What are the understandable causes for blacks' dissatisfaction with the way American history has been written?
4. How have American black attitudes toward Africa changed? What two paths of action might result from this change?
5. What is deculturation? acculturation?
6. Should black history be left entirely to black historians? Why?
7. What does Woodward mean when he says "all Americans are part Negro"?
8. What are some of the ironic elements in black history?
9. What is the historian's creed?
10. What is the major proposition or hypothesis on which Woodward bases his argument?

Style

1. What is Woodward's point of view?
2. Who is Woodward's audience? How is his style appropriate to his audience?
3. What specific stylistic techniques does Woodward use to convince his readers to agree with his major proposition? Does he convince you?
4. What specific stylistic techniques does Woodward use to make his argument formal?
5. Is the allusion to Hemingway at the end effective? Why?
6. What do Woodward's quotations from Du Bois, Herskovits, Crèvecoeur, and others add to his argument?

7. What is the tone of the last sentence of paragraph (47)? Is this comment suitable in this position? Why?

Application of Stylistic Techniques

1. Write one paragraph in which you summarize, briefly and clearly, Woodward's argument.
2. Throughout this essay, Woodward is restrained. For contrast, write an emotional introduction to this essay.

Suggestions for Writing

1. Write an essay on one of the following topics suggested by Woodward's essay:
   Who Should Teach Black History and Literature?
   Paradoxes of American History
   Search for Identity
   American Myths
   The Afro-American Culture
   Misguided Philanthropy
2. Write a formal argument of hypothesis on one of the following hypotheses. Do not become emotional.
   Abortion laws should be liberalized.
   The draft should be abolished.
   The population explosion must be curbed.
   Contributors to environmental pollution must be punished.
   Final examinations should be abolished.
   The seniority system in Congress should be abolished.

Carolyn Dillon (1939–   ) is head psychiatric social worker, Austin Unit, Boston State Hospital; an assistant clinical professor of psychiatry at Tufts Medical School; a fieldwork instructor at the Boston University School of Social Work; and a psychotherapist in private practice in the Boston area. At the time this article was written, she was a caseworker for the Family Service Association in Boston. She has delivered papers to Boston professional groups, has assisted in predictive predelinquency research at Putnam Children's Center in Roxbury, Massachusetts, and has contributed articles to *Smith College Studies in Social Work* and *Social Casework.*

The Professional Name Game *(Formal Argument of Policy)*

CAROLYN DILLON

[1] Despite Sisyphean efforts to disabuse ourselves of the art and science of categorizing, social workers continue to produce whole new generations of Mrs. A, the hapless client whose fate is sealed by the terms *anal character* or *pseudoneurotic schizophrenic, borderline state* or *depressive core,* flesh melted from bone and reduced to a record-fattening conundrum of syndrome and synthesis. It is our Name Game, and we like to think it brings us closer to meeting burgeoning requests for service with a limited number of hearts and heads. We also like to think it brings us closer, through understanding, to the people who make the requests.

[2] I suggest that the Name Game has had an adverse effect; that we have succeeded in finding increasingly sophisticated and intellectually palatable labels for people who are caught up in the vicissitudes of life and with whom it is often

From *Social Casework,* June 1969. Reprinted by permission of Family Service Association of America.

difficult to relate; that the labels tend to set off clients as distinct from the worker; that the resultant groups overlap diagnostic categories; and that the clients have subtly become simply Them. The device that had once promised to bring us closer to our clients through "shorthand" understanding may actually have caused a breach between us and the people who need our closeness. The clients seem to read us quickly and accurately, however, even though we cannot read them, mainly because we have considerable knowledge about them but still do not *know* them well at all.

[3] Our Name Game has focused so steadily on histories of misery, problems, limitations, and deficient differences from a mythical norm that it has blurred our ability to see clients as fellow human beings who, like ourselves at times, are in trouble and exceedingly hard to love. Perhaps the painful similarity has been the cause of our seeking increasingly subtle labels—labels that separate groups of clients not only from other groups but also, and more important, from ourselves.

[4] Social workers prefer to think that long ago we purged ourselves of Lady Bountiful and her designations Deserving and Unworthy. We seemed to take a great step forward when we substituted Character Disorder and Borderline. Unfortunately, in spite of such useful distinctions, so many clients continued to "terminate" us before we thought they ought to that we moved into subcategorizing and the appellations Hard to Reach, Hard to Engage, Hard to Hold. To date we seem to emphasize the characteristics that make the client "hard"—hard to do almost anything with except close the case.

[5] Befuddled, we go on to bigger and better categories, all the while intoning that diagnostic "boxes" are too rigid and depersonalizing! Currently the person who is not a Neurotic (like us?) can knowledgeably be called Deprived, Culturally and Spiritually Impoverished, Ghetto Dweller, Multi-problem Client, Hard (there it is again) Core, and Urban Isolate. (When in doubt, use Crisis Families.) In short, ever since Michael Harrington came upon the scene, it has become insidiously all right to call people who do not live the way we live or in the place in which we live The Poor, and we are

back where Lady Bountiful was a century ago. Technically I would agree with anyone who argues that social work has undergone changes in the past hundred years. Attitudinally I am concerned because of a deep conviction that our attitudes are decisive in regard to whether a client will grow—or simply go—after his initial contact with us. And when professional social workers can once again be heard to say casually, "In general, this is a hard working, deserving family," certainly we have reason to wonder how long it will be before "deserving" and "poor" once again fall naturally together in our parlance.

[6] In any event we have our Name Game, and within it the tendency to view clients as Them is, perhaps, the most disturbing. The tendency is evident in our requests for "good" counseling cases, although our caseloads are full and waiting lists are lengthy. It is evident in our wish for "a different kind of case," despite our life building basic premise that each person is different and merits respect for his uniqueness. The trouble with seeing clients as Them is that, although it reassures us that we do not have "problems like that," it can feed a sense of inadequacy and hopelessness. We may eventually feel overwhelmed by undifferentiated masses of Them in comparison with few of Us, whose energy and time are limited.

[7] Why, then, do we persist in playing the Name Game that seems only to distance and dishearten rather than to bring clients and workers closer together? Why have we so easily learned to call people everything but people and managed to have so many Thems suspended on waiting lists? And when they are able to gain entrance to our office, how is it that so many become lost in the quagmire of recording that is resplendent with jargon and theoretical speculation but often devoid of the simplest sense of personhood or pathos?

[8] We like to say we find it difficult to describe the Less-Well-Put-Together client or to form a relationship with him because of the differences between us. It seems to me that the major difficulty is his similarity to us—the many aspects of ourselves that we prefer not to have to examine or to have stirred up week after weary week. The closer we are to our clients, the more painfully aware we are that they

spare us nothing in bombarding us with raw impulse and unambiguous imagery. They are incredibly quick and accurate in perceiving our underlying feelings toward them and our subtler feelings about ourselves. Having no Name Game, they often overwhelm us with undiluted anger, with a desperate sense of their unimportance, and with a terrible, enervating despair that comes from mattering to no one. I think we are more aware, in a visceral way, of such client characteristics than we choose to admit. Our labels, waiting lists, and ponderous records shield us mainly from ourselves. We shall continue to resist case openings and essential relating as long as we fear to look in mirrors, intolerant of seeing ourselves at one with the people we want to call Bad Counseling Cases and regard as strange and different. (Little wonder that the mere utterance of *Multiproblem,* laden as it has become with poor prognosis and menacing visions of a twenty-four-hour day, tempts us to hang onto Productive Mrs. B a little longer so that "just no time" is available to see Mrs. A—on the borderline or off).

[9] Perhaps we can stop labeling long enough to come to grips with a reality that may be unpleasant for some of us but, nevertheless, relentlessly begs our attention: The "cases" we say we "cannot counsel" are likely to remain in the majority of cases we shall *be* counseling. I think all social workers can agree that unless we want to continue to have abrupt and "unexplained" client terminations, to reduce caseloads in order to mount textbook attacks, or to accept seven to ten years of therapy as a satisfactory treatment solution, we must search out effective means of connecting with and mobilizing—of counseling—the people whose human wants require an equally human response. Few of us would have remained in metropolitan agencies if we had not been secretly and somewhat tenaciously committed to improving our relationships with the very people we, in our weariness, say are abhorrent.

[10] If we are to make such improvement we must honestly acknowledge that despite our tutoring and analysis, we remain subject to infirmity, anxiety, and myopia. We continue to be people and may easily be seen as Them. Continuing honesty in the observation and discipline of our own

prejudices and predispositions is required in order to diminish the mutual anxiety between us and our clients. As long as we remain estranged from our own humanity we will bring estrangement to our clients, and as long as our acceptance of our own imperfections is uneasy our acceptance of the imperfect client will be uneasy.

[11] Moreover, we need to rekindle the no longer fashionable conviction that there is a reachable, mobilizable something in everyone that can be dug out, nurtured, and expanded not by Me and Him, but by the two as We. I find it unfortunate, for example, that we try to rid casework students of their testy assurance that everyone could be cured if it were not for all us professionals! The students' dogged insistence on the impossible is precisely that which so often distinguishes their work and sparks their clients, enabling students to leap hurdles before which you and I pale. Perhaps they suffer delusions of grandeur. If so, I think social work needs them, and I think our Name Game has turned on us most destructively in this area, with the result that one label can weight us in advance with the certain difficulty of our work.

[12] We should remember that fifty years ago the schizophrenic person was Untreatable, growing up and dying in a secret room or back ward with the equally Hopeless retarded person. Twenty years ago only neurotic patients were considered able to gain from introspection; today we ask many and different people to look within and tell us what they see and feel. Not long ago we were assured that any discussion at the intellectual level was a waste of the client's time, if not outright support of a poor defense. Today we know the intellect as an ever promising ally.

[13] Habitually we stressed caution, always wary of the client's tender underside and wondering which honestly confronting statement, unambiguous piece of advice, or direct display of real feeling would cause the client to fall apart. We have stressed his fear and resistance in confronting truths; his vulnerability to breakdown when pushed too far too soon; his inability to do almost anything you and I say you and I do in the normal course of things. Slowly we stressed ourselves right out of tirelessly searching for what the client has done,

can do, and would like to do if he dared hope someone—any-one—believed he could do it.

[14] I see that belief—the belief that the client can succeed—as the primary force for change we have to offer people who seek us out. I think they recognize the absence of such belief immediately and respond accordingly—with apathy, withdrawal, foot dragging, manipulation, and frequently termination. Clearly the transmission of that belief, as well as the hope-for-change companion to it, is the major continuing task of casework, from first contact to last.

[15] We will have to risk, and experiment boldly in, being more responsive and warm, so that we may provide flesh-and-blood models toward or against which clients can grow. Curiously, all caseworkers currently speak easily of client growth through identification with the worker, while many maintain that the exposure of worker identity through honest reaction or comment may work such grievous results as destructive transferences, fury because of the worker's humanity, and fright because of the worker's closeness.

[16] It seems to me that clients need a consistently graspable and real person that they can identify before identifying with if they are to grow. Surely we, too, grow as we are reminded of the resiliency and durability of human beings and their ability to tolerate almost anything said or done in a relationship of mutual respect and faith. We should ask ourselves how many nodding enigmas we should want to trust, be like, or try to feel close to week after week. Perhaps we, too, would find low back pain a welcome alternative!

[17] In brief, the suggestions made here are intended to replace the Name Game with a reaffirmation that people who turn to social workers now do so for the same reasons people have always turned to other people: in search of love and encouragement, a place of importance, and a chance to be somebody. We need to respond in a more freely personal way to that turning; not as one to one, but as one *with* one and with him all the way. In all their guises and despite all our labels, clients are likely to continue to seek in us an opportunity for a kind of essential, human reality testing by virtue of their long experience with credibility gaps, with distance, and

with strangers who remain strangers. They ask us for something different, not more of the distance, strangeness, and hopelessness with which they are already burdened.

[18] We, in turn, need to search ourselves to see whether it is just the client who is hard to reach, to feel close to, and to define as a person. We need to realize that, as fallible human beings, we are already "meeting the client where he is" if only we can rest there comfortably and operate there as courageously as we do at a distance. Our clients' search requires that we be ourselves, that we deal with our fantasies of objective detachment, and that we feel, respond, and extend ourselves to reach them. If we cannot do these things, who will?

EXERCISES—*THE PROFESSIONAL NAME GAME*

Content

1. What is "the professional name game"?
2. What has been the result of the "name game"?
3. What makes a social worker's job difficult?
4. What must be done to improve social work?

Style

1. Who is Dillon's audience? Explain.
2. Is this essay tightly or loosely structured? Why?
3. Why is this an argument of policy instead of an argument of hypothesis?
4. What is the effect of Dillon's use of rhetorical questions in paragraph (7)? in paragraph (18)?
5. What is Dillon's tone?
6. Point out some examples of connotative language in this essay. Why is such language justifiable in this formal argument?
7. Why does Dillon use first person point of view in her argument?

Application of Stylistic Techniques

1. Rewrite paragraph (2), substituting third person for first person.
2. Rewrite paragraph (7) in declarative instead of interrogative sentences.
3. Compare and contrast Dillon's style to Woodward's.

Suggestions for Writing

1. Write an essay in which you criticize the jargon, slang, or specialized language of a group, such as teenagers, hippies, scientists, educators, businessmen, doctors, or mechanics.
2. Write a formal argument of policy on some situation which you believe should be changed. Be sure to include your solution to the problem, and try to incite your chosen audience to action. Use a topic of your own or one of the following hypotheses:
   The present grading system in college should be changed.
   Television ratings are invalid.
   There is too much violence on television.
   A student should have more freedom in high school.
   A student should be given more responsibility in college.

K. Ross Toole (1920–   ), born in Missoula, Montana, is a professor of United States history at the University of Montana. He has contributed to numerous historical journals, *Reader's Digest,* and *U.S. News & World Report.* He has also written *Probing the American West* and *Montana: An Uncommon Land.*

I Am Tired of the Tyranny of Spoiled Brats

(Informal Argument)

K. ROSS TOOLE

[1] I am 49 years old. It took me many years and considerable anguish to get where I am—which isn't much of anyplace except exurbia. I was nurtured in depression; I lost four years to war; I am invested with sweat; I have had one coronary; I am a "liberal," square and I am a professor. I am sick of the "younger generation," hippies, Yippies, militants and nonsense.

[2] I am a professor of history at the University of Montana, and I am supposed to have "liaison" with the young. Worse still, I am father of seven children. They range in age from 7 to 23—and I am fed up with nonsense. I am tired of being blamed, maimed and contrite; I am tired of tolerance and the reaching out (which is always my function) for understanding. I am sick of the total irrationality of the campus "rebel," whose bearded visage, dirty hair, body odor and "tactics" are childish but brutal, naïve but dangerous, and the essence of arrogant tyranny—the tyranny of spoiled brats.

From Billings, Montana, *Gazette,* February 8, 1970. Reprinted by permission.

[3] I am terribly disturbed that I may be incubating more of the same. Our household is permissive, our approach to discipline is an apology and a retreat from standards—usually accompanied by a gift in cash or kind.

[4] It's time to call a halt: time to live in an adult world where we belong, and time to put these people in their places. We owe the "younger generation" what all "older generations" have owed younger generations—love, protection to a point, and respect when they deserve it. We do not owe them our souls, our privacy, our whole lives—and above all, we do not owe them immunity from our mistakes, or their own.

[5] Every generation makes mistakes, always has and always will. We have made our share. But my generation has made America the most affluent country on earth. It has tackled, head-on, a racial problem which no nation on earth in the history of mankind had dared to do. It has publicly declared war on poverty and it has gone to the moon; it has desegregated schools and abolished polio; it has presided over the beginning of what is probably the greatest social and economic revolution in man's history. It has begun these things, not finished them. It has declared itself, and committed itself, and taxed itself, and damn near run itself into the ground in the case of social justice and reform.

[6] Its mistakes are fewer than my father's generation —or his father's, or his. Its greatest mistake is not Vietnam; it is the abdication of its first responsibility, its pusillanimous capitulation to its youth, and its sick preoccupation with the problems, the mind, psyche, the *raison d'être* of the young.

[7] Since when have children ruled this country? By virtue of what right, by what accomplishment should thousands of teen-agers, wet behind the ears and utterly without the benefit of having lived long enough to have either judgment or wisdom, become the sages of our time?

[8] The psychologists, the educators and preachers say the young are rebelling against our archaic mores and morals, our materialistic approaches to life, our failures in diplomacy, our terrible ineptitude in racial matters, our narrowness as parents, our blindness to the root ills of society. Balderdash!

[9] Society hangs together by the stitching of many

threads. No 18-year-old is simply the product of his 18 years: He is the product of 3,000 years of the development of mankind—and throughout those years, injustice has existed and been fought; rules have grown outmoded and been changed; doom has hung over men and been avoided: unjust wars have occurred; pain has been the cost of progress—and man has persevered.

[10] As a professor and the father of seven, I have watched this new generation and concluded that most of them are fine. A minority are not—and the trouble is that minority threatens to tyrannize the majority and take over. I dislike that minority; I am aghast that the majority "takes" it and allows itself to be used. And I address myself to both the minority and the majority. I speak partly as a historian, partly as a father and partly as one fed-up, middle-aged and angry member of the so-called "Establishment"—which, by the way, is nothing but a euphemism for "society."

[11] Common courtesy and a regard for the opinions of others is not merely a decoration on the pie crust of society—it is the heart of the pie. Too many "youngsters" are egocentric boors. They will not listen: they will only shout down. They will not discuss but, like 4-year-olds, they throw rocks and shout.

[12] Arrogance is obnoxious; it is also destructive. society has classically ostracized arrogance without the backing of demonstrable accomplishment. Why, then, do we tolerate arrogant slobs who occupy our homes, our administration buildings, our streets and parks—urinating on our beliefs and defiling our premises? It is not the police we need—our generation and theirs—it is an expression of our disgust and disdain. Yet we do more than permit it; we dignify it with introspective flagellation. Somehow it is our fault. Balderdash again!

[13] Sensitivity is not the property of the young, nor was it invented in 1950. The young of any generation have felt the same impulse to grow, to reach out, to touch stars, to live freely and to let the minds loose along unexplored corridors. Young men and young women have always stood on the same hill and felt the same vague sense of restraint that sep-

arated them from the ultimate experience—the sudden and complete expansion of the mind, the final fulfillment. It is one of the oldest, sweetest and most bitter experiences of mankind.

[14] Today's young people did not invent it; they do not own it. And what they seek to attain, all mankind has sought to attain throughout the ages. Shall we, therefore, approve the presumed attainment of it through heroin, "speed," LSD and other drugs? And shall we, permissively, let them poison themselves simply because, as in other respects, we feel vaguely guilty because we brought them into this world?

[15] Again, it is not police raids and tougher laws that we need; it is merely strength. The strength to explain, in our potty, middle-aged way, that what they seek, we sought; that it is somewhere but not here—and sure as hell not in drugs; that, in the meanwhile, they will cease and desist the poison game. And this we must explain early and hard—and then police it ourselves.

[16] Society, "the Establishment," is not a foreign thing we seek to impose on the young. We know it is far from perfect. We did not make it; we have only sought to change it. The fact that we have only been minimally successful is the story of all generations—as it will be the story of the generation coming up. Yet we have worked a number of wonders. We have changed it. We are deeply concerned about our failures; we have not solved the racial problem but we have faced it; we are terribly worried about the degradation of our environment, about injustices, inequities, the military-industrial complex and bureaucracy. But we have attacked these things.

[17] We have, all our lives, taken arms against our sea of troubles—and fought effectively. But we also have fought with a rational knowledge of the strength of our adversary; and, above all, knowing that the war is one of attrition in which the "unconditional surrender" of the forces of evil is not about to occur. We win, if we win at all, slowly and painfully. That is the kind of war society has always fought—because man is what he is.

[18] Knowing this, why do we listen subserviently to the violent tacticians of the new generation? Either they have

total victory by Wednesday next or burn down our carefully built barricades in adolescent pique; either they win now or flee off to a commune and quit; either they solve all problems this week or join a wrecking crew of paranoids.

[19] Youth has always been characterized by impatient idealism. If it were not, there would be no change. But impatient idealism does not extend to guns, fire bombs, riots, vicious arrogance, and instant gratification. That is not idealism; it is childish tyranny.

[20] The worst of it is that we (professors and faculties in particular) in a paroxysm of self-abnegation and apology, go along, abdicate, apologize as if we had personally created the ills of the world—and thus lend ourselves to chaos. We are the led, not the leaders. And we are fools.

[21] As a professor I meet the activists and revolutionaries every day. They are inexcusably ignorant. If you want to make a revolution, do you not study the ways to do it? Of course not! Ché Guevara becomes their hero. He failed; he died in the jungles of Bolivia with an army of six. His every move was a miscalculation and a mistake. Mao Tse-tung and Ho Chi Minh led revolutions based on a peasantry and an overwhelmingly ancient rural economy. They are the patternmakers for the SDS [Students for a Democratic Society] and the student militants. I have yet to talk to an "activist" who has read Crane Brinton's "The Anatomy of Revolution," or who is familiar with the works of Jefferson, Washington, Paine, Adams or even Marx or Engels. And I have yet to talk to a student militant who has read about racism elsewhere and/or who understands, even primitively, the long and wondrous struggle of the NAACP [National Association for the Advancement of Colored People] and the genius of Martin Luther King—whose name they invariably take in vain.

[22] An old and scarred member of the wars of organized labor in the U.S. in the 1930s recently remarked to me: "These 'radicals' couldn't organize well enough to produce a sensible platform, let alone revolt their way out of a paper bag." But they can—because we let them—destroy our universities, make our parks untenable, make a shambles of our streets, and insult our flag.

[23] I assert that we are in trouble with this younger generation not because we have failed our country, not because of affluence or stupidity, not because we are antediluvian, not because we are middle-class materialists, but simply because we have failed to keep that generation in its place, and we have failed to put them back there when they got out of it. We have the power; we do not have the will. We have the right; we have not exercised it.

[24] To the extent that we now rely on the police, Mace, the National Guard, tear gas, steel fences and a wringing of hands, we will fail.

[25] What we need is a reappraisal of our own middle-class selves, our worth and our hard-won progress. We need to use disdain, not Mace; we need to reassess a weapon we came by the hard way, by travail and labor: firm authority as parents, teachers, businessmen, workers and politicians.

[26] The vast majority of our children from 1 to 20 are fine kids. We need to back this majority with authority and with the firm conviction that we owe it to them and to ourselves. Enough of apology, enough of analysis, enough of our abdication of responsibility, enough of the denial of our own maturity and good sense.

[27] The best place to start is at home. But the most practical and effective place, right now, is our campuses. This does not mean a flood of angry edicts, a sudden clamp-down, a "new" policy. It simply means that faculties should stop playing chicken, that demonstrators should be met not with police but with expulsions. The power to expel (strangely unused) has been the legitimate recourse of universities since 1209.

[28] More importantly, it means that at freshman orientation, whatever form it takes, the administration should set forth the ground rules—not belligerently but forthrightly.

[29] A university is the microcosm of society itself. It cannot function without rules for conduct. It cannot, as society cannot, legislate morals. It is dealing with young men and women, 18 to 22. But it can, and must, promulgate rules. It cannot function without order—and, therefore, who disrupts order must leave. It cannot permit students to determine when,

what and where they shall be taught. It cannot permit the occupation of its premises, in violation both of the law and its regulations, by "militants."

[30] There is room within the university complex for basic student participation, but there is no room for slobs, disruption and violence.

[31] The first obligation of the administration is to lay down the rules early, clearly and positively, and to attach to this statement the penalty for violation. It is profoundly simple—and the failure to state it, in advance, is the salient failure of university administrations in this age.

[32] Expulsion is a dreaded verdict. The administration merely needs to make it clear, quite dispassionately, that expulsion is the inevitable consequence of violation of the rules. Among the rules, even though it seems gratuitous, should be these:

1. Violence—armed or otherwise—the forceful occupation of buildings, the intimidation by covert or overt act of any student or faculty member or administrative personnel, the occupation of any university property, field, park, building, lot or other place, shall be cause for expulsion.
2. The disruption of any class, directly or indirectly, by voice or presence or the destruction of any university property, shall be cause for expulsion.

[33] This is neither new nor revolutionary. It is merely the reassertion of an old, accepted and necessary right of the administration of any such institution. And the faculty should be informed, firmly, of this reassertion, before trouble starts.

[34] This does not constitute provocation. It is one of the oldest rights and necessities of the university community. The failure of university administrators to use it is one of the mysteries of our permissive age—and the blame must fall largely on faculties, because they have consistently pressured administrators not to act.

[35] Suppose the students refuse to recognize expulsions —suppose they march, riot, strike. The police? No. The matter, by prearrangement, publicly stated, should then pass to the courts. If buildings are occupied, the court enjoins the participating students. It has the lawful power to declare them

in contempt. If violence ensues, it is in violation of the court's order. Courts are not subject to fears, not part of the action. And what militant will shout obscenities in court with contempt hanging over his head?

[36] Too simple? Not at all. Merely an old process which we seem to have forgotten. It is too direct for those who seek to employ Freudian analysis, too positive for "academic senates" who long for philosophical debate, and too prosaic for those who seek orgastic self-condemnation.

[37] This is a country full of decent, worried people like myself. It is also a country full of people fed up with nonsense. We need—those of us over 30: tax-ridden, harried, confused, weary and beat-up—to reassert our hard-won prerogatives.

[38] It is our country, too. We have fought for it, bled for it, dreamed for it, and we love it. It is time to reclaim it.

EXERCISES—*I AM TIRED OF THE TYRANNY OF SPOILED BRATS*

Content

1. According to Toole, what does the older generation owe the younger generation? What does the older generation not owe the younger generation?
2. What have been the positive contributions of Toole's generation to America and the world? Why did they do these things?
3. What is the greatest mistake of Toole's generation?
4. How do a minority of the young tyrannize our society?
5. What can be done to stop this tyranny?
6. How is a university a microcosm of society?
7. What is the first obligation of a college administration?

Style

1. What is Toole's angle of vision?
2. Who is Toole's intended audience?
3. What is the tone of this essay?
4. What makes this essay informal instead of formal?
5. Does Toole avoid alienating his audience? Support your answer.
6. Is this essay an argument of hypothesis or an argument of policy? Why?

7. What is the effect of Toole's use of rhetorical questions in paragraph (7)? paragraph (14)?
8. What is the effect of Toole's use of "Balderdash" at the end of paragraph (8)?
9. Is Toole's diction primarily denotative or connotative?

Application of Stylistic Techniques

1. Rewrite paragraph (38), making it six short sentences. Is Toole's version better?
2. Study and analyze paragraph (1). Then using that paragraph (especially the sentence structure) as a pattern, write a paragraph describing yourself.

Suggestions for Writing

1. Write an essay in which you agree or disagree with Toole's main idea.
2. Write an informal argument. You may use a topic of your own or refer to the suggestions following the Woodward essay and the Dillon essay.

This fragment of a larger document was found in the Men's Room in Low Library at Columbia University following the police removal of revolutionary students from that building on April 30, 1968. It was marked "Preamble" and was the opening of a statement titled "A Declaration of Liberation."

A Declaration of Liberation

(Emotional Argument)

[1] Look, there are certain truths that no one can deny. Everybody is created good and beautiful and equal. So we're as great as anybody else in this sick culture, and probably a hell of a lot better. Second, everybody has their rights, lots of them, and no one on earth, not even a professor or a mother, has any business interfering with any of them. Among these is the right to Life, a big, full, beautiful life—without middle-class hangups like money, responsibility, examinations and grades, the Puritan ethic, military service, and pressures. Another is Liberty, the right to come and go as you please, whenever you please, without the government manipulators, crummy businessmen, religious spooks, uptight parents, the stupid CIA, the sadistic cops, and the really out-of-it college Administrators imposing their totalitarianism. Also, there is the pursuit of Happiness, the moral right to have a fun time, to blow your mind, to sleep around, to turn on, however and whenever you like—so long as you don't interfere with anybody else.

[2] Now, it's only because you sometimes have to protect these rights from right-wing idiots and jocks that governments have any right to exist at all. But politicians and everybody in authority must be totally and at every minute responsible to the people in the streets and the students. That's where all power comes from. As soon as government or authority of any kind, starts pushing people around or impinging on any liberties with their decrees, the people have a perfect right to tear down that power structure and build a better one based on love and total freedom.

EXERCISES—*A DECLARATION OF LIBERATION*

Content

1. What are the four truths no one can deny?
2. Where does all power come from?
3. What is the main idea of this declaration?

Style

1. What specific techniques does the writer use to appeal to emotion?
2. Who is the intended audience? What audiences would this emotional argument alienate?
3. What is the writer's angle of vision?
4. Is the diction primarily denotative or connotative? Why?
5. Is the connotation of the author's use of the following words favorable or unfavorable: *sick* (paragraph (1)); *professor* (1); *middle-class* (1); *Liberty* (1); *businessmen* (1); *a fun time* (1); *authority* (2)?
6. Point out the cliches in this declaration.
7. Point out the unsupported generalizations in the declaration.
8. Why is this declaration not logical?
9. Is the declaration formal, informal, or colloquial? Explain.

Application of Stylistic Techniques

1. Rewrite paragraph (1) to make it formal and objective.
2. Find an example of emotional argument in an editorial or letter to the editor in a newspaper or magazine. Compare and contrast its effectiveness to the effectiveness of this declaration.

Suggestions for Writing

1. Write an essay explaining how advertisers or politicians use emotional argument to persuade. Be sure to use specific examples.
2. Write a logical argument in which you explain some aspect of what you think is wrong with our society and how it can be changed.

PART FOUR

Fiction and Criticism

The common meaning of "criticism" is to find fault with, as in "My sister criticized my new outfit; she said it was too tight." or "The teacher criticized my speech; she said I mumbled." But criticism in its broader sense means to examine all aspects in order to evaluate.

Every day we exercise our critical powers in many ways. The housewife decides which brand of tomatoes is best for her family. The husband decides which car will best suit his needs for commuting to work. The teenager determines whether he should attend college or not. The boss decides which computer to buy. The citizen chooses one candidate to vote for. Whenever we make a decision or express an opinion or make an evaluation, we are using criticism as a basic method of thought. As a student you use your critical faculty in class discussions, debates, themes, research papers, and examinations.

If a literature instructor asks you to write a paper on the theme of Shakespeare's *Macbeth* or on the imagery in Crane's *The Open Boat,* he is asking you to write a particular type of exposition—literary criticism. The purpose of this type of criticism is to analyze, evaluate, and explain a piece of literature or some aspect of it.

The literary critic examines the faults and the virtues, the weaknesses and the strengths, of a piece of literature to arrive at a valid estimation of the value of the literature. The professional critic's job is to help his readers understand and appreciate literature more fully; he accomplishes his task by analyzing and judging the quality of literary works. As a student critic, you have the same job. You have studied *Macbeth* or *The Open Boat* thoroughly, and you want to share your conclusions with your audience to help them understand and appreciate the work as well as you do.

Because of different backgrounds and different frames of reference, critics might come to different conclusions, all valid. Perhaps one critic will say that the theme of *Macbeth* focuses on greed, but another will say on ambition, or another on evil. The test of the validity of any interpretation is the evidence from the literature the critic offers in support of his idea.

Most literary criticism is written for a limited audience—

those interested in understanding literature better, usually students, teachers, and scholars.

The style of literary criticism suits this specific purpose and this limited audience. The level is informal except in the most scholarly instances. The point of view is usually first person or third person singular subjective or a combination of the two. The tone is generally straightforward, but sometimes satiric or sarcastic. The language should be primarily denotative and very precise in shades of meaning to prevent ambiguity and confusion in understanding.

If you can write effective exposition, you can adapt your style to this special type of exposition.

John Steinbeck (1902–1968), before becoming one of America's best known novelists and short story writers, was a jack-of-all-trades. His works demonstrate his special interest in the depressed economic classes of U.S., especially the migrant workers of California. In 1962 he received the Nobel Prize in literature. His best known works include *Tortilla Flat, Of Mice and Men, The Grapes of Wrath, The Moon Is Down, East of Eden,* and *The Winter of Our Discontent.*

Flight

JOHN STEINBECK

About fifteen miles below Monterey, on the wild coast, the Torres family had their farm, a few sloping acres above a cliff that dropped to the brown reefs and to the hissing white waters of the ocean. Behind the farm the stone mountains stood up against the sky. The farm buildings huddled like little clinging aphids on the mountain skirts, crouched low to the ground as though the wind might blow them into the sea. The little shack, the rattling, rotting barn were grey-bitten with sea salt, beaten by the damp wind until they had taken on the color of the granite hills. Two horses, a red cow and a red calf, half a dozen pigs and a flock of lean, multicolored chickens stocked the place. A little corn was raised on the sterile slope, and it grew short and thick under the wind, and all the cobs formed on the landward sides of the stalks.

Mamma Torres, a lean, dry woman with ancient eyes, had ruled the farm for ten years, ever since her husband tripped over a stone in the field one day and fell full length on a rattlesnake. When one is bitten on the chest there is not much that can be done.

Mamma Torres had three children, two undersized black ones of twelve and fourteen, Emilio and Rosy, whom Mamma kept fishing on the rocks below the farm where the sea was kind and when the truant officer was in some distant part of Monterey County. And there was Pepé, the tall smiling son of nineteen, a gentle, affectionate boy, but very lazy. Pepé had a tall head, pointed at the top, and from its peak, coarse black hair grew down like a thatch all around. Over his smiling little eyes Mama cut a straight bang so he could see. Pepé had sharp Indian cheekbones and an eagle nose, but his mouth was as sweet and shapely as a girl's mouth, and his chin was fragile and chiseled. He was loose and gangling, all legs and feet and wrists, and he was very lazy. Mama thought him fine and brave, but she never told him so. She said, "Some lazy cow must have got into thy father's family, else how could I have a son like thee." And she said, "When I carried thee, a sneaking lazy coyote came out of the brush and looked at me one day. That must have made thee so."

Pepé smiled sheepishly and stabbed at the ground with his knife to keep the blade sharp and free from rust. It was his inheritance, that knife, his father's knife. The long heavy blade folded back into the black handle. There was a button on the handle. When Pepé pressed the button, the blade leaped out ready for use. The knife was with Pepé always, for it had been his father's knife.

One sunny morning when the sea below the cliff was glinting and blue and the white surf creamed on the reef, when even the stone mountains looked kindly, Mama Torres called out the door of the shack, "Pepé, I have a labor for thee."

There was no answer. Mama listened. From behind the barn she heard a burst of laughter. She lifted her full long skirt and walked in the direction of the noise.

Pepé was sitting on the ground with his back against a box. His white teeth glistened. On either side of him stood the two black ones, tense and expectant. Fifteen feet away a redwood post was set in the ground. Pepé's right hand lay limply in his lap, and in the palm the big black knife rested. The blade was closed back into the handle. Pepé looked smilingly at the sky.

Suddenly Emilio cried, "Ya!"

Pepé's wrist flicked like the head of a snake. The blade

seemed to fly open in mid-air, and with a thump the point dug into the redwood post, and the black handle quivered. The three burst into excited laughter. Rosy ran to the post and pulled out the knife and brought it back to Pepé. He closed the blade and settled the knife carefully in his listless palm again. He grinned self-consciously at the sky.

"Ya!"

The heavy knife lanced out and sunk into the post again. Mama moved forward like a ship and scattered the play.

"All day you do foolish things with the knife, like a toy-baby," she stormed. "Get up on thy huge feet that eat up shoes. Get up!" She took him by one loose shoulder and hoisted at him. Pepé grinned sheepishly and came half-heartedly to his feet. "Look!" Mama cried. "Big lazy, you must catch the horse and put on him thy father's saddle. You must ride to Monterey. The medicine bottle is empty. There is no salt. Go thou now, Peanut! Catch the horse."

A revolution took place in the relaxed figure of Pepé. "To Monterery, me? Alone? *Si*, Mama."

She scowled at him. "Do not think, big sheep, that you will buy candy. No, I will give you only enough for the medicine and salt."

Pepé smiled. "Mama, you will put the hatband on the hat?"

She relented then. "Yes, Pepé. You may wear the hatband."

His voice grew insinuating. "And the green handkerchief, Mama?"

"Yes, if you go quickly and return with no trouble, the silk green handkerchief will go. If you make sure to take off the handkerchief when you eat so no spot may fall on it. . . ."

"*Si*, Mama. I will be careful. I am a man."

"Thou? A man? Thou art a peanut."

He went into the rickety barn and brought out a rope, and he walked agilely enough up the hill to catch the horse.

When he was ready and mounted before the door, mounted on his father's saddle that was so old that the oaken frame showed through torn leather in many places, then Mama brought out the round black hat with the tooled leather band,

and she reached up and knotted the green silk handkerchief about his neck. Pepé's blue denim coat was much darker than his jeans, for it had been washed much less often.

Mama handed up the big medicine bottle and the silver coins. "That for the medicine," she said, "and that for the salt. That for a candle to burn for the papa. That for *dulces* for the little ones. Our friend Mrs. Rodriguez will give you dinner and maybe a bed for the night. When you go to the church say only ten Paternosters and only twenty-five Ave Marias. Oh! I know, big coyote. You would sit there flapping your mouth over Aves all day while you looked at the candles and the holy pictures. That is not good devotion to stare at the pretty things."

The black hat, covering the high pointed head and black thatched hair of Pepé, gave him dignity and age. He sat the rangy horse well. Mama thought how handsome he was, dark and lean and tall. "I would not send thee now alone, thou little one, except for the medicine," she said softly. "It is not good to have no medicine, for who knows when the toothache will come or the sadness of the stomach. These things are."

"Adios, Mama," Pepé cried. "I will come back soon. You may send me often alone. I am a man."

"Thou art a foolish chicken."

He straightened his shoulders, flipped the reins against the horse's shoulder and rode away. He turned once and saw that they still watched him, Emilio and Rosy and Mama. Pepé grinned with pride and gladness and lifted the tough buckskin horse to a trot.

When he had dropped out of sight over a little dip in the road, Mama turned to the black ones, but she spoke to herself. "He is nearly a man now," she said. "It will be a nice thing to have a man in the house again." Her eyes sharpened on the children. "Go to the rocks now. The tide is going out. There will be abalones to be found." She put the iron hooks into their hands and saw them down the steep trail to the reefs. She brought the smooth stone *metate* to the doorway and sat grinding her corn to flour and looking occasionally at the road over which Pepé had gone. The noonday came and then the afternoon, when the little ones beat the abalones on a rock to make them tender and Mama patted the tortillas to make them thin.

They ate their dinner as the red sun was pluging down toward the ocean. They sat on the doorsteps and watched the big white moon come over the mountain tops.

Mama said, "He is now at the house of our friend Mrs. Rodriguez. She will give him nice things to eat and maybe a present."

Emilio said, "Some day I too will ride to Monterey for medicine. Did Pepé come to be a man today?"

Mama said wisely, "A boy gets to be a man when a man is needed. Remember this thing. I have known boys forty years old because there was no need for a man."

Soon afterwards they retired, Mamma in her big oak bed on one side of the room, Emilio and Rosy in their boxes full of straw and sheepskins on the other side of the room.

The moon went over the sky and the surf roared on the rocks. The roosters crowed the first call. The surf subsided to a whispering surge against the reef. The moon dropped toward the sea. The roosters crowed again.

The moon was near down to the water when Pepé rode on a winded horse to his home flat. His dog bounced out and circled the horse yelping with pleasure. Pepé slid off the saddle to the ground. The weathered little shack was silver in the moonlight and the square shadow of it was black to the north and east. Against the east the piling mountains were misty with light; their tops melted into the sky.

Pepé walked wearily up the three steps and into the house. It was dark inside. There was a rustle in the corner.

Mama cried out from her bed. "Who comes? Pepé, is it thou?"

"*Si*, Mama."

"Did you get the medicine?"

"*Si*, Mama."

"Well, go to sleep, then. I thought you would be sleeping at the house of Mrs. Rodriguez." Pepé stood silently in the dark room. "Why do you stand there, Pepé? Did you drink wine?"

"*Si*, Mama."

"Well, go to bed then and sleep out the wine."

His voice was tired and patient, but very firm. "Light the candle, Mama. I must go away into the mountains."

"What is this, Pepé? You are crazy." Mama struck a sulphur match and held the little blue burr until the flame spread up the stick. She set light to the candle on the floor beside her bed. "Now, Pepé, what is this you say?" She looked anxiously into his face.

He was changed. The fragile quality seemed to have gone from his chin. His mouth was less full than it had been, the lines of the lips were straighter, but in his eyes the greatest change had taken place. There was no laughter in them any more, nor any bashfulness. They were sharp and bright and purposeful.

He told her in a tired monotone, told everything just as it had happened. A few people came into the kitchen of Mrs. Rodriguez. There was wine to drink. Pepé drank wine. The little quarrel—the man started toward Pepé and then the knife—it went almost by itself. It flew, it darted before Pepé knew it. As he talked, Mama's face grew stern, and it seemed to grow more lean. Pepé finished. "I am a man now, Mama. The man said names to me I could not allow."

Mama nodded. "Yes, thou art a man, my poor little Pepé. Thou art a man. I have seen it coming on thee. I have watched you throwing the knife into the post, and I have been afraid." For a moment her face had softened, but now it grew stern again. "Come! We must get you ready. Go. Awaken Emilio and Rosy. Go quickly."

Pepé stepped over to the corner where his brother and sister slept among the sheepskins. He leaned down and shook them gently. "Come, Rosy! Come, Emilio! The mama says you must arise."

The little black ones sat up and rubbed their eyes in the candlelight. Mama was out of bed now, her long black skirt over her nightgown. "Emilio," she cried. "Go up and catch the other horse for Pepé. Quickly, now! Quickly!" Emilio put his legs in his overalls and stumbled sleepily out the door.

"You heard no one behind you on the road?" Mama demanded.

"No, Mama. I listened carefully. No one was on the road."

Mama darted like a bird about the room. From a nail on the wall she took a canvas water bag and threw it on the floor.

She stripped a blanket from her bed and rolled it into a tight tube and tied the ends with string. From a box beside the stove she lifted a flour sack half full of black stringy jerky. "Your father's black coat, Pepé. Here, put it on."

Pepé stood in the middle of the floor watching her activity. She reached behind the door and brought out the rifle, a long 38-56, worn shiny the whole length of the barrel. Pepé took it from her and held it in the crook of his elbow. Mama brought a little leather bag and counted the cartridges into his hand. "Only ten left," she warned. "You must not waste them."

Emilio put his head in the door. " *'Qui'st 'l caballo,* Mama."

"Put on the saddle from the other horse. Tie on the blanket. Here, tie the jerky to the saddle horn."

Still Pepé stood silently watching his mother's frantic activity. His chin looked hard, and his sweet mouth was drawn and thin. His little eyes followed Mama about the room almost suspiciously.

Rosy asked softly, "Where goes Pepé?"

Mama's eyes were fierce. "Pepé goes on a journey. Pepé is a man now. He has a man's thing to do."

Pepé straightened his shoulders. His mouth changed until he looked very much like Mama.

At last the preparation was finished. The loaded horse stood outside the door. The water bag dripped a line of moisture down the bay shoulder.

The moonlight was being thinned by the dawn and the big white moon was near down to the sea. The family stood by the shack. Mama confronted Pepé. "Look, my son! Do not stop until it is dark again. Do not sleep even though you are tired. Take care of the horse in order that he may not stop of weariness. Remember to be careful with the bullets—there are only ten. Do not fill thy stomach with jerky or it will make thee sick. Eat a little jerky and fill thy stomach with grass. When thou comest to the high mountains, if thou seest any of the dark watching men, go not near to them nor try to speak to them. And forget not thy prayers." She put her lean hands on Pepé's shoulders, stood on her toes and kissed him formally on both cheeks, and Pepé kissed her on both cheeks. Then he went to Emilio and Rosy and kissed both of their cheeks.

Pepé turned back to Mama. He seemed to look for a little softness, a little weakness in her. His eyes were searching, but Mama's face remained fierce. "Go now," she said. "Do not wait to be caught like a chicken."

Pepé pulled himself into the saddle. "I am a man," he said.

It was the first dawn when he rode up the hill toward the little canyon which let a trail into the mountains. Moonlight and daylight fought with each other, and the two warring qualities made it difficult to see. Before Pepé had gone a hundred yards, the outlines of his figure were misty; and long before he entered the canyon, he had become a gray, indefinite shadow.

Mama stood stiffly in front of her doorstep, and on either side of her stood Emilio and Rosy. They cast furtive glances at Mama now and then.

When the gray shape of Pepé melted into the hillside and disappeared, Mama relaxed. She began the high, whining keen of the death wail. "Our beautiful—our brave," she cried. "Our protector, our son is gone." Emilio and Rosy moaned beside her. "Our beautiful—our brave, he is gone." It was the formal wail. It rose to a high piercing whine and subsided to a moan. Mama raised it three times and then she turned and went into the house and shut the door.

Emilio and Rosy stood wondering in the dawn. They heard Mama whimpering in the house. They went out to sit on the cliff above the ocean. They touched shoulders. "When did Pepé come to be a man?" Emilio asked.

"Last night," said Rosy. "Last night in Monterey." The ocean clouds turned red with the sun that was behind the mountains.

"We will have no breakfast," said Emilio. "Mama will not want to cook." Rosy did not answer him. "Where is Pepé gone?" he asked.

Rosy looked around at him. She drew her knowledge from the quiet air. "He has gone on a journey. He will never come back."

"Is he dead? Do you think he is dead?"

Rosy looked back at the ocean again. A little steamer

drawing a line of smoke sat on the edge of the horizon. "He is not dead," Rosy explained. "Not yet."

Pepé rested the big rifle across the saddle in front of him. He let the horse walk up the hill and he didn't look back. The stony slope took on a coat of short brush so that Pepé found the entrance to a trail and entered it.

When he came to the canyon opening, he swung once in his saddle and looked back, but the houses were swallowed in the misty light. Pepé jerked forward again. The high shoulder of the canyon closed in on him. His horse stretched out its neck and sighed and settled to the trail.

It was a well-worn path, dark soft leaf-mould earth strewn with broken pieces of sandstone. The trail rounded the shoulder of the canyon and dropped steeply into the bed of the stream. In the shallows the water ran smoothly, glinting in the first morning sun. Small round stones on the bottom were as brown as rust with sun moss. In the sand along the edges of the stream the tall, rich wild mint grew, while in the water itself the cress, old and tough, had gone to heavy seed.

The path went into the stream and emerged on the other side. The horse sloshed into the water and stopped. Pepé dropped his bridle and let the beast drink of the running water.

Soon the canyon sides became steep and the first giant sentinel redwods guarded the trail, great round red trunks bearing foliage as green and lacy as ferns. Once Pepé was among the trees, the sun was lost. A perfumed and purple light lay in the pale green of the underbrush. Gooseberry bushes and blackberries and tall ferns lined the stream, and overhead the branches of the redwoods met and cut off the sky.

Pepé drank from the water bag, and he reached into the flour sack and brought out a black string of jerky. His white teeth gnawed at the string until the tough meat parted. He chewed slowly and drank occasionally from the water bag. His little eyes were slumberous and tired, but the muscles of his face were hard set. The earth of the trail was black now. It gave up a hollow sound under the walking hoofbeats.

The stream fell more sharply. Little waterfalls splashed on the stones. Five-fingered ferns hung over the water and dripped spray from their fingertips. Pepé rode half over in his saddle, dangling one leg loosely. He picked a bay leaf from a tree beside the way and put it into his mouth for a moment to flavor the dry jerky. He held the gun loosely across the pommel.

Suddenly he squared in his saddle, swung the horse from the trail and kicked it hurriedly up behind a big redwood tree. He pulled up the reins tight against the bit to keep the horse from whinnying. His face was intent and his nostrils quivered a little.

A hollow pounding came down the trail, and a horseman rode by, a fat man with red cheeks and a white stubble beard. His horse put down his head and blubbered at the trail when it came to the place where Pepé had turned off. "Hold up!" said the man and he pulled up his horse's head.

When the last sound of the hoofs died away, Pepé came back into the trail again. He did not relax in the saddle any more. He lifted the big rifle and swung the lever to throw a shell into the chamber, and then he let down the hammer to half cock.

The trail grew very steep. Now the redwood trees were smaller and their tops were dead, bitten dead where the wind reached them. The horse plodded on; the sun went slowly overhead and started down toward the afternoon.

Where the stream came out of a side canyon, the trail left it. Pepé dismounted and watered his horse and filled up his water bag. As soon as the trail had parted from the stream, the trees were gone and only the thick brittle sage and manzanita and chaparral edged the trail. And the soft black earth was gone, too, leaving only the light tan broken rock for the trail bed. Lizards scampered away into the brush as the horse rattled over the little stones.

Pepé turned in his saddle and looked back. He was in the open now: he could be seen from a distance. As he ascended the trail the country grew more rough and terrible and dry. The way wound about the bases of great square rocks. Little gray rabbits skittered in the brush. A bird made a monotonous high creaking. Eastward the bare rock mountaintops were pale and powder-dry under the dropping sun. The horse plodded up and up the trail toward a little V in the ridge which was the pass.

Pepé looked suspiciously back every minute or so, and his eyes sought the tops of the ridges ahead. Once, on a white barren spur, he saw a black figure for a moment, but he looked quickly away, for it was one of the dark watchers. No one knew who the watchers were, nor where they lived, but it was better to ignore them and never to show interest in them. They did not bother one who stayed on the trail and minded his own business.

The air was parched and full of light dust blown by the breeze from the eroding mountains. Pepé drank sparingly from his bag and corked it tightly and hung it on the horn again. The trail moved up the dry shale hillside, avoiding rocks, dropping under clefts, climbing in and out of old water scars. When he arrived at the little pass he stopped and looked back for a long time. No dark watchers were to be seen now. The trail behind was empty. Only the high tops of the redwoods indicated where the stream flowed.

Pepé rode on through the pass. His little eyes were nearly closed with weariness, but his face was stern, relentless and manly. The high mountain wind coasted sighing through the pass and whistled on the edges of the black blocks of broken granite. In the air, a red-tailed hawk sailed over close to the ridge and screamed angrily. Pepé went slowly through the broken jagged pass and looked down on the other side.

The trail dropped quickly, staggering among broken rock. At the bottom of the slope there was a dark crease, thick with brush, and on the other side of the crease a little flat, in which a grove of oak trees grew. A scar of green grass cut across the flat. And behind the flat another mountain rose, desolate with dead rocks and starving little black bushes. Pepé drank from the bag again for the air was so dry that it encrusted his nostrils and burned his lips. He put the horse down the trail. The hooves slipped and struggled on the steep way, starting little stones that rolled off into the brush. The sun was gone behind the westward mountain now, but still it glowed brilliantly on the oaks and on the grassy flat. The rocks and hillsides still sent up waves of the heat they had gathered from the day's sun.

Pepé looked up to the top of the next dry withered ridge. He saw a dark form against the sky, a man's figure standing on top of a rock, and he glanced away quickly not to appear curious. When a moment later he looked up again, the figure was gone.

Downward the trail was quickly covered. Sometimes the horse floundered for footing, sometimes set his feet and slid a little way. They came at last to the bottom where the dark chaparral was higher than Pepé's head. He held up his rifle on one side and his arm on the other to shield his face from the sharp brittle fingers of the brush.

Up and out of the crease he rode, and up a little cliff. The grassy flat was before him, and the round comfortable oaks. For a moment he studied the trail down which he had come, but there was no movement and no sound from it. Finally he rode out over the flat, to the green streak, and at the upper end of the damp he found a little spring welling out of the earth and dropping into a dug basin before it seeped out over the flat.

Pepé filled his bag first, and then he let the thirsty horse drink out of the pool. He led the horse to the clump of oaks, and in the middle of the grove, fairly protected from sight on all sides, he took off the saddle and the bridle and laid them on the ground. The horse stretched his jaws sideways and yawned. Pepé knotted the lead rope about the horse's neck and tied him to a sapling among the oaks, where he could graze in a fairly large circle.

When the horse was gnawing hungrily at the dry grass, Pepé went to the saddle and took a black string of jerky from the sack and strolled to an oak tree on the edge of the grove, from under which he could watch the trail. He sat down in the crisp dry oak leaves and automatically felt for his big black knife to cut the jerky, but he had no knife. He leaned back on his elbow and gnawed at the tough strong meat. His face was blank, but it was a man's face.

The bright evening light washed the eastern ridge, but the valley was darkening. Doves flew down from the hills to the spring, and the quail came running out of the brush and joined them, calling clearly to one another.

Out of the corner of his eye Pepé saw a shadow grow out of the bushy crease. He turned his head slowly. A big spotted wildcat was creeping toward the spring, belly to the ground, moving like thought.

Pepé cocked his rifle and edged the muzzle slowly around. Then he looked apprehensively up the trail and dropped the hammer again. From the ground beside him he picked an oak twig and threw it toward the spring. The quail flew up with a roar and the doves whistled away. The big cat stood up; for a long moment he looked at Pepé with cold yellow eyes, and then fearlessly walked back into the gulch.

The dusk gathered quickly in the deep valley. Pepé muttered his prayers, put his head down on his arm and went instantly to sleep.

The moon came up and filled the valley with cold blue light, and the wind swept rustling down from the peaks. The owls worked up and down the slopes looking for rabbits. Down in the brush of the gulch a coyote gabbled. The oak trees whispered softly in the night breeze.

Pepé started up, listening. His horse had whinnied. The moon was just slipping behind the western ridge, leaving the valley in darkness behind it. Pepé sat tensely gripping his rifle. From far up the trail he heard an answering whinny and the crash of shod hooves on the broken rock. He jumped to his feet, ran to his horse and led it under the trees. He threw on the saddle and cinched it tight for the steep trail, caught the unwilling head and forced the bit into the mouth. He felt the saddle to make sure the water bag and the sack of jerky were there. Then he mounted and turned up the hill.

It was velvet dark. The horse found the entrance to the trail where it left the flat, and started up, stumbling and slipping on the rocks. Pepé's hand rose up to his head. His hat was gone. He had left it under the oak tree.

The horse had struggled far up the trail when the first change of dawn came into the air, a steel grayness as light mixed thoroughly with dark. Gradually the sharp snaggled edge of the ridge stood out above them, rotten granite tortured and eaten by the winds of time. Pepé had dropped his reins on the horn, leaving direction to the horse. The brush grabbed at his legs in the dark until one knee of his jeans was ripped.

Gradually the light flowed down over the ridge. The starved brush and rocks stood out in the half light, strange and lonely in high perspective. Then there came warmth into the light. Pepé drew up and looked back, but he could see nothing in the darker valley below. The sky turned blue over the coming sun. In the waste of the mountainside, the poor dry brush grew only three feet high. Here and there, big outcroppings of unrotted granite stood up like mouldering houses. Pepé relaxed a little. He drank from his water bag and bit off a piece of jerky. A single eagle flew over, high in the light.

Without warning Pepé's horse screamed and fell on its side. He was almost down before the rifle crash echoed up from the valley. From a hole behind the struggling shoulder, a stream of bright crimson blood pumped and stopped and pumped and stopped. The hooves threshed on the ground. Pepé lay half stunned beside the horse. He looked slowly down the hill. A piece of sage clipped off beside his head and another crash echoed up from side to side of the canyon. Pepé flung himself frantically behind a bush.

He crawled up the hill on his knees and one hand. His right hand held the rifle up off the ground and pushed it ahead of him. He moved with the instinctive care of an animal. Rapidly he wormed his way toward one of the big outcroppings of granite on the hill above him. Where the brush was high he doubled up and ran, but where the cover was slight he wriggled forward on his stomach, pushing the rifle ahead of him. In the last little distance there was no cover at all. Pepé poised and then he darted across the space and flashed around the corner of the rock.

He leaned panting against the stone. When his breath came easier he moved along behind the big rock until he came to a narrow slit that offered a thin section of vision down the hill. Pepé lay on his stomach and pushed the rifle barrel through the slit and waited.

The sun reddened the western ridges now. Already the buzzards were settling down toward the place where the horse lay. A small brown bird scratched in the dead sage leaves directly in front of the rifle muzzle. The coasting eagle flew back toward the rising sun.

Pepé saw a little movement in the brush far below. His grip tightened on the gun. A little brown doe stepped daintily out on the trail and crossed it and disappeared into the brush again. For a long time Pepé waited. Far below he could see the little flat and the oak trees and the slash of green. Suddenly his eyes flashed back at the trail again. A quarter of a mile down there had been a quick movement in the chaparral. The rifle swung over. The front sight nestled in the v of the rear sight. Pepé studied for a moment and than raised the rear sight a notch. The little movement in the brush came again. The sight settled on it. Pepé squeezed the trigger. The explosion crashed down the mountain and up the other side, and came rattling back. The whole side of the slope grew still. No more movement. And then a white streak cut into the granite of the slit and a bullet whined away and a crash sounded up from below. Pepé felt a sharp pain in his right hand. A sliver of granite was sticking out from between his first and second knuckles and the point protruded from his palm. Carefully he pulled out the sliver of stone. The wound bled evenly and gently. No vein or artery was cut.

Pepé looked into a little dusty cave in the rock and gathered a handful of spider web, and he pressed the mass into the cut, plastering the soft web into the blood. The flow stopped almost at once.

The rifle was on the ground. Pepé picked it up, levered a new shell into the chamber. And then he slid into the brush on his stomach. Far to the right he crawled, and then up the hill, moving slowly and carefully, crawling to cover and resting and then crawling again.

In the mountains the sun is high in its arc before it penetrates the gorges. The hot face looked over the hill and brought instant heat with it. The white light beat on the rocks and reflected from them and rose up quivering from the earth again, and the rocks and bushes seemed to quiver behind the air.

Pepé crawled in the general direction of the ridge peak, zig-zagging for cover. The deep cut between his knuckles began to throb. He crawled close to a rattlesnake before he saw it, and when it raised its dry head and made a soft beginning whirr, he backed up and took another way. The quick gray lizards flashed in front of him, raising a tiny line of dust. He found another mass of spider web and pressed it against his throbbing hand.

Pepé was pushing the rifle with his left hand now. Little drops of sweat ran to the ends of his coarse black hair and rolled down his cheeks. His lips and tongue were growing thick and heavy. His lips writhed to draw saliva into his mouth. His little dark eyes were uneasy and suspicious. Once when a gray lizard paused in front of him on the parched ground and turned its head sideways he crushed it flat with a stone.

When the sun slid past noon he had gone a mile. He crawled exhaustedly a last hundred yards to a patch of high sharp manzanita, crawled desperately, and when the patch was reached he wriggled in among the tough gnarly trunks and dropped his head on his left arm. There was little shade in the meager brush, but there was cover and safety. Pepé went to sleep as he lay and the sun beat on his back. A few little birds hopped close to him and peered and hopped away. Pepé squirmed in his sleep and he raised and dropped his wounded hand again and again.

The sun went down behind the peaks and the cool evening came, and then the dark. A coyote yelled from the hillside. Pepé started awake and looked about with misty eyes. His hand was swollen and heavy; a little thread of pain ran up the inside of his arm and settled in a pocket in his armpit. He peered about and then stood up, for the mountains were black and the moon had not yet risen. Pepé stood up in the dark. The coat of his father pressed on his arm. His tongue was swollen until it nearly filled his mouth. He wriggled out of the coat and dropped it in the brush, and then he struggled up the hill, falling over rocks and tearing his way through the brush. The rifle knocked against stones as he went. Little dry avalanches of gravel and shattered stone went whispering down the hill behind him.

After a while the old moon came up and showed the jagged ridge top ahead of him. By moonlight Pepé traveled more easily. He bent forward so that his throbbing arm hung away from his body. The journey uphill was made in dashes and rests, a frantic rush up a few yards and then a rest. The wind coasted down the slope rattling the dry stems of the bushes.

The moon was at meridian when Pepé came at last to the sharp backbone of the ridge top. On the last hundred yards of the rise no soil had clung under the wearing winds. The way was on solid rock. He clambered to the top and looked down on the other side. There was a draw like the last below him, misty with moonlight, brushed with dry struggling sage and chaparral. On the other side the hill rose up sharply and at the top the jagged rotten teeth of the mountain showed against the sky. At the bottom of the cut the brush was thick and dark.

Pepé stumbled down the hill. His throat was almost closed with thirst. At first he tried to run, but immediately he fell and rolled. After that he went more carefully. The moon was just disappearing behind the mountains when he came to the bottom. He crawled into the heavy brush feeling with his fingers for water. There was no water in the bed of the stream, only damp earth. Pepé laid his gun down and scooped up a handful of mud and put it in his mouth, and then he spluttered and scraped the earth from his tongue with his finger, for the mud drew at his mouth like a poultice. He dug a hole in the stream bed with his fingers, dug a little basin to catch water; but before it was very deep his head fell forward on the damp ground and he slept.

The dawn came and the heat of the day fell on the earth, and still Pepé slept. Late in the afternoon his head jerked up. He looked slowly around. His eyes were slits of wariness. Twenty feet away in the heavy brush a big tawny mountain lion stood looking at him. Its long thick tail waved gracefully, its ears were erect with interest, not laid back dangerously. The lion squatted down on its stomach and watched him.

Pepé looked at the hole he had dug in the earth. A half inch of muddy water had collected in the bottom. He tore the sleeve from his hurt arm, with his teeth ripped out a little square, soaked it in the water and put it in his mouth. Over and over he filled the cloth and sucked it.

Still the lion sat and watched him. The evening came down but there was no movement on the hills. No birds visited the dry bottom of the cut. Pepé looked occasionally at the lion. The eyes of the yellow beast drooped as though he were about to sleep. He yawned and his long thin red tongue curled out. Suddenly his head jerked around and his nostrils quivered. His big tail lashed. He stood up and slunk like a tawny shadow into the thick brush.

A moment later Pepé heard the sound, the faint far crash of horses' hooves on gravel. And he heard something else, a high whining yelp of a dog.

Pepé took his rifle in his left hand and he glided into the brush almost as quietly as the lion had. In the darkening evening he crouched up the hill toward the next ridge. Only when the dark came did he stand up. His energy was short. Once it was dark he fell over the rocks and slipped to his knees on the steep slope, but he moved on and on up the hill, climbing and scrabbling over the broken hillside.

When he was far up toward the top, he lay down and slept for a little while. The withered moon, shining on his face, awakened him. He stood up and moved up the hill. Fifty yards away he stopped and turned back, for he had forgotten his rifle. He walked heavily down and poked about in the brush, but he could not find his gun. At last he lay down to rest. The pocket of pain in his armpit had grown more sharp. His arm seemed to swell out and fall with every heartbeat. There was no position lying down where the heavy arm did not press against his armpit.

With the effort of a hurt beast, Pepé got up and moved again toward the top of the ridge. He held his swollen arm away from his body with his left hand. Up the steep hill he dragged himself, a few steps and a rest, and a few more steps. At last he was nearing the top. The moon showed the uneven sharp back of it against the sky.

Pepé's brain spun in a big spiral up and away from him. He slumped to the ground and lay still. The rock ridge top was only a hundred feet above him.

The moon moved over the sky. Pepé half turned on his

back. His tongue tried to make words, but only a thick hissing came from between his lips.

When the dawn came, Pepé pulled himself up. His eyes were sane again. He drew his great puffed arm in front of him and looked at the angry wound. The black line ran up from his wrist to his armpit. Automatically he reached in his pocket for the big black knife, but it was not there. His eyes searched the ground. He picked up a sharp blade of stone and scraped at the wound, sawed at the proud flesh and then squeezed the green juice out in big drops. Instantly he drew back his head and whined like a dog. His whole right side shuddered at the pain, but the pain cleared his head.

In the gray light he struggled up the last slope of the ridge and crawled over and lay down behind a line of rocks. Below him lay a deep canyon exactly like the last, waterless and desolate. There was no flat, no oak trees, not even heavy brush in the bottom of it. And on the other side a sharp ridge stood up, thinly brushed with starving sage, littered with broken granite. Strewn over the hill there were giant outcroppings, and on the top the granite teeth stood out against the sky.

The new day was light now. The flame of the sun came over the ridge and fell on Pepé where he lay on the ground. His coarse black hair was littered with twigs and bits of spider web. His eyes had retreated back into his head. Between his lips the tip of his black tongue showed.

He sat up and dragged his great arm into his lap and nursed it, rocking his body and moaning in his throat. He threw back his head and looked up into the pale sky. A big black bird circled nearly out of sight, and far to the left another was sailing near.

He lifted his head to listen, for a familiar sound had come to him from the valley he had climbed out of; it was the crying of hounds, excited and feverish, on a trail.

Pepé bowed his head quickly. He tried to speak rapid words but only a thick hiss came from his lips. He drew a shaky cross on his breast with his left hand. It was a long struggle to get to his feet. He crawled slowly and mechanically to the top of a big rock on the ridge peak. Once there, he arose slowly, swaying to his feet, and stood erect. Far below he could see the dark brush where he had slept. He braced his feet and stood there, black against the morning sky.

There came a ripping sound at his feet. A piece of stone flew up and a bullet droned off into the next gorge. The hollow crash echoed up from below. Pepé looked down for a moment and then pulled himself straight again.

His body jarred back. His left hand fluttered helplessly toward his breast. The second crash sounded from below. Pepé swung forward and toppled from the rock. His body struck and rolled over and over, starting a little avalanche. And when at last he stopped against a bush, the avalanche slid slowly down and covered up his head.

Dan Vogel (1927–   ) was born in Brooklyn, New York, where he now resides. Having majored in American literature, he is a professor of English at Stern College for Women, Yeshiva University. He has contributed to *Nineteenth Century Fiction, Esquire, College English,* and *Criticism;* other works include *Roger Clullingworth: The Satantic Paradox in* The Scarlet Letter and *Dramatic Chapters in* Moby Dick.

Steinbeck's "Flight": The Myth of Manhood

DAN VOGEL

In "Flight," a narrative of the Monterey country, John Steinbeck tells the story of Pepé, an immature 19-year-old who grows up in a moment when he kills a man. As a result of this murder, Pepé must flee to the desert and the hills, but he is chased relentlessly, fights thirst and gangrene, and finally is shot down. Peter Lisca has called the tale an "uncomplicated plot" which veils the theme of man's "reduction to the state of a wild animal," and his retention nevertheless of "something more than an animal." In the plot, Mr. Lisca discerns "a thread of moral allegory—the growth of a boy to manhood and the meaning of that manhood."[1]

More than a mere allegory, "Flight" reveals characteristics of myth and tragedy. A myth is a story that tries to explain some practice, belief, institution, or natural phenomenon, and is especially associated with religious rites and beliefs. The natural phenomenon, for Steinbeck, is not the facts of nature, with which historical myths deal; rather, it is, as Mr. Lisca points out, the development of innocent childhood into

[1] Peter Lisca, *The Wide World of John Steinbeck,* pp. 99-100.

From *College English,* December 1961. Reprinted with the permission of the National Council of Teachers of English and Dan Vogel.

disillusioned manhood. The myth that Steinbeck wrought also contains another quality of myth, the rite. The plot of "Flight" narrates symbolically the ritual: the escape from the Mother, the divestiture of the Father, and the death and burial of Childhood. To discern these mythic symbols, it is necessary to review the narrative facts.

At the beginning of the story, Pepé, though 19 years of age, has all the innocence of the "toy-baby" his mother calls him. He is called lazy, but "his mouth was as sweet as a girl's mouth";[2] he was perhaps lazy, but his most significant trait was a girlish purity. He has also the universal childish characteristic of eagerness to do things by himself, evident in the alacrity with which he goes on an errand alone into Monterey.

In these days of childish innocence, his most prized possession is his father's switchblade knife. It is an inheritance, with which he proudly plays at sticking the post, to the delight of his little brother and sister. When his rather domineering mother—who constantly taunts him with his inability to be "a man"—asks him to go to Monterey, "a revolution took place in the relaxed figure of Pepé" (p. 5). He is asked, surprisingly, to go alone; he is permitted to wear his father's hat and his father's hatband and to ride in his father's saddle. In departing, Pepé says, "You may send me often alone. I am a man." To which his mother retorts, "Thou art a foolish chicken" (pp. 6-7).

When Pepé returns, he has killed a man with his father's knife, left behind him at the scene of the crime. The look of innocence is gone; he has been shocked by a fact of life, an extreme independent act. His mother quickly understands and helps him outfit himself for the flight into the mountains. She gives him especially his father's black coat and rifle. Weighted down by the accoutrements of his father, Pepé separates himself from his mother. She recognizes the change. She tells the little boy, "Pepé is a man now. He has a man's thing to do" (p. 10). Logically, however, this is not necessarily so. A man might possibly have been expected to give himself up and pay

[2] John Steinbeck, "Flight," in *The Portable Steinbeck* (1943), p. 4. Page references in the article are to this edition.

for his crime. It seems to me, then, that Pepé's mother perceived that her son is entering manhood and must stand alone. This he must do.

The ordeal of transformation from innocence to experience, from purity to defilement begins. There is the physical pain of the ordeal, symbolized by a cut hand that soon becomes gangrenous. There is the psychological pain—the recognition of a strangeness in this life that is omnipresent, silent, watchful and dark—the sense of Evil, or Tragedy, or Retribution. This realization is symbolized by the narratively gratuitous, unrealistic presence of the black figures, the "dark watchers" who are seen for a moment on the tops of ridges and then disappear. "No one knew who the watchers were," Steinbeck tells us, "nor where they lived, but it was better to ignore them and never to show interest in them. They did not bother one who stayed on the trail and minded his own busness" (pp. 14-15). They are not the posse, who are physcal figures behind Pepé with horses and guns and dogs. These are the silent inscrutable watchers from above, the universal Nemesis, the recognition of which signals a further step into manhood.

Pepé meets wild animals face to face, but they are quiescent and harmless. They seem to recognize a fellow creature who also lives for a moment in a wilderness, they in the throes of an instinctive existence, he in the playing out of an inevitable phenomenon. He is no danger to them.

Clambering over rocks, staggering across sunbaked flats, fleeing before sounds and shapes, Pepé forgets his father's hat; his father's horse is shot out from under him and his father's saddle is now useless; he divests himself of his father's coat because it pains his swollen, gangrenous arm; and in his pain he leaves his father's rifle on the trail behind him.

Only now, having been separated from his mother and having cleansed himself of all the accouterments and artifacts of his father, can the youth stand alone. But to Steinbeck this is far from a joyous or victorious occasion. It is sad and painful and tragic. Pepé rises to his feet, "black against the morning sky" (p. 25), astride a ridge. He is a perfect target and the narrative ends with the man against the sky shot down. The body rolls down the hillside, creating a little avalanche, which follows him in his descent and covers up his head. Thus innocence is killed and buried in the moment that Man stands alone.

Thus the myth ends, as so many myths do, with violence and melodrama. What the myth described is the natural miracle of entering manhood. When serenity of childhood is lost, there is pain and misery. Yet there is nevertheless a sense of gain and heroism which are more interesting and dramatic. It is a story that has fascinated many from Wordsworth to Hemingway, and what Steinbeck has written is a myth that describes in symbols what has happened to each of us.

Chester F. Chapin (1922–) was born in Greensboro, N.C.; he now resides in Ann Arbor, Michigan. Having majored in eighteenth century literature, he is a professor of English at the University of Michigan. He has contributed to *College English, Modern Philology, The Philogical Quarterly,* and other periodicals. He is also the author of *Religious Thought of Samuel Johnson.*

Pepé Torres: A Steinbeck "Natural"

CHESTER F. CHAPIN

I would like to take issue with Professor Dan Vogel's interpretation of John Steinbeck's short story "Flight" (*CE,* December 1961). Professor Vogel sees in this story of the painful flight from home and heroic death of an immature 19-year-old boy a universal "myth of manhood," a myth "that describes in symbols what has happened to each of us." As each of us, like Pepé Torres, must undergo the painful process of separating ourselves from our parents and from our childish innocence if we are to achieve responsible manhood, so, according to Professor Vogel, "Flight" is to be read as a description in symbolic terms of "the natural miracle of entering manhood," a miracle fraught with pain but redeemed by "a sense of gain and heroism." Pepé Torres, in Mr. Vogel's interpretation, is Everyman; Pepé's story is our story.

Mr. Vogel's interpretation, excellently supported as it is, overlooks evidence that Pepé is not like "each of us" in one important respect: that he is in fact, not merely innocent and immature, but a boy of subnormal intelligence, a mental defective. Pepé, Steinbeck says, "had a tall head, pointed at the top,

From *College English,* May 1962. Reprinted with permission of the National Council of Teachers of English and Chester F. Chapin.

and from its peak, coarse black hair grew down like a thatch all around" (*The Portable Steinbeck,* pp. 3-4). A pointed or "pinhead" is everywhere popularly understood as a sign of subnormal intelligence. Pepé's hat, we are told elsewhere, "covering the high pointed head and black thatched hair," gives him "dignity and age" (p. 6). When Pepé is finally shot down, a little avalanche covers up his head. As in life Pepé's hat gives him dignity by concealing his defective part, so in death the avalanche performs this function. Pepé's deformed head is mercifully concealed; his body, his "dignified" part, is revealed. Pepé, dying as a man should, deserves this consideration.

Pepé's mother understands clearly enough that Pepé is different from other immature 19-year-olds. It is something more than "immaturity" when a 19-year-old cannot be trusted to perform the simple errand that Mama Torres asks of Pepé. For the first time in his life she sends him alone to Monterey to buy medicine, but even then only because she considers the occasion an emergency: "I would not send thee now alone, thou little one, except for the medicine," she says "softly" (p. 6).

Pepé, in short, is another of Steinbeck's "naturals." He is hardly better fittted to cope with the world of men than Lennie in *Of Mice and Men,* who is shot, or than Tularecito in *The Pastures of Heaven,* who is committed to an insane asylum. Pepé's first and only contact with the world of men ends in disaster, a conclusion not unanticipated by Mama Torres. "Yes," she says, when Pepé has returned home with his tale of woe, "thou art a man, my poor little Pepé. . . . I have seen it coming on thee. I have watched you throwing the knife into the post, and I have been afraid" (p. 9). Mama Torres has been "afraid," I suggest, because she senses how potentially dangerous addiction to this habit of knifethrowing can be in a boy who is weak mentally but fully developed physically.

What, then, is Steinbeck saying to us in this story? Not, I think, that Pepé, with his abnormality, is Everyman; rather that man is *still* man even when defective in that part—intellect—which most clearly distinguishes him from the animals, a conclusion in harmony with Steinbeck's frequent insistence upon the human worth of the Lennies and Tularecitos of this world.

John J. Iorio (1925–   ) was born in Italy. An associate professor at the University of South Florida in Tampa, he teaches American and modern literature and creative writing. He was fiction editor of *Northeast,* an international literary magazine, and is now completing a novel. He has contributed reviews, articles, and short stories to various periodicals, including *Colby Quarterly, University of Kansas City Review, Artesian, The Southern Review, Prairie Schooner, Colorado Quarterly,* and *Arizona Quarterly*. He has also written two movie scripts. For the years 1960, 1966, and 1968 he won Honorable and Distinctive Mention in Martha Foley's *Best American Short Stories.*

The Man in the Black Apron

JOHN J. IORIO

Skipping and darting like a skittish animal, Stephen steps on the cracks of the broken pavement as he accompanies his father. He whispers the barely remembered song his mother sang when she rocked him on her knees:

See-saw master Stephen,
Go and catch a butterfly;
If you hold it in your hand,
It will never fly again.
See-saw . . .

Mateo scowls his son into mature propriety. For a while Stephen feels locked and restless between obedience and impulse. But soon the rhythms of spontaneity and energy of a ten year old boy reassert themselves, and he begins to hum and skip until the admonition falls again.

His father is unusually preoccupied. His purpose has a grim edge to it. He had risen early this morning and moved not by his own volition but by some force conceived and issued in the blind necessity of time. During a depression a man, an

From *Southern Review*, Autumn 1967, vol. 3, no. 4. Reprinted with permission.

immigrant half defeated by language, must fight harder to feed a family of seven, and so Mateo is going to a friend at the slaughterhouse to borrow a knife, a pulley, and chains.

The slaughterhouse is a massive building of sooted red brick. The date 1886 is fading on its pediment. Mateo tells his son to wait outside while he goes into the office to see what he can borrow. Across the street is the unbroken red brick wall of a steel factory, also sooted. A spring sun, hot for this time of year, beats against the bricks and asphalt. The entire street vibrates in coppery brilliance. It all appears dusty.

Stephen sees a truck turning a corner. It straightens out and appears motionless. He cups his ears against the tunneled noise as the truck backs against the mammoth and scarred wooden doors of the slaughterhouse. The jangle of doors, tail-gate, and ramps are like the sounds of ancient torture chambers. Inside the truck are animals, squealing and nervous, their tumid bodies sliding against one another. A giant of a man with a scarred lip and frayed overalls does what has to be done.

Before long Stephen sees a trickle of blood, luminous in the sun, on the man's hand, on the fat of his palm. Coppery strands embrace the fingers.

Pigs cower in the still center of their blending cries, their eyes red with the certainty of doom. They stand massed at the far end of the truck, their snouts raised like horns in cacaphonous defiance.

The man licks the blood off his hand and sucks at the source of the blood where the splintery two by four had ripped across the palm. He doesn't look at it again, but keeps his eyes fixed on the animals as he calculates the ratio of resistance to punishment and fear. His face is warped abetted by the scar. Climbing to the side of the truck where truck and ramp meet, the man works the pole in and out smashing wood against hump, shoulder, back, and belly. Animals smash into one another. Some start down the ramp. Narrow the eyes as the ramp is narrow, the pig enters the compass of his doom and he knows it and he refuses to move, held immobile by his legs fixed in an angle of strength and desperation. The man smacks with his pole; the squeal echoes the fury of the man. The wood falls again and again on the pig's snout—the squinting eyes are hurt, the bone is crushed, the flesh pulsates like a gong of pain. The pig shakes his head dumbly to throw off the pain, and the drops of blood hit Stephen. He withdraws sharply and his stomach feels knotted.

Another man climbs the opposite side and pushes the pig with a sharp spike and draws a trickle of blood. The pig, now dazed and uncertain, the drive behind his eyes gone, the desperation diffused, shudders down the ramp. The others follow enclosed in terror and protest.

Stephen slips inside. Haunt of death—smoking flesh and wool and scalding skin, the boiling pots and the bodies emerging pink and white in purification. No more squealing. No more sound. Animals, now motionless and painless, heaved upon stone slabs—set to cooling in the full surrendered arch of their backs and crumpled small legs.

Stephen watches. The bloodied men in their black aprons, like black apparitions, laughing, cursing, shouting through unshaven faces appear as killer giants. Stephen feels dizzy and sees only dimly the shapes of horror. A red, sticky, hypnotic dream. He cringes from life.

His eye is drawn by the cry of a lamb to the death corner. The eye of the lamb fixes on his tormentors, his hind legs chained and raised inexorably until he is dangling, his front legs uselessly pawing the concrete. Then the knife thrust while the eyes are still fixed on the yawning half barrel beneath. The ears are held by a hunched man. In its convulsive dance of death, the animal spits a fine rain of blood in a wide circle, and the steam of his blood leaps to the folded flesh. The droplets of blood touch the boy, who trembles, screams and sees only blackness where God should have been.

The man, job finished, carelessly dips a cup into another barrel, arches his back and drinks it down. Then he laughs abrasively at another man. Stephen hates the huge man in his black and red apron.

Home. The children, all younger than Stephen, find excitement in the three lambs. It is as much a part of the Easter holiday as the ritual cooking of noodle pies, cheese cakes, meat pies, and pastries. "The lambs will bring us good fortune," Matalena says in her mood of abundance. But Stephen does not participate. He stares out the window at the animals tied to a large pine tree.

He watches his father preparing the equipment for the next day when he will kill the lambs. His father is solemn in his purpose as if all the frustrations and fears of the year will be vanquished by this one act. It had always been part of his way of life as it had been for his father before him—the way it had been part of the Easter celebration to grow white wheat in the cellar to deck the altars. But in the new world they had lost many of the old habits and their sons would lose all of them. Stephen's mind retreats to happier days. He thinks hard. He thinks of Christmas and of the green tree fresh from the cold and the silver strips shimmering in carressing lights. He asks his mother why Easter can't be like Christmas.

"If you have Christmas you gotta have Easter," she tells him. But he is not convinced. When he persists in his questioning she tells him to help his father. "If you love someone you try to help him—do something for him—now go!" She raises her hand in a feigned gesture of punishment.

But he does not help his father. He sees in him the man in the black apron, and he wants to run away to another world of Christmasy colors, of pastures and sunlight. He withdraws to his room. He is hot and begins to sweat. He thinks of the animals, of the pain pricking his own skin. His eyes redden and burn. But he will not cry. The contamination has made him too bitter. He wonders why others do not feel the same way, why he alone is in this prison.

That night his brothers and sisters are asleep, but he continues to stare into the darkness and listen to the squeal of cars turning the corner and throwing shadows on the bedroom walls. Somehow he does not fear the darkness the way he had on other nights. His anger has diluted his fears and there is too much to think about. When his eyes begin to hurt he shuts them against the darkness. But there is darkness on the inside as well—shiny, wet-black like the black apron. He feels he is running—endless rows of sheep . . .

The animals make no sound, forelegs clawing at the concrete. The scene shimmers and Stephen feels his legs weaken. The knowledge is artificial, uncertain, grim. The animals are hairless and pink and ribbed. Endless rows like the ribs of St. Mary's Cathedral. The smoke of burnt candles and incense is consoling and the dark booth he enters is cool and musty of old, old church wood.

"Father, I have lied and disobeyed my father and mother."

"Ah—that's very bad. Very bad indeed. One lie since your last confession?"

"Yes."

"Well then—you are sorry for your sin are you not?"

"Yes, Father."

"Good. Hell, you know, is a terrible place for sinners."

"And is killing a sin, too, Father?"

"Oh indeed it is—a very bad sin."

"Is it worse than lying?"

"My yes—very much worse. Why do you ask?"

"But if I save someone from being killed by lying is that a sin?"

"Well—that is a problem, isn't it. That depends . . ."

"Father—what makes people cruel?"

"When the devil is in them."

"How?"

"When they have evil thoughts. Now you say seven 'Our Fathers' and seven 'Hail Marys.' Now for the 'Act of Contrition.' "

Again Stephen wants to run. He does not feel cleansed. He feels more engorged with sin than ever. He is running among the sheep now scattering them to safety. He runs with them, becomes one of them. Then he sees a fleshless hand reach for him and he knows what it is to be irrevocably fixed, appointed, chosen, and sacrificed. No! His voice awakens him and it is a long time before the protest of his heart returns to normal and before he falls asleep again. He awakens before dawn and makes his way silently through the dark downstairs to the backyard where the lambs are waiting.

"Matalena! The lambs—they are gone! Stolen!"

Her face is at first uncomprehending. She wrings her hands without bothering to dry them. "Stolen? But how? We would have heard, no?" Her face slumps into weariness, her eyes narrow in bitter rage as the words sink in.

"Stolen!" he repeats. He curses. He makes a fist and raises it above his head. "I would break the thief in two," he shouts. "Taking food from the mouths of children." He searches for names, seizing on past indiscretion, past suspicions, and rolls them into accusations. Finally the rage spends itself in futility and there are tears in his eyes.

Stephen is fearful, but he is glad the lambs are safe.

"I'm going out," Mateo says.

"Where?"

"Out! Out! Where do you think? To look for them."

Matalena shuts off the gas under the kettle and slumps into a chair. Her head is cupped in crooked palms. Her disheveled hair hides her face.

Stephen sits at the far end of the table, his body quivering from the consequences of what he had done. He wants to talk to her but the words do not come. The children are up. Their morning cacaphony feeds her anger. "Go back to bed—all of you," she yells.

When Mateo returns later that morning his face is wet from exertion.

She says nothing at first. She knows too well the look of failure. When she speaks she says, "What do we do now?"

"How do I know what we do—how do I know? A month's wages!" He chops the air with his hand. "That's if I work—*if I work*!" he emphasizes. He dashes water on his face and rubs it vigorously. "And where do we get the money to pay Luigi and Domenico for their shares? Aah!" He shakes his head.

"It's terrible," she said. A look of frantic desperation pinches her face appearing even darker now. She holds her crooked index finger between her teeth in a gesture of despair.

"But who would do it," he returns to the incomprehensible. "And on Easter! Who is such a beast to do something like this? They got the rich to steal from—why us? Why us?" He curses his plight, his neighbors, the country, and his predicament.

When Matalena breaks into sobs, the boy's lips quiver, but he does not cry. The drawn look of guilt is on his face; he feels he might have broken some sacred rhythm of their lives.

He breaks away and runs towards the stairs. His father calls to him but he does not respond.

Mateo looks at his wife. The peasant squint of his eyes reveals some intuition. He calls again sternly. Stephen does not come. Mateo walks slowly to the stairs and orders his son to come down. His voice is menacing.

Stephen descends slowly and he runs to his mother.

"What's wrong with you?" Mateo asks. "Why did you get up so early this morning? And where did you go?" He thrusts his whiskered face towards him. "Huh?"

Overcome with confusion he throws himself into his mother's arms and hides his face.

"Come here," the father commands.

The boy clings.

"Go to your father."

Mateo takes him by the wrist forcefully. "Now tell me—what happened? What did you do? What? What?" His voice rises.

Stephen trembles. His tolerance for pain is low, but he does not cry. He says softly, "I let them go."

The father releases the wrist involuntarily and gazes at him in a stupefied stare, uncomprehending. Then he slammed his hands into one another. "You let them go!" He slams the table with his fist. "Why?" He slaps Stephen's face. The water in Stephen's eyes turns bitter and his face rings with pain. He thinks of the pain of the animals.

"What's in your head—sawdust?"

Matalena sobs softly.

"Come with me!" Mateo shouts. "Come on. If we don't find them I'm gonna send *you* to the cemetery."

They walk down the street of row houses and three more similar streets to the slaughterhouse where Stephen stands fixed in all his fears. He expects to see another truck turn the corner. He wants to run to some land he no longer can see clearly. But the sadness overwhelms him and his imagination bogs down in a world of darkness. He watches his father knock at the door of the office. He sees him waiting nervously in his embarrassment. A man comes to the door, frowns and shakes his head.

His father stands as if confused. Then they walk six blocks to a police station. Stephen sees the perspiration on his father's face as he pauses outside the station as if something about his demeanor or dress would indicate some hidden crime, some violation of which he was not aware. Then slamming his hands together as if he had reached some decision, he walks through the darkened entrance.

Someone is speaking to the police at the desk. A woman. It is not about police matters. Mateo dares not interrupt. When they finish he would speak. But when would they finish? He sits on a curved mahogany bench and waits, wringing his hands, listening to the buzz of incomprehensible voices.

Stephen sits immobile in the hard surroundings. He feels an oppression. The scenes of the slaughterhouse come back to him and he does not like the police. His eyes are brought together in meditation, and his mind goes back to happier days —his father playing the guitar slightly off key and singing songs of another world, a lost world, while the children danced in wild abandonment, the joyous gyrations filling the house. It seems so distant now.

Suddenly his father rises, his face hard. He takes Stephen's arm and moves towards the door. The man at the desk turns his head and says, "Can we do anything for you, mister?"

Mateo is caught unexpectedly. He tries to smile, but nothing comes. He shrugs instead as if what he was about to say was unimportant, did not warrant the interruption of police affairs. "I lost some sheeps," he says hesitantly in his best English.

"Sheep, eh?" The policeman asks his name and writes something down on a pad. "Where do you live?"

Mateo shows apprehension at the question. "Clocka Street."

"Clark?"

"Yes—Clocka Street."

"What number?"

"Twenty-four."

"Near the woods?"

"Yes."

"Okay. If anything turns up we'll get in touch with you."

Mateo nods and thanks the policeman. He almost bows. But once he crosses the sharp shadows into the sunlight, he curses the police and mutters that it was all a mistake, that he had lost valuable time. Temporarily he seems lost in the full sunlight. He turns to Stephen. "Did you hide them anywhere? Did you take them anyplace?" He does not wait for an answer. He takes Stephen's arm and pulls him along with him.

They walk back to their street and pass their house. The street turns to a dirt road and leads to a wooded area. Mateo stops at a country gas station. Stephen waits by unused gas pumps while his father walks to the door of the clapboard house and waits. Stephen watches his father rubbing his hands together. He knows his father does not like to knock on strange doors. His language is bad and he is easily embarrassed. His father waits a long time for someone to come to the door and then receives an annoyed headshake.

They continue down the road towards the woods. A group of boys on vacation are walking towards a creek with their fishing poles and tire tubes. "Did you see sheeps?" Mateo asks.

The boys answered in a disheveled chorus. One of them imitates the sound of sheep.

Stephen does not like the boys. He hears his father mutter something about people being cruel who don't know what misery is.

Soon they stand at the edge of the woods. Mateo stops to survey it. It appears so endless that it brings a look of defeat to his face. Then he heads into the woods warning his son to stay close behind him.

The ground is soft and damp from spring rains, and virgin green is on most of the trees. Every few minutes Mateo stops to check his direction. After more than half an hour of meandering and backtracking Mateo stops and looks at his son. "Don't you have any idea where they are? No idea, huh?"

The scenes of the slaughterhouse return and Stephens shuts his eyes.

"Is that all you do? Shut yourself up? Smart in school but at home you're an idiot!"

In a few minutes the father again asks, "Why did you do it?" Believing that the training of children was always some mysterious process of imitation and re-enactment, he senses some profound failure. When the boy does not answer, Mateo turns to him in a rage and slaps his face. "Answer me!"

"I didn't want to hurt them."

Mateo shakes his head despairingly. The answer seems to irritate him. "And what do we eat, eh? Eh?" He shoves his boy back. Stephen trips and falls on a decaying tree trunk, cutting his hand on a splintery branch. His hand bleeds. Still he does not cry, but accepts the bruise.

His father becomes more conciliatory. "You think I like to kill them? You think so? You think I enjoy it?" He shakes his head and closes his eyes. "It's for you we do these things—you think the animals are more important than us? The rich let others do it for them—we must do it ourselves."

The cut on his hand burns. The fine grains of decaying wood mingle with the blood. Stephen seems on the verge of crying, or fainting and again he feels like running and again the imagination collapses. "Where did you take them?" he hears his father say. And then, "Come on—come on . . ."

He follows his father and hears his talking to himself. "Work like a beast to pull the family ahead and then they betray you—ah—ugly beast of life—and where do I get the money to pay the others—where?" He turns his head and spits out a remark, "What got into your head?" Then he pauses, waits for Stephen to reach him, takes his arm and gives it a hurting twist.

As if without thinking Mateo charges into a field of heavy underbrush and flowers. He picks up a thick branch and begins to strike at the growth. Soon he finds himself in a field of thorns. Stephen halts at the edge of the field.

Mateo strikes harder at the foliage and his anger mounts. The thorns rip into him. Violence meets violence. His hands, legs and arms are scratched and begin to bleed. Mateo curses and looks wild. He beats the earth; he beats the bushes; he swings at the air, at the trees wildly without direction, without reason. Then exhaustion. He breathes heavily and slumps down on a burnt tree stump, his head between his arms.

Stephen watches his father and his face breaks into sobs. He sees the blood on his father's hands and he feels an overwhelming sense of loss. Nothing is as it should be. He feels he has broken the pattern and blames himself and he cries his mournful cry.

He turns away and runs. His father yells after him. "Runaway—sure, sure, run! Come back here!" He curses him. He rises and follows him. The boy moves faster—through the woods and down to a small creek, to a small pasture between the creek and the woods, rimmed by pine trees and rosebud trees in their pink-purplish effusions.

Stephen sees the lambs by the bank and walks toward them. He walks as if in slow motion, the movements not his. The animals jerk away at first and then settle down and await the approaching hands of their benefactor. Stephen throws his arms around the neck of one lamb and rubs his face on the woolly head. He feels an intimacy he cannot release. He takes the ropes and turns his face towards his approaching father. "Come on," he sobs to the animals. "Come on."

The father waits. There is a new look on his face. Then he takes the ropes, his eyes still on his son. He ties the ropes to his belt. He takes Stephen to the creek and washes his bruised hand and face. He examines the boy's hand and kisses it. "You will be all right," he says. He pulls the boy's head against his side and holds it for a long while in the silence that encompasses them. "Tonight we will celebrate," he tells his son.

Stephen is solemn. It was something that had to be done, he tells himself. But he would always hate the man in the black apron. That he would always do.

PART FIVE

Selections for Analysis of Style: Angles of Vision

Frederick Douglass (1817?–1895) was an American lecturer and writer called in consultation by Abraham Lincoln. His major work is his autobiography relating his experiences as the illegitimate son of a white man and a Negro slave and his final escape to freedom: *The Narrative of the Life of Frederick Douglass* (1845).

A Child's Reasoning

FREDERICK DOUGLASS

The incidents related in the foregoing chapter led me thus early to inquire into the origin and nature of slavery. Why am I a slave? Why are some people slaves and others masters? These were perplexing questions and very troublesome to my childhood. I was very early told by some one that *"God up in the sky"* had made all things, and had made black people to be slaves and white people to be masters. I was told too that God was good, and that He knew what was best for everybody. This was, however, less satisfactory than the first statement. It came point blank against all my notions of goodness. The case of Aunt Esther was in my mind. Besides, I could not tell how anybody could know that God made black people to be slaves. Then I found, too, that there were puzzling exceptions to this theory of slavery, in the fact that all black people were not slaves, and all white people were not masters.

An incident occurred about this time that made a deep impression on my mind. My Aunt Jennie and one of the men slaves of Captain Anthony ran away. A great noise was made about it. Old master was furious. He said he would follow them and catch them and bring them back, but he never did, and somebody told me that Uncle Noah and Aunt Jennie had gone to the free states and were free. Besides this occurrence, which brought much light to my mind on the subject, there were several slaves on Mr. Lloyd's place who remembered being brought from Africa. There were others who told me that their fathers and mothers were stolen from Africa.

This to me was important knowledge, but not such as to make me feel very easy in my slave condition. The success of Aunt Jennie and Uncle Noah in getting away from slavery was, I think, the first fact that made me seriously think of escape for myself. I could not have been more than seven or eight years old at the time of this occurrence, but young as I was, I was already, in spirit and purpose, a fugitive from slavery.

Up to the time of the brutal treatment of my Aunt Esther, already narrated, and the shocking plight in which I had seen my cousin from Tuckahoe, my attention had not been especially directed to the grosser and more revolting features of slavery. I had, of course, heard of whippings and savage mutilations of slaves by brutal overseers, but happily for me I had always been out of the way of such occurrences. My play time was spent outside of the corn and tobacco fields, where the overseers and slaves were brought together and in conflict. But after the case of my Aunt Esther I saw others of the same disgusting and shocking nature. The one of these which agitated and distressed me most was the whipping of a woman, not belonging to my old master, but to Col. Lloyd. The charge against her was very common and very indefinite, namely, "*impudence.*" This crime could be committed by a slave in a hundred different ways, and depended much upon the temper and caprice of the overseer as to whether it was committed at all. He could create the offense whenever it pleased him. A look, a word, a gesture, accidental or intentional, never failed to be taken as impudence when he was in the right mood for such an offense. In this case there were all the necessary conditions for the commission of the crime charged. The offender was nearly white, to begin with; she was the wife of a favorite hand on board of Mr. Lloyd's sloop, and was, besides, the mother of five sprightly children. Vigorous and spirited woman that she was, a wife and a mother, with a predominating share of the blood of the master running in her veins, Nellie (for that was her name) had all the qualities essential to impudence to a slave overseer. My attention was called to the scene of the castigation by the loud screams and curses that proceeded from the direction of it. When I came near the parties engaged in the struggle the overseer had hold of Nellie, endeavoring with his whole strength to drag her to a tree against her resistance. Both his and her faces were bleeding, for the woman was doing her best. Three of her children were present, and though quite small, (from seven to ten years old, I should think), they gallantly took the side of their mother against the overseer, and pelted him well with stones and epithets. Amid the screams of the children, "Let my mammy go! Let my mammy go!" the hoarse voice of the maddened overseer was heard in terrible oaths that he would teach her how to give a white an *impudence*. The blood on his face and on hers attested her skill in the use of her nails, and his dogged determination to conquer. His purpose was to tie her up to a tree and give her, in slaveholding parlance, a "genteel flogging," and he evidently had not expected the stern and protracted resistance he was meeting, or the strength and skill needed to its execution. There were times when she seemed likely to get the better of the brute, but he finally overpowered her and succeeded in getting her arms firmly tied to the tree towards which he had been dragging her. The victim was now at the mercy of his merciless lash. What followed I need not here describe. The cries of the now helpless woman, while undergoing the terrible infliction, were mingled with the hoarse curses of the overseer and the wild cries of her distracted children. When the poor woman was untied her back was covered with blood. She was whipped, terribly whipped, but she was not subdued, and continued to denounce the overseer and to pour upon him every vile epithet of which she could think.

Such floggings are seldom repeated on the same person by overseers. They prefer to whip those who are the most easily whipped. The doctrine that submission to violence is the best cure for violence did not hold good as between slaves and overseers. He was whipped oftener who was whipped easiest. That slave who had the courage to stand up for himself against the overseer, although he might have many hard stripes at first, became while legally a slave virtually a freeman. "You can shoot me," said a slave to Rigby Hopkins, "but you can't whip me," and the result was he was neither whipped nor shot. I do not know that Mr. Sevier ever attempted to whip Nellie again. He probably never did, for he was taken sick not long after and died. It was commonly said that his deathbed was a wretched one, and that, the ruling passion being strong in death, he died flourishing the slave whip and with horrid oaths upon his lips. This deathbed scene may only be the imagining of the slaves. One thing is certain, that when he was in health his profanity was enough to chill the blood of an ordinary man. Nature, or habit, had given to his face an expression of uncommon savageness. Tobacco and rage had ground his teeth short, and nearly every sentence that he uttered was commenced or completed with an oath. Hated for his cruelty, despised for his cowardice, he went to his grave lamented by nobody on the place outside of his own house, if, indeed, he was even lamented there.

In Mr. James Hopkins, the succeeding overseer, we had a different and a better man, as good perhaps as any man could be in the position of a slave overseer. Though he sometimes wielded the lash, it was evident that he took no pleasure in it and did it with much reluctance. He stayed but a short time here, and his removal from the position was much regretted by the slaves generally. Of the successor of Mr. Hopkins I shall have something to say at another time and in another place.

For the present we will attend to a further description of the businesslike aspect of Col. Lloyd's "Great House" farm. There was always much bustle and noise here on the two days at the end of each month, for then the slaves belonging to the different branches of this great estate assembled here by their representatives to obtain their monthly allowances of cornmeal and pork. These were gala days for the slaves of the outlying farms, and there was much rivalry among them as to who should be elected to go up to the Great House farm for the "Allowances," and indeed to attend to any other business at this great place, to them the capital of a little nation. Its beauty and grandeur, its immense wealth, its numerous population, and the fact that uncles Harry, Peter, and

Jake, the sailors on board the sloop, usually kept on sale trinkets which they bought in Baltimore to sell to their less fortunate fellow-servants, made a visit to the Great House farm a high privilege, and eagerly sought. It was valued, too, as a mark of distinction and confidence, but probably the chief motive among the competitors for the office was the opportunity it afforded to shake off the monotony of the field and to get beyond the overseer's eye and lash. Once on the road with an oxteam and seated on the tongue of the cart, with no overseer to look after him, one felt comparatively free.

Slaves were expected to sing as well as to work. A silent slave was not liked, either by masters or overseers. "Make a noise there! Make a noise there!" and "bear a hand," were words usually addressed to slaves when they were silent. This, and the natural disposition of the Negro to make a noise in the world, may account for the almost constant singing among them when at their work. There was generally more or less singing among the teamsters, at all times. It was a means of telling the overseer, in the distance, where they were and what they were about. But on the allowance days those commissioned to the Great House farm were peculiarly vocal. While on the way they would make the grand old woods for miles around reverberate with their wild and plaintive notes. They were indeed both merry and sad. Child as I was, these wild songs greatly depressed my spirits. Nowhere outside of dear old Ireland, in the days of want and famine, have I heard sounds so mournful.

In all these slave songs there was some expression of praise of the Great House farm—something that would please the pride of the Lloyds.

> I am going to the Great House farm,
> O, yea! O, yea! O, yea!
> My old master is a good old master,
> O, yea! O, yea! O, yea!

These words would be sung over and over again, with others, improvised as they went along—jargon, perhaps, to the reader, but full of meaning to the singers. I have sometimes thought that the mere hearing of these songs would have done more to impress the good people of the North with the soul-crushing character of slavery than whole volumes exposing the physical cruelties of the slave system, for the heart has no language like song. Many years ago, when recollecting my experience in this respect, I wrote of these slave songs in the following strain:

"I did not, when a slave, fully understand the deep meaning of those rude and apparently incoherent songs. I was, myself, within the circle, so that I could then neither hear nor see as those without might see and hear. They breathed the prayer and complaint of souls overflowing with the bitterest anguish. They depressed my spirits and filled my heart with ineffable sadness."

The remark in the olden time was not unfrequently made, that slaves were the most contented and happy laborers in the world, and their dancing and singing were referred to in proof of this alleged fact; but it was a great mistake to suppose them happy because they sometimes made those joyful noises. The songs of the slaves represented their sorrows, rather than their joys. Like tears, they were a relief to aching hearts. It is not inconsistent with the constitution of the human mind that it avails itself of one and the same method for expressing opposite emotions. Sorrow and desolation have their songs, as well as joy and peace.

It was the boast of slaveholders that their slaves enjoyed more of the physical comforts of life than the peasantry of any country in the world. My experience contradicts this. The men and the women slaves on Col. Lloyd's farm received, as their monthly allowance of food, eight pounds of pickled pork, or its equivalent in fish. The pork was often tainted, and the fish were of the poorest quality. With their pork or fish, they had given them one bushel of Indian meal, unbolted, of which quite fifteen per cent was more fit for pigs than for men. With this, one pint of salt was given, and this was the entire monthly allowance of a full-grown slave, working constantly in the open field from morning till night every day in the month except Sunday. There is no kind of work which really requires a better supply of food to prevent physical exhaustion than the field-work of a slave. The yearly allowance of clothing was not more ample than the supply of food. It consisted of two tow-linen shirts, one pair of trousers of the same coarse material, for summer, and a woolen pair of trousers and a woolen jacket for winter, with one pair of yarn stockings and a pair of shoes of the coarsest description. Children under ten years old had neither shoes, stockings, jackets, nor trousers. They had two coarse tow-linen shirts per year, and when these were worn out they went naked till the next allowance day—and this was the condition of the little girls as well as of the boys.

As to beds, they had none. One coarse blanket was given them, and this only to the men and women. The children stuck themselves in holes and corners about the quarters, often in the corners of huge chimneys, with their feet in the ashes to keep them warm. The want of beds, however, was not considered a great privation by the field hands. Time to sleep was of far greater importance. For when the day's work was done most of these had their washing, mending, and cooking to do, and having few or no facilities for doing such things, very many of their needed sleeping hours were consumed in necessary preparations for the labors of the coming day. The sleeping apartments, if they could have been properly called such, had little regard to comfort or decency. Old and young, male and female, married and single, dropped down upon the common clay floor, each covering up with his or her blanket, their only protection from cold or exposure. The night, however, was shortened at both ends. The slaves worked often as long as they could see, and were late in cooking and mending for the coming day, and at the first gray streak of the morning they were summoned to the field by the overseer's horn. They were whipped for oversleeping more than for any other fault. Neither age nor sex found any favor. The overseer stood at the quarter door, armed with stick and whip, ready to deal heavy blows upon any who might be a little behind time. When the horn was blown there was a rush for the door, for the hindermost one was sure to get a blow from the overseer. Young mothers who worked in the field were allowed an hour about ten o'clock in the morning to go home to nurse their children. This was when they were not required to take them to the field with them, and leave them upon "turning row," or in the corner of the fences.

As a general rule the slaves did not come to their quarters to take their meals, but took their ashcake (called thus because baked in the ashes) and piece of pork, or their salt herrings, where they were at work.

But let us now leave the rough usage of the field, where vulgar coarseness and brutal cruelty flourished as rank as weeds in the tropics and where a vile wretch, in the shape of a man, rides, walks, and struts about, with whip in hand, dealing heavy blows and leaving deep gashes on the flesh of men and women, and turn our attention to the less repulsive slave life as it existed in the home of my childhood. Some idea of the splendor of that place sixty years ago has already been given. The contrast between the condition of the slaves and that of their masters was marvelously sharp and striking. There were pride, pomp, and luxury on the one hand, servility, dejection, and misery on the other.

Eleanor Wait (1946–   ) won first prize in the poetry division of the *Story* College Creative Awards Contest of 1967–1968 while she was a student at Chatham College. A drama major, she worked several summers at the Booth Bay Playhouse in Maine. She considers Emily Dickinson, T. S. Eliot, and Walt Whitman her favorite poets.

Ellie: An Inventory of Being

ELEANOR WAIT

I am Ellie.

I am twenty years old.

I am a student, but never a co-ed.
A girl, afraid to be a woman.

If I stand very tall I am 65 inches high.
I have blue eyes streaked with gray
And tarnished brown hair
That gets in them.
Sometimes I wear it in a bun and am Emily Dickinson or
    Louisa Alcott
Or in pigtails, and play hopscotch in front of Mellon Institute.
Or just let it hang,
And run down Chapel Hill anyway.

I am a student, and a lady, and a child;
Almost a woman, but always a girl.

I love rare steak and burnt potato chips.

I am older than Neenie,
Younger than Lea;
I love the smell of Arpege and mud flats.

I drink tea with lemon and sugar with coffee.

Daffodils laugh, but blue-bells depress me.
I'm afraid of trolls.

I like raisins in oatmeal, and in the sun.
I work best under pressure.

I like shiny fingernails and jazz, but
I hate Altman's and mini-skirts.

I like small rooms lined with books, and braided rugs, and
Pillows, because I like to sit on the floor.

I like fountain pens and brown notebooks and blue ink and
I don't believe in god, but I don't tell anyone anymore,
And my children will go to church,
Because I love Christmas.

I love pearls.
I like garnets better than rubies,
And topaz more than diamonds.
But someday I want a diamond
And a gold band
Forever.

But not just now.

Someday I want a girl named Jeannie and a boy named Mike—
But they'll have to wait.
Because I want to be a person first.

Subject to change.

I believe that women are more than equal, but keep quiet about it.
I know there are 435 members of the House of Representatives
But I don't understand why more of them aren't Negroes and women.

Rachel Carson and Margaret Chase Smith were my high school ideals.
Now I'd add (quietly) Jean Kerr.

I'm an anti-feminist.
I love to travel alone.

I'm crazy about noodles and tuna fish and pizza with pepperoni
and Jello.
I hate clutter, unless it's books.

I love cosy slippers and lacy underwear and going barefoot in
the mud.
I make spaghetti in a popcorn popper, and always add paprika.
I am in love with chipmunks, pigeons, and 4 x 6 envelopes.
I read Dickens and Ferlinghetti.

I love wind and rain and snowmen
And Baroque music and Barbra Streisand, even if she's trite.
And I don't like earrings or hair spray or soap operas and
I adore commercials.

I love fireplaces with real fires, and front porches with creaky
swings, and noisy typewriters.

I like strawberry milkshakes and frosted lipsticks.
I'd like to be cultured, but I love WABC and
I daydream at the symphony.

I love to get dressed up, but I don't waste time doing it.
I hate alarm clocks and television sets. But I couldn't live
without them.

I'd rather walk than ride. But I'll drive anywhere.

I'm honest to a proudly self-conscious fault, and I'm
Corrupt to a deeper meaning.
I wish sex were legal—but I went through a phase of wishing
human sacrifice were too.

I don't want to grow up, but I'm scared to stay young.

I eat too much, sometimes, and talk too much, often, and
Wish I could sleep too much, always.

If the world were a stage I'd feel more comfortable in it.

I'm a loner, but I love being lonely.
I'm a conformist, except when I think.
I have horrible nightmares, and wild daydreams,
And I couldn't live without either.

I spend too much money on velvet hair ribbons and funny cards
and books of plays.
Hamlet and Antigone are my ideals, but
Creon and I are one.

I think too fast.
I hate greasepaint, but I love crowds.

I love Degas, but I don't think I like horses or ballet.
I've always wanted to be the first woman president, and a marine biologist, and a literary lionness,
And an archaeologist,
But I'm allergic to dust.

I don't want anyone to understand me,
But people think they do, and
They're probably right.

If I were rich the first place I'd go would be Scotland.
The second would be Stratford.
And the third would be Disneyland.

I need someone to need me, because then I need them too.
I'm a deadly realist, but I pretend to be idealistic.
I used to think there was no such thing as love.
Now I'm not so sure.

I never want to go to the moon, but I'd love to see penguins.
I've always felt that horses were incomplete zebras.

I'm funny.
But most of the time it's intentional.

I get migraine heartaches.

I either love or hate October and March; I haven't decided yet.
I like men who know that women are people too,
And I hate crew cuts and red hair.

I'm a drama major because there are only five of us.
I support the minority, but
If I were Jewish, I'd be conservative.
If I were a Democrat, I'd be liberal.
I'm in favor of staying in Viet Nam,
But I hate war.

I may be in love, but it scares me.
But he doesn't.

I love to see the sun rise, but hate to get up in the morning.

I'm perennially frustrated because I can't know everything.
And I'm annually concerned about self.

My name is Ellie, and this is 1967.

E. B. White was born in Mount Vernon, New York on July 11, 1899. In 1921 he was graduated from Cornell. He is well known for his essays, short stories, and poems. He has held various jobs in journalism and has contributed regularly to *Harper's Magazine* and *The New Yorker*. He is still on the salaried staff of *The New Yorker,* working from his home in Maine. His books include *Quo Vadimus?, One Man's Meat, The Second Tree from the Corner,* and *The Points of My Compass*. He is also the author of two juvenile classics, *Charlotte's Web* and *Stuart Little,* for which he won the 1970 Laura Ingalls Wilder Award, which is presented by the Children's Services Division of the American Library Association every five years to an author of books that have, over a period of years, "made a substantial and lasting contribution to literature for children." In June, 1970, Mr. White's long awaited third book for children, *The Trumpet of the Swan,* was published. He edited and amplified *The Elements of Style* by William Strunk, Jr. In 1963 he received the Presidential Medal of Freedom.

The Sword

E. B. WHITE

"Make me a sword!"

(Man lives alone and by the sword.)

"What for? [You mean the wars, the debatable
 wars?] You get the stick from the cellar."

"For the scabbard?"

"No, for the sword."

"You have to saw a piece off, to nail across, and
 smooth a place where my hand goes around."

"The grip?"

"Smoothened for the hand, the edges rounded."

"This stick is dusty. Get a cloth. Don't dust
 it here it'll dirty the room take it out

and dust it not with that new cloth it'll
ruin it."

"Where is the saw?"

"Hold it, hold the end."

(The first stroke, sawblade against thumbside. On this point, my hearty, impale the world. "Hold the end while I saw a piece off." On this point, which isn't even sharpened yet, impale the enemy only don't get hurt. "Hold it steady and don't fool.")

(Man lives alone and by the sword,
youth dreams alone and girds for right
and dulls his blade against the stone;
the dream fails in the short night.
Man is disarmed and still alone.)

keep your feet dry
don't take cold
be polite shake hands with Mr. Hecatomb
marry a nice girl
pay your bills
look at those hands
don't put your mouth on that dirty old rail

Povl W. Toussieng 1918-   ) was born in Nysted, Denmark. He now resides in Oklahoma City. Having received his M.D. degree, he majored in child psychiatry and is now a professor of child psychiatry. He has contributed to the *American Journal of Orthopsychiatry, Journal of the American Academy of Child Psychiatry, International Journal of Adolescence, Mental Hygiene,* and numerous other periodicals. He is also the author of two chapters in the *Handbook on Psychopathology,* and he is now preparing a book entitled *Renewal without Rebellion.*

Arthur Henley (1921–   ) lives in Forest Hills, New York. He majored in psychology and is now a writer and lecturer. He has contributed to *Ladies Home Journal, Mental Hygiene, Saturday Evening Post, McCall's, Today's Health* and many other periodicals. His major works include *Demon in My View,* and *Make Up Your Mind.*

Defiant Kids Will Make the Best Adults

DR. POVL W. TOUSSIENG
with ARTHUR HENLEY

It has become increasingly apparent that more and more children do *not* want to be like their parents; they dress differently, think differently and aspire to different goals. Youth seems to be going its own way, not the way its elders want it to go. But is this necessarily so bad?

My answer, as a child psychiatrist, is a resounding "No!"

Working with teen-agers has always been one of the things I enjoyed most and thought I did best. We always seemed to "dig" each other. About a year ago, I became aware that I wasn't getting through to them any longer, and I began to worry about it. Finally, after a lengthy and intense personal crisis, I began to understand why these young people and I had ceased to communicate. It wasn't the kids who had become estranged from me; it was I who had not kept pace with them. This changed my thinking a great deal, as well as my views on what is happening in our increasingly youthful society.

As things fell into place for me, I made a surprising discovery. The "ideal children" who are the envy of the neighborhood because they are "such good kids and no trouble to anyone" aren't really growing up, or even trying to solve the crucial problems of adolescence. Yet many children whose behavior worries their elders most *are* actively struggling with the tasks of growing up and are likely to do better as adults than their "ideal" contemporaries.

The last task of childhood, the one that makes it possible to reach maturity, is the adolescent's achievement of a firm sense of knowing just who he is in relation to others and to events around him. For the child to become a stable adult, these relationships must have stability—a difficult task in our uncertain world.

From the time of these youngsters' birth, mankind has shuddered under the menace of possible nuclear conflict. Electronic communications have shrunk the world into one village where everyone everywhere shares the impact of any emotional experience anywhere. Almost all aspects of our lives change so abruptly, so frequently and so unpredictably that many adults have a terrible time adapting to such changes.

Fear is the result of such profound and constant change in one's accustomed way of life. Adults, by and large, have become so insecure, anxious and bewildered that fears of all kinds tend to dominate their lives: fear of death, fear of Communism, fear of growing old, fear of bad breath and body odor, fear of atheism, fear of breast-feeding and mother's milk (only in America!), fear of homosexuality, fear of nonconformity, fear of losing, fear of being alone (without a television set), fear of silence, fear of other social classes and other ethnic groups, fear of boys with long hair and girls with short skirts, and so on.

The increase in attacks on our social order has increased adult fearfulness. Those who rightly seek to protect the young from such legitimate dangers as narcotics addiction and sexual promiscuity sometimes extend their protection to include dangers, such as those imposed by social change, that they themselves fear. So their protectiveness is sometimes a disguised appeal to the younger generation to save *them* from perils *they* feel threatened by.

However, today's youth is not generally persuaded by such emotional appeals, nor are young people deluded by the double standards practiced by too many adults. While still very young, children learn from references in the news media and from conversations in their own homes about important grown-ups who are caught lying, cheating and stealing and often get away with breaking the rules.

Such hypocrisy leaves youngsters with fewer admirable adult models to pattern themselves after, and they must work out their own answers to the key questions of adolescence: *Who am I? Who should I be?* These used to be difficult questions to answer even with adult support; they are overwhelming when the young have to do it alone, while being undermined for trying to be themselves, and pressed to identify with outmoded styles of living—especially in the middle and upper classes. The only kids choosing to follow in their parents' footsteps are America's "ideal children." This large group of youngsters has neither the courage nor the stamina to fight back against adult attempts to keep them chained to a world that no longer exists. Despite their high intelligence generally, these young people question nothing. They are products of schools that still resist relevance to contemporary life.

Our affluent society emphasizes the joys of leisure, and the once-sturdy virtues of hard work and long hours are not esteemed as highly as they used to be. Unfortunately, many who cling to these virtues feel so guilty about their leisure time that they fail to learn how to enjoy and use it constructively.

Yesterday's moral standards have taken a battering, too. It is no longer a simple question of to steal or not to steal. More sophisticated ethical questions are now being raised. For example, how should we resolve the problem of pesticides that preserve the crops but endanger the food? Or the problem of industrial wastes that are by-products of increased production vital for today's living standards—but pollute the air, jeopardizing the health of all?

"Ideal children" rarely weigh such issues or entertain doubts. They follow orders of authority figures with the blind obedience that their parents condemned at the time of the Nuremburg Trials, which condemned Nazi officials for having followed orders instead of listening to their consciences. Yet these same adults applaud obedience by their children, cheering these brain-washed youngsters on in hope that somehow they will bring back the "good old days."

Since such hopes are futile, these "ideal" young people have sacrificed their dignity and individuality for a fictitious cause. They are walking backward into the future, so far removed from what is happening that they are nothing more than their grandparents disguised in teen-age bodies. I have begun to call them "the living dead."

They will grow up going through all the right motions but will rarely touch the real world. For a time they will manage well enough—completing their education, marrying and procreating, doing what is "proper" and delighting their parents with their tractability—but sooner or later they will begin to experience the same kinds of fears, uncertainties and anxieties that beset their parents. They will seek escape in the protected suburban environment, only to discover that this protection is a sham. Many will be forced to seek escape through other means, perhaps alcohol, drugs or illicit sex. Like most contemporary adults, they will become people for whom love is nothing more than a flight from loneliness; sex nothing but a more acceptable form of masturbation; social relationships nothing but occasions to get drunk together; for whom religious faith is measured only by tithing and weekly church attendance; for whom "truth" comes neatly pre-packaged in hygienic "see-through" cellophane—and who are senile before they have been young.

They will, in short, become a dangling generation, detached from their contemporaries and from their time, perpetuating their discomfort in their own children who will come crippled into a world they cannot comprehend.

The younger generation has *never* known a world that did not bristle with overwhelming stimulation, and was not always in ferment. So it seems to me tragic that so many adults choose to look down on young people (except the "ideal kids") with dismay, equating "decadence" of youth and such manifestations as legitimate student protests with juvenile delinquency, teen-age vandalism, illegitimacy, venereal disease, and youthful abuse of drugs and alcohol.

Such behavior represents serious, even dangerous, national problems and many youngsters will be scarred permanently by such experiences. But adults tend to label *all* vigorously independent behavior as "delinquent," and seem convinced that these "misbehaving" kids either have deep-seated character disorders or are emotionally disturbed. Some of these young people *are* warped psychologically, but we find that an increasingly large percentage do not show sufficient signs of emotional disturbance or character defects to explain their behavior. So the question is whether their defiant behavior really reflects a wish to be bad or to rebel, or whether they are fighting in the only way they know how to avoid "living death."

In my experience, many of these "bad" youngsters, unruly though some may be, are searching stubbornly for a workable and meaningful identity that will lead them to maturity in the style of the second half of the 20th century. They do not see their behavior as being bad, nor do they want to be bad.

Adults make an even bigger mistake when they automatically view the behavior of all young people who drink, sample drugs, indulge in sex, drop out of school or run away as passive, escapist behavior. I, too, deplore such excesses. But 100 million "grown-up" Americans regularly turn to alcohol and tranquilizers to banish anxiety and discomfort—impressive evidence that it is the adult generation that seeks oblivion by "copping out." Nearly all researchers agree that these "bad" young people are not looking for escape, but are actively seeking—sometimes in foolish, even dangerous, ways

—how to tolerate and integrate the intense overstimulation that is built into the society they have inherited from us. They want to *find* out, not *drop* out; to learn to live with and conquer the pain, not bury it as so many of their elders do.

Actually, adults need not be afraid of this search by the young. They are simply taking the old value systems and trying to give them new form, new expression and new, intensely personal meanings that require deep commitment—not to escape or indulge in empty rebellion, but to seek a more meaningful life for themselves and all of society.

In this category are those youngsters who disdain business careers because they do not think making money is that important; who participate in the Peace Corps, Vista and other people-to-people enterprises; who leave their church when they feel it does not respond to the social responsibilities of our time—departing not because of a loss of faith but to practice through unselfish service to others what they consider the essence of the Judaeo-Christian ethic.

It behooves us to listen to these kids, to their music, to their protests, and not turn our backs on them even if they choose not to emulate us. Although most older people feel like fish out of water in this youthful society, the parent generation still has a wider perspective on many things. And young people *are* eager to listen to their elders, so long as they are not given sermons. Supportive concern and understanding by adults would go a long way to keeping our sometimes "wayward" youth from getting sidetracked dangerously en route to self-discovery and self-realization.

It's these youngsters—not the "ideal" ones—who are most likely to find ways to build a bridge from a disordered present to a more substantial future for themselves, their children and us as well. The times are indeed changing, and we have to change with them.

Arthur Schopenhauer (1788–1860), German philosopher, was born in Danzig and educated in France, Germany, and England. He had an unhappy childhood and thereafter spent a wandering, lonely life, working on his philosophical writings. Only in the last ten years of his life did he receive some measure of recognition. To Schopenhauer, complete salvation for man is achieved only by negation of the will or denial of self and desire through a passionless ascetic life. His principal work is *The World as Will and Idea.*

On Women

ARTHUR SCHOPENHAUER

Schiller's poem in honour of women, *Worde der Frauen,* is the result of much careful thought, and it appeals to the reader by its antithetic style and its use of contrast; but as an expression of the true praise which should be accorded to them, it is, I think, inferior to these few words of Jouy's: *Without women the beginning of our life would be helpless; the middle, devoid of pleasure, and the end, of consolation.* The same thing is more feelingly expressed by Byron in *Sardanapalus:—*

The very first
Of human life must spring from woman's breast,
Your first small words are taught you from her lips,
Your first tears quench'd by her, and your last sighs
Too often breathed out in a woman's hearing,
When men have shrunk from the ignoble care
Of watching the last hour of him who led them.
(Act I, Scene 2.)

These two passages indicate the right standpoint for the appreciation of women.

You need only look at the way in which she is formed to see that woman is not meant to undergo great labour, whether of the mind or of the body. She pays the debt of life not by what she does but by what she suffers; by the pains of childbearing and care for the child, and by submission to her husband, to whom she should be a patient and cheering companion. The keenest sorrows and joys are not for her, nor is she called upon to display a great deal of strength. The current of her life should be more gentle, peaceful and trivial than man's, without being essentially happier or unhappier.

Women are directly fitted for acting as the nurses and teachers of our early childhood by the fact that they are themselves childish, frivolous and short-sighted; in a word, they are big children all their life long—a kind of intermediate stage between the child and the full-grown man, who is man in the strict sense of the word. See how a girl will fondle a child for days together, dance with it and sing to it; and then think what a man, with the best will in the world, could do if he were put in her place.

With young girls Nature seems to have had in view what, in the language of the drama, is called *a coup de théâtre.* For a few years she dowers them with a wealth of beauty and is lavish in her gift of charm, at the expense of the rest of their life, in order that during those years they may capture the fantasy of some man to such a degree that he is hurried into undertaking the honourable care of them, in some form or other, as long as they live—a step for which there would not appear to be any sufficient warranty if reason only directed his thoughts. Accordingly Nature has equipped woman, as she does all her creatures, with the weapons and implements requisite for the safeguarding of her existence, and for just as long as it is necessary for her to have them. Here, as elsewhere, Nature proceeds with her usual economy; for just as the female ant, after fecundation, loses her wings, which are then superfluous, nay, actually a danger to the business of breeding; so, after giving birth to one or two children, a woman generally loses her beauty; probably, indeed, for similar reasons.

And so we find that young girls, in their hearts, look upon domestic affairs or work of any kind as of secondary importance, if not actually as a mere jest. The only business that really claims their attention is love, making conquests, and everything connected with this—dress, dancing, and so on.

The nobler and more perfect a thing is, the later and slower it is in arriving at maturity. A man reaches the maturity of his reasoning powers and mental faculties hardly before the age of twenty-eight; a woman, at eighteen. And then, too, in the case of woman, it is only reason of a sort—very niggard in its dimensions. That is why women remain children their whole life long; never seeing anything but what is quite close to them, cleaving to the present moment, taking appearance for reality, and preferring trifles to matters of the first importance. For it is by virtue of his reasoning faculty that man does not live in the present only, like the brute, but looks about him and considers the past and the future; and this is the origin of prudence, as well as of that care and anxiety which so many people exhibit. Both the advantages and the disadvantages which this involves, are shared in by the woman to a smaller extent because of her weaker power of reasoning. She may, in fact, be described as intellectually shortsighted, because, while she has an intuitive understanding of what lies quite close to her, her field of vision is narrow and does not reach to what is remote: so that things which are absent or past or to come have much less effect upon women than upon men. This is the reason why women are more often inclined to be extravagant, and sometimes carry their inclination to a length that borders upon madness. In their hearts women think that it is men's business to earn money and theirs to spend it—if possible during their husband's life, but, at any rate, after his death. The very fact that their husband hands them over his earnings for purposes of housekeeping strengthens them in this belief.

However many disadvantages all this may involve, there is at least this to be said in its favour: that the woman lives more in the present than the man, and that, if the present is at all tolerable, she enjoys it more eagerly. This is the source of that cheerfulness which is peculiar to woman, fitting her to amuse man in his hours of recreation, and, in case of need, to console him when he is borne down by the weight of his cares.

It is by no means a bad plan to consult women in matters of difficulty, as the Germans used to do in ancient times; for their way of looking at things is quite different from ours, chiefly in the fact that they like to take the shortest way to their goal, and, in general, manage to fix their eyes upon what lies before them; while we, as a rule, see far beyond it, just because it is in front of our noses. In cases like this, we need to be brought back to the right standpoint, so as to recover the near and simple view.

Then, again, women are decidedly more sober in their judgment than we are, so that they do not see more in things than is really there; whilst, if our passions are aroused, we are apt to see things in an exaggerated way, or imagine what does not exist.

The weakness of their reasoning faculty also explains why it is that women show more sympathy for the unfortunate than men do, and so treat them with more kindness and interest; and why it is that, on the contrary, they are inferior to men in point of justice, and less honourable and conscientious. For it is just because their reasoning power is weak that present circumstances have such a hold over them, and those concrete things which lie directly before their eyes exercise a power which is seldom counteracted to any extent by abstract principles of thought, by fixed rules of conduct, firm resolutions, or, in general, by consideration for the past and the future, or regard for what is absent and remote. Accordingly, they possess the first and main elements that go to make a virtuous character, but they are deficient in those secondary qualities which are often a necessary instrument in the formation of it.

Hence it will be found that the fundamental fault of the female character is that it has *no sense of justice.* This is mainly due to the fact, already mentioned, that women are defective in the powers of reasoning and deliberation; but it is also traceable to the position which Nature has assigned to them as the weaker sex. They are dependent, not upon strength, but upon craft; and hence their instinctive capacity for cunning, and their ineradicable tendency to say what is not true. For as lions are provided with claws and teeth, and elephants and boars with tusks, bulls with horns, and the cuttle fish with its cloud of inky fluid, so Nature has equipped woman, for her defence and protection, with the arts of dissimulation; and all the power which Nature has conferred upon man in the shape of physical strength and reason has been bestowed upon women in this form. Hence dissimulation is innate in woman, and almost as much a quality of the stupid as of the clever. It is as natural for them to make use of it on every occasion as it is for animals to employ their means of defence when they are attacked; they have a feeling that in doing so they are only within their rights. Therefore a woman who is perfectly truthful and not given to dissimulation is perhaps an impossibility, and for this reason they are so quick at seeing through dissimulation in others that it is not a wise thing to attempt it with them. But this fundamental defect which I have stated, with all that it entails, gives rise to falsity, faithlessness, treachery, ingratitude, and so on. Perjury in a court of justice is more often committed by women than by men. It may, indeed, be generally questioned whether women ought to be sworn at all. From time to time one finds repeated cases everywhere of ladies, who want for nothing, taking things from shop-counters when no one is looking and making off with them.

Nature has appointed that the propagation of the species shall be the business of men who are young, strong and handsome; so that the race may not degenerate. This is the firm will and purpose of Nature in regard to the species, and it finds its expression in the passions of women. There is no law that is older or more powerful than this. Woe, then, to the man who sets up claims and interests that will conflict with it; whatever he may say and do, they will be unmercifully crushed at the first serious encounter. For the innate rule that governs women's conduct, though it is secret and unformulated, nay, unconscious in its working, is this: *We are justified in deceiving those who think they have acquired rights over the species by paying little attention to the individual, that is, to us. The constitution and, therefore, the welfare of the species have been placed in our hands and committed to our care, through the control we obtain over the next generation, which proceeds from us; let us discharge our duties conscientiously.* But women have no abstract knowledge of this leading principle; they are conscious of it only as a concrete fact; and they have no other method of giving expression to it than the way in which they act when the opportunity arrives. And then their conscience does not trouble them so much as we fancy; for in the darkest recesses of their heart they are aware that, in committing a breach of their duty towards the individual, they have all the better fulfilled their duty towards the species, which is infinitely greater.

And since women exist in the main solely for the propagation of the species, and are not destined for anything else, they live, as a rule, more for the species than for the individual, and in their hearts take the affairs of the species more seriously than those of the individual. This gives their whole life and being a certain levity; the general bent of their character is in a direction fundamentally different from that of man; and it is this which produces that discord in married life which is so frequent, and almost the normal state.

The natural feeling between men is mere indifference, but between women it is actual enmity. The reason of this is that trade-jealousy which, in the case of men, does not go beyond the confines of their own particular pursuit but with women embraces the whole sex; since they have only one kind of business. Even when they meet in the street women look at one another like Guelphs and Ghibellines. And it is a patent fact that when two women make first acquaintance with each other they behave with more constraint and dissimulation than two men would show in a like case; and hence it is that an exchange of compliments between two women is a much more ridiculous proceding than between two men. Further, whilst a man will, as a general rule, always preserve a certain amount of consideration and humanity in speaking to others, even to those who are in a very inferior position, it is intolerable to see how proudly and disdainfully a fine lady will generally behave towards one who is in a lower social rank (I do not mean a woman who is in her service), whenever she speaks to her. The reason of this may be that, with women, differences of rank are much more precarious than with us; because, while a hundred considerations carry weight in our case, in theirs there is only one, namely, with which man they have found favour; as also that they stand in much nearer relations with one another than men do, in consequence of the one-sided nature of their calling. This makes them endeavour to lay stress upon differences of rank.

It is only the man whose intellect is clouded by his sexual impulses that could give the name of *the fair sex* to that undersized, narrow-shouldered, broad-hipped, and short-legged race: for the whole beauty of the sex is bound up with this impulse. Instead of calling them beautiful, there would be more warrant for describing women as the unaesthetic sex. Neither for music, nor for poetry, nor for fine art, have they really and truly any sense or susceptibility; it is a mere mockery if they make a pretence of it in order to assist their endeavour to please. Hence, as a result of this, they are incapable of taking a *purely objective interest* in anything; and the reason of it seems to me to be as follows: A man tries to acquire *direct* mastery over things, either by understanding them or by forcing them to do his will. But a woman is always and everywhere reduced to obtaining this mastery *indirectly,* namely through a man; and whatever direct mastery she may have is entirely confined to him. And so it lies in woman's nature to look upon everything only as a means for conquering man; and if she takes an interest in anything else it is simulated —a mere roundabout way of gaining her ends by coquetry and feigning what she does not feel. Hence even Rousseau declared: *Women have, in general, no love of any art; they have no proper knowledge of any, and they have no genius.*

No one who sees at all below the surface can have failed to remark the same thing. You need only observe the kind of attention women bestow upon a concert, an opera, or a play —the childish simplicity, for example, with which they keep on chattering during the finest passages in the greatest masterpieces. If it is true that the Greeks excluded women from their theatres, they were quite right in what they did; at any rate you would have been able to hear what was said upon the stage. In our day, besides, or in lieu of saying, *Let a woman keep silence in the church,* it would be much to the point to say, *Let a woman keep silence in the theatre.* This might, perhaps, be put up in big letters on the curtain.

And you cannot expect anything else of women if you consider that the most distinguished intellects among the whole sex have never managed to produce a single achievement in the fine arts that is really great, genuine, and original; or given to the world any work of permanent value in any sphere. This is most strikingly shown in regard to painting, where mastery of technique is at least as much within their power as within ours—and hence they are diligent in cultivating it; but still, they have not a single great painting to boast of, just because they are deficient in that objectivity of mind which is so directly indispensable in painting. They never get beyond a subjective point of view. It is quite in keeping with this that ordinary women have no real susceptibility for art at all; for Nature proceeds in strict sequence—*non facit saltum.* The case is not altered by particular and partial exceptions; taken as a whole, women are, and remain, thoroughgoing philistines, and quite incurable. Hence, with that absurd arrangement which allows them to share the rank and title of their husbands, they are a constant stimulus to his ignoble ambitions. And, further, it is just because they are philistines that modern society, where they take the lead and set the tone, is in such a bad way. Napoleon's saying—that *women have no rank*—should be adopted as the right standpoint in determining their position in society; and as regards their other qualities Chamfort makes the very true remark: *They are made to trade with our own weaknesses and our follies, but not with our reason. The sympathies that exist between them and men are skin-deep only, and do not touch the mind or the feelings or the character.* They form the *sexus sequior*—the second sex, inferior in every respect to the first; their infirmities should be treated with consideration; but to show them great reverence is extremely ridiculous, and lowers us in their eyes. When nature made two divisions of the human race, she did not draw the line exactly through the middle. These divisions are polar and opposed to each other, it is true; but the difference between them is not qualitative merely, it is also quantitative.

This is just the view which the ancients took of woman, and the view which people in the East take now; and their judgment as to her proper position is much more correct than ours, with our old French notions of gallantry and our preposterous system of reverence—that highest product of Teutonico-Christian stupidity. These notions have served only to make women more arrogant and overbearing; so that one is occasionally reminded of the holy apes of Benares, who in consciousness of their sanctity and inviolable position think they can do exactly as they please.

But in the West the woman, and especially the *lady*, finds herself in a false position; for woman, rightly called by the ancients *sexus sequior*, is by no means fit to be the object of our honour and veneration, or to hold her head higher than man and be on equal terms with him. The consequences of this false position are sufficiently obvious. Accordingly it would be a very desirable thing if this Number Two of the human race were in Europe also relegated to her natural place, and an end put to that lady-nuisance, which not only moves all Asia to laughter but would have been ridiculed by Greece and Rome as well. It is impossible to calculate the good effects which such a change would bring about in our social, civil and political arrangements. There would be no necessity for the Salic law: it would be a superfluous truism. In Europe the *lady*, strictly so-called, is a being who should not exist at all; she should be either a housewife or a girl who hopes to become one; and she should be brought up, not to be arrogant, but to be thrifty and submissive. It is just because there are such people as *ladies* in Europe that the women of the lower classes, that is to say, the great majority of the sex, are much more unhappy than they are in the East. And even Lord Byron says: *Thought of the state of women under the ancient Greeks—convenient enough. Present state, a remnant of the barbarism of the chivalric and the feudal ages—artificial and unnatural. They ought to mind home—and be well fed and clothed—but not mixed in society. Well educated, too, in religion—but to read neither poetry nor politics—nothing but books of piety and cookery. Music—drawing—dancing—also a little gardening and ploughing now and then. I have seen them mending the roads in Epirus with good success. Why not, as well as hay-making and milking?*

The laws of marriage prevailing in Europe consider the woman as the equivalent of the man—start, that is to say, from a wrong position. In our part of the world where monogamy is the rule, to marry means to halve one's rights and double one's duties. Now when the laws gave women equal rights with man, they ought to have also endowed her with a masculine intellect. But the fact is that, just in proportion as the honours and privileges which the laws accord to women exceed the amount which Nature gives, there is a diminution in the number of women who really participate in these privileges; and all the remainder are deprived of their natural rights by just so much as is given to the others over and above their share. For the institution of monogamy, and the laws of marriage which it entails, bestow upon the woman an unnatural position of privilege, by considering her throughout as the full equivalent of the man, which is by no means the case; and seeing this men who are shrewd and prudent very often scruple to make so great a sacrifice and to acquiesce in so unfair an arrangement.

Moreover, the bestowal of unnatural rights upon women has imposed upon them unnatural duties, and nevertheless a breach of these duties makes them unhappy. Let me explain. A man may often think that his social or financial position will suffer if he marries, unless he makes some brilliant alliance. His desire will then be to win a woman of his own choice under conditions other than those of marriage, such as will secure her position and that of the children. However fair, reasonable, fit and proper these conditions may be, if the woman consents by foregoing that undue amount of privilege which marriage alone can bestow, she to some extent loses her honour, because marriage is the basis of civic society; and she will lead an unhappy life, since human nature is so constituted that we pay an attention to the opinion of other people which is out of all proportion to its value. On the other hand, if she does not consent, she runs the risk either of having to be given in marriage to a man whom she does not like, or of being landed high and dry as an old maid; for the period during which she has a chance of being settled for life is very short. And in view of this aspect of the institution of monogamy, Thomasius' profoundly learned treatise *On Concubinage* is well worth reading; for it shows that, amongst all nations and in all ages, down to the Lutheran Reformation, concubinage was permitted; nay, that it was an institution which was to a certain extent actually recognized by law, and attended with no dishonour. It was only the Lutheran Reformation that degraded it from this position. It was seen to be a further justification for the marriage of the clergy; and then, after that, the Catholic Church did not dare to remain behindhand in the matter.

The first love of a mother for her child is, with the lower animals as with men, of a purely *instinctive* character, and so it ceases when the child is no longer in a physically helpless condition. After that, the first love should give way to one that is based on habit and reason; but this often fails to make its appearance, especially where the mother did not love the father. The love of a father for his child is of a different order, and more likely to last; because it has its foundation in the fact that in the child he recognizes his own inner self; that is to say, his love for it is metaphysical in its origin.

In almost all nations, whether of the ancient or the modern world, even amongst the Hottentots, property is inherited by the male descendants alone; it is only in Europe that a departure has taken place; but not amongst the nobility, however. That the property which has cost men long years of toil and effort, and been won with so much difficulty, should afterwards come into the hands of women, who then, in their lack of reason, squander it in a short time, or otherwise fool it away, is a grievance and a wrong, as serious as it is common, which should be prevented by limiting the right of women to inherit. In my opinion the best arrangement would be that by which women, whether widows or daughters, should never receive anything beyond the interest for life on property secured by mortgage, and in no case the property itself, or the capital, except where all male descendants fail. The people who make money are men, not women; and it follows from this that women are neither justified in having unconditional possession of it, nor fit persons to be entrusted with its administration. When wealth, in any true sense of the word, that is to say, funds, houses or land, is to go to them as an inheritance, they should never be allowed the free disposition of it. In their case a guardian should always be appointed; and hence they should never be given the free control of their own children, wherever it can be avoided. The vanity of women, even though it should not prove to be greater than that of men, has this much danger in it that it takes an entirely material direction. They are vain, I mean, of their personal beauty, and then of finery, show and magnificence. That is just why they are so much in their element in society. It is this, too, which makes them so inclined to be extravagant, all the more as their reasoning power is low. But with men vanity often takes the direction of non-material advantages, such as intellect, learning, courage.

That woman is by nature meant to obey may be seen by the fact that every woman who is placed in the unnatural position of complete independence, immediately attaches herself to some man, by whom she allows herself to be guided and ruled. It is because she needs a lord and master. If she is young, it will be a lover; if she is old, a priest.

Sara Davidson (1943–) was born in Los Angeles, California, and resides in New York City. Her major field is social and political currents; she is a freelance writer-journalist. She has contributed to *Harper's, Life, New York, New York Times Magazine, Nova,* and the *London Sunday Times.*

An Oppressed Majority Demands Its Rights

SARA DAVIDSON

To demonstrate against the Miss America pageant was a glorious idea! "Protest the mindless boob girlie symbol of American womanhood. Help crown a live sheep Miss America. Burn bras, fashion magazines and cosmetic goop in a freedom trash can." The handbills were signed, "Women's Liberation." It was September 1968 and my immediate reaction was, "Beautiful." After a fling at modeling as a teen-ager, I had long resented the plastic (buy-me!) images of the fashion press, and beauty contests where women are paraded like prize cattle. If I had had free time, I would have wandered out to Atlantic City. Women's liberation was a grand joke, the supreme, anarchist zap to the system.

Three weeks later, I was at Columbia University for a political meeting when a member of women's liberation asked to speak. She was a pretty, soft-featured brunette who wore a loose gray sweater and no bra, and she was dead earnest. She said women are the most oppressed and underprivileged class in any society. The audience laughed and hooted. One man drew vulgar pictures on the blackboard, S.D.S. members yelled obscenities, and the girl walked out near tears. I remember laughing and feeling, inexplicably, embarrassed.

From *Life*, December 12, 1969. Reprinted by permission of the author.

Today women's liberation has become a serious national movement. In less than two years, it has grown in numbers and militancy, embracing a wide spectrum of women: housewives, professionals, students, women who are married, single, divorced, with children or childless. Fifty years after American women were granted the right to vote, a new feminist movement, predominantly middle-class and centered around universities and the cities, has begun at the grass roots level. The movement, which some say is 10,000 strong, has no national organization, no formal title, but "women's liberation" is the collective name most often used to describe it. The groups vary in every community, but all raise common themes: women are denied opportunity to fulfill their talents; traditional sex roles and family structure must be changed; women must relate in new ways to one another and to men.

Members of women's liberation point to civil rights, radical activism and the black liberation struggle as having inspired them. The birth control pill, which gave women more options, was also a factor. But perhaps most important, women in the last few decades were allowed small measures of equality, which aroused greater expectations. In colleges, women received the same education as men, only to find they could not use it upon graduation.

As I read more about the movement, I felt certain chords in my own experience were being hit. Almost every woman, even if she is happy in her role, has buried within her rankling resentment. From our earliest years, we were taught our lives would be determined not by ourselves but by the men we married. We sang rhymes about whom we would marry: "Rich man, poor man, beggar man, thief; doctor, lawyer, Indian chief." Little boys do not sing, "Actress, heiress, social worker, nurse." If our mothers pursued careers on top of being housewives, our situation was more ambiguous. We were encouraged to become self-sufficient, but to stay flexible enough so that we could adapt our life work, or give it up, for the right man. We worried ceaselessly about getting married and if we did not do so by our early 20s, we were pressured and insulted. "What's wrong with you? How come you're not married?"

When we did marry, our husbands usually determined where and how we lived.

Early this fall I set out to contact women's liberation in New York, not an easy task, because the groups are not listed in the phone book. You have to find someone who knows the number of someone, or learn about a demonstration and attend it. The first group I was able to locate was the Feminists, who appeared one afternoon at the Marriage License Bureau to protest the marriage contract. Ti-Grace Atkinson, a tall blonde from Louisiana who is a doctoral candidate in philosophy and a longtime radical feminist, told the women reporters, who stifled smiles, that husbands should pay wives for all labor in the house. She grimaced. "Tony Bennett sings these songs of propaganda: get married and everything will be all right. Marriage means rape and lifelong slavery." A reporter asked, "What about pregnancy?" Ti-Grace (her name is Cajun for petite, or little, Grace) constricted her face, as if suffering. "It's very painful. It's so immature to grow babies in people's bodies. If we had test-tube babies, there would be less chance of deformed fetuses."

Five of the Feminists, who ranged from 25 to 30, met with me later in the one-room, one-windowed apartment of Pamela Kearon in a Greenwich Village tenement. They said they joined forces a year ago to annihilate sex roles. The group is highly regimented; all tasks are assigned by lot, members cannot miss meetings or disagree with the Feminists' line, and no more than a third of the group can be married or living with a man. "The purpose of our quota is to show that we mean what we say," Ti-Grace said. "We reject marriage both in theory and in practice." I began to feel self-conscious about the wedding ring on my finger. "Aren't there any positive differences between the sexes?" I asked. Linda Feldman, a heavy-set office worker, said, "I don't know if there are any differences between men and women. What differences could there be except genitals?" I said men are physically stronger. She said, "I don't think that would be true if women exercised more strenuously while growing up."

On to love. Ti-Grace said, "Love has to be destroyed. It's

an illusion that people care for each other. Friendship is reciprocal, love isn't." And sex? "In the good society, we can't tell what will happen to sexual attraction. It may be that sex is a neurotic manifestation of oppression. It's like a mass psychosis."

"The more I understand what's going on with men," Ti-Grace said, "the less I miss male companionship and sex. Men *brag* about domination, conquest, trickery, exploitation. It gets so I can't even respond. Male chauvinism comes out in waves—every gesture, every word."

After three hours on this subject, I was depressed. What had led these women to the point where they could coldly dismiss feeling and touching, sex and love? Some of them are quite beautiful, which creates political contradictions. Women's liberation rejects the glossy magazines' vision of the liberated girl, who wears see-through clothes, smokes Virginia Slims and gives free love. The feminists say this fake liberated girl is a sex object, a bigger and better prostitute, not a human being. Women's liberation members avoid makeup, fancy hair styles and seductive clothes. If they go without bras, it is to be natural, not erotic. A girl in Chicago described the progression of giving up short skirts, then makeup, and recently, shaving her legs. "I still look at my legs and think, oh my God, I cannot go through with this. I'll die for the revolution, but don't ask me not to shave my legs! I have to keep reminding myself that there's nothing wrong with body hair, and no reason for one sex to scrape a razor over their legs."

Even the most radical feminists, however, retain many female character traits: soft-spokenness; talkiness (interviews and phone calls are difficult to terminate) ; and a proclivity for handwork. There was hardly a meeting I attended where someone was not knitting. While they condemn seductiveness, many want to look attractive. Pam Kearon of the Feminists said, "People like to look nice for other people. It's a statement of respect. It's just not true that we want to look like ugly freaks."

Some of the Feminists were active in the National Organization for Women (NOW), which they left in 1968 because they felt it was not radical enough. NOW was founded by Betty Friedan, whose book, *The Feminine Mystique,* was the signal flare of the new feminism in 1963. NOW members are, for the most part, professional women who want to end sex discrimination in hiring, promotions and salaries; repeal abortion laws; establish comprehensive child care; and place women in policy-making posts. NOW has been called "the NAACP of the women's movement," but in the past year it has moved left, influenced by the younger activists.

In an apartment on the Lower East Side, Redstockings, a group which takes its name from "Blue Stockings," a term used in the past for intellectual women, meets each Sunday. A poster on the wall reads: "Speak pains to recall pains—the Chinese Revolution. Tell it like it is—the black revolution. Bitch, sisters, bitch!—the final revolution." The group employs consciousness-raising, or the bitch session, to gain political insights from shared feelings. More than 30 young women sit crowded on the floor of the small, stuffy room for five to six hours. A question is posed, such as, "Did you choose to stay single or marry?" Each girl relates specific incidents in her life, and at the end, the "testimony" is analyzed. They find that problems they thought were their own private sorrows are shared by everyone in the group. "If all women share the same problem, how can it be personal? Women's pain is not personal, it's political."

In the past month Redstockings has been considering, "How do you feel about sexual commitment and fidelity? Have you ever wanted to have more than one sex relationship at a time?" Several said their boyfriends or husbands felt women should be faithful while men could be free. One said she'd mind less if her husband had affairs with people he didn't care about than if he were emotionally involved. Another disagreed: "Since I've been in women's liberation, I object to my husband using other women like that."

One girl said, "I would like to be able to be tolerant and understanding if I learned my husband was having an affair, but I don't think I would be." Another said, "We say we'd like to be that way, but no one in this room would not feel hurt and angry. Maybe infidelity is a bad thing, and our feelings are right." The point struck me. Why should women not listen to their feelings; why should they feel guilty about them? The group was split on the desire for sexual commitment. Some felt it was imprisonment; others saw it as true freedom. At length they hit on the idea that women might write up their own marriage contract that would spell out commitment to fidelity or lack of it, priorities in life, and what division of labor there would be in the home.

Members of Redstockings have spent much time analyzing why women feel competitive and suspicious of one another, why so many like to say, "I'm a man's woman," and place little value on female friendships. Those who succeed in careers often feel they are special and look down on other women. Redstockings members say they identify with all women, and will always take the woman's side. "In fighting for our liberation . . . we will not ask what is 'revolutionary' or 'reformist,' only what is good for women."

About the time of the Redstockings meeting, I began to encounter hostility, fear and a distressing contrariness in some of the women's groups. I called a member of WITCH (Women's International Terrorist Conspiracy from Hell), a feminist revolutionary group which, in its manifesto, sees witches as the first guerrilla fighters against women's oppression: "Witches have always been women who dared to be groovy, courageous, aggressive, intelligent, nonconformist, sexually liberated, revolutionary." We spoke for an hour with what I felt was warmth and rapport, and arranged to meet the next week. When I called later to set the time, the woman hung up. I thought it was a mistake; I called back, and she said, "I've decided I don't want to be used as an object by LIFE magazine." In the background, a woman was screaming, "Don't apologize, just hang up."

Members of another group said they would vote at their meeting on whether to talk with me. I was informed the decision had been affirmative. When I appeared at the appointed hour, one of the women said she had changed her mind. "We've been ridiculed by so many journalists. I don't think we should cooperate." The group flipped over like a row of cards.

In Boston, a girl active in a new group, Bread and Roses, invited me to stay at her home. I declined, but asked to meet her. When I arrived, she said nervously that a mistake had been made. She had spoken with others, who urged her not to talk to me. I made further calls. Several people cursed and hung up. One girl said she was torn between wanting to communicate about women's liberation and fear of the American public's reaction. "We've been attacked as lesbians, or sick, frustrated bitches." Others ranted at me as a member of the "corrupt, bourgeois press," asked for money, and insisted they be allowed to censor anything I would write.

These experiences unnerved me, despite reminders that I should not take it personally and an understanding of what lay behind the fear and hostility. The negative reactions toward me expressed a great deal of what women's liberation is about: women's long-suppressed anger at being used; women's sense of vulnerability and defenselessness; women's suspicion and mistrust of other women; women's insecurity, lack of confidence in their judgments, the "secret fear," as one girl put it, "that maybe we are inferior."

I had dinner with Diana Gerrity, a staff editor at the *Atlantic*, who sympathized with my frustration. She said people in women's liberation are just getting in touch with the anger pent up inside them. "It takes a long time for any girl to realize she can register her outrage." Diana, tall and willowy, with long chestnut hair, was a fashion model while doing graduate work at the University of Chicago. She is 25, has been married two years, and joined a liberation group last May. "We've gotten to know each other very well. I don't think I ever trusted women before or really thought they were valuable people to be with. Friendships were based on competing for men."

As Diana spoke she would interrupt herself and say, "I don't know if I'm making sense." There is not a woman I know who doesn't feel, at some points, that she is rambling, not being rational. This must stem from expectations that women will be imprecise and fuzzy in their logic. In universities, a compliment paid to bright women is, "You think like a man." Women who are successful in professions come to think they have male attributes. A girl who was telling me about the difficulties of her job made an interesting slip: "I'm harassed by all the other men."

Diana is studying Tao Kwon Do, the Korean form of karate, two nights a week. "I've always felt great fear whenever I had to go out alone. Several friends of mine have been raped. Karate is as much psychological as it is physical training. It gives you the confidence to be able to judge a situation, or maybe fight your way out, instead of just collapsing."

The karate class is taught by Jayne West, a member of Boston Female Liberation, formerly called Cell 16. Female Liberation is a tight-knit, fiercely committed and clannish group which includes Abby Rockefeller, daughter of David Rockefeller, chairman of the Chase Manhattan Bank, and Roxanne Dunbar, who grew up on a poor white farm in the South and has been writing and lecturing on women's liberation for more than six years.

There were 12 women in the class, three of them teenagers, and one 7-year-old who said she wanted to be able to beat up the 16-year-old bully on her block. Wearing coarse white uniforms, the women worked in precise, military rows, punching, jabbing and kicking, biting their lips and yelling "Kee-up!" Jayne West, a blue belt, who wears a headband Indian style over her long dark hair, rammed the floor with a board as she called out instructions. She kicked at the girls' legs and shoved them from behind. "You've got to be very steady. Your punch has to be accurate. You want to hit the person's solar plexus." I was watching from the back of the room when suddenly Jayne said, "Bricks!" The women wheeled and stampeded toward me. My blood froze. Bricks? I found I was sitting next to a pile of bricks; each woman grabbed one, tore back to line and began pounding it with her fists.

In their journal, *No More Fun and Games,* Female Liberation members urge women to leave their husbands and children and to avoid pregnancy. Women should dress plainly, chop their hair short, and begin to "reclaim themselves" by dropping their husbands' or fathers' names. They should live alone and abstain from sexual relationships.

Women's liberation has flowered in Boston to the point where it is impossible to attend a social gathering without hearing the subject discussed. There are probably more than 1,000 women in the area engaged in feminist study groups, theater, groups of secretaries and clerical workers, groups to legalize abortion, child care groups, encounter groups and women's communes.

A longtime friend of mine, Jane Harriman, joined a women's liberation group last May, and we stayed up through the night talking about the movement. Jane is 29, an expressive, blue-eyed, affection-giving woman who likes to play sad sack and be humorous at her own expense. She is not married and supports herself and her 2-year-old son by working as a writer for a social research firm. Members of her group, which meets once a week, have been examining their personal lives to see where options were narrowed, restrictions imposed because of sex. When Jane was 14, she decided she wanted to be a doctor. "I began working in a hospital and studied science like mad. Gradually I got the idea I should be a nurse instead. My father told me I was bright, so I would be an exceptional nurse, but as a woman I would be only a fair doctor." After high school, she was urged to go to college, primarily, she thinks, to meet college men. Then when she had been at Bennington College two years, her father began sending her brochures for secretarial schools.

Along with the pressure to pursue a womanly career, Jane remembers the pressure to get a man. "As a teen-ager, your whole personality had to change to be popular with boys. You had to be empty-headed and amusing. You wore falsies and a girdle, and bleached your hair. I remember the horror of thinking, what if boys see me without makeup?"

Since women's liberation, Jane believes sex roles should be redefined. "Why shouldn't men share the responsibility for raising children and keeping house? I used to laugh about that, but I don't now. Why shouldn't a woman, if she's attracted to a man, be able to call and invite him to a movie? Why aren't there Playboy Clubs for women where we could go after work and have a very attractive man serve us drinks and say, 'Hi, I'm your bull, Mike'?"

Jane feels women's liberation is not anti-male. "Because you believe women are human beings, not objects, doesn't mean you don't like men. It's terrible to need a man for your identity. You want a man as an enrichment to your life."

The next morning, I drove from Boston to Windham College in Putney, Vt., where women's liberation members had been invited to speak. The college of 840 students is an arresting sight: white double-decker buildings with domed skylights set in a wooded field. About 100 people were waiting in the science auditorium. Janet Murray, a social worker who was wearing an orange blouse with the sleeves rolled up, a tweed skirt and oxford shoes, said: "The most painful and the greatest cause of women's oppression is the nuclear family. We think it should be broken up or radically changed, so that men and women share the economic responsibility, the child-care and the drudgery. As it is now, women get all the drudgery. It's a bad division of labor." Marya Levenson, a young graduate student and member of Bread and Roses, said people are experimenting with communal child-raising and cooperative play groups, where the fathers put in equal time. "The men begin to see taking care of children is boring and it's not all groovy being mother earth."

When they asked for questions, only male hands went up. Marya smiled. "You can see that in a mixed group the men tend to dominate and the women don't talk. That's why women's liberation groups have to be all women." After a pause, a fair-skinned girl rose and said, "I'm married, I have two children, and I'm happy as a clam. Some people naturally enjoy the passive role. I'd hate to see a society where there was no choice of being a housewife." Marya said, "There's no choice under the present society. If women resent being a housewife, or don't want to get married, they're told to see a psychiatrist." About 25 women, many faculty wives, stayed afterward to talk about forming a women's liberation group.

We slept that night on cots in the farmhouse of a political science professor. Next morning, as we drove back to Boston, Janet Murray, who is married and has a 3-year-old daughter, said: "I miss my nuclear family."

The first feminist movement in America took 50 years to gain mass support. Toward the end, the struggle for women's suffrage, won in 1920, eclipsed the deeper social changes the suffragettes had been calling for. Since 1920, the social and economic position of women has advanced little. Women's liberation has already revived national interest in feminism. Some of the groups, which grew out of the New Left, believe socialism is a prerequisite for women's liberation, and that women must confront racism and imperialism as well as their own oppression. Other groups do not feel associated with the left, and see male chauvinism, not capitalism, as the main enemy.

All the groups have more members than they know what to do with. "We don't have money to even distribute literature," a member of Redstockings said. "It's enough at this point for people to just start thinking and talking about women's liberation." Several groups are publishing feminist journals—*Aphra* in New York and *Women: A Journal of Liberation* in Baltimore. The Caravan Theater in Boston performs *How To Make a Woman* every weekend, followed by audience discussions. The New Feminist Repertory Theater in New York, directed by Anselma dell'Olio, is preparing a revue to tour the country. One sketch shows a man's reaction when he finds an impregnated uterus has been placed in his body.

Those who have been in women's liberation for many months are trying to incorporate their politics in their personal lives. Some have formed communes—all women, or mixed, with work divided equally. Many are restructuring their nuclear families. Robin Morgan, a member of WITCH, who is a poet, editor and former child actress (she played Dagmar in the television series *Mama*), has been married seven years and has a 5-month-old son. Robin and her husband, Poet Kenneth Pitchford, have consciously worked to share all roles. Both have part-time jobs, he in the mornings, she afternoons; while one works, the other takes care of the baby. "We're both mothers," Robin says. "He bottle feeds, I breast feed." Before the baby was born, they chose a name they felt was genderless—Blake, after the English romantic poet, William Blake, who, Robin says, was an early feminist. If the baby had been a girl, she would have taken her mother's last name instead of her father's. Robin hopes they will be living in a commune before Blake grows up. "Our arrangement is one attempt at an interim solution. But no personal solution will work until we have a complete social and economic revolution which stresses the liberation of 51% of the people."

Overexposure to women's liberation leads, I found, to headaches, depression and a fierce case of the shakes. A friend of mine retreated to her kitchen after a weekend of meetings to lose herself in an orgy of baking pies. I stayed home for three days and stopped answering the phone. But women's liberation was accelerating each day.

In New York court suits were filed to have the state abortion laws declared unconstitutional.

Women's liberation in San Francisco learned a group of radical men were publishing a pornographic magazine to raise money for politics. They confronted the editor, convinced him he could not advance his cause at the expense of women, and burned the magazine layouts.

A WITCH coven, carrying pails and brooms, performed guerrilla skits on Wall Street to shocked and amused crowds.

NOW picketed the headquarters of the three candidates for mayor of New York for failing to take a stand on women's rights. At John Lindsay's headquarters on Fifth Avenue, Nancy Seifer, who works for Lindsay, brought out a statement of partial support. Nancy told me, "I agree with their ideas, but some of their demands are unrealistic." We began arguing, casually, about what women should demand, when a young salesman, tall and beanpole thin, with crew-cut blond hair, interrupted us: "Woman aren't discriminated against! Women aren't capable of certain types of work, just like men aren't capable of raising children. A woman will fold under pressure more easily than a man. A woman can't make decisions or quick judgments."

Nancy and I both got mad. The salesman, Hugh Wessell, said, "Women aren't open about sex."

Nancy cried, "What has that got to do with making decisions?"

I asked Wessell, "Would you say the same things about black people?" He grew sober. "I have nothing against black people."

"But you wouldn't make jokes about their abilities," I said. "Why do you joke about women?"

Wessell grinned. "Well, most of the women I know are not that sensitive about it."

I smiled back at him. "Not for long."

Sue Smart (1932–   ) was born in Chicago, Illinois, and now resides in Cambridge, Massachusetts. She is a poet and writer who has contributed to *New Yorker, Poet and Critic, Antioch Review,* and other periodicals. She is also the co-author of *The Abnormal Personality Through Literature* and co-author of *Social Problems Through Literature.*

Certain Women

SUE SMART

Marvelous as young, blue stars
Are women obsessed by their own composition:
Beautiful women scrubbed like beaten plate,
Whose simplest movements are whipped stitches.

Every part of them has a tender name
Which you cannot know. But if you follow,
They will lead you into their forests
Where light is felt as heat on velvet.

Remember the women of the bible,
Elbows dipping into the cool water of wells
Or barefoot husking the sheaves of corn
So calm, muscular and ample in the distance.

Your eyes add to their pleasure.

Think of the girls you know, flushed
And whirling, secretive in the shadow
Of their future giving.

If they were empty, they would not
Excite you. But they are full of
Tension and change like the surface
Of a drop of water.

From *Antioch Review,* Fall 1969. Reprinted by permission.

e. e. cummings (1894–   ) was born in Cambridge, Massachusetts. He was graduated from Harvard in 1915 and remained to take his M.A. in 1916. He is known for the eccentricity of his typography and punctuation. His works consist of love poems, humorous character sketches, and satires on the foibles of his time. His major works include *Tulips and Chimney, XLI Poems, &, is 5, No Thanks, him, The Enormous Room,* and *Tom.*

mrs

e. e. cummings

& mr across the way are kind of
afraid) afraid

of what (of

a crazy man) don't
ask me how i know (a he of head
comes to some dirty window every) twilight i

feel (his lousy eyes roaming) wonderful all

sky (a little mouth) stumbling (can't
keep up with how big very
them) now (it tears
off rag its

of

mind chucks away flimsy
which but) always (they're
more much further off) further these
those three disappear finally what's left

behind is (just a head of he

is) merely (a pair of ears with some
lipe plus a couple of) holes probably that's what
(mr & mrs are

sort of really

really kind
of afraid of) these (down pull & who'll

shades

) when what hugs stopping earth than silent is
more silent than more than much more is or
total sun oceaning than any this
tear jumping from each most least eye of star

and without was if minus and shall be
immeasurable happenless unnow
shuts more than open could that every tree
or than all life more death begins to grow

end's ending then these dolls of joy and grief
these recent memories of future dream
these perhaps who have lost their shadows if
which did not do the losing spectres mime

until out of merely not nothing comes
only one snowflake (and we speak our names

Rupert Brooke (1887–1915) was an English poet educated at Rugby. His best-known poems are *Granchester, The Great Lover,* and his series of war sonnets entitled *1914.* He died in service during World War I. His major works include *The Bastille, Selected Poems,* and *The Collected Poems.*

Jealousy

RUPERT BROOKE

When I see you, who were so wise and cool,
Gazing with silly sickness on that fool
You've given your love to, your adoring hands
Touch his so intimately that each understands,
I know, most hidden things; and when I know
Your holiest dreams yield to the stupid bow
Of his red lips, and that the empty grace
Of those strong legs and arms, that rosy face,
Has beaten your heart to such a flame of love,
That you have given him every touch and move,
Wrinkle and secret of you, all your life,
—Oh! then I know I'm waiting, lover-wife,
For the great time when love is at a close,
And all its fruit's to watch the thickening nose
And sweaty neck and dulling face and eye,
That are yours, and you, most surely, till you die!
Day after day you'll sit with him and note
The greasier tie, the dingy wrinkling coat;
As prettiness turns to pomp, and strength to fat,
And love, love, love to habit!

And after that,
When all that's fine in man is at an end,
And you, that loved young life and clean, must tend

A foul sick fumbling dribbling body and old,
When his rare lips hang flabby and can't hold
Slobber, and you're enduring that worst thing,
Senility's queasy furtive love-making,
And searching those dear eyes for human meaning,
Propping the bald and helpless head, and cleaning
A scrap that life's flung by, and love's forgotten,—
Then you'll be tired; and passion dead and rotten;
And he'll be dirty, dirty!

O lithe and free
And lightfoot, that the poor heart cries to see,
That's how I'll see your man and you!—

But you
—Oh, when *that* time comes, you'll be dirty too!

Howard Luck Gossage (1917–1969) was a writer and business consultant whom *Atlantic* has called "an advertising and propaganda genius and an irrepressible wit." Stricken with leukemia, he wrote the following article. He contributed to *Harper's*, *Atlantic*, and *Ramparts*. He is also the author of *Dear Miss Afflerbach* and *Ist die Werbung noch zu Retten.*

"Tell Me, Doctor, Will I Be Active Right Up to the Last?"

HOWARD LUCK GOSSAGE

Our society views dying as being in questionable taste despite the fact that ten out of ten still do it. Perhaps it is part of our emphasis on eternal youthfulness as opposed to maturity. The life-span expands, and we have chosen to put the stretch on the early part. We apparently like to think of ourselves as being young or youngish right up to the moment when we proceed with bouncy step to retirement communities, there to live on forever in spry clusters of ranch-style death houses.

The word "death" is almost never employed nowadays except as a legal term or for intentional shock. I note the increasing use of "passed on," a usage confined until recently to Christian Scientists and others who deny death categorically.

It is therefore not surprising that our funerals are no longer scenes of terrible grief, nor are there purging wakes, celebrated from the dawn of history, to confirm that we are still alive. Overt performance of death rituals is not considered good form unless televised nationwide. But this, too, has diminishing returns. Over the years from J. F. Kennedy to Eisenhower we have seen that a TV formula can turn even death into a bore.

This refusal to recognize a threatening phenomenon, or even to utter its name lest it gain power over you, is magical thinking of a primitive order. One of the choicer recent examples is the substitution in many newspaper horoscopes of "Moon Children" for the zodiac sign Cancer. A sardonic friend of mine was recently cornered at a cocktail party by one of those horoscope-spouting sibyls. He was asked, "How did your mother go?" He replied, "She was taken by Moon Children"; thus passing on two birds with one stone.

The price we pay for this pastel-washed denial of the only inevitable experience of life may be higher than we know. Our abnegation, as a people, of death may be the chief reason we seem to get so little genuine joy out of everyday life. For when life stretches out indefinitely, world without end, there is no yardstick for momentary pleasures, and passing pains are blown up out of all proportion.

One might say that this never-never thinking is a natural evolution of the Greco-Judeo-Christian ethic, but this is not supportable. The ancient Greeks did not hold with a personal, defined afterlife, nor does Judaism even now. Christianity, since it does believe in a hereafter, necessarily recognizes life as a prerequisite. However, it is notable that the more specific a given religious society's acceptance of death as a finality, at least of life as we know it, the more importance its members are likely to assign both to funerals and to day-to-day living. Whatever else may be said of this mode of thought, it is apparently not boring. A modern Greek, a Spaniard, an Irishman-in-Ireland will still put on a funeral worth going to. At the same time their countries have the lowest suicide rates in the world and an enviable relish of dinky temporal joys.

As an aside, the ancient Egyptians, because of their notable death rituals, elaborate preparation of bodies, and staggering devotion to necropolises, are popularly supposed to have had a morbid preoccupation with dying, so that it hung over their entire lives like an immense pall.[1] I think, however, just the opposite must have been true: that the Egyptians, because they had death so well sorted out, must have led vigorous, rewarding, and even sunny lives. It is hard to imagine how a civilization could have lasted for all those thousands of years—much longer than anyone else's—unless life itself had been purposeful and worth the living.

In spite of my citing these national and cultural examples, I don't think that dying is or ever has been a mass phenomenon: it is something that each man ought to do for himself, without assigning a proxy. What a society can do is grant him permission to die so that he need think no more about it, but can go ahead and live until the time comes—staving it off as long as possible, of course. In America, we seem to walk around this subject entirely, so that with the passing of old-time religious sureties—and the stretching-out of life so that three score and ten is no longer a goal, but a mere norm—we simply do not know how to think about death at all. Nobody has given us permission to die, or to live, for that matter. So what we do is sort of happen until one day we sort of stop happening.

In our culture dying has a vocabulary, surely, but it is mostly expressed in figurative terms and by euphemistic rituals derived from popular art forms. Nature imitating art is no new thing, but thanks to mass communication, it is probably more pervasive today than at any other time in man's history. It extends to acts so commonplace that one would suppose they had always existed as they are. The matter of closing one's eyes when kissing, for example. I understand that it became a social convention only with the birth of motion pictures. Some early director must have noticed that his actors looked funny kissing while staring at one another, so he told them to close their eyes. If you find this hard to believe, observe how small children as yet unimpressed by movie

[1] As I write this it occurs to me that "pall" cannot possibly mean coffin, as in "pallbearer." Checking the dictionary, I find this to be so: the pall is a cloth, usually black, purple, or white velvet, lofted over the coffin by six attendants. So, whatever those men carrying the box are, they are not pallbearers.

love scenes will kiss eyeball-to-eyeball. Seventy years ago presumably everybody did; at any rate, it was not considered bad manners to do so.

I had graphic proof of this conditioning-by-media one time when I was informed that I had contracted a fatal disease. "Contracted" seems a strange word to use in this connection; it sounds as though you have to sign up for it, with codicils, and all. Well, codicils is what I had, all right, terminal codicils, with maybe six months to live.

On the basis of this one experience I found out where doctors acquire their graveside manner. There were two of them in there to break the news, and from the first clearing of the throat it was pure *déjà vu.* It was uncanny. I knew exactly the words they were going to say, and I made the responses automatically.

Then it dawned on me why. They had picked it up the same place I had, at the knee of old Auntie Procter & Gamble. What we were enacting was an amberized sequence from an antique episode of Helen Trent or Young Dr. Kildare. Honest to God, I found myself saying at one point, "Tell me, Doctor, will I be active right up to the last?"

Not to keep you on tenterhooks, the deal was stalled off before the deadline. On that day, however, neither I nor the doctors suspected that the cavalry was going to gallop up waving a reprieve. I believed it was a moment cast in bronze: it still is: there is nothing like it.

I believed it, but had no intention of abiding by it, and began thinking how I could turn this disaster to an advantage. This quick reaction (the soap opera dialogue was still going on) was due to life-long conditioning, I suspect, for I have made a career out of the notion that if you are stuck with a lemon, make lemonade. Still, I recall that the part of one's brain that observes such things was surprised and even pleased at this unexpected burst of objective activity. It may have illustrated Bertrand Russell's thesis that "all unusual energy is inspired by an unusual degree of vanity." But the line that passed through my thoughts just then was Samuel Johnson's, "Depend upon it, Sir, when a man knows he is to be hanged in a fortnight, it concentrates his mind wonderfully."

None of this prevented me from feeling perfectly happy. Bertrand Russell describes this sensation, though it sprang from an obverse experience, as I shall try to explain. He had been given up for dead (at about the age I was, fifty), but was making an unexpected recovery. He says: "Lying in my bed feeling that I was not going to die was surprisingly delightful. I had always imagined till then that I was fundamentally pessimistic and did not greatly value being alive. I discovered that in this I had been completely mistaken, and that life was infinitely sweet to me. . . . I have known ever since that at bottom I am glad to be alive. Most people, no doubt, always know this, but I did not."

I question the long-term endurance of this gladness-to-be-alive unless it is preceded and accompanied by an equally poignant revelation that one will die; whether soon or sometime is academic. I have found that the gratitude for life that follows mere escape from death, however vivid and narrow, is not likely to stick to one's ribs. I am sure you can confirm this from your own experience: in the glorious, shaken aftermath you swear never to worry about anything trivial again; you do, of course, usually within hours. On the other hand, it is possible to acquire and retain this bone-deep feeling of life *because* there is no reprieve, for one is alive now. Lord Russell, no doubt, has always known this; I did not.

Let me try to clarify this uncomplicated awareness by separating it from two other types of life-before-death recognition which, unlike the other, are familiar even to those who haven't experienced them personally—possibly because they are not usually private, but involve other people. Also, both are perversions of real life and are therefore more recognizable. The first occurs when the doctor assigns what John Steinbeck calls "one of those carefully named difficulties which are the whispers of approaching age," and with it a lecture that ends, "slow down." You know that you're going to die, but it doesn't make you feel more alive. You do cut down, but these diminutions of activity are not limitations which concentrate energy, but are truncations of manhood. It is, in fact, a reversion to babyhood, and is encouraged by others, especially wives. It is all extremely comfortable, for "who," Steinbeck asks, "doesn't like to be a center for concern? A kind of second childhood falls on so many men. They trade their violence for the promise of a small increase of life span."

The above is from *Travels With Charley,* and was the reason he took the trip. "I did not want to surrender fierceness for a small gain in yardage. My wife married a man; I saw no reason why she should inherit a baby. And in my own life I am not willing to trade quality for quantity." This was no mere retroactive dress-up. And he was complimentary enough to assume the same attitude in others. When I told him of my own prognosis, he looked at me gravely and said, "If you tell your friends you're going to die in six months you'd better do it or they'll be pissed off at you."

The second variety of death recognition to be sorted out from the above is, in fact, a ghastly parody of it. Flat acceptance that one is going to die does constitute a proof of one's own uniqueness as a man distinct from others; is not unpleasant, even heady; and lends immediacy and importance to matters that were routine before. But what I am talking about is a perversion, a monstrous contained exultation. It is manifested in certain daredevils, paranoid psychopaths who, after nebbish lives, suddenly feel themselves invulnerable in the certain wooing of sweet death; or it can be the Götterdämmerung complex that gripped the Nazi mind. Such a delusion may arise because life appears so meaningless that some significance must be assigned to it, even if it is only death. In turn, death must be justified to remove it from nothingness and give it certain worth. The commonest of the resulting delusions is called martyrdom, for whatever cause. If this seems an unusually harsh judgment, recall that it is invariably on a volunteer basis. A drafted martyr is not a martyr, but a victim. Gibbon recounts that one of the more exhausting aspects of Roman soldering was a shooing off of hordes of early Christian volunteers. I'm not sure that being men of goodwill had much to do with it at bottom. People to a man regard themselves as men of goodwill; even a Hitler, especially a Hitler, for how otherwise could he have justified such dreadful acts? And he, in the end, showed martyrdom, the only glorious form of suicide.

The key notion here, and the common thread in the two examples of death anticipation I have just cited, seems to be the scampering after certainty. In each instance the scamperer is metamorphosed into a subnormal or abnormal creature. The trick, it seems to me, lies in the opposite direction. Bertrand Russell, again, states it well: "Uncertainty, in the presence of vivid hopes and fears, is painful, but must be endured if we wish to live without the support of comforting fairy tales." He proposes as an ideal, "to live without certainty, and yet without being paralyzed by hesitation," and suggests that this admirable state may be attained through the study of philosophy. When I first read these words many years ago, I thought them the noblest view of man I had ever seen, but thought it probably unrealizable except through the toughest self-discipline. I have since found, to my surprise, that it is attainable and that whatever portion one gets through discipline or logic is subject to backslide without notice, for it is a very fugitive state of mind. It is something like an account I once read of a game Tolstoy and his little chums used to play at Yasna Polyana: they would sit around the nursery trying not to think about the Great Bear who sits on top of the North Pole. They found this difficult.

If there is any doubt that to learn to live without certainty is a worthwhile aim, it's not as though we had any choice about it: it's another of those ten-out-of-ten things. And the problem is fiercer in our age than in any which has preceded it. The basic reasons for this, I think, are neither as confused nor hopeless as we are led to believe. They are really quite simple, but, nevertheless, have never existed before in the history of man. I shall get around to them in a minute . . .

James Thurber (1894–1961) was born in Columbus, Ohio, where he was educated at Ohio State University. He was on the staff of the *Columbus Dispatch, The Chicago Tribune* in Paris, *The New York Evening Post*, and the *New Yorker*. One of America's foremost humorists, Thurber's works include *Is Sex Necessary* (with E. B. White), *The Male Animal* (with Elliott Nugent), *The Thurber Carnival, Men, Women, and Dogs, The Owl in the Attic, My Life and Hard Times, Fables for Our Time, My World—and Welcome to It,* and *Thurber Country.*

The Night the Ghost Got In

JAMES THURBER

The ghost that got into our house on the night of November 17, 1915, raised such a hullabaloo of misunderstandings that I am sorry I didn't just let it keep on walking, and go to bed. Its advent caused my mother to throw a shoe through a window of the house next door and ended up with my grandfather shooting a patrolman. I am sorry, therefore, as I have said, that I ever paid any attention to the footsteps.

They began about a quarter past one o'clock in the morning, a rhythmic, quick-cadenced walking around the dining-room table. My mother was asleep in one room upstairs, my brother Herman in another; grandfather was in the attic, in the old walnut bed which, as you will remember, once fell on my father. I had just stepped out of the bathtub and was busily rubbing myself with a towel when I heard the steps. They were the steps of a man walking rapidly around the dining-room table downstairs. The light from the bathroom shone down the back steps, which dropped directly into the dining-room; I could see the faint shine of plates on the plate-rail; I couldn't see the table. The steps kept going round and round the table; at regular intervals a board creaked, when it was trod upon. I supposed at first that it was my father or my brother Roy, who had gone to Indianapolis but were expected home at any time. I suspected next that it was a burglar. It did not enter my mind until later that it was a ghost.

After the walking had gone on for perhaps three minutes, I tiptoed to Herman's room. "Psst!" I hissed, in the dark, shaking him. "Awp," he said, in the low, hopeless tone of a despondent beagle—he always half suspected that something would "get him" in the night. I told him who I was. "There's something downstairs!" I said. He got up and followed me to the head of the back staircase. We listened together. There was no sound. The steps had ceased. Herman looked at me in some alarm: I had only the bath towel around my waist. He wanted to go back to bed, but I gripped his arm. "There's something down there!" I said. Instantly the steps began again, circled the dining-room table like a man running, and started up the stairs toward us, heavily, two at a time. The light still shone palely down the stairs; we saw nothing coming; we only heard the steps. Herman rushed to his room and slammed the door. I slammed shut the door at the stairs top and held my knee against it. After a long minute, I slowly opened it again. There was nothing there. There was no sound. None of us ever heard the ghost again.

The slamming of the doors had aroused mother: she peered out of her room. "What on earth are you boys doing?" she demanded. Herman ventured out of his room. "Nothing," he said, gruffly, but he was, in color, a light green. "What was all that running around downstairs?" said mother. So she had heard the steps, too! We just looked at her. "Burglars!" she shouted intuitively. I tried to quiet her by starting lightly downstairs.

"Come on, Herman," I said.

"I'll stay with mother," he said. "She's all excited."

I stepped back onto the landing.

"Don't either of you go a step," said mother. "We'll call

the police." Since the phone was downstairs, I didn't see how we were going to call the police—nor did I want the police—but mother made one of her quick, incomparable decisions. She flung up a window of her bedroom which faced the bedroom windows of the house of a neighbor, picked up a shoe, and whammed it through a pane of glass across the narrow space that separated the two houses. Glass tinkled into the bedroom occupied by a retired engraver named Bodwell and his wife. Bodwell had been for some years in rather a bad way and was subject to mild "attacks." Most everybody we knew or lived near had *some* kind of attacks.

It was now about two o'clock of a moonless night; clouds hung black and low. Bodwell was at the window in a minute, shouting, frothing a little, shaking his fist. "We'll sell the house and go back to Peoria," we could hear Mrs. Bodwell saying. It was some time before mother "got through" to Bodwell. "Burglars!" she shouted. "Burglars in the house!" Herman and I hadn't dared to tell her it was not burglars but ghosts, for she was even more afraid of ghosts than of burglars. Bodwell at first thought that she meant there were burglars in his house, but finally he quieted down and called the police for us over an extension phone by his bed. After he had disappeared from the window, mother suddenly made as if to throw another shoe, not because there was further need of it but, as she later explained, because the thrill of heaving a shoe through a window glass had enormously taken her fancy. I prevented her.

The police were on hand in a commendably short time: a Ford sedan full of them, two on motorcycles, and a patrol wagon with about eight in it and a few reporters. They began banging at our front door. Flashlights shot streaks of gleam up and down the walls, across the yard, down the walk between our house and Bodwell's. "Open up!" cried a hoarse voice. "We're men from Headquarters!" I wanted to go down and let them in, since there they were, but mother wouldn't hear of it. "You haven't a stitch on," she pointed out. "You'd catch your death." I wound the towel around me again. Finally the cops put their shoulders to our big heavy front door with its thick beveled glass and broke it in: I could hear a rending of wood and a splash of glass on the floor of the hall. Their lights played all over the living-room and crisscrossed nervously in the dining-room, stabbed into hallways, shot up the front stairs and finally up the back. They caught me standing in my towel at the top. A heavy policeman bounded up the steps. "Who are you?" he demanded. "I live here," I said. "Well, whattsa matta, ya hot?" he asked. It was, as a matter of fact, cold; I went to my room and pulled on some trousers. On my way out, a cop stuck a gun into my ribs. "Whatta you doin' here?" he demanded. "I live here," I said.

The officer in charge reported to mother. "No sign of nobody, lady," he said. "Musta got away—whatt'd he look like?" "There were two or three of them," mother said, "whooping and carrying on and slamming doors." "Funny," said the cop. "All ya windows and doors was locked on the inside tight as a tick."

Downstairs, we could hear the tromping of the other police. Police were all over the place; doors were yanked open, drawers were yanked open, windows were shot up and pulled down, furniture fell with dull thumps. A half-dozen policemen emerged out of the darkness of the front hallway upstairs. They began to ransack the floor: pulled beds away from walls, tore clothes off hooks in the closets, pulled suitcases and boxes off shelves. One of them found an old zither that Roy had won in a pool tournament. "Looky here, Joe," he said, strumming it with a big paw. The cop named Joe took it and turned it over. "What is it?" he asked me. "It's an old zither our guinea pig used to sleep on," I said. It was true that a pet guinea pig we once had would never sleep anywhere except on the zither, but I should never have said so. Joe and the other cop looked at me a long time. They put the zither back on a shelf.

"No sign o' nuthin'," said the cop who had first spoken to mother. "This guy," he explained to the others, jerking a thumb at me, "was nekked. The lady seems historical." They all nodded, but said nothing; just looked at me. In the small silence we all heard a creaking in the attic. Grandfather was turning over in bed. "What's 'at?" snapped Joe. Five or six cops sprang for the attic door before I could intervene or explain. I realized that it would be bad if they burst in on grandfather unannounced, or even announced. He was going through a phase in which he believed that General Meade's men, under steady hammering by Stonewall Jackson, were beginning to retreat and even desert.

When I got to the attic, things were pretty confused. Grandfather had evidently jumped to the conclusion that the police were deserters from Meade's army, trying to hide away in his attic. He bounded out of bed wearing a long flannel nightgown over long woolen underwear, a nightcap, and a leather jacket around his chest. The cops must have realized at once that the indignant white-haired old man belonged in the house, but they had no chance to say so. "Back, ye cowardly dogs!" roared grandfather. "Back t' the lines, ye goddam lily-livered cattle!" With that, he fetched the officer who found the zither a flat-handed smack alongside his head that sent him sprawling. The others beat a retreat, but not fast enough; grandfather grabbed Zither's gun from its holster and let fly. The report seemed to crack the rafters; smoke filled the attic. A cop cursed and shot his hand to his shoulder. Somehow, we all finally got downstairs again and locked the door against the old gentleman. He fired once or twice more in the darkness and then went back to bed. "That was grandfather," I explained to Joe, out of breath. "He thinks you're deserters." "I'll say he does," said Joe.

The cops were reluctant to leave without getting their hands on somebody besides grandfather; the night had been distinctly a defeat for them. Furthermore, they obviously didn't like the "layout;" something looked—and I can see their viewpoint—phony. They began to poke into things again. A reporter, a thin-faced, wispy man, came up to me. I had put on one of mother's blouses, not being able to find anything else. The reporter looked at me with mingled suspicion and interest. "Just what the hell is the real lowdown here, Bud?" he asked. I decided to be frank with him. "We had ghosts," I said. He gazed at me a long time as if I were a slot machine into which he had, without results, dropped a nickel. Then he walked away. The cops followed him, the one grandfather shot holding his now-bandaged arm, cursing and blaspheming. "I'm gonna get my gun back from that old bird," said the zither-cop. "Yeh," said Joe. "You—and who else?" I told them I would bring it to the station house the next day.

"What was the matter with that one policeman?" mother asked, after they had gone. "Grandfather shot him," I said. "What for?" she demanded. I told her he was a deserter. "Of all things!" said mother. "He was such a nice-looking young man."

Grandfather was fresh as a daisy and full of jokes at breakfast next morning. We thought at first he had forgotten all about what had happened, but he hadn't. Over his third cup of coffee, he glared at Herman and me. "What was the idee of all them cops tarryhootin' round the house last night?" he demanded. He had us there.

Winston Weathers (1926–   ) was born in Pawhuska, Oklahoma, and now resides in Tulsa, Oklahoma, where he is Professor of English at the University of Tulsa. He has contributed to *Literary Review, Antioch Review, Cimarron Review, Texas Quarterly,* and others. His major works include *Messages from the Asylum* (sonnets), *Archetype and Psyche: Essays in World Literature,* and *The Lonesome Game* (short stories).

For Those of You Who Are Obviously Smarter Than I Am: A Sonnet

WINSTON WEATHERS

My mind is an empty soupcan filled with cold
water. My mind is a black crab biting the thoughts
that feed it. My mind is a spur-line railroad track,
discontinued and abandoned with
permission of the I.C.C.
My mind is a ghost in my brain, and my brain is square
in an oval hatbox. Look in my eyes and see
tunnels fading into a flooded mine.

I wish I had yours: a solid aluminum sphere,
precision made, guaranteed not to rust,
floating in perfumed intellectual oils,
purring to quiet motors. If I had yours
I, too, could suck like a brand-new vacuum cleaner
softly, from the world, a tumescent bag of wisdom.

Marshall McLuhan (1911–   ) is Canadian. In 1933, he received his B.A. from the University of Manitoba; he received his M.A. in 1939, his Ph.D. in 1942. His numerous articles on mass media are well known. His major works include *The Mechanical Bride, Studies in Communication, The Gutenberg Galaxy, Understanding Media, The Extensions of Man,* and *The Medium Is the Massage.*

Sight, Sound and Fury

MARSHALL McLUHAN

In his recent visit to America, Roy Campbell mentioned that when Dylan Thomas had discovered he could read poetry on the radio, this discovery transformed his later poetry for the better. Thomas discovered a new dimension in his language when he established a new relation with the public.

Until Gutenberg, poetic publication meant the reading or singing of one's poems to a small audience. When poetry began to exist primarily on the printed page, in the seventeenth century, there occurred that strange mixture of sight and sound later known as "metaphysical poetry" which has so much in common with modern poetry.

American colonization began when the only culture available to most men was that of the printed book. European culture was then, as now, as much an affair of music, painting, sculpture, and communication as it was of literature. So that to this day North Americans associate culture mainly with books. But, paradoxically, it is in North America that the new media of sight and sound have had the greatest popular sway. Is it precisely because we make the widest separation between culture and our new media that we are unable to see the new media as serious culture? Have four centuries of book-culture

From *Commonweal,* April 9, 1954. Reprinted by permission of Commonweal Publishing Co., Inc.

hypnotized us into such concentration on the content of books and the new media that we cannot see that the very form of any medium of communication is as important as anything that it conveys?

Ireland is perhaps the only part of the English-speaking world where the oral tradition of culture has strongly persisted in spite of the printed page. And Ireland has given us Wilde, Shaw, Yeats, Synge, and Joyce in recent years—all of them masters of the magic of the spoken word. A Ballynooley farmer who returned to Ireland from America said to his neighbor: "In three years I didn't meet a man who could sing a ballad, let alone compose one on his feet."

The printed page was itself a highly specialized (and spatialized) form of communication. In 1500 A.D. it was revolutionary. And Erasmus was perhaps the first to grasp the fact that the revolution was going to occur above all in the classroom. He devoted himself to the production of textbooks and to the setting up of grammar schools. The printed book soon liquidated two thousand years of manuscript culture. It created the solitary student. It set up the rule of private interpretation against public disputation. It established the divorce between "literature and life." It created a new and highly abstract culture because it was itself a mechanized form of culture. Today, when the textbook has yielded to the classroom project and the classroom as social workshop and discussion group, it is easier for us to notice what was going on in 1500. Today we know that the turn to the visual on one hand, that is, to photography, and to the auditory media of radio and public address systems on the other hand, has created a totally new environment for the educational process.

André Malraux has recently popularized the notion of the art revolution of our time in his *Museum without Walls*. His theme is that the picture book today can embrace a greater range of art than any museum. By bringing such a range of art within portable compass, however, it has changed even the painter's approach to painting. Again, it is not just a question of message, image, or content. The picture-book as a museum without walls has for the artist a new technical meaning, just as for the spectator, pictorial communication means a large but unconscious shift in his ways of thought and feeling.

We have long been accustomed to the notion that a person's beliefs shape and color his existence. They provide the windows which frame, and through which he views, all events. We are less accustomed to the notion that the shapes of a technological environment are also idea-windows. Every shape (gimmick or metropolis), every situation planned and realized by man's factive intelligence, is a window which reveals or distorts reality. Today, when power technology has taken over the entire global environment to be manipuated as the material of art, nature has disappeared with nature-poetry. And the effectiveness of the classroom has diminished with the decline of the monopoly of book-culture. If Erasmus saw the classroom as the new stage for the drama of the printing press, we can see today that the new situation for young and old alike is classrooms without walls. The entire urban environment has become aggressively pedagogic. Everybody and everything has a message to declare, a line to plug.

This is the time of transition from the commercial age, when it was the production and distribution of commodities which occupied the ingenuity of men. Today we have moved from the production of packaged goods to the packaging of information. Formerly we invaded foreign markets with goods. Today we invade whole cultures with packaged information, entertainment, and ideas. In view of the instantaneous global scope of the new media of sight and sound, even the newspaper is slow. But the press ousted the book in the nineteenth century because the book arrived too late. The newspaper page was not a mere enlargement of the book page. It was, like the movie, a new collective art form.

To retrace some of this ground, it will help to recall that in the *Phaedrus,* Plato argued that the new arrival of writing would revolutionize culture for the worse. He suggested that it would substitute reminiscence for thought and mechanical learning for the true dialectic of the living quest for truth by discourse and conversation. It was as if he foresaw the library of Alexandria and the unending exegesis upon previous exegesis of the scholiasts and grammarians.

It would seem that the great virtue of writing is its power

to arrest the swift process of thought for steady contemplation and analysis. Writing is the translation of the audible into the visual. In large measure it is the spatialization of thought. Yet writing on papyrus and parchment fostered a very different set of mental habits from [that achieved by] those who associate with print and books. In the first place, silent reading was unknown until the macadamized, streamlined surfaces of the printed page arrived to permit swift traverse of the eye alone. In the second place, difficulty of access to manuscripts impelled students to memorize so far as possible everything they read. This led to encyclopedism, but also to having on tap in oral discourse one's entire erudition.

The child at school in the Middle Ages had first to make his own copies of texts from dictation. He had next to compile his own grammar and lexicon and commonplace book. The arrival of plenty of cheap, uniform, printed texts changed all this. The mechanization of writing by means of the assembly line of movable type speedily expanded the range of available reading and just as quickly reduced the habit of oral discourse as a way of learning. During the sixteenth century, however, a degree of equilibrium persisted between oral and written learning which we associate with the special excellence of Elizabethan drama, sermon, and poetry.

In the reverse direction, much of the vivid energy of American speech and writing in the twentieth century is the result of the movement away from book-culture toward oral communication. This nonliterary direction of speech has been felt to a much smaller degree in England and in Europe during the same period. Radio in particular has encouraged the return to the panel discussion and the round table. But the spontaneous move toward the seminar and class discussion as learning process has been helped by press and photography too, in so far as these have challenged the monopoly of the book.

Above all, the habits of the business community in demanding conference and discussion as the swift way of establishing insight into method and procedure in various specialized branches of business—these have prompted the new reliance on speech as a means of discovery. It is significant, for example, that the atomic physicists found that only by daily, face-to-face association could they get on with their tasks during the past war.

It has long been a truism that changes in material culture cause shifts in the patterns of the entire culture. The ancient road made possible armies and empires and destroyed the isolated city states of Greece. But the road depended in the first place on writing. Behind the imperial command of great land areas stood the written word in easily transportable form. In the nineteenth century, the newspapers, especially after the telegraph, paid for new roads and faster transport by land and sea. The press altered the forms of government, and the telegraph brought secret diplomacy to an end. When events in Egypt or Russia, London, Paris, or New York were known everywhere at once, the time for secret negotiation was reduced to hours and minutes. And the great national populations of the world, alerted and emotionalized by the press, could confront one another immediately for a showdown.

Printing had from the first fostered nationalism because the vernaculars with their large reading publics were more profitable to commercial publishers than Latin. The press has pushed this nationalism to its ultimate point. There it remains. But photography and movies, like music and painting, are international in their power of appeal. The power of pictures to leap over national frontiers and prejudices is well-known, for good and ill.

One aspect of the press deserves special comment in this same respect. The contents of newspapers, their messages and information, have steadily promoted nationalism. But the form of the newspaper page is powerfully intercultural and international. The unformulated message of an assembly of news items from every quarter of the globe is that the world today is one city. All war is civil war. All suffering is our own. So that regardless of the political line, or the time or the place, the mere format of the press exerts a single pressure. Basic acceptance of this fact is recorded in the steady weakening of interest in political parties everywhere.

From the point of view of its format, the press as a daily cross-section of the globe is a mirror of the technological instruments of communication. It is the popular daily book, the great collective poem, the universal entertainment of our age. As such it has modified poetic techniques and in turn has already been modified by the newer media of movie, radio, and television. These represent revolutions in communication as radical as printing itself. In fact, they are "magic casements opening on the foam of perilous seas," on which few of us have yet ventured in thought, art or living. If Erasmus was the first to size up and exploit the printing press as a new force in art and education, James Joyce was the first to seize upon newspaper, radio, movie, and television to set up his "verbivocovisual" drama in *Finnegans Wake.* Pound and Eliot are, in comparison with Joyce, timid devotees of the book as art form. But most of the difficulties which the ordinary person encounters with the poetry of Pound and Eliot disappear if it is viewed as a historical newsreel of persons, myths, ideas, and events with thematic musical score built in. Joyce had a much greater trust of language and reality than Pound or Eliot. By contrast they give their language and reality the Hollywood glamor treatment. Joyce is closer to a De Sica film with its awareness of the intimate riches of the most ordinary scenes and situations.

But the reader who approaches Pound, Eliot, and Joyce alike as exploiters of the cinematic aspects of language will arrive at appreciation more quickly than the one who unconsciously tries to make sense of them by reducing their use of the new media of communication to the abstract linear forms of the book page.

The basic fact to keep in mind about the movie camera and projector is their resemblance to the process of human cognition. That is the real source of their magical, transforming power. The camera rolls up the external world on a spool. It does this by rapid still shots. The projector unwinds this spool as a kind of magic carpet which conveys the enchanted spectator anywhere in the world in an instant. The camera records and analyzes the daylight world with more than human intensity because of the forty-five degree angle of the camera eye. The projector reveals this daylight world on a dark screen where it becomes a dream world.

The wonderful resemblance in all this to human cognition extends at least this far: in cognition we have to interiorize the exterior world. We have to recreate in the medium of our senses and inner faculties the drama of existence. This is the work of the *logos poietikos,* the agent intellect. In speech we utter that drama which we have analogously recreated within us. In speech we make or *poet* the world even as we may say that the movie parrots the world. Languages themselves are thus the greatest of all works of art. They are the collective hymns to existence. For in cognition itself is the whole of the poetic process. But the artist differs from most men in his power to arrest and then reverse the stages of human apprehension. He learns how to embody the stages of cognition (Aristotle's "plot") in an exterior work which can be held up for contemplation.

Even in this respect the movie resembles the cognitive process since the daylight world which the camera rolls up on the spool is reversed and projected to become the magical dream world of the audience. But all media of communication share something of this cognitive character which only a Thomist vision of existence and cognition dare do justice to.

Television, for example, differs from the movie in the immediacy with which it picks up and renders back the visible. The TV camera is like the microphone in relation to the voice. The movie has no such immediacy of pickup and feedback. As we begin to look into the inevitably cognitive character of the various media we soon get over the jitters that come from exclusive concern with any one form of communication.

In his *Theory of the Film,* Bela Balazs notes how "the discovery of printing gradually rendered illegible the faces of men. So much could be read from paper that the method of conveying meaning by facial expression fell into desuetude. Victor Hugo wrote once that the printed book took over the part played by the cathedral in the Middle Ages and became the carrier of the spirit of the people. But the thousands of books tore the one spirit . . . into thousands of opinions . . . tore the church into a thousand books. The visible spirit was thus turned into a legible spirit and visual culture into a culture of concepts."

Before printing, a reader was one who discerned and probed riddles. After printing, it meant one who scanned, who skipped along the macadamized surfaces of print. Today at the end of that process we have come to equate reading skill with speed and distraction rather than wisdom. But print, the mechanization of writing, was succeeded in the nineteenth century by photography and then by the mechanization of human gesture in the movie. This was followed by the mechanization of speech in telephone, phonograph and radio. In the talkies, and finally with TV, came the mechanization of the totality of human expression, of voice, gesture, and human figure in action.

Each of these steps in the mechanization of human expression was comparable in its scope to the revolution brought about by the mechanization of writing itself. The changes in the ways of human association, social and political, were telescoped in time and so hidden from casual observers.

If there is a truism in the history of human communication it is that any innovation in the external means of communication brings in its train shock on shock of social change. One effect of writing was to make possible cities, roads, armies, and empires. The letters of the alphabet were indeed the dragon's teeth. The printed book not only fostered nationalism but made it possible to bring the world of the past into every study. The newspaper is a daily book which brings a slice of all the cultures of the world under our eyes every day. To this extent it reverses the tendency of the printing press to accentuate merely national culture. Pictorial journalism and reportage tend strongly in the same international direction. But is this true of radio? Radio has strengthened the oral habit of communication and extended it, via the panel and round table, to serious learning. Yet radio seems to be a form which also strengthens the national culture. Merely oral societies, for example, are the ultimate in national exclusiveness.

A group of us recently performed an experiment with a large group of students. We divided them into four sections and assigned each section to a separate communication channel. Each section got the identical lecture simultaneously, but one read it, one heard it as a regular lecture in a studio, one heard it on radio and one heard and saw it as a TV broadcast. Immediately afterwards we administered a quiz to determine apprehension and understanding of this new and difficult material. The TV section came out on top, then the radio section, then the studio, and reading sections at the bottom. This was a totally unexpected result and it is too soon to generalize; but it is quite certain that the so-called mass media are not necessarily ordained to be channels of popular entertainment only.

It is "desirable" in thinking about the new media that we should recall that buildings are mass communications and that the first mechanical medium was print from movable type. In fact, the discovery of movable type was the ancestor of all assembly lines, and it would be foolish to overlook the impact of the technological form involved in print on the psychological life of readers. To overlook this would be as unrealistic as to ignore rhythm and tempo in music. Likewise it is only common sense to recognize that the general situation created by a communicative channel and its audience is a large part of that in which and by which the individuals commune. The encoded message cannot be regarded as a mere capsule or pellet produced at one point and consumed at another. Communication is communication all along the line.

One might illustrate from sports. The best brand of football played before fifty people would lack something of the power to communicate. The large enthusiastic crowd is necessary to represent the community at large, just as the players enact a drama which externalizes certain motivations and tensions in the communal life which would not otherwise be visible or available for audience participation. In India huge crowds assemble to experience *darshan,* which they consider to occur when they are massed in the presence of a visible manifestation of their collective life.

The new media do something similar for us in the West. Movies, radio, and TV establish certain personalities on a new plane of existence. They exist not so much in themselves but as types of collective life felt and perceived through a mass medium. L'il Abner, Bob Hope, Donald Duck, and Marilyn Monroe become points of collective awareness and communication for an entire society. And as technology increasingly undertakes to submit the entire planet as well as the contents of consciousness to the purposes of man's factive intelligence, it behooves us to consider the whole process of magical transformation involved in the media acutely and extensively.

From this point of view it should be obvious, for example, that the framers of the Hollywood morality code were operating with a very inadequate set of perceptions and concepts about the nature of the movie medium. Modern discussions of censorship, in the same way, are helplessly tied to conceptions borrowed from book-culture alone. And the defenders of book-culture have seldom given any thought to any of the media as art forms, the book least of all. The result is that their "defense" might as well be staged on an abandoned movie lot for all the effect it has on the actual situation.

When I wrote *The Mechanical Bride* some years ago I did not realize that I was attempting a defense of book-culture against the new media. I can now see that I was trying to bring some of the critical awareness fostered by literary training to bear on the new media of sight and sound. My strategy was wrong, because my obsession with literary values blinded me to much that was actually happening for good and ill. What we have to defend today is not the values developed in any particular culture or by any one mode of communication. Modern technology presumes to attempt a total transformation of man and his environment. This calls in turn for an inspection and defense of all human values. And so far as merely huma aid goes, the citadel of this defense must be located in analytical awareness of the nature of the creative process involved in human cognition. For it is in this citadel that science and technology have already established themselves in their manipulation of the new media.

Charles A. Fairbanks (1900–   ) was born in Springfield, Vermont. In 1963 he moved from Massachusetts to St. Petersburg, Florida. He is a retired Civil Service employee (railway mail) and an instructor of arts and crafts at the Holy Family Parish. He has contributed to *The Floridian.*

Liberalism: Too High a Price?

CHARLES A. FAIRBANKS

To me "liberalism" means "communism made acceptable." Like communism and socialism, liberalism holds that the citizen is the servant of the state, which is just the opposite of our American concept. It equates changes with progress, advances the idea that whatever is new must necessarily be better (contrary to the conservative position of no change without benefit) and seeks to discard old and tried principles and ideas for the new and radical. It seems to have but one solution to all problems: Government intervention. Among its pet programs are: Elimination of God and prayer in the public schools, birth control, abolition of the death penalty, disarming American citizens, unilateral civil rights, de-escalation of the war in Vietnam without corresponding de-escalation by the enemy and trade with countries which in turn trade with the enemy.

Despite the tendency of some liberals to move without knowing where they're going, there are many American liberals who know exactly what their goal is, just how to get there and are deadly determined to reach it. Their goal is one world government.

From "A Point of View," in *Floridian,* March 24, 1968. Reprinted by permission.

However desirable a one world government may sound, it can be achieved only at the price of losing national sovereignty. Just as the family is the unit of society, the nation is the unit of world society. A world government which could override any national government can be no more acceptable than a neighborhood association which could override a family's right to regulate its own family affairs.

The continued sovereignty of the United States is the last barrier to the fulfillment of the liberals' dream. Our sovereignty is based on our spiritual, economic and military strength. The assault on our spiritual or cultural strength is evident in today's grotesque art, lurid books and plays and heroes whose characters are of doubtful worth to society. Books so obscene that they never would have reached print a few decades ago are published now because of "their compensating literary value." When examined, the authors, the artists of this cultural trash almost invariably will be found to be persons of extreme political and moral views.

Our economic status has been weakened by foreign give-away programs, resulting in confiscatory taxes, inflation and the cheapening of our currency. Even now the liberals are contemplating the removal of the last bit of gold backing our dollar.

Liberalism needs a military build-up to keep industry busy and then points to a thriving economy bought by American blood and tears.

Unless a citizen is old enough to have been voting at least 20 years, he does not know what it is to live in a free country. The American people have lost about 60 per cent of the freedoms they had at the beginning of the century. Then a man could take home his pay, pay his taxes once a year and the rest was his. He did not have to hire someone to fill out complicated forms or spend hours figuring out how much more he owed or if he might get some back. His money was not thrown all over the world for all kinds of purposes. New parents of a boy were not tortured by the thought that someday their baby might have to die on a foreign battlefield. There was no draft to disrupt the lives of young men and young families. Boys could work alongside men learning a man's trade.

But because child labor was sometimes abused, it was eliminated instead of being corrected as if cutting off the head is the only way to cure the headache. Instead of young people working and earning and achieving something in which they could take pride, they have been deprived of that satisfaction.

If this is a government of the people, by the people and for the people, just what does the mess we are in today say for American people.

We have forgotten the advice and warnings of our first president: "Beware of foreign entanglements" or "Eternal vigilance is the price of liberty," or "Tyranny thrives when good people do nothing." I wonder what the good people were doing when slaves were being imported. Their indifference eventually caused a war between states and has left us with a very poignant problem. I wonder what the good people were doing when the Pandora's box of communism was loosed on the world as a four-times elected president and his rubber stamp Congress recognized Russia in the name of foreign trade and built her up to be a menace to the world. It was then that the seeds of our troubles in Korea and Vietnam, our riots and student demonstrations were sown.

We spend millions of dollars building athletic facilities to develop the physical side of our young people and millions more to develop the intellectual side, but the moral and spiritual side is allowed to grow wild. Our schools and universities are turning out individuals who are only two-thirds educated as human beings.

Our intellectuals have been so "hell-bent for progress" in the scientific, industrial and intellectual fields that we have slipped back into the moral Dark Ages. In the coming months, we will hear much about the greatest problems facing the country from candidates.

The greatest problem is not the Vietnam war; it is not our economy; it is not inflation; it is not even crime in our streets. It is the liberals' Godless education. It has brought America to the verge of anarchy. There can be no freedom except through the framework of restraint. Without restraint liberty becomes license. The society that can not or will not protect itself eventually must perish.

To save our country, we must go back to the morality of our fathers and refuse to let the liberals define for us what is moral. We must refuse to let the editors, columnists and professors do our thinking and form our opinions for us. We must break out of the paper curtain behind which we have lived so long.

Langston Hughes (1902–   ) is an American poet and writer who has written musical scores and radio scripts, was a visiting Professor in Creative Writing at Atlanta University, and a columnist for the *Chicago Defender*. His major publications include *The Sun Do Move, Troubled Island and the Banner, Freedom's Plow,* lyrics for *Streetscene,* and a collection of short stories.

Evenin' Air Blues

LANGSTON HUGHES

Folks, I come up North
Cause they told me de North was fine.
I come up North
Cause they told me de North was fine.
Been up here six months—
I'm about to lose my mind.

This mornin' for breakfast
I chawed de mornin' air.
This mornin' for breakfast
Chawed de mornin' air.
But this evenin' for supper,
I got evenin' air to spare.

Believe I'll do a little dancin'
Just to drive my blues away—
A little dancin'
To drive my blues away,
Cause when I'm dancin'
De blues forgets to stay.

But if you was to ask me
How de blues they come to be,
Says if you was to ask me
How de blues they come to be—
You wouldn't need to ask me:
Just look at me and see!—

Charles Gordone (1925?–), author of *No Place to be Somebody,* the long-running play he describes as "a black-black comedy," distinguished himself as an entertainer, actor, and director before he turned to playwriting in the early Sixties. He attended Los Angeles City College, following two years of Special Services duty in the U.S. Air Force, and was a drama major at Los Angeles State College, where he received a B.A. in 1952. Gordone was co-founder in 1962 and chairman, with Godfrey Cambridge, of the Committee for the Employment of Negro Performers. He worked as production manager for a USIA documentary on the Negro in America, and in 1967 was on the research team in Newark and New Haven for the President's Commission on Civil Disorders. Now he is continuing his writing and acting. *No Place to Be Somebody,* which took seven years to complete to the author's satisfaction, won a Drama Desk Award as well as a Pulitzer Prize.

A Quiet Talk with Myself

CHARLES GORDONE

And a prayer for the Sixties:
Please bless the Prez we's
Got now. Mistah Mill-house Nix.
He ain't much, Lawd.
But he's all we's got!

Q: Let's get down to the nitty-gritty right away. What do you think of the possibility of a "race war"?

A: There's always been a race war in this country.

Q: How do you mean that?

A: Well, from the moment them Europeans landed we can say that was the beginnin'. Dig, right after the Revolutionary War, them Europeans who fought the mother country to take this one began to kill off the Indians. An' the propaganda against the Indian about how he was inferior an' a savage was one of the most diabolical in the history of man.

Q: And you believe that the annihilation of the Indian was racist?

A: Sure I do. What you call it, genocide? White Anglo-Saxon, Judeo-Christian practice has always needed some excuse for its own brand of "man's inhumanity to man."

Q: Historically, how does this apply today?

A: Well, you gotta go back to the time when them Europeans sent over to Africa to git about as many Africans as they could git, to put 'em in slavery. But you see, when you put a man in bondage against his will, call him inferior because his skin happens to be a different color than yours, an' you do it for your own greed an' gain, he will begin to show you in any way he can that he is not inferior. An' in order to do that, he will have to consider you his enemy. An' to me, man, that is war.

Q: But there has never been an out-and-out armed conflict between whites and blacks in this country of any real consequence.

A: That depends on how you wanna look at it. In the history of the black man in this country, no matter what your New England-headed history books tell you, there have been many armed rebellions by black people. Of course they was never successful, but the psychology of it happenin' in these times, an' on a bigger scale, sits heavy on the minds of a awful lotta white people, along with their guilt.

Q: In these days of black militancy, do you think there is a strong possibility of an armed clash on any whole scale?

A: If things keep goin' the way they have been, you will always have a segment of the poor an' disenfranchised who will preach an' carry out acts, either by violent means or with civil disturbance. As long as the rights of certain people are violated, be they black or white, you can usually predict what will come.

Q: What do you predict as of now?

A: Well, up to now there has never been any strong union among all the people of color in this country. Sure, all these Civil Rights groups agree on one thing, "Civil Rights." But none of 'em agree on the methods to use. An' the thing that sticks in the minds of the black militants is the fact that no matter how many B.M.'s you git, no matter how many guns, ammo an' equipment you come up with, you will still be outnumbered an' out-armed. It would be nothin' but a slaughter.

Q: So what you are really saying is that there will never be a "race war" in this country.

A: Not the kind we been talkin' about. But as long as you have bad housing, no jobs, people poor an 'hungry, you gonna have some kinda outbreak. An' the people stayin' in these ghettos are gonna always find ways to git back at what they consider to be the enemy.

Q: Just who is this "enemy"? Surely not all white people in this country are racists.

A: I'm hip. But them exceptions ain't never been very impressive. But you gotta take into account another very important point. The majority of the blacks in this country don't wanna do anything to hurt it an' most of 'em wanna stay aroun' to git a piece of the action that everybody else seems to be gittin'. An' deep down inside they wanna believe that this country is all that it says it is. Then, too, I think there is a awful lotta people, both white an' black, who are beginnin' to git hip to the idea that the thing to aim at is the bad thinkin' in the country as a whole.

Q: Bad thinking?

A: Yeah. First lemme say that the subject of race is really beginnin' to bore the hell outta me. The most important thing to come outta the Civil Rights movement was that it showed to some people in this country an' to the world that there was a lotta things wrong other than it bein' racist. An' the main reason why it's been takin' such a helluva long time doin' anything about blacks, poor people or anything else is because most everybody's head ain't been in the right place. An' to me this is far more dangerous. An' if we don't all do somethin' damned fast, somethin' will happen much more terrible than a "race war."

Q: Can you be more specific?

A: Like I say about the thinkin'? Well, we got a whole

lotta people in this country who don't want no kinda change. You got these slow, time-clock-headed people on one hand an' then on the other you got these blind-sheep, plastic-headed, status quo-minded "patriots" who live in small towns or out in suburbia.

Q: Are you really speaking of the comfortable American middle class?

A: An' I'm speakin' of some that ain't comfortable too. Because if they ain't comfortable, they are busy as hell, spendin' all their time tryin' to git comfortable. An' gittin' comfortable means either workin' your butt off or stealin' all the money you can git. An' there is some poor people even on welfare who are steady schemin' up ways so's they can git comfortable too. An' when you got the majority of people in this country thinkin' about nothin' but gittin' some money an' gittin' comfortable, they ain't gonna have no time to be thinkin' about the conditions of blacks, themselves, poor people, criminals, kids, the Vietnam war or nothin' else.

Q: Well, everyone should want to be comfortable, at least.

A: I sure ain't gonna argue that point. But dig this. We have become the richest an' most powerful nation in the world. We have not only produced, in the process, a racist society but we have moved further into a class society as well. An' this kinda thinkin' "class kinda thinkin'," has been happenin' to people all over this country.

Q: Tell me, how does this kind of thinking lead to the danger of a greater uprising than a race war?

A: For example, let's take this group of people who been carryin' aroun' the idea that this country can do no wrong. They don't fool me. They're only sayin' that because they are scared an' don't wanna lose what they think they got. They are usually a bunch of white Anglo-Saxon Protestants who been preachin' all along that "all men was created equal," but they been practicin' "some is more equal than others." For instance, if I put myself in one of them Wasper's shoes an' I don't want nothin' to change: "I might condemn those blacks who demonstrate for their own Civil Rights. I will lack the insight or understanding as to why they burn down their own ghettos. I will compare their action with criminal action and urge the authorities to deal with these blacks in the same way that criminals are dealt with. I might condemn black students who demand a Black Studies Program or refuse to pay my son's tuition because he wants a hand in his own educational destiny and because he had the nerve to burn his draft card. I have little tolerance for poor people because I was once poor and had the ambition and guts to pull myself up by my own bootstraps. I condemn hippies who wear long hair, smoke marijuana and take LSD. I am opposed to any kind of change even if it could be in the interest or for the betterment of the country I love so well. I will be opposed to change because my intelligence and imagination may be warped and tainted in my desperate effort to 'keep up with the Joneses.' I will look at only what I want to see in the world for that is the 'American way.' If I want to be a bit 'liberal,' I can always hold onto the old idea that if there *is* something wrong, I can content myself with the thought that these 'wrongs' cannot, will not and must not be changed overnight. And, like a true 'American,' begin to believe that I, myself, can do no wrong. I make a good wage, own my home, pay my bills always on time. I own two cars. Have life insurance, family insurance, fire, auto-theft and accident insurance. A checking account, savings account and credit cards. My politics are conservative. I'm loyal to my party. I go on jury duty when called. Go to church each Sunday and pay my tithe. I have good friends, go to parties, the theatre and attend movies regularly. I read all the best sellers, belong to the Elks Lodge, the Kiwanis, and I'm a member of the American Legion Post. I am devoted to my fraternity and my College Alumni Association. I have sacrificed a great deal for my family. I don't have a mistress. I love my wife, still. I eat good food. Drink good drink. Take a well-earned vacation every year. My name is John Doe Jones. I am forty-three years of age. I would say that I am comfortable. I don't want anything to change it before I die and I don't want to die before my time because I have a bad heart, you know."

Q: What is this man you have just described? Has he accomplished the "American dream"?

A: I call this man "public-enemy number one." Because it has always been this kinda man that has been killin' the American dream. This kinda man has always found a way to keep race prejudice goin', even though he might not admit it openly. He is the kinda man that creates a climate for the Ku Klux Klan, for the John Birch Society an' for every reactionary group in the United States. He will hide behin' the church an' "the strong arm of the law." He doesn't want anything to do with change. He agrees with J. Edgar Hoover that "law and order is more important than justice."

Q: Don't you agree that law and order must be maintained?

A: Only when you know somethin' about what justice is. It is pure common sense to know that if justice is broken down in a country, a whole lotta people are gonna git mad. Now, how you gonna call somebody a criminal when it is obvious that he is simply fightin' for his rights an' self-respect? The reason that there is so much crime in this country could be that the kind of justice that is bein' practiced has provided a reason for it. An' as long as cats like Mister Hoover are in there carryin' on their kinda justice, we are gonna have more an' more crime an' violence. As a matter of fact, he is voicin' the opinions an' wishes of people who think just like he does.

Q: It is obvious that you are calling for a radical change. What kinds of changes should we begin to implement? And where should we start?

A: Here again we'll have to rap a litle bit about violence. I say that to say, you can't call for any kinda organized violent overthrow. That's what a lotta these here "plastic-heads" would like to see. Anyway, nobody wants that who is thinkin'. Unless they are gonna be pushed into it. The thinkin' people, the people who really care about this country, never want anything like that. They have had it up to here with violence. We are a violent nation. We live with violence every day. We see it on the streets. We read about it in all the newspapers. We see it all the time in the home on television. We even have it in our schools an' practically anyplace else you can name. We took this country through violence an' we think we have to keep it by usin' violence, even if we have to go to other countries to do it. We are foolin' ourselves by thinkin' that the landin' on the moon will bring peace to the world. But will it bring peace just to the United States? You see, the institutions an' government of this country has a pattern. First of all, the people behin' the moon shot are usin' the same old pattern of thought. An' the cats they sent up there was all "gung-ho, all-American type cats."

Q: What was wrong with that?

A: Nothin' *could* be wrong with it. But the question I'm askin' is, "Do they really represent what this country is all about?"

Q: What would you have done?

A: Do I have to remind you that we gotta awful lotta different kinda cats just as "American" fightin' over there in Vietnam.

Q: Could it be that they picked the best men for the job?

A: That's always a good "white" excuse. It's my guess that the cats they picked to go to the moon were perfect "white American" types for the kinda thinkin' that sent 'em there.

Q: Seems to me, it was pretty good thinking indeed.

A: Yeah, what they did was outta sight! Man, I don't deny that. I couldn't an' wouldn't. But I'm still askin': "Why are these cats always the first on the list?"

Q: And you think there should have been a better American representation among the crew?

A: That would be more "American," don't you think? Now, my next point is more important. Do people really think that plantin' the American flag up there is really gonna bring peace to the world?

Q: We certainly hope it does.

A: Well, it seems to me, if they really wanted to show the world that we had peace in mind, why did they just plant the American flag?

Q: We were the first to land there, of course.

A: Now, suppose there was somebody up there when they got there?

Q: Well, as far as scientists were able to determine, there was no reason to expect that there would be.

A: I know, I know, but just suppose if there was?

Q: I presume that we would make every effort to communicate with them.

A: Would "we" have still planted the American flag?

Q: I don't understand what you are getting at.

A: I'm just tryin' to think if plantin' the American flag is *really* gonna do anythin' about havin' peace in the world an' how?"

Q: Well, uh—we certainly hope so. Don't we?

A: An' I'm also wonderin', why if we was gonna show the world we had peace in mind an' we wasn't gonna lay no claim on the moon, why we couldn't have planted the U.N. flag? Or maybe no flag at all!

Q: So you suspect this gesture of peace?

A: I can't help but *suspect* it! Dig? If I can't keep the peace in my own family, I sure ain't got no business goin' aroun' to no other family, tryin' to keep the peace there. Or even believin' I can show my family how groovy I can keep the peace someplace else, so that my family will cool it.

Q: A-hem. Well now, I think we'll have to get back to the problems here on earth.

A: I would say that we have to. Now these "plastic-heads," these—

Q: Excuse me. Now, you have used that term a few times in this interview. What exactly is a "plastic-head"?

A: People who are "straight." People who ain't real an' can't change their heads, let alone their hearts.

Q: I see....

A: Anyway, like I was sayin'. We are beginnin' to develop two kinds of opposin' sides. If it ain't happened yet. It's the people who don't want no change against the people who wants some change. Dig, if there's one thing that TV did, it showed people in this country an' all over the world that segregation an' prejudice was not just a figment of the black man's mind. It showed cats like Faubus an' Wallace in all their racist glory. An' it showed to the world a whole lotta American Nazi police brutality. This made an impression on a awful lotta people. An' the hip ones began to see that not only blacks was bein' cheated outta their rights as individuals but they was bein' cheated too. Some of 'em didn't know what they could do about it, 'cause a lot of 'em was young an' was tired a'bein' kicked aroun' by a lotta old heads who couldn't see further than their nose. Now, git to this: When I was a kid, I used to hear my Mama an' Daddy say that the world they grew up to live in had been a pretty rotten place. They said they hoped an' prayed that me an' all them kids my age would grow up to make this world a better place. I didn't know what they had in mind when they said it but you can believe they ain't never agreed to the way I been tryin' to make that dream come true.

Q: Do you feel that there is a larger civil rights movement ahead of us? I mean one that will include the problems of many whites as well as blacks?

A: Well, it looks like it. Mind you, I ain't sayin' that all those uptight whites are gonna join up with blacks in general. But there will be a awful lotta sympathy for one another because all them "straight people" are gonna try to put a terrible hurtin' on 'em, just like they been tryin' to do to these black movements. Dig, there is like a campaign goin' on right now all aroun' the country to git rid of the hippies. An' the hip head is gonna be aroun' in the nex' generation. But now the "straight people" are tryin' to exterminate 'em. They are too embarrassin'. An' the hippies remind their parents of their own failures as parents. I mean in the same way that blacks remind the whole country of its failures as a country. Dig this: I go see my publisher yesterday. We had to take care some business. After we get through, he says: "Shall we go to lunch?" Now, here he is with a suit on with a tie stick in his shirt an' he's got this groovy distinguished beard on. I forgot about havin' lunch because, you know I don't think about no kinda food until I git hungry. I got on this old leather hat, a striped tank shirt that ain't got no sleeves on it an' that leather vest on an' I'm barefooted with my shoes tied together an' hangin' over my shoulder. Before we git up to go, I says, "Now wait a minute, Bob; we is goin' to lunch?" An' he says; "Yeah, ain't you hungry?" I start thinkin' how I ain't too together an' I got these kinky-ass braids hangin' down with a big turkey feather stickin' out of one of 'em. But I walk on out with him to this nowhere type Madison Avenue type restaurant. When we git in the restaurant, the atmosphere was like, wide apart!

An' when we git over to the eatin' room, the atmosphere gits very narrow. I was gittin' very bad vibrations from everybody. "The Man," he comes up. He knows Bob. Spoke to him, said: Mister Amussen an' so on an' so on. He's steady lookin' at me while he's rappin' to Bob. Then he says to Bob: "This gentleman has gotta wear a jacket. Now, how the f— was I gonna wear a jacket over what I was wearin'? What was I gonna look like? A idiot? "Do I gotta git on a shirt an' a tie too?" No! He just wants me to git on a jacket! All them plastic-headed bastards sittin' aroun' just gobblin' up the food an' lookin' stupid lookin' at me lookin' stupid, 'cause I can't git in *lookin'* like I *look*! They ain't complainin' about me bein' a nigger. Just complainin' because I ain't dressed right to suit 'em! You know in a lotta places in this country you could starve to death simply because you ain't dressed right! Ain't that a bitch? We got no respect for differences in this country.

Q: A-hem! Well now, can you sum up some of the factions that will, in other words, join in some kind of coalition against those that are against social change?

A: Well, these "factions" as you call 'em always been here in one form or another. It's just they have just about come to the end of their rope. That's the only difference. Right now, you got a whole lotta mothers uptight about their sons dyin' over there in Vietnam. You got a whole lotta students dissatisfied either about the war or the way they are bein' educated. There are thousands of people slowly starvin' to death here in many places an' the Welfare rolls ain't gittin' no smaller. The little workin' man is grumblin' an' gittin' more hip about the way he is bein' used. The prisoners in the prisons don't like the way they are bein' treated nor the conditions there neither. Many hospitals, institutions an' asylums are goin' to the dogs in many ways. We still have slums an' ghettos an' the people there ain't changed their minds one damned bit about it gittin' any better an' they hate the police more than ever. The Civil an' Criminal Courts are filled every day with blacks, Puerto Ricans, Mexicans, drunks, junkies an' prostitutes while organized crime goes on an' on. There is an awful lotta footloose kids panhandlin' in the streets in every big city an' soldiers comin' home to nothin'. An' of course blacks will still be ploddin', ploddin' along.

Q: So then, you see a pretty grim future?

A: If nothin' ain't done damned quick, it'll turn out to be a new kinda Civil War!

Q: But what you describe doesn't sound like this "Civil War" will be a coalition. Not to mention having any kind of organization.

A: I didn't say nothin' about no coal-ishun. You did. But I do believe all these peoples that I named will rise up one day soon. Rise up hard in their *own* way separately because any organization, if they could git one, wouldn't stand a chance against all them people who don't want no change.

Q: A-hem. Well, thank you for the interview. Is there anything else you would like to add before we close?

A: Yeah. I'd like to leave you with a little prayer called A Prayer For The Sixties:

Lawd, do you 'member whut happen to us durin' the Civil Rights Movement? An' whut happen with
our Po' Peoples' in March?

We thanks ya, Lawd, jus' the same that we no longer
Minds bein' called niggers.
An' thoo yo' he'p, we kin finally say:
"Ah's black an' ah's proud!"
Along with yo' lovin' servant, Brother James Brown.

We is provin' that we's proud, Lawd.
We's lettin' our hair go nachul.
An's we's wearin' Dashikis too.

We thanks ya, Lawd, fuh Reb'm Adam Cee.
He got a big mouf, Lawd.
But whut he do, he do all to the glory of Thee.

An' we thanks ya fuh Muhammad Ali.
He got a big mouf, too, Lawd.

But he was a man, Lawd.
Who stuck to his gloves.

We prays fuh them brothers who been callin' fuh
Sum "Black Power," Lawd.
'Cause sum of 'em got a terrible hurtin' put on 'em
An' had to split over to a place called Fiddla-Cuba.
An' sum of 'em stayed home an' got kilt!

An', Lawd, put a special blessin' on all them
Thousands of orphans who grew their hair long
'Cause they couldn't grow it kinky.
But they speak the language pretty good, Lawd.
An' tha's cool.

One thing we don't understan', Lawd.
Why you keep lettin' them Poah-leece do all them
Dirty things they been doin' to us,
While you let them other bad people who been
Puttin' 'em up to it go Scot free?

We thanks ya fuh lettin' us have all them
Student demonstrations of one kind or another.
An' Lawd, we thanks ya fuh chicks.
Specially them that wears mini-skirts.

Lawd, we prays fuh sum a'them brothers an' sisters.
Both white an' black who groove on pot, pills an' LSD.
They is jus' tryin' to git nex' to you, Baby!

We also thanks ya fuh sendin' all them Gurus that
Went back to India.
We thanks ya too fuh givin 'us sum groovy music
To go 'long with them neon lights ya give us.
Bless The Beatles an' Jimi Hendrix.
Bless the Rollin' Stones.

An' bless Broadway Joe Namath.
He's still out there groovin' as usual.
Thank ya fuh changin' his heart so's he wouldn't
Quit an' blow everything fuh the Jets.

An' please. Lawd! Lay yo' sweet evah lovin' foot
On Jimmie Brown the actor's ass
So he don't blow his cool so much.

We gotta 'member in our prayers, Lawd,
The great Mickey Mantle.
An' of course, Mistah "Say Hey," himself.
        Brother Willie Mays.

Put yo' lovin' arms aroun' Sidney Poitier.
We's waitin' on him to grow a beard but we knows
West Indians ain't got no use for 'em.

By the way, Lawd, we wants to thank ya fuh inventin'
Them bell-bottom pants.
We also thanks ya fuh these old pioneer clothes
An' fuh them Indian an' cowboy outfits
We been seein' fuh so long in the movies.
We's wearin' 'em now, to 'member our dear ancestors by.

Now, Lawd, we particularly wanna
        'member in our prayers
Prez Jay F. Kay.
He was a very han'some, cool cat who
        made a lotta groovy moves.
'Member Miss Jackie too, Lawd.
Fuhgive her, 'cause she know not whut she do!

An' we thanks ya fuh the good li'l time we had with
Li'l Bobby Kay. He was another outta sight cat who
Was caught by the spirit an' cut down by the ghost.
An' of course we all got to 'member the gret Reb'm
Doctah King who loved evahbody.

An' our dear blessed brother, Malcolm X who blew
A lotta people's minds.

We is now puttin' in a gassy word fuh brother Teddy Kay,
        too, Lawd. But we know you gonna cross that bridge
        when you come to it.

Bless them Astro-Nuts who grooved with a spoon on the Moon, fuh the sak'a peace on earth and good will to mens.

Don't wanna fuhgit "Mistah Fas' Draw," El Bee Jay neither, Lawd. 'Cause he wuz the fust real cowboy to become Prez.
Provin' that even cowboys kin become President.

An' above all, Lawd. Please, please bless the
Prez we's got now. Mistah Mill-house Nix.
He ain't much, Lawd.
But he's all we's got!
Thank ya, Lawd, an' Ay-man!

P.S.—Bless all them swingin' dudes who been kilt over there in Vee-eat-Numb.
Ay-man again.

e. e. cummings (1894–   ) was born in Cambridge, Massachusetts. He was graduated from Harvard in 1915 and remained to take his M.A. in 1916. He is known for the eccentricity of his typography and punctuation. His works consist of love poems, humorous character sketches, and satires on the foibles of his time. His major works include *Tulips and Chimney, XLI, Poems, &, is 5, No Thanks, him, The Enormous Room,* and *Tom.*

!blac

e. e. cummings

!blac
k
agains
t

(whi)

te sky
?t
rees whic
h fr

om droppe

d

,
le
af

a:;go

e
s wh
IrlI
n

.g

From *Fifty Poems* by e. e. cummings. Copyright © 1939, 1940 by e. e. cummings. Published by D. Appleton Century Co., Inc.

Frank Trippett (1926–) was born in Columbus, Mississippi, and now resides in Larchmont, New York. Having majored in journalism, he is a writer who has contributed to *Look, Newsweek, New Republic,* and *Reader's Digest.* He is also the author of *The States: United They Fell.*

The Epic of Garbage

FRANK TRIPPETT

Conspicuous consumption of valuable goods is a means of reputability to the gentleman of leisure.

—The Theory of the Leisure Class

If the appropriate sanitation services are not provided, the counterpart of increasing opulence will be deepening filth.

—The Affluent Society

The way to end glut was to produce gluttons.

—The Waste Makers

America's materialistic fever was first clearly charted by Thornstein Veblen. He diagnosed the waning 19th century's leisure class. His prognosis anticipated John Kenneth Galbraith's assay of mid-20th-century affluence as well as Vance Packard's vision of the nation as a herd of waste-making status-seekers. Onto Veblen's theory, Galbraith and Packard grafted a corollary: A leisure *society* behaves as formerly did the leisure *class.*

The imperatives of leisure, Veblen's "conspicuous consumption" and "conspicous waste," have been democratized. Thus the national soul is more egalitarian today, but it remains the avaricious sump that Veblen plumbed. We stand at two convenient ways to verify this: One is to study Veblen, Galbraith and Packard; the other is to study our national garbage. The garbage speaks with possibly less grace, but its reeking eloquence rises beyond the gifts of our prophets, and its message is clear.

It speaks with a tidal roar, because it is rising tidelike about us, our garbage, an ever-stinking, ever-festering, ever-swelling tide. It tells of a people indentured to excess. Even in the abstract, the national garbage exudes an epic aroma. Each average one of us issues nearly 5½ pounds of refuse a day, some four trillion pounds a year in all. It is an awful flow of gunk and junk, and it frightens the mind charged with finding a place for it all to go.

Where on earth to put it? This question (and not how to reduce it) inevitably preoccupies a society entranced by obvious technique, a society that has solved its traffic problem by building more parking spaces. So across the land, from New York to San Francisco, city fathers are dreaming of new and more and better dumping grounds, while the inundation of garbage that lies ahead takes on an ever more menacing shape. The sheer mass of the present garbage tests the very limits of graphic prose. Each year, *Nation's Business* calculated, our "garbage, rubbish, junked cars and scrap" would "fill the Panama Canal four times." California's 71.5 million annual tons alone would make "a mass . . . 100 feet wide and 30 feet high [from] Oregon to the Mexican border," said *Solid Wastes Management*. Our common litter? It would make a "drift" five feet high from New York to Seattle, said Keep America Beautiful, Inc., adding that the Memorial Day litter alone would suffice to "create a 3,800 mile memorial wreath two feet wide and four inches high covering an area the size of Minnesota, Ohio, Texas and Wyoming."

Garbage that impels witnesses to such picturesqueness is nothing if not vast. And it is growing vaster still. Since 1920, the per capita garbage has doubled, and the national total is up 60 percent since 1950, growing twice as rapidly as the population. Officials who contrast this horrendous vista with the primitive disposal apparatus at hand are driven to the language of crisis and the metaphor of apocalypse.

Our festering dumps and air-poisoning incinerators are

"a national disgrace," says the Public Health Service; and in the garbage explosion itself, a Chicago expert sees looming cataclysm: "We're running in front of an avalanche, and it's already begun to bury us." In the rhetoric of waste-disposal men, this notion of literal burial recurs with dismaying regularity. "People are up to their knees in garbage, but they don't really care," says a New York specialist. "In three more years, when they're up to their waists in it, they'll start screaming."

Skeptics may sniff. Still, skepticism must pale in the light of archaeological fact: Of seven cities that have thrived at the site of Troy, each of the last six was erected on the refuse of its predecessor. America so far has avoided burial by garbage only by methodically building on top of it. There among other hallowed monuments in Washington's Tidal Basin stands the Lincoln Memorial, serenely gracing acres of refuse that began accumulating at the founding of the nation's capital city. Some 17 percent of New York City rises from refuse-filled land.

So technique has saved us so far from interment. But new troubles are upon us, not only because of the rate at which the garbage tide is rising but because of its changing character. Full of aluminum cans (48 billion a year) that won't rust away and exotic plastics that seem to endure forever, it is becoming less and less destructible. And this at a moment when city after city is running out of landfill space. San Francisco long and diligently (and so far with utter futility) has tried to work out a plan to ship its garbage by rail for dumping some 375 miles away—a scheme that must seem more preposterous in some places than in New York, where the cost of collecting and disposing of a ton of garbage ($30) is higher than the cost (at $23) of mining and shipping a ton of Kentucky coal to Manhattan.

Indubitably, what to do with all this waste remains a compelling question, and technicians are busy looking for answers. A Japanese technique for converting solid waste into building blocks is commanding interest, and so are high-temperature incinerators that burn waste without stinking up the air. As important, industry is showing fresh interest (under fresh pressure) in exploring ways to recycle the materials in our cornucopia of cast-off products. With it all we may just escape entombment. No doubt the escape is worth the $4.5 billion we spend yearly handling our variegated garbage. Whatever its drain on money, energy and resources, the tide of waste as a logistical issue is unavoidable.

Yet, the person who sees this epic spillage only as a disposal problem should think on, should consider, perhaps, the ineptness of a physician who, discovering a man wallowing in his own excretions, conceives only of a problem of sanitation. An organism's waste is symptomatic, and the heaping, cascading waste of this land speaks amply of a certain quenchless greed. Of its implications perhaps too little has been said. We know the brighter side: Yes, our lust for goods and goodies keeps the technology thrumming, it enraptures the fiscal soul. But it does other things, too, things not so clearly seen because they lie on greed's dark nether side, and not so easily said because they rise bitter in the mouth. Someone must say them: Singular greed has blurred this country's vision and muffled the generous beat of its heart. Today, we fear floundering in the pungent excrescences of plenty while we quibble drily and ceaselessly over a question whose starkness impales the breast of decency: Shall we feed the poor?

As a question, how to dispose of our garbage engages us more. Those baleful minions of poverty in Resurrection City could induce only fizzling yawns in Washington (Shall we feed the poor?), but a long strike of garbage men in Memphis spawned the lethal tensions that delivered to the nation one of its exalted martyrs. Martin Luther King's murder is not severable from his presence in Memphis, nor from the insuperable anger of the Memphis garbage men, nor is their anger severable from the diurnal rage of discovering in every genteel, galvanized refuse can more food than they could afford to put in their pantries on payday. King survived the darkness of race hate only to perish in a fluke close by the shadow of engrossing greed and mindless waste.

Our history, for all its sweetness, casts up sometimes an eerie reek.

Ralph Nader (1934–   ) often called the "People's Crusader," received his A.B. from Princeton and LL.B. from Harvard. He is well known for his disclosures of practices unfair to the consumer and is responsible for legislation to protect the consumer. He is a lawyer and lecturer who has contributed to numerous periodicals. His best-known work is *Unsafe at Any Speed*.

Fashion or Safety

RALPH NADER

Auto manufacturers, with a corporate brutality unsurpassed since the railroads in post-Civil War days, have been steadily rejecting a life-saving technology that could reduce our annual highway death toll from 40,000 a year to 12,000 or less. For more than ten years, many scientists and lawmakers have been pointing the way to this technology, which involves no more than the redesigning of cars in accordance with principles as old as Archimedes. Their struggle so far has been almost entirely in vain.

I say "*almost* entirely" because grudgingly, slowly, the auto industry has given way on some points. Safety belts, newly designed steering wheels, padded dashboards have become, if not standard equipment, at least available as extras. A few manufacturers have discarded the deadly, sharp fins and pointed radiator ornaments—lethal weapons even on a slow-moving vehicle—that were so popular only a few years ago. But by and large the industry continues to reject safety for speed, power, decor; and, under the leadership of General Motors, the "big three" of Detroit—GM, Ford and Chrysler—have forged what amounts to a united front against any outside interference with their designs.

In a speech before the National Safety Congress, John F. Gordon, president of GM, ridiculed "amateur engineers" who

From *The Nation*, October 12, 1963. Reprinted by permission.

were trying to take over responsibilities that belong to "competent engineers in the industry." But it has been through engineers and medical scientists at Cornell, Harvard, California, Minnesota and other universities, and through research carried out by the Liberty Mutual Insurance Company, that the relationship has been uncovered between auto designs and our annual 40,000 fatalities and four million injuries on the highways. Pop-open doors, cardboard-like roof structures, uprootable seats, flying cushions, jutting metal dashboards, bone-crushing knobs, chisel-like rear-view mirrors and, above all, dangerous shafts and steering wheels are a few of the more than a hundred design deficiencies that Mr. Gordon's "competent" engineers seem to have overlooked.

Item: A team of optometrists, on funds provided by the American Optometric Foundation, is producing a series of studies on some fifty late-model cars. Dr. Merrill J. Allen, the project's director, offers this comment: "Not a single car provides a suitable visual environment for daytime driving." Serious obstructions to visibility include dashboard and panel reflections, windshield distortions, hood and chrome reflections, corner posts and sun-shades. "It almost appears," Allen stated, "that automobile manufacturers believe that vision has nothing to do with driving."

Item: Henry Wakeland, New York automobile consultant, has collected photographs showing children and elderly women killed when their hearts or lungs were pierced by the fins of automobiles moving as slowly as four miles per hour.

Item: Public service Research, Inc., of Stamford, Conn., analyzed the accident experience of several large commercial fleets under a U.S. Public Health Service grant. The findings showed that some car makes are more accident-prone than others—a clear indication that safety is a function of the car as well as of the driver. Similarly, a Cornell group established substantial variations in the strength of door latches among various makes, but all were below minimum adequate safety regulations. *Both the Public Service and Cornell Studies were supported by public funds, yet the findings of neither have been made available to the consumer.*

Item: Dr. Horace Campbell, an expert on the effects of

collisions on car passengers, insists that the instrument panels and dashboards of GM cars are the most dangerous in the industry. Further, the Chevrolet Corvair's steering box, from which ascends the steering shaft, is mounted *forward* of the front axle and so gets the first blow in any head-on collision. (GM is an exponent of the policy that any safety component on its cars, such as crash padding, should be offered as an "extra"—i.e., if you want it, you pay extra for it.)

The list could be lengthened almost indefinitely. And what this list contributes to are a couple of appalling statistics: (1) half of all the cars now on the road will be involved, at some time or another, in an injury-producing crash; (2) an American's chance of escaping injury in a vehicular crash during the whole of his lifetime is no better than fifty-fifty.

This is not to say that manufacturers are uniformly culpable. American Motors has publicly condemned the glamorizing of horsepower and speed. It pioneered in the adoption, in moderate-priced cars, of independent braking systems for front and rear wheels, so that if either system fails, the remaining one can bring the car to a halt. Studebaker's president, Sherwood Egbert, has registered vigorous dissent from the proposition that safety advances should wait for public demand. Studebaker's Lark and Avanti are free of many sharp edges and projections, both inside and outside. Ford has made some significant advances since 1956, and probably has the sincerest injury-prevention program operating in the industry.

The auto industry is perfectly aware of the mounting tide of criticism leveled against its product. It is equally aware of the remedies—practical and effective—that have been offered. Why does it respond so little? One thing is certain: *in terms of immediate production costs, safety can be purchased for pennies.* Liberty Mutual's experience in constructing "survival" cars is instructive in this respect. The company took four stock 1960 Chevrolets, removed the gingerbread, gewgaws and unsafe features and replaced them with dozens of safety improvements that *added no more than $10 to the cost of production.* Among these improvements were collapsible steering assemblies, automatic fire-protection systems, roll bars to strengthen roofs and in-the-line safety-brake devices. *Every* *one of these safety features has been known to Detroit for years.*

It isn't production costs that makes Detroit so safety-unconscious; it is the fear that its *policy of obsolescence* will become obsolescent. Safety engineering sponsors constant values which conflict with automobile "fashions" that alone justify yearly model change-overs. The industry is built on calculated, non-functional obsolescence—the appeal of the new color, the new gimmick, the new silhouette, the added horsepower or wheelbase or wheel track. What else is it that makes the '64 model different from the '63? The emphasis that Detroit places on style over safety is clearly revealed in its payrolls: the chief automobile stylist and his associates get much more money, much more authority, and enjoy much greater prestige, than the largely ignored safety engineers. But once a sensible, sturdy, safe car is produced, "fashion" to a large extent flies out of the window, and no justification remains for the annual style changeover.

And there's a second reason why the auto makers don't want to listen to outsiders: they fear that once they do so, they will be inviting government regulation. In this respect, the auto industry today enjoys an immunity shared by no other transportation industry. Trains, airplanes and ships must all meet federal safety specifications. The only controls the auto makers have to worry about are the *minutiae* of state standards: laws requiring windshield wipers and directional signals, for example.

Headed by the "big three," the Automobile Manufacturers Association is following a threefold strategy to preserve its present policies and protect its members against the threat of government control:

1. Common agreement on safety-design policy so that no company can offer the public substantially more than its competitors in the way of safety improvements. (The "big three," in particular General Motors, fought for years against the use of seat belts before succumbing to public pressure.)

2. Generous contributions to, and support of, traffic-safety groups which emphasize *driver responsibility* exclusively. Here, the manufacturers find themselves in a common front with such organizations as the Automobile Safety Coun-

cil, the National Safety Council and the Association of Motor Vehicle Administrators. Pushing the driver responsibility theme diverts attention from the automobile and gives the manufacturers a "responsible" public image.

3. Reliance on the safety-performance specifications of the Society of Automotive Engineers (SAE), which is supposed to impose "impartial, authoritative standards." But SAE, in large measure, is a "company" society; the men who lay down the standards are the men who work for the companies that are supposed to adhere to the standards. Thus, for instance, the society's Vehicle Latch Subcommittee is composed of seven men, all paid employees of one or another of the major automobile companies; no non-industry interest is represented. The presumption is that the only standards set by the SAE are those that have already been agreed upon by the auto makers.

But it may be that the industry's biggest safeguard is its very bigness and power. Americans are never permitted to forget that one in every six workers in the country owes his job directly or indirectly to Detroit. Currently the industry has been touted as "holding up the national economy," with sales rushing toward a record. Such arguments in the hands of a lobbyist are very powerful indeed. Did it just happen that Congress stripped the Armed Forces Epidemiological Board of authority to finance crash-injury research on the ground that this work was civilian in nature? In 1956 Congressman Kenneth A. Roberts' Subcommittee on Health and Safety held dramatic hearings on car-safety problems; why did its findings go unheeded? Why was its work in the field cut short?

Domestic air fatalities rarely exceed 1,200 annually, compared to the automobiles' 40,000. Yet the federal government spends tens of millions or more on air safety—and just about $5 million on automobile research.

Recently, Professor J. Douglas Brown of Princeton University asked his engineering colleagues:

> *If engineers can design space ships to go to the moon, why can't they design a safer automobile? Who is to be the bridge between science and human fulfillment, the professional engineer or the Madison Avenue pollster?*

The lessons of the past in such fields as meat and drugs teach that the decisive pressures come from an aroused public. But the public, to be aroused, must be *informed.* Slaughter on the highways has been a perennial phenomenon for nearly half a century—and still an industry is permitted to produce, unhindered, vehicles full of accidents and tragedies waiting to happen.

W. H. Auden (1907–), born at York, England, was educated at Oxford where he became a leader of the young poets of his generation. His early poetry is social criticism and protest, and demonstrates the influences of psychoanalytical and Marxist ideas; but his later verse is written from a position of Christian commitment. In 1939 he emigrated to the United States and later became an American citizen; however, since 1945 he has lived much in Italy, Austria, and England. His collections of verse include *Poems, The Age of Anxiety, Homage to Clio,* and *About the House*. He has also published *The Dyer's Hand,* a collection of literary criticism.

Moon Landing

W. H. AUDEN

It's natural the Boys should whoop it up for
so huge a phallic triumph, an adventure
    it would not have occurred to women
    to think worthwhile, made possible only

because we like huddling in gangs and knowing
the exact time: yes, our sex may with reason
    hurrah the deed, although the motives
    that primed it were somewhat less than *menschlich.*

A grand gesture. But what does it period?
What does it osse? We were always adroiter
    with objects than lives and more facile
    at courage than kindness: from the moment

the first flint was flaked, this landing was merely
a matter of time. But our selves, like Adam's,
    still don't fit us exactly, modern
    only in this—our lack of decorum.

Homer's heroes were no braver than Armstrong,
Aldrin, Collins, but more fortunate: Hector
    was excused the insult of having
    his valor covered by television.

Worth *going* to see? I can well believe it.
Worth *seeing*? Much! I once rode through a desert
    and was not charmed: give me a watered
    lively garden, remote from blatherers

about the New, the von Brauns and their ilk, where
on August mornings I can count the morning
    glories, where to die has a meaning,
    and no engine can shift my perspective.

Unsmudged, thank God, my Moon still queens the Heavens
as She ebbs and fulls, a Presence to glop at,
    Her Old Man, made of grit not protein,
    still visits my Austrian several

with His old detachment, and the old warnings
still have power to scare me: Hybris comes to
    a nasty finish, Irreverence
    is a greater oaf than Superstition.

Our apparatniks will continue making
the usual squalid mess called History:
    all we can pray for is that artists,
    chefs and saints may still appear to blithe it.

author-title index

Acapulco Confidential, 149
Age of Dust, The, 54
Alienation: Sign of Sickness or Symbol of Health?, 291
American History (White Man's Version) Needs an Infusion of Soul, 326
Anonymous, 360
Artificial Respiration and Other First-Aid Measures, 169
Assassination, The, 110
Auden, W. H., 510

Baker, James, 291
Baker, Russell, 26
Baldwin, James, 159
Beyond the Moon, 191
!blac, 499
Blenheim, Laurence C., 310
Brooke, Rupert, 454
Buchwald, Arthur, 139
Bull Fighting A Tragedy, 201

Carlyle, Thomas, 260
Central Park, 187
Certain Women, 451
Changing Times Staff, 316
Chapin, Chester F., 391
Child's Reasoning, A, 407
Childlike Adult, The, 16
Commercial Shrimping, 92
Confessions of a Kite Hustler, 154
Corson, John J., 66
Council for National Cooperation in Aquatics, 169
cummings, e. e., 452, 499

Davidson, Sara, 439
Death of All Children, The, 75
Decade of Destiny, 227
Declaration of Liberation, A, 360
Defiant Kids Will Make the Best Adults, 421
Dickinson, Emily, 107
Dillon, Carolyn, 343
Distant Music of the Hounds, The, 182
Douglass, Frederick, 407
Dyson, Freeman, 38

Ego, The, 8
Ellie: An Inventory of Being, 415
Epic of Garbage, The, 500
Evenin' Air Blues, 484

Fairbanks, Charles A., 480
Fall of the Bastille, The, 260
Farrell, Barry, 154
Fashion or Safety, 504
Faulkner, William, 213
Fichte, Johann Gottlieb, 8
Flight, 367
For Those of You Who Are Obviously Smarter Than I Am: A Sonnet, 469
Frazier, George, 298

Gibbon, Edward, 254
Gordone, Charles, 485
Gossage, Howard Luck, 456

Hemingway, Ernest, 201
Henley, Arthur, 421

How to Hunt for Bargains, 316
Hughes, Langston, 484
Human Consequences of the Exploration of Space, 38
Huxley, Thomas Henry, 240

I Am Tired of the Tyranny of Spoiled Brats, 351
I Taste a Liquor Never Brewed, 107
Iorio, John, 393

Jealousy, 454
Joe Namath and the Problem of Heroic Virtue, 143
John Steinbeck! John Steinbeck! How Still We See Thee Lie, 298
Jolidon, Laurence A., 227
Joyce, Edwin A., 92

Keats, John, 266

Liberalism: Too High a Price?, 480
Lucid Eye in Silver Town, The, 279

McLuhan, Marshall, 470
Man in the Black Apron, The, 393
Modest Proposal, A, 123
Monster, The, 248
Moon Landing, 510
Morris, Desmond, 16
mrs, 452
My Heart Leaps Up, 106

Nader, Ralph, 504
Night the Ghost Got In, The, 463
No Dodo, 134

On Privacy: The American Dream, What Happened to It?, 213
On Running Away, 266
On Women, 427
Oppressed Majority Demands Its Rights, An, 439

Pepé Torres: A Steinbeck Natural, 391
Piece of Chalk, A, 240
Professional Name Game, The, 343

Quiet Talk with Myself, A, 485

Rediscovery, 177
Richardson, Jack, 143
Rome Besieged, 254
Rosenfeld, Albert, 191

Schopenhauer, Arthur, 427
Shakespeare, William, 105
Sight, Sound and Fury, 470
Smart, Sue, 451
Social Change and the University, 66
Spring Rain, 244
Steinbeck, John, 367
Steinbeck's Flight: The Myth of Manhood, 387
Sternglass, Ernest J., 75
Sweet Lorraine, 159
Swift, Jonathan, 123
Sword, The, 419

Taylor, Deems, 248
Television Teaching by Professional Performers, 310
Tell Me, Doctor, Will I Be Active Right Up to the Last?, 456
Thurber, James, 115, 463
Toole, K. Ross, 351
Toussieng, Povl W., 421
Trial of Jack the Ripper, The, 139
Trippett, Frank, 500

University Days, 115
Updike, John, 110, 134, 187, 244, 279

Vogel, Dan, 387

Wait, Eleanor, 415
Wanted: New Heads for Old Ivy, 26
Weathers, Winston, 469
When in Disgrace with Fortune, 105
White, E. B., 54, 177, 182, 419
Whyte, William H., Jr., 58
Winchell, Earl Cameron, 149
Woodward, C. Vann, 326
Wordsworth, William, 106

You, Too, Can Write the Casual Style, 58

index of terms

Analogy, 167
Analysis, 238
Angle of vision, 5–7
Attitude, 5
Argument, 235, 238–39
  emotional, 238–39
  hypothesis, 238
  informal, 239
  policy, 238
Audience, 5–7

Balance, 103–4
Burlesque, 103

Cause to effect, 238
Classification, 238
Colloquial, 6–7
Comparison, 238
Connotation, 166–67, 236
Contrast, 238
Coordination, 197
Criticism, 363–66

Definition, 238
Denotation, 166–67, 235–36, 366
Description, 235–36
Development, 238

Example, 238
Exposition, 235, 237–38, 365–66
  loose, 238
  process, 238
  tight, 238

Fiction, 236, 363–66
Figurative language, 167
Formal, 6, 238

Humor, 102–3
Hyperbole, 167

Illustration, 238
Imagery, 167, 236
Imperative mood, 34
Informal, 6–7, 238, 239
Innuendo, 103
Invective, 103
Irony, 102–3

Language
  levels, 5–7, 366
  patterns, 197–200
  scientific, 167–68

Metaphor, 167
Method, 233–39
Mood, 102–4, 236

Narration, 235, 236–37
  experiential, 237
  historical, 236
  reminiscent, 237
  speculative, 237
Nonfiction, 236–37

Objective, 35–36, 235–37
One, 35–36
Organization
  chronological, 236
  spatial, 235

Parody, 103
Personification, 167

Point of view, 33–37, 366
impersonal, 33, 35–37
personal 33–35
Pronoun, 33–36
impersonal, 33–36
indefinite, 33–34
personal, 33–36
Purpose, 235–39

Sarcasm, 102–3
Satire, 102–3
Horatian, 103
Juvenalian, 103
Scientific writing, 35–37, 236
Sentence patterns, 199–200
normal, 199
parallel, 199–200
periodic, 199–200
Sentence structure, 197–200
complex, 197–99
compound, 197–98
compound-complex, 197–99
simple, 197–98
Sentimentalism, 103–4, 236
Simile, 167
Style, 1–5
colloquial, 6–7
formal, 6
informal, 6–7
Subjective, 35–36, 235–36, 237
Subordination, 197–99

Technical writing, 36–37, 236
Tone, 102–4, 366

Voice, 36–37
active, 37
passive, 36–37

We, 34–35
editorial, 34–35
personal, 34–35
Word order, 199–200

You, 33–34